PHYSICAL EDUCATION AND SPORT IN A CHANGING SOCIETY

Third Edition

William H. Freeman
Durham, North Carolina

MACMILLAN PUBLISHING COMPANY

New York

COLLIER MACMILLAN PUBLISHERS

London

Development editor: Anne E. Heller
Assistant development editor: Charlene J. Brown
Copy editor: Lawrence J. Zwier
Production editor: Jean R. Starr
Cover design: Terry Dugan

Macmillan Publishing Company
866 Third Avenue, New York, New York 10022

Collier Macmillan Canada, Inc.

Library of Congress Cataloging in Publication Data
Freeman, William Hardin, 1943–
    Physical education and sport in a changing
society

    Bibliography: p.
    Includes index.
    1. Physical education and training — History.
2. Sports — History.   I. title.
GV211.F73   1987   613.7'1   86-23895
ISBN 0-02-339702-0

Printing: 1 2 3 4 5 6 7 8   Year: 7 8 9 0 1 2 3 4 5

ISBN 0-02-339702-0

Dedicated to
Betty McCue Slater-Hammel—
scholar, mentor, friend

CONTENTS

PREFACE

This text is written to introduce new students to the field of physical education and sport. It defines the field, shows how it has developed over the years, describes what its specialists study, discusses employment opportunities, and looks at the current concerns and future directions of the field.

This third edition brings the developing disciplines and interests of the broad field of physical education and sport up to the late 1980s. It is much changed from the earlier editions, but the concepts underlying its structure remain the same.

Although this edition places much stress on the combined interests of physical education and sport, its main emphasis is still on the field of physical education. Physical education is presented as a broad field of interests that includes both a professional side (in which teaching is emphasized) and a disciplinary side (in which scholarship is emphasized). These two sides are facets of the same broad interests, not antagonistic competitors. The essential interest in physical activity draws us together, whatever our more specific professional or disciplinary interests may be.

Part I serves as an introduction by defining the field of physical education and sport. Part II provides a broad overview of the history of physical education and sport. Part III discusses the foundations of knowledge in physical education and sport. This part of the book looks first at the philosophical aspects of the field, including ethical problems, then at the disciplines in the biological, physical, and social sciences that have implications for physical education and sport. Part IV examines the work world in physical education and sport, including the traditional field of teaching, new directions in employment outside the schools, and the new world of the technological workplace. Part V considers physical education and sport in today's world, with chapters on current issues in American education, physical education, and sport and on the future of society, education, physical education, and sport as we move close to the 21st century.

Though their relative share of space in the text has changed, history and philosophy are presented as forming the cornerstone of the study of physical education and sport as a profession and as a discipline. I take this view because I believe that we can more easily find our directions for the future when we know our past, both in action and in thought. Ethics and ethical problems are still treated as of critical importance, as in the earlier editions. The scientific bases are described in some detail for the first time. The depth of coverage is not great, because those bases are traditionally studied in separate courses or course sequences, and this text emphasizes material that is less often examined in other required courses.

The essential treatment of the concepts and issues presented is for the beginning student rather than for the upper-level student. The primary goal is to discuss the matters in a clear and simplified manner, but each student should pursue the subjects to more scholarly levels. The readings listed after each chapter can expand the student's exposure to the work of specialists in those areas covered in the chapter, but the lists should simply serve as a starting point for the interested student. I do not list these works as "approved" readings; they will give diverse and, at times, conflicting ideas that the student should learn to examine critically. More basic works and periodicals are included in the section on resources at the end of the book.

I want to express my sincere appreciation to the people who had a formative influence on this book. The late Professor F. W. Clonts, of Wake Forest University, helped as my advisor, and as an historian who possessed a broad view of history and who insisted on clear, precise prose. Professor Betty F. McCue, of the University of Oregon, was an invaluable, supportive advisor and critic during and after my graduate studies. Professor Bill Bowerman, of Oregon, assisted in many ways by providing developmental experiences, an association of lasting value and meaning, and an example of commitment to the broad view of the university experience.

I also wish to express my appreciation to my first advisor in physical education, Professor Clay Costner, for the excellent advice and encouragement that he provided. People who were especially helpful during the production of this edition of the text include Dr. Peter Batke, of Duke University, for his help with the Kurzweil Optical Character Reader; Chip Spann, of the Duke University Preventive Approach to Cardiology; James Daniell and Neil Moore, of Duke University; and my wife.

I want to thank the reviewers of this manuscript for their helpful suggestions. I am most appreciative of the many teachers and students who have used the previous editions of this text. Comments from the users of this edition will be welcomed.

PART I

THE FIELD OF PHYSICAL EDUCATION AND SPORT

Courtesy Duke University Sports Information

chapter 1

What *Are* Physical Education and Sport?

When we speak of physical education and sport, to what are we referring? Many people are confused by the terms and are not sure exactly what physical education is or what its teachers do. In many cases this confusion is shared by the college students who have chosen physical education as their major field. The purpose of this chapter is to explain what physical education and sport really are. We will look at them separately.

A BROAD FIELD OF INTERESTS

When we speak of physical education, we are referring to a broad field of interests. The basic concern is the improvement of human movement, primarily in the sense of gross (larger) movements rather than the more minute or finer movements of the body. More specifically, physical education is concerned with the relationship between human movement and other areas of education—that is, with the relationship of the body's physical development to the mind and soul as they are being developed. This concern for the effect of physical development on other areas of human growth and development contributes to the uniquely broad scope of physical education, for no other single field— except education, when viewed as broadly as possible— is concerned with the *total* development of the human.

Definitions of Physical Education

While many definitions have been given for physical education, one of the most lasting was expressed by Jesse Feiring Williams: "Physical education is the sum of man's physical activities selected as to kind, and conducted as to outcomes."[1] He explains his definition by considering the question of whether educating only the physical aspect of the body is sufficient to define the field:

> When mind and body were thought of as two separate entities, physical education was obviously an education *of* the physical. . . . With new understanding of the nature of the human organism in which wholeness of the individual is the outstanding fact, physical education becomes education *through* the physical. With this view operative, physical education has concern for and with emotional responses, personal relationships, group behaviors, mental learnings, and other intellectual, social, emotional, and esthetic outcomes.[2]

Williams is stressing the point that even though physical education seeks to educate people through physical means by working with physical activities, it is concerned with educational results that are not entirely physical. The goal of physical education is to influence all areas of educational development, including the mental and social growth of the student. While the body is being improved physically, the mind should be learning and expanding, and there should be some social development, such as learning to work with others.

Other authors have sought to convey this broad definition of the goal of physical education. John H. Jenny, for example, also discusses this "education *through* the physical":

> The unique contribution that physical education has to make to general education is that of general body development through physical activity. When this physical activity is guided by competent teachers so that the other general outcomes of education accompany the physical activity, then, and only then, does the physical activity become more than physical culture or physical training.[3]

In this definition, education that is simply "*of* the physical," or has a goal that focuses on only the physical aspects of education, is too limited in scope to be considered true physical education.

Harold M. Barrow puts physical education into the context of education's traditional goal of developing the liberally (broadly) educated person:

> Physical education may be defined as "an education of and through human movement where many of the educational objectives are achieved by means of big-muscle activities involving sports, games, gymnastics, dance and exercise."...The product...is a *physically educated person*. This value becomes one of many values of the liberally educated person, and it has meaning only when it is related to the totality of the individual's life.[4]

In placing physical education within the context of the total educational experience, Barrow stresses that the physical education experience should relate to the total educational process and to each person's whole life. If the physical education experience makes no contribution to the other educational experiences, the proper function expected of a true physical education program is not being fulfilled.

John E. Nixon and Ann E. Jewett also stress the total educational experience in defining physical education as

> that phase of the total process of education which is concerned with the development and utilization of the individual's voluntary, purposeful, movement capabilities, and with directly related mental, emotional and social responses.[5]

This definition is a bit more limited, as it does not include all the educational areas affected by a good program of physical education. The authors do, however, point out that the education is not purely physical, for "movement potential" is a broad area, particularly when the "related responses" are included in the educational process.

James A. Baley and David A. Field describe physical education with more emphasis on its use of gross physical activities that are not generally easy:

> Physical education is a process through which favorable adaptations and learnings—organic, neuromuscular, intellectual, social, cultural, emotional, and esthetic—result from and proceed through selected and fairly vigorous physical activities.[6]

The activities noted here are selected, as in Williams's earlier definition, in relation to the desired outcomes they can produce in the student. That the education uses physical means is emphasized by the statement that the activities considered a part of physical education are "fairly vigorous physical activities." While physical activities requiring little effort might be considered recreational or beneficial under this definition, they would not be considered genuine physical education.

Jan Felshin has discussed the definition of physical education by suggesting that its body of knowledge is based on human movement, but not on all human movement; it focuses on gross muscular efforts and activities. The notion of physical prowess underlies physical education, as she defines it. Moreover, physical education's prime concern has not been with the human use of movement in work activities but with physical movement in play and sport and with the basic functioning of the human body.[7]

As we can see from these various definitions of physical education, the basic points that define the field are brought forth consistently by different scholars. First, physical education is conducted through physical means; that is, some sort of physical activity is involved. This physical activity is usually (though not always) moderately vigorous, it consists primarily of gross motor movements, and the skills involved do not have to be very finely developed or of high quality for the student to benefit from such activity. Finally, although the educational means—the process by which the student gains these benefits—is physical, the benefits for the student include improvements in nonphysical areas of educational development such as intellectual, social, and aesthetic growth or the cognitive and affective domains.

In other words, physical education tries to develop each person's whole being by the use of physical means, which is a characteristic that physical education shares with no other area of education. Since the educational results of the physical experience are not limited to the physical or body-improving benefits, our definition does not refer solely to the traditional meaning of physical activity. We must view the term *physical* on a broader, more abstract plane—as a condition of mind as well as body. Indeed, this physical education *should* bring about improvements in mind and body that affect all aspects of the person's daily living, and the whole person should benefit by the experience. This mind–body holistic approach includes an emphasis on all three domains: the psychomotor, the cognitive, and the affective.

The Relationship to Play and Sport

In defining physical education, we must also consider its relationship to play and sport. Numerous physical educators have begun to study play and its implications for our well-being. While many of these studies consider sport and physical education to be one and the same, we will consider play, sport, and physical education as three different but overlapping entities.

Play is essentially activity used as amusement. We think of play as a noncompetitive type of physical amusement, though play does not have to be physical. Play is not necessarily sport or physical education, though elements of play may be found in both.

Sport is an organized, competitive form of play. Some people view sport simply as an organized form of play, which might put it closer to physical education as we have defined it. However, close consideration will show that sport has traditionally involved competitive activities.

When we refer to sport as "organized," competitive activity, we mean that the activity has been refined and formalized to some degree, that is, some definite form or process is involved. Rules, whether they are written or not, are used in this form of activity, and those rules or procedures cannot be changed during the competition, though new ones may evolve from one episode to the next.

Sport is, above all, competitive activity. We cannot think of sport without thinking of competition, for without the competition, sport becomes simply play or recreation. Play can at times be sport, but, strictly speaking, sport is never simply play; the competitive aspect is essential to sport.

Physical education has elements of both play and sport, but it is not exclusively either one nor is it a balanced combination of the two. By its very title,

Children get an early start in physical education in their play. Because play involves physical movement, elements of it are evident in both physical education and sport. (From R. P. Pangrazi and V. P. Dauer, *Movement in Early Childhood and Primary Education*, p. 335, Burgess Publishing, Minneapolis, 1981)

physical education is physical activity with an educational goal. It is physical and it seeks to educate, but neither play nor sport— even though both can be used in the educational process—always includes the educational portion of the physical experience as a vital aim.

Play, sport, and physical education all involve forms of movement, and all can fit within the context of education if they are used for some educational purpose. Play can be for relaxation and entertainment without any educational aim, just as sport can exist for its own sake without any educational aim. For example, professional sports (some people prefer the term *athletics*) have no educational goals, yet we consider them no less sport, for an activity need not be amateur to be considered sport. Sport and play can exist purely for pleasure, purely for education, or for any combination of the two. Pleasure and education are not mutually exclusive; they can and should exist together.

The concepts of play, games, sport, and athletics are discussed more fully later in this chapter. Work by scholars such as John Loy[8] and Allen Guttmann[9] has helped to clarify our understanding of these concepts. In fact, most of the work of defining and studying these concepts has taken place only in the last two decades.

THE ALLIED AREAS: HEALTH EDUCATION, RECREATION, AND DANCE

In our attempt to explain physical education in its broadest sense, we should not overlook the areas allied to physical education. We have defined physical education as basically concerned with the development or education of the individual, both *of* the physical and *through* physical means. To complete our description of this very broad concept, three areas allied to the field of physical education and sport need to be introduced.

Health Education

Health education is perhaps the largest of the areas allied to physical education and sport. We speak of health education most often in the sense of total fitness of the person: physical, mental, emotional, and social fitness. Three subareas, which can be included in a description of the larger area of health education,[10] are also functions or goals of health education.

The first of these areas is *health instruction*, which is concerned with teaching the basics of healthful living to people. This instruction is provided in various ways at every level of education from preschool through college and by various public and private information programs. Health instruction can include information n caring for the body and general disease prevention, as well as sex instruction. It also can provide help for more specific problems, such as alcohol or drug abuse, coping with stress, or coping with the death of a family member or friend.

Dancing, gymnastics, and other types of movement are allied to the general field of physical education. This ancient Greek vase shows such activities. (Courtesy, Museum of Fine Arts, Boston)

Providing *health services* is the second area included in health education. In educational institutions, health services are necessary to develop and maintain a reasonable state of health among the students. The nurses and doctors who work in this area of health education provide routine health care services, such as dental, hearing, and eye examinations, and outpatient services at the college level. It is increasingly a facet of employee programs in the business world.

Health environment is the third area within health education. Its goal is to develop settings that provide better health and safety standards for the people who study, work, or live in a given environment. For example, the concerns of the health environment include examining the cleanliness of schools and public or private facilities and seeing that people are not needlessly exposed to disease or injury.

Health educators are not always teachers, but they are concerned with education and physical well-being, though the means by which they educate may not be physical.

Recreation

Recreation is the second of the three areas allied to physical education and sport. We generally think of recreation as leisure-time activity. However, recreation has been defined as fulfilling the earlier educational goal of "the worthy use of leisure."[11] In this view, activities are selected by the individual to serve a constructive purpose, and they are not so much time consuming as time using. Jenny refers to them as activities that are physically, mentally, and socially healthful.[12] Jay B. Nash has referred to recreation as a complement to work and therefore a need of all individuals.[13] The emphasis of recreation in this sense is the "re-creation" of the person—the revitalization of body and mind that is a result of getting away from the stressful things in life. Like physical education, recreation is a broad and rapidly growing field. For example, the growth of park programs across the country has led to an expansion of outdoor education and related activities. The educational base of recreation also has been broadened by increasing amounts of leisure time in people's lives, for they need to be educated in how to use their leisure time.

Dance

Dance is the third area allied to physical education. Although dance is not necessarily a specialty of a large number of physical education professionals, it is quite a large area in terms of the popularity of dance-oriented activities for people of all ages. Dance activities have been something of a stepchild of physical education, for dance hangs on the periphery of physical education.

While dance activities can definitely be considered a part of physical education, dance itself is strongly a part of the arts. Dance, with its orientation to body movement, has perhaps come naturally into the realm of physical education, and this bit of the arts may do much to temper the sometimes excessively athletic orientation of physical education. However, most dance programs in schools have now joined fine arts and performance arts programs.

HISTORICAL TERMS FOR PHYSICAL EDUCATION

Physical education has been known by many other titles in the past, but most of them are now considered too narrow and exclusive to express the full scope of the field.

The earliest of those titles was *gymnastics*. During the 19th century, *gymnastics* referred to exercises or activities that took place in a gymnasium, rather than to the activities that today are part of a particular sport. The term was very popular with European programs, but in the United States it came to be used for only one phase of the total physical education program. Because of the limited nature of its meaning, the term, where it is still used, carries an explanatory subtitle, such as Olympic gymnastics or corrective gymnastics.

Another popular term of the 19th century, *hygiene*, really referred to the science of preserving people's health. This term was applied to activities similar to those of today's health education programs, which developed at the turn of the century as state legislatures began passing laws requiring instruction in hygiene, or the teaching of basic health practices. Many of the early leaders in American physical education were MDs concerned with improving overall health.

Physical culture, which was a popular term during the late 19th century, was often used parallel to the term *physical training*. *Physical culture* was a fad term often used in trying to sell programs of physical training designed to bring about certain physical and (often) health benefits. While *physical training* was also used as a sales promotional term in the United States, it properly refers exclusively to physical conditioning exercises and programs. The term is still commonly used to describe programs in the armed services, but it implies a far too narrow concept of physical education to be used by educators in the United States today.

PHYSICAL EDUCATION: THE BEST NAME FOR OUR FIELD?

For years physical educators have been dissatisfied with the term *physical education*, because they feel that it does not make clear exactly what the concern of the field is. An allied problem is that many physical educators believe that the term recalls close ties between physical education and school athletics, or sports programs, which have all too often had little relationship to education in the schools. Many physical educators have wanted to divorce themselves of this tie to sports in the belief that only in this way can physical education show its true worth in the educational arena. For reasons such as these, physical educators have been seeking a new name for physical education, one that will clearly tell people what physical education is all about while giving a new image free of ties to the past.

Physical educators are attempting to resolve the name problem by trying to establish the focus of the field. The American Academy of Physical Education devoted an issue of *The Academy Papers*[14] to the question of what constitutes the theoretical base for physical education—that is, the area of knowledge on which physical education is based. The discussions also considered whether the designation *physical education* should be replaced as the title for the field, and if so, what title should be used as its replacement.

Defining the Theoretical Base

The discussions of the theoretical base of physical education presented in *The Academy Papers* centered on four different areas. Lois Ellfeldt stated the case for *human movement* as the base of theory by stressing that we need to remember that movement is an open concept, more of a process than an absolute.[15] The American Alliance for Health, Physical Education, Recreation and Dance (AAHPERD)* has outlined a discipline centered on human movement phenomena (Figure 1.1). In this view, there can be no physical education without movement.

The second area of theory was suggested by Paul Hunsicker, who proposed *fitness* as the theoretical base.[16] He discussed fitness as including mental and physical fitness and thus used a broadened definition of fitness. He suggested that one of the benefits of using fitness as the theoretical base is that the public generally understands and accepts the relationship between physical education and fitness.

Thomas J. Sheehan had earlier suggested *sport* as the focal point of physical education and showed the difficulty of studying physical fitness, human movement, and social values derived from physical education activities. He suggested sport science as physical education's area of work and study.[17] Later, Edward J. Shea also argued the case for sport as physical education's theoretical base. He pointed out that, because his definition of sport does not exclude the less physically gifted person, it is broader than the traditional view.[18]

Other physical educators considered the broad base of physical education to be its greatest appeal. Warren Fraleigh argued that physical education is *multitheoretical* and is not based on a single area of theory.[19] In essence, he stressed that several different kinds of theory are included in the broader context of physical education (Figures 1.2 and 1.3). Celeste Ulrich further elaborated on this point by noting that while each of the areas we have already cited was called the base that underlies all of physical education, each is actually part of a greater whole.[20] As she pointed out:

*This organization was formerly termed the American Association for Health, Physical Education and Recreation (AAHPER). In 1980, the name was changed to reflect a growing involvement in dance. In this text, the abbreviation AAHPERD will be used for all references to the organization, regardless of the actual organization name at the time.

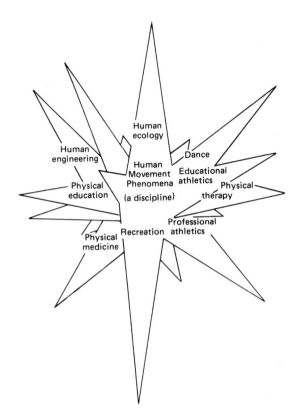

Figure 1.1. The suggested components of a discipline based on human movement phenomena. (From AAHPERD, *Tones of Theory,* Reston, Va., 1972, p. 13. Reprinted by permission of the American Alliance for Health, Physical Education, Recreation and Dance, 1900 Association Drive, Reston, VA 22091)

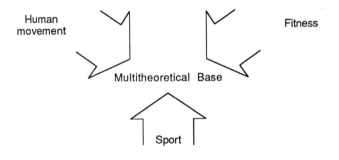

Figure 1.2. Suggested theoretical bases of physical education.

The concepts cannot be isolated. One moves to be active. Sport is based upon specific patterns of activity. Fitness results from activity carefully "selected as to kind and conducted as to outcome."...But there may be a way of putting it all together. If physical educators will stop seeking a uni-theoretical approach and agree that the uniqueness of physical education is in its multi-theoretical approach.[21]

From this point of view, physical education draws from many areas of theory, which sets it apart from many other areas of educational concern. In other words, we need not limit ourselves to any single area of theory to say that we are working with the theoretical base of physical education.

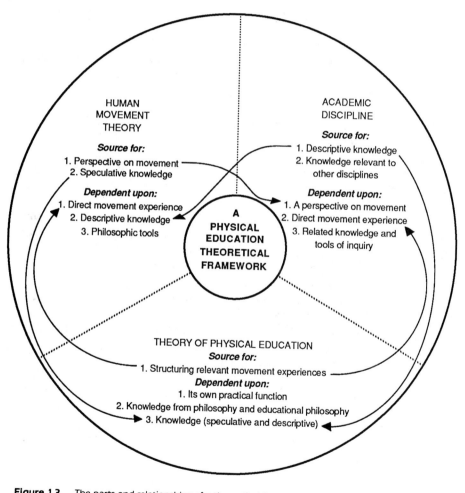

Figure 1.3.   The parts and relationships of a theoretical framework. (From Warren P. Fraleigh, "Developing a Physical Education Theoretical Framework," a paper presented at the Conference on the Theoretical Structure of Physical Education, June 3, 1969, Zion, Illinois. Used by permission)

Daryl Siedentop considered these discussions of the focus of study and the theoretical base of physical education, then pointed out the risks of losing sight of the task of physical education. He believes physical educators may get so carried away with semantic battles, fighting over the definitions and implications of the terms they use when speaking of physical education, that they will forget what they are trying to do with physical education. He suggests that physical educators not spend so much time arguing over these questions that they fail to concentrate on the battle to improve the teaching of physical education in the schools.[22]

Possible New Names for Physical Education

The American Academy of Physical Education also considered several possible new designations that would more clearly define the field and help people to understand what physical education really is. First, there were some preliminary discussions, led by Rosalind Cassidy, of whether the older term needed to be dropped for a new name.[23] Then, brief presentations in *The Academy Papers* were made in support of the various proposed designations.[24]

Movement arts and sciences was suggested as one possible new name, since movement is a vital concern of the field. Physical education, however, goes beyond simple science; dance, for example, cannot be called a science so much as an art. Nevertheless, while this designation is not broad enough in this area, it does give some indication of the breadth of physical education's concerns.

Movement arts, which also was suggested, is really a slightly less broad version of the *movement arts and sciences* title already mentioned. Using this title could eliminate some of the overlap of study within the sciences that are concerned with certain aspects of human movement, but it also could cause the problem of disregard for the precision of science within physical education. Much science is involved in physical education; it is not primarily an art any more than it is purely a science.

Movement education refers to the broader meaning of physical education, but there has been some confusion over the use of the term, as Marion R. Broer pointed out. Many educators have interpreted the term as referring primarily to dance activities, which are only a narrow part of physical education. Others have confused it with the movement education that has developed at the elementary school level and come to the United States from England.[25] While movement education is rarely used to refer to the broad field of physical education, nothing in its meaning contradicts what physical education seeks to do.

Developmental motor performance, another designation that was advanced, expresses physical education's concern with motor performance and its development. The problems involved in using this designation lie in its breadth as well as its clarity: Does it describe the whole work of physical education?

Would a typical educator in another field know what physical educators do according to this title?

Kinesiology is a term that a number of physical educators began using as their designation for the field in the 1970s. The term, which is primarily scholar oriented, refers to the study of human movement. However, in the sense that the term refers to a particular study, it gives no indication of the breadth of what is taught. A student in physical education does not necessarily study movement; movement is used to teach the student something, but a student does not always study the movement itself. Teaching the strategy involved in playing a team game, for example, is definitely a part of physical education, but it is not kinesiology or the study of movement per se. Since we are not always involved in studying the movement itself, kinesiology is too narrow in scope to define the whole field, even though it does get at the heart of much of what physical education is about.

Human physical sciences, as a suggested designation for physical education, points out a number of the characteristics of the field, for it is concerned with studying areas of the physical sciences (such as physics and the laws of mechanics) as they relate to people. To understand its use as a descriptive title for physical education, however, people must know exactly what the physical sciences are as well as the difference between physical education and the overlapping areas within the sciences.

Physical fitness, or simply *fitness*, has been used at times to refer primarily to the bodily aspects of fitness, which makes it simply a more modern version of the older title *physical training*. Physical fitness is basically a state of health or the body's ability to withstand the stresses of daily life. Since programs of physical fitness concentrate primarily on these physical goals, the term is too narrow to include the broader goals of physical education.

Athletics, sport sciences, and simply *sport* have increasingly come into use as designations for physical education, but these titles are too narrow by definition to represent the whole field of physical education. We have discussed sport and what it represents. Athletics is essentially the same thing, though scholars will debate this statement at the philosophical level. *Athletics* refers to competitive activities, organized games and sports, either on a team or on an individual basis. Competitive activities are only one phase of education, and as we have mentioned, they need not be educational. Unless sport and athletics are properly channeled and oriented, they can easily result in education or learning directly contrary to what the physical educator is seeking to accomplish.

Physical education and sport is another suggested designation that is becoming more common. This title broadens the concerns of physical education by making it clear that sport is a concern of the field, but at the same time it shows that sport is not the only concern. This title has two inherent benefits: (1) it retains the traditional designation, which is basically familiar to the public, yet (2) it includes sport, which is vitally involved in physical education and which is seen by an increasing number of educators as the primary area of physical education's concern.

Last, some arguments were advanced for retaining the title *physical education*. Although many physical educators are not satisfied with this title, they recognize that the public does at least have some idea of what physical education is and that developing a new image for the old term may be easier than trying to teach the public to recognize a new, unfamiliar title.

Although no agreement has been reached, this preference for the traditional title is the most likely direction for the next few years. However, when the arguments have all been studied and the dust has settled, perhaps the most likely replacement will be the title *physical education and sport*. The largest movement away from the *physical education* designation at this time is toward the use of various designations that include the word *sport*, though perhaps *human movement studies*, which E. O. Ojeme prefers,[26] will eventually become the title of choice.

No matter what the final designation, we should keep in mind that each of the proposals to define and represent physical education by a particular name depends heavily on individual interpretations of the focus within the field. Perhaps this diversity of opinion is a virtue in itself, for it represents our earlier definition of physical education as a broad area of work and study that includes many people who seem to have little relationship to each other in their interests and tasks.

THE FIELD OF PHYSICAL EDUCATION: DISCIPLINE OR PROFESSION?

In recent years, many physical educators have been debating the exact status of the field of physical education. Is it a profession, a discipline, or both? Where does physical education fit into the academic scheme of things? This study need not divide our field, for physical education has many dimensions. One of these is a body of knowledge, which is one essential characteristic of a discipline, while other dimensions of physical education bear the traits of a profession. To determine the status of physical education, we need to understand exactly what a profession and a discipline are, then see whether physical education has the characteristics of either one. A field does not have to be *only* a discipline *or* a profession, however.

Physical Education as a Profession

For many years, physical educators have referred to themselves as members of a profession, in this case the teaching profession. Although we often argue that we are members of a profession, the characteristics we use to show such a status are sometimes limited to our advantage. First we will look at a commonly accepted set of criteria for professional status suggested by Abraham Flexner.[27] Flexner suggested six criteria or characteristics that determine whether a field is really a profession:

1. Intellectual activity (a body of knowledge)
2. A practical use
3. Research resulting in new knowledge and ideas
4. Self-organization
5. The capacity for communication (internal and external)
6. A dedication to helping others (altruism and service)

The first characteristic is that the activities of a profession are basically intellectual. While physical skills may be involved in performing the work, it must have an intellectual base, or body of knowledge. The intellectual nature of the field must be a more important aspect of the work than the physical or other skills used to apply the knowledge. This is perhaps where physical education is on the weakest ground when we say it is a profession, for some physical educators exhibit an anti-intellectual bent. This attitude may result in heated arguments with educators outside the field.

The second characteristic is that the work must be practical. It must have a genuine use. Even though it is based on knowledge, that knowledge has no value unless it is used. Most physical educators will agree that physical education has an intellectual base, and every physical educator will agree that the work is practical. The knowledge is applied to the practical use of developing and improving people's health, skills, and fitness.

The third characteristic of a profession is constant research resulting in new knowledge and ideas that are then tested and applied in the professional work. This characteristic does apply to physical education, though many educators are dissatisfied with the small amount of research as well as the tendency to experiment only in the most narrowly practical areas. Some critics also have suggested that physical educators and coaches are the most resistant of all groups to change, even when research has shown that changes would be more useful.

The fourth characteristic of a profession is formal self-organization. Examples of such organization in physical education are the numerous professional groups such as AAHPERD; many of these will be discussed elsewhere. This characteristic is closely related to the fifth characteristic, the capacity for communication. A profession sets up formal means of communication among its members not only to enable them to work together toward the solution of common problems but also to spread information. AAHPERD is the largest group that assists physical educators in meeting those communication requirements, not only by holding regular meetings at the state, district, and national levels but also by sponsoring many publications.

The sixth characteristic of a profession is altruism and service; that is, the people who work in a profession are dedicated to helping others. The profession is characterized by concern for people's welfare, and it exists, at least in part, to help improve or protect the lives of others. Few people would dispute the claim that this characteristic applies to teaching.

Most physical educators consider their field a profession. It does meet all of Flexner's criteria to some degree (though there might be some arguments over the importance given to some of the criteria). However, Charles A. Bucher has given convincing arguments that physical education is not a fully matured profession.[28] He suggested that it is an *emerging* profession, and his arguments seem to hold true even today.

Do people see physical educators as rendering a "unique and essential social service," one that could not be rendered by a nonprofessional? Many people believe physical educators are doing a job that most well-coordinated people could do. Are physical educators selective about the people admitted to the field? Research has indicated consistently that the students majoring in the teacher-preparation programs in our colleges are the least intelligent and the least academically trained of our nation's college students—and that certification requirements sometimes vary so widely as to be almost meaningless. Are "rigorous training programs" provided for future members? There are many doubts in this area also. Finally, is physical education "self-regulatory"? Are unethical or ill-prepared members dealt with within the field? This has rarely been the case. Bucher suggests, rightly, that physical education still has not earned the full status of a profession—that it is still an emerging profession. Although some educators have argued that it has spent a long time emerging, its basic shortcomings are undeniable. While physical education's goals equal the characteristics of a profession, its public status has not yet risen to that level.

Physical Education as a Discipline

The difference between a discipline and a profession can be confusing, for a field can be a discipline while its members are the members of a profession. In essence, a discipline is an area of knowledge and theory that can exist purely for itself; a profession must have a practical application. We have shown that physical education has practical uses—such as developing people's health and fitness—and thus can be considered a profession. What, then, is necessary for physical education to be considered a discipline? Franklin M. Henry defines an academic discipline as

> an organized body of knowledge collectively embraced in a formal course of learning. The acquisition of such knowledge is assumed to be an adequate and worthy objective as such, without any demonstration or requirement of practical application. The content is theoretical and scholarly as distinguished from technical and professional.[29]

Henry's definition, which is a synthesis of a number of definitions of a discipline, makes it clear that for physical education to be considered a discipline it must have what is often called a body of knowledge; that is, some scholarly knowledge with an important focus of attention. Is this the case with physical education? Henry and others believe that it is.

We might view a discipline as an area of basic science, a field concerned with the discovery of new knowledge but not obligated to find any use for that knowledge or to apply it in any way. The primary objective of a discipline is to *gain* knowledge, while that of a profession is to *apply* knowledge in a way that serves others.

Gerald S. Kenyon suggests that three criteria are necessary for a field to be a discipline: a focus of attention, a unique body of knowledge, and a particular mode of inquiry.[30] Others have suggested that the focus of attention of physical education as a discipline is the *human movement phenomena*,[31] or as Kenyon puts it, the study of "man in motion." While there is some argument over whether physical education also possesses a unique body of knowledge, many physical educators believe that such a body of knowledge does exist and that it is expanding rapidly.

Kenyon suggests that physical education's problem in developing or claiming a discipline lies in the characteristic of having our own particular mode of inquiry or research method used throughout the discipline, for several different research methods are used. Kenyon suggests that the field of study is still too broad and that the question of research method still must be settled.

Many physical educators see a discipline of physical education emerging not necessarily *from* the profession but rather *parallel to* the profession; that is, they see a division of the field into the educators (profession) and the scholars (discipline). While neither the discipline nor the profession is fully developed, both are making rapid progress in physical education today. We need to remember that one need not exclude the other, however.

WHAT IS SPORT?

If we want to grasp what the specialist in the study of sport is doing, we need a more thorough understanding of that field of study. Though we already have discussed briefly the field of physical education and its related elements, including sport, we need a more detailed discussion of the terms related to sport studies at this point. Our basic areas of concern will be the meanings and relationships of *play, games, sport*, and *athletics*, or what Hal A. Lawson has called "ludic activities" because they are forms of playing.[32] These meanings and relationships are the focal points at which the philosophic study of sport begins.

Sociologists have perhaps spent more time than philosophers in trying to define precisely the terms related to sport. Play has been described in a number of ways, for the true meaning of play is not all that clear (Figure 1.4). Perhaps the most common definition of play is actually a contrast, with play defined as the opposite of work.[33] As work is considered utilitarian— effort applied to some useful purpose—play is considered nonutilitarian. That is, play serves no useful purpose, at least as we currently define "useful pur-

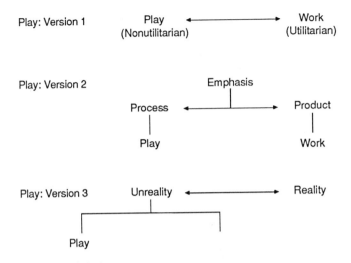

Figure 1.4.   Definitions of *play* by contrast.

pose." Not only is play nonutilitarian but also it is pursued simply for its own sake. It is *autotelic*, too; that is, the pleasure of play is in performing the activity rather than in the accomplishment of the activity. Performance itself serves as the purpose of play. Because of this quality, play offers a type of freedom not available as part of the workaday world.

At the same time, play can be defined without contrasting it to work. Stephen Miller has defined play and its importance in terms of the relative importance of means and ends.[34] In play, the means is more important than the end result. This can also be rephrased using the terms *process* and *product*; in play, the process is more important than the product. Klaus Meier suggests that play has two aspects: it is voluntary, and it is autotelic.[35] The voluntary aspect makes play different from work; the autotelic aspect—pleasure in the doing—does not necessarily contrast to work, for play can be pleasurable in and of itself. Meier reveals the crux of play, however, when he states that "the prize of play is play itself."

A third way of defining play comes from Sigmund Freud, who suggested that the opposite of play is reality.[36] Play is unreality, different from the real world. As such, play is an escape from reality. This aspect of play can be both a strength and a weakness. Some escape from reality is useful in maintaining a balanced, harmonious life, for it can act as a pressure release. On the other hand, a person can be too anxious to escape from reality and seek that release too often, choosing instead to live in a dream world where the pressures of reality can be ignored.

In his work *Man, Play, and Games*, Roger Caillois defines play in terms of *paidia*, which might be called "child's play," and *ludus*, which might be called "complex play" or "adult play."[37] He states:

[Games can] be placed on a continuum between two opposite poles. At one extreme an almost invisible principle, common to diversion, turbulence, free improvisation, and carefree gaiety is dominant. It manifests a kind of uncontrolled fantasy that can be designated by the term *paidia*. At the opposite extreme, this frolicsome and impulsive exuberance is almost entirely absorbed or disciplined by...a growing tendency to bind it with arbitrary, imperative, and purposely tedious conventions...in order to make it more uncertain of attaining its desired effect. This latter principle...requires an ever greater amount of effort, patience, skill, or ingenuity. [This second component is called] *ludus*.[38]

The *paidia-ludus* continuum is used by Daryl Siedentop to show ways of playing and their part in physical education. As he explains, "As play moves from *paidia* to *ludus*, an ever increasing amount of skill, effort, patience, and ingenuity is required in order to be a successful player."[39] The free-spirited, no-limits play that is *paidia* has rules and structure forced on it, making it less free yet much more complicated and challenging. While the relatively formless play of children is not appropriate for organized education, the more structured *ludic* form of play can be used well in an educational setting.

To understand the relationship among play, games, and sport, we can use a diagram suggested by Guttmann in which contrasting terms show the elements forming each term, beginning with *play* (Figure 1.5).[40] Guttmann uses the definition of play as "any nonutilitarian activity performed for its own sake," and then subdivides play into two categories: spontaneous and organized. While we usually think of play as being spontaneous or spur-of-the-moment, Guttmann suggests that "most play is regulated and rule-bound." This is particularly true when play loses its restriction to an individual and involves more than one person; some organization becomes necessary when this occurs. The more people involved, the higher the level of organization required.

Organized play is called games, and to Guttman, "games symbolize the willing surrender of absolute spontaneity for the sake of playful order." He further divides games into competitive and noncompetitive games, with competitive games called contests. He then divides contests into two catego-

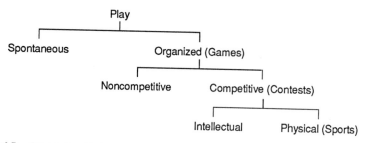

Figure 1.5.   The relationship between play and sport. (Adapted from Guttmann, *From Ritual to Record: The Nature of Modern Sports*, p. 9. © 1978 Columbia University Press. By permission)

ries, intellectual and physical, with the physical contests called sports. According to Guttmann, this gives a final definition of *sports* as "'playful' contests which include an important measure of physical skill."

None of the subdivisions suggested in Guttmann's model is absolute; play is not either totally spontaneous or totally organized. Contests are not totally intellectual or totally physical. Each category exists along a continuum, with different activities appearing at different points between opposite ends. As an example, even a chess match, which is basically intellectual, has its physical side: The pieces must be moved, which requires physical effort. Furthermore, long periods of mental effort at a high level require physical stamina; even chess masters have gone into physical training to increase their stamina for a major match or set of matches.

A variation of Guttmann's model might be used to draw a slightly different distinction between sports and contests, and at the same time, to clarify the distinction that philosophers use in discussing sport as opposed to athletics (Figure 1.6). While Guttmann presents sports as always being competitive and therefore contests, he cites Huizinga as showing an intersection of games and contests that, when blended, also could be described as "sport."[41] While Guttmann rejects this choice, he notes that it does have its supporters. We might view the contest as a higher order of sport that is further along the line toward organization and further away from the "pure play" concept than sport, for the contest moves more closely toward the emphasis on the victory—the ends—than toward the joy of the means.

This brings us to the distinction that philosophers make between sport and athletics. The distinction is, at the heart, one of emphasis. In athletics the

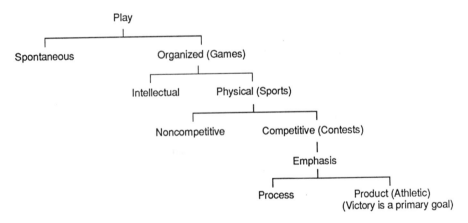

Figure 1.6.   The relationship of play, sport, and athletics. (Adapted from Guttmann, *From Ritual to Record: The Nature of Modern Sports*, and modified by Freeman. © 1978 Columbia University Press. By permission)

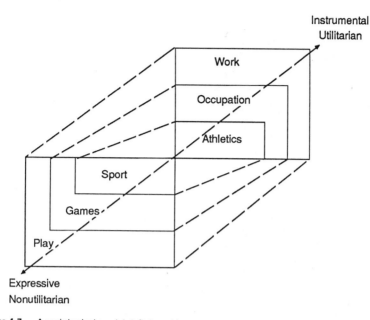

Figure 1.7. A sociological model defining play, sport, and athletics. (From J. Loy, B. McPherson, & G. Kenyon, *Sport and Social Systems*, © 1978, Addison-Wesley Publishing Company, Inc., Reading, Massachusetts. Pg. 23, Fig. 1.4. Reprinted with permission)

emphasis is on the victory; the product, or end (victory), is more important than the process, or means (play or sport), that leads to it. Indeed, as Harper and others point out, the word *athletics* comes from a Greek word that means "to contend for a prize."[42] The end, rather than the joy or spontaneity of the competition, is stated as the real goal.

To add to the confusion, we often fail to make the distinction between professional sports, which are purely goal centered and therefore athletics (if not purely entertainment, rather than sport), and intercollegiate athletics, which are supposedly genuinely sports and less goal centered. Our references to the college activities are probably far more accurate in philosophical terms than our references to the professional activities.

One further example can show how sociologists have attempted to develop a model to define *play* and *sport* in relation to other activities (Figure 1.7). John W. Loy has placed play, sport, and athletics on a continuum running from the utilitarian and instrumental to the nonutilitarian and expressive.[43] He defines work and play as entirely separate categories or sets (though actually they can intersect or cross over). He places games as a subset of play, and then notes sport as a subset of games; that is, a sport will always be a game, but a game will not always be a sport.

On the work side, Loy lists occupation as being a subset of work. He then lists athletics as a subset of occupation, for its goal emphasis or utilitarian emphasis makes it more work than play. Loy has athletics and sport meet or intersect—in reality the distinction between sport and athletics is equally unclear—for they also form a continuum because any given sport may have a different degree of emphasis on the victory, depending on the situation of the activity and the level at which the activity occurs.

These definitions are open to considerable argument from both philosophic and semantic approaches. Play can be described as an opposite of work or as an emphasis on process (the joy of participation). Games can be described as an organized form of play, and sport as games with a primarily physical interest. All of these concepts are very complex. The complexity results in the considerable overlapping of one term or concept with another. Only when each concept is more clearly defined can we determine how each fits into life as it is lived and how each can be best used in the physical education program. At this time, the definition of each varies from person to person, from region to region, and from nation to nation. As Guttmann puts it, "I shall be less intent on *whether* the sport appears than with *how* it appears."[44] The concepts are too complex and too variable to permit simple definition.

Modern society is more involved in athletics than in sport. As a result, philosophers are beginning to give more attention to the differences between sport and athletics, particularly philosophers such as James Keating and Paul Weiss. Keating has described the distinction between sport and athletics as follows:

> In essence, port is a kind of diversion which has for its direct and immediate end, fun, pleasure, and delight and which is dominated by a spirit of moderation and generosity. Athletics, on the other hand, is essentially a competition activity, which has for its end victory in the contest and which is characterized by a spirit of dedication, sacrifice and intensity.[45]

In his book *Sport: A Philosophic Inquiry*, Paul Weiss's theme for athletics is the pursuit of excellence.[46] Indeed, the first chapter of his book is called "Concern for Excellence," and VanderZwaag correctly suggests that Weiss's book might have been entitled *Athletics* rather than *Sport*.[47] The theme of excellence and the idea of the pursuit of excellence as a major goal of athletics reappears throughout Weiss's work.

VanderZwaag maintains that sport and athletics cannot be contrasted as if they were exact opposites. He suggests another continuum running from play to athletics, with sport between them and athletics viewed as an extension of sport.[48] He further suggests that games can be placed along the continuum from play through sport and into the realm of athletics (Figure 1.8), though it does not reach the extreme ends of the continuum; instead, its nature changes as the activity moves toward pure play or pure athletics. VanderZwaag also points out another contrast between sport and athletics. In sport, the spectator is unimportant, while in athletics the spectator is always important and may even become more important than the participant. An

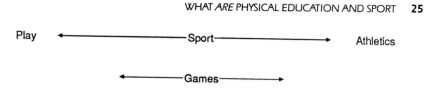

Figure 1.8. The relation of play, sport, games, and athletics. (From VanderZwaag, *Toward a Philosophy of Sport*, p. 72. Used with permission)

athletics event frequently is changed in some manner simply for the sake of convenience or appeal to the spectator. Thus, while athletics differs from sport by the importance of the outcome of a contest, it also differs by the importance it places on the spectator.

SPORT AS A LEGITIMATE FIELD OF ACADEMIC STUDY

Sport holds a prominent place in modern life. Millions of people participate in sporting activities, watch and read about them, and spend billions of dollars annually on sports-related activities and equipment. Though this massive interest in sport was noticed many decades ago, little attention was paid to actually studying sport except by sports journalists and by the occasional scholar, whose professional co-workers often saw the pursuit of such interests as scholarly slumming. The impact of sport on modern society, however, has made it clear that sport is a very legitimate field of academic study, one that has slowly crept into the academic mainstream. As Max Scheler noted more than half a century ago, "Scarcely an international phenomenon of the day deserves social and psychological study to the degree that sport does. Sport has grown immeasurably in scope and in social importance, but the meaning of sport has received little in the way of serious attention."[49]

We now see sport used at the international level for many blatantly political purposes: prestige, a show of friendship, a show of international acceptance, propaganda, and influencing public opinion. In the early 1970s, China invited the United States to send a table tennis team on a tour as a sign of improving relations between the countries. Cuba used the 1976 Olympic victories of Alberto Juantorena as an argument for the superiority of their political system in improving life in their nation. Just as Hitler used the 1936 Olympics to show the "superiority" of his Nazi system, so did the Soviet Union use the 1980 Olympics to serve the same flagrant propaganda purposes for their communist system. The United States used the 1984 games to show the strength of its free-enterprise system.

The increasing political use of the Olympic games, with threats of boycotts for political reasons, is the greatest threat to the survival of the games. The obvious political nature of sport was made more clear when the United States and many other nations withdrew from the Moscow games, using their absence more as a protest against the Soviet Union's political actions than against the Russian political use of the Olympics, a "favor" that was returned in 1984 by the Soviet bloc boycott. Indeed, just as in 1936, the International

Olympic Committee has shown no sign of protest or penalty against the use of the games for political means by the host nation.

Sometimes we fail to recognize the extent of our interest in sport in modern times. As Guttmann notes:

> One reason that sports are not understood is that familiarity has made their significance seem obvious when it is not. Another reason is that the philosophers, historians, sociologists, and psychologists who have concerned themselves with sports have only rarely written for the ordinary reader. They have communicated mainly with each other.[50]

Over the last decade and a half we have seen the rise of "sport science," the discipline arm of physical education. Though arguments for human movement as the focus of the discipline were advanced, more popularity seems to have settled on sport as the focus. Human movement has been called too broad, as it can include things such as learning to hold a pencil or to walk, while sport is more specific to the types of activities that are used in the field.

THE EMERGENCE OF A DISCIPLINE IN PHYSICAL EDUCATION

We defined a discipline as "an area of knowledge and theory that can exist purely for itself," that is, one with no need to show that it has a practical application. The interest in this side of physical education began to develop in the mid-1960s. It was helped along by the impetus of Franklin M. Henry's JOHPER article on the subject, in which he defined an academic discipline as

> An organized body of knowledge collectively embraced in a formal course of learning. The acquisition of such knowledge is assumed to be an adequate and worthy objective as such, without any demonstration or requirement of practical application. The content is theoretical and scholarly as distinguished from technical and professional.[51]

Henry's article caused a flurry of interest in whether physical education was a discipline—whether it had the required focus of attention and particular mode of inquiry. The question of whether a body of knowledge could be demonstrated caused particular concern.

Daryl Siedentop discussed the idea of a discipline by describing a discipline as "value-free," since it tries to study "what is" rather than "what should be." He suggested that the difference between a discipline and a profession could be summarized by the idea that "a discipline describes while a profession prescribes."[52] A discipline avoids bias in research. On the other hand, a profession tries to solve a specific problem and must therefore study a specific group, which results in a biased study and results.

The interest in a discipline centered on Henry's 1964 article and its implications. While various scholars, such as Kenyon, worked to define a discipline and its area of study,[53] AAHPERD worked to organize and present a document that would demonstrate physical education's "body of knowledge." At the same time, scholars in the Big Ten Athletic Conference schools organized a series of annual conferences to discuss the different newly emerging disciplines or subdisciplines in what some scholars were beginning to call "sport studies." By the early 1970s, a publication had appeared from AAHPERD that attempted to organize the theoretical base underlying physical education.[54] Meanwhile, the American Academy of Physical Education debated whether a new name was needed for physical education—one that would better demonstrate the true focus of its study.[55]

In the years since Henry's article first appeared and spurred interest in a discipline, many changes in direction have affected—and are continuing to affect—physical education. The first notable change has been the split in physical education between the professional interests and the disciplinary interests. Many conflicts have arisen that seem to pit physical education against sport studies and "teachers" against "researchers." The more practical appearance of the profession side of studies has created problems with those interested in the discipline or research side, as each sometimes questions the other's validity or importance. In truth, both groups contribute to physical education in important ways. Their conflicts often seem to be little more than arguments of different points of view, though sometimes the real argument has been over which group wields the power in a department. The scholarly side of physical education, however, is far more prominently displayed today than it has been in the past.

A second notable change has been the appearance of new professional societies representing the disciplinary subgroups and their particular scholarly focus of interests. These new societies, which represent areas such as sport philosophy, sport sociology, sport history, and sport psychology, have promoted scholarship in their areas by initiating national conferences and by publishing journals that provide more scholarly and wide-ranging outlets of research than those provided by the older organizations of physical education. By the late 1970s, AAHPERD had belatedly recognized the growth of the scholarly interests and had started "academies" within its professional structure. These organizations will be discussed more fully elsewhere.

A third notable change in the direction of physical education has been evident in the last decade or so. These years have seen a great burst of scholarly research and writing. The need to revise extensively books of readings in scholarly areas as the quality and quantity of research continues to rise reflects this growth. This growth of scholarship has perhaps done the most to revive physical education and to present it to the outside world as an academically respectable field of study and work.

At the same time, we should note that in recent years more scholars have begun to question the value of the discipline movement. As Lawrence Locke points out and Elizabeth Bressan emphasizes, we did not develop disciplines—we simply *declared* that they were present.[56] Locke says that disciplines do not appear by being declared or proven. "They are created by the labor of inquiry, the accumulation of knowledge and theory, the fortunes of social recognition, and the accidents of history."[57]

Bressan notes that young scholars in the disciplines are, in fact, trained in the language and bases of fields other than physical education, so that "there is no real community of scholars who study physical education, or human movement or sport or whatever particular delineation of content upon which we might settle. A sound disciplinary structure is supposed to promote such communal identity and effort."[58]

Jan Broekhoff suggests that a discipline is not as necessary as we originally believed. As he says,

> The assumption...is that persons who have mastered the formal content of the academic discipline will be better prepared to teach than those who possess only professional and applied knowledge. Unfortunately, there is no evidence to support such an assumption....Theory and practice should stand in a reciprocal relationship.[59]

He argues that we must recognize that our field is concerned with educating people. Thus we need to focus our disciplines into an educational context, so they will contribute to what physical educators do. He notes the weakness of a theory-based program that is not rooted in practice, saying, "I should like to throw in a Latin phrase of my own: *Primum vivere, deinde philosophari.* Freely translated this means that people have to live first before they can philosophize."[60] Theory must be grounded in practice.

Indeed, Christopher Hopper joins in the call for increased emphasis on the professional side, arguing that "the emphasis in academic and research-related areas of knowledge and the neglect of personal competency in activities is leaving the prospective teacher inadequately prepared to offer a variety of physical education experiences to children and adults."[61] He calls for integration of the theoretical and the practical, with a return to "pedagogical commitment," suggesting that "such a mission would facilitate the integration of knowledge from research to practice."[62]

This call for a "return to the original mission" of physical education, the concern for helping others in areas related to health, for teaching physical activities, is echoed increasingly in the field, as it was decades ago with C. H. McCloy's article of challenge and complaint, "How About Some Muscle?"[63] Indeed, we need to remember Charles Poskanzer's remark:

> Having agonized for years over the proper title for my own academic department...I have come to an inescapable conclusion. Academic respectability is acquired and maintained through intellectual honesty and professional integrity. The name matters not, and the label is unimportant. The ingredients are the important things. It's the substance, not the style, that counts.[64]

THE DISCIPLINES IN PHYSICAL EDUCATION

The fields of study or subdisciplines of sport are shown in Figure 1.9. Similar groupings have been suggested by other scholars, though Siedentop is one of the few who has called for the inclusion of pedagogy in the disciplines.[65] The figure shows the generally accepted subdisciplines within sport science and, at the same time, indicates their relationships to each other.

If we include sport pedagogy as a subdiscipline, we have seven recognizable scholarly specialties within the field of physical education and sport. They are (in the order of our study):

1. Sport history
2. Sport philosophy
3. Sport sociology
4. Sport psychology
5. Sport physiology
6. Sport biomechanics
7. Sport pedagogy

Sport biomechanics and sport physiology are the areas traditionally considered the "hard sciences" of physical education and sport. Biomechanics is concerned with the effects of natural laws and forces on the human body during sporting activities. It has developed from the field of kinesiology, which is also the study of movement. Kinesiology has two basic areas: anatomical kinesiology, which is concerned with the construction and working mechanisms of the body, and mechanical kinesiology, which is biomechanics or the mechanics of the human body. In sum, sport biomechanics is the study of the human body and how the laws of physics apply to it.

Sport physiology is concerned with how the body functions during exercise. The effects of training are a critical facet of sport physiology research, which makes it perhaps the most important of the sport studies, for it is concerned with all aspects of how the body adapts to exercise. At the same time, this area may include sport medicine, an equally important and growing area of study. Sport medicine is concerned with both preventing and treating athletic injuries.

Sport psychology and sport sociology study human behavior in the sport setting. Sport psychology is studied in two respects: motor skill learning and motor performance. The study is concerned with the psychological factors affecting the learning and performance of physical skills—with how individuals are affected by both internal and external factors.

Sport sociology is concerned with the social behavior of people in the sport setting, both their individual and group behavior. This broad area is sometimes described as studying the sociocultural processes and institutions as they relate to and are affected by sport and sporting behavior. The sport sociologist studies how people interact with each other in a sport setting so

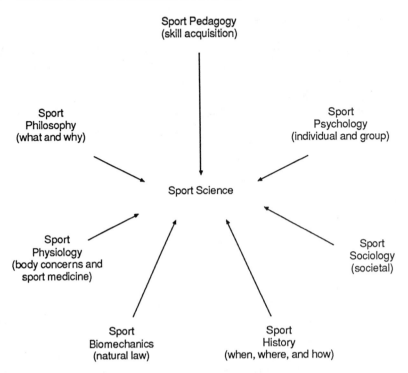

Figure 1.9.   The fields of study of subdisciplines of sport.

we can determine how the process of sport affects their development and socialization, or how they fit into society.

Sport history is the study of sport in the past. It can show us how things came to be as they are today, and it can direct us to problems that need to be solved. We can learn not only how things developed but also what things were tried and did not work. This may help us to see better ways of doing things, or at least help us to avoid the mistakes of the past.

Sport philosophy attempts to define and clarify sport and the sporting experience in order to determine the place and meaning of sport in our lives. The sport philosopher looks at the sport setting, so that the circumstances under which sporting experiences take place can be understood. The critical elements of the experience itself are studied, that is, the elements that contributed to the experience. Finally, the broader meaning and implications of the experience are studied. In essence, the sport philosopher is concerned with what is significant about the sport experience.

Sport pedagogy is concerned with teaching, particularly teaching play and the skills used in sporting situations. It includes the study of teaching methods and many other elements tied to the concerns of the profession of physical education. These concerns will be discussed more fully in later chapters.

Physical education and sport indeed form a house of many rooms. Although communications between those working and studying within each of the rooms may sometimes be difficult, it is still one house, and its inhabitants have but one goal—that of physical education and sport as it has been broadly defined in this chapter.

NOTES

1. Jesse Feiring Williams, *The Principles of Physical Education*, 8th ed., W. B. Saunders, Philadelphia, 1964, p. 13.
2. Ibid., p. 8.
3. John H. Jenny, *Physical Education, Health Education and Recreation: Introduction to Professional Preparation for Leadership*, Macmillan, New York, 1961, p. 5.
4. Harold M. Barrow, *Man and Movement: Principles of Physical Education*, 3d ed., Lea & Febiger, Philadelphia, 1983, pp. 23, 24.
5. John E. Nixon and Ann E. Jewett, *An Introduction to Physical Education*, 9th ed., W. B. Saunders, Philadelphia, 1980, p. 27.
6. James A. Baley and David A. Field, *Physical Education and the Physical Educator*, 2d ed., Allyn & Bacon, Boston, 1976, p. 4.
7. Jan Felshin, "Physical Education: An Introduction," in *Physical Education: An Interdisciplinary Approach*, ed. Robert N. Singer, Macmillan, New York, 1972, pp. 3–12.
8. John W. Loy, "The Cultural System of Sport," *Quest* 29 (Winter 1978), 73–102.
9. Allen Guttmann, *From Ritual to Record: The Nature of Modern Sports*, Columbia University Press, New York, 1978.
10. Jenny, p. 25.
11. Jay B. Nash, "Education for Leisure: A Must," *JOHPER* 31 (January 1960), 17–18, 62.
12. Jenny, p. 43.
13. Nash, pp. 17–18, 62.
14. *The Academy Papers* 7 (1973).
15. Lois Ellfeldt, "Movement as a Theoretical Base for Physical Education," *The Academy Papers* 7 (1973), 12–13.
16. Paul Hunsicker, "Fitness as a Theoretical Base for Physical Education," *The Academy Papers* 7 (1973), 14–15.
17. Thomas J. Sheehan, "Sport: The Focal Point of Physical Education," *Quest* 10 (May 1968), 62–63, 66.
18. Edward J. Shea, "Sport as a Theoretical Base for Physical Education," *The Academy Papers* 7 (1973), 16–17.
19. Warren Fraleigh, "Resolved that Physical Education is Multi-Theoretical Rather than Uni-Theoretical," *The Academy Papers* 7 (1973), 10–11.
20. Celeste Ulrich, "A Multi-Theoretical Crusade," *The Academy Papers* 7 (1973), 18–20.
21. Ibid., 19.
22. Daryl Siedentop, "On Tilting at Windmills While Rome Burns," *Quest* 18 (June 1972), 94–97.
23. Rosalind Cassidy, "Should We Drop the Designation *Physical Education* in Favor of a Different Name?" *The Academy Papers* 6 (1972), 14.

24. *The Academy Papers* 7 (1973), 26–32.

25. Marion R. Broer, "Movement Education: Wherein the Disagreement?" *Quest* 2 (April 1964), 19–24.

26. E. O. Ojeme, "Has the Name, Physical Education, Outlived Its Usefulness?" *The Physical Educator* 41 (December 1984), 190–194.

27. Abraham Flexner, cited in Walter P. Kroll, *Graduate Study and Research in Physical Education*, Human Kinetics, Champaign, Ill., 1983, pp. 119–122.

28. Charles A. Bucher, *Foundations of Physical Education*, 6th ed., C. V. Mosby, St. Louis, 1972, pp. 9–18.

29. Franklin M. Henry, "The Discipline of Physical Education," *JOHPER* 37 (September 1964), 32.

30. Gerald S. Kenyon, "On the Conceptualization of Sub-Disciplines within an Academic Discipline Dealing with Human Movement," reprinted in *Contemporary Readings in Physical Education*, 3d ed., ed. Aileene S. Lockhart and Howard S. Slusher, Wm. C. Brown, Dubuque, 1975, pp. 343–347.

31. Celeste Ulrich and John E. Nixon, *Tones of Theory*, AAHPERD, Reston, Va., 1972, pp. 11–13.

32. Hal A. Lawson, *Invitation to Physical Education*, Human Kinetics, Champaign, Ill., 1984, pp. 57–58.

33. Guttmann, pp. 3–4.

34. Stephen Miller, "Ends, Means, and Galumphing: Some Leitmotifs of Play," *American Anthropologist* 75 (1973), 87–98.

35. Klaus Meier, "In Defense of Mediocrity: A Re-Visioning of Play," paper presented at American Alliance for Health, Physical Education, Recreation and Dance convention, Detroit, 14 April 1980.

36. Sigmund Freud, quoted in *Motivations in Play, Games, and Sports*, ed. Ralph Slovenko and James A. Knight, Charles C Thomas, Springfield, Ill., 1967, p. xxvii.

37. Roger Caillois, *Man, Play, and Games*, trans. Meyer Barash, Free Press, New York, 1961, pp. 13, 27–33.

38. Ibid., p. 13.

39. Daryl Siedentop, *Physical Education: Introductory Analysis*, 3d ed., Wm. C. Brown, Dubuque, 1980, p. 261.

40. Guttmann, p. 9.

41. Ibid., pp. 6–7.

42. William A. Harper et al., *The Philosophic Process in Physical Education*, 3d ed., Lea & Febiger, Philadelphia, 1977, p. 255.

43. Loy, "Cultural System of Sport," 73–102, and John W. Loy, Barry D. McPherson, and Gerald Kenyon, *Sport and Social Systems*, Addison-Wesley, Reading, Mass., 1978, pp. 21–23.

44. Guttmann, p. 11.

45. James W. Keating, "Sportmanship as a Moral Category," *Ethics* 75 (October 1964), 25–35.

46. Paul Weiss, *Sport: A Philosophic Inquiry*, Southern Illinois University Press, Carbondale, 1969, pp. 3–17.

47. Harold J. VanderZwaag, *Toward a Philosophy of Sport*, Addison-Wesley, Reading, Mass., 1972, pp. 70–72.

48. Ibid., pp. 72–74.

49. Cited in Guttmann, p. vii.
50. Ibid.
51. Henry, 32.
52. Siedentop, *Physical Education: Introductory Analysis*, pp. 126–127.
53. Kenyon, "On the Conceptualization of Sub-Disciplines," pp. 343–347.
54. Ulrich and Nixon.
55. *The Academy Papers* 7 (1973), entire issue.
56. Lawrence F. Locke, "Disciplines by Declaration: Verities and Balderdash," *Proceedings, National Association for Physical Education in Higher Education Annual Conference* 1 (1979), 96–100; and Elizabeth S. Bressan, "An Academic Discipline for Physical Education: What a Fine Mess!" *Proceedings, National Association for Physical Education in Higher Education Annual Conference* 3 (1982), 22–27.
57. Locke, 100.
58. Bressan, 26–27.
59. Jan Broekhoff, "A Discipline—Who Needs It?" *Proceedings, National Association for Physical Education in Higher Education Annual Conference* 3 (1982), 31, 33.
60. Ibid., 32.
61. Christopher Hopper, "Knowledge—Toward an Integration." *JOPERD* 55 (March 1984), 66–68.
62. Ibid., 68.
63. C. H. McCloy, "How About Some Muscle?" in *Philosophical Bases for Physical Education*, F. S. Crofts, New York, 1940.
64. Charles Poskanzer, Editorial letter, *JOPERD* 53 (February 1983), 7.
65. Daryl Siedentop, *Developing Teaching Skills in Physical Education*, Houghton Mifflin, Boston, 1976, pp. 12–14.

SUGGESTED READINGS

American Academy of Physical Education. *The Academy Papers* 7 (1973). Given largely to discussions of the focus and proper designation of the field of physical education.

American Academy of Physical Education. *The Academy Papers* 9 (1975). Discussions on the topic "Realms of Meaning."

American Academy of Physical Education. *The Academy Papers* 11 (1977). Discussions on the topic "Relationships in Physical Education."

Aronson, Richard M. "Physical Education: A Thought for Reform." *JOPERD* 57 (August 1986), 29–31.

Brackenbury, Robert L. "Physical Education, an Intellectual Emphasis?" *Quest* 1 (December 1963), 3–6.

Bressan, Elizabeth S. "An Academic Discipline for Physical Education: What a Fine Mess!" *Proceedings, National Association for Physical Education in Higher Education Annual Conference* 3 (1982), 22–27.

———. "2001: The Profession Is Dead—Was It Murder or Suicide?" *Quest* 31, no. 1 (1979), 77–82.

Broekhoff, Jan. "A Discipline—Who Needs It?" *Proceedings, National Association for Physical Education in Higher Education Annual Conference* 3 (1982), 28–36.

———. Physical Education as a Profession." *Quest* 31, no. 2 (1979), 244–254.

Corbin, Charles B. "First Things First, But Don't Stop There." JOPERD 52 (June 1981), 12–13.

Czula, Roman. "Sport as an Agency of Change." *Quest* 31, no. 1 (1979), 45–49.

"The Discipline of Physical Education," in *Contemporary Readings in Physical Education,* 3d ed., ed. Aileene S. Lockhart and Howard S. Slusher, pp. 331–365. Dubuque: Wm. C. Brown, 1975.

Gardner, David Pierpont. "Excellence: As Difficult as It Is Rare." *The Academy Papers,* 16 (1982), 105–112.

Haag, Herbert. "Development and Structure of a Theoretical Framework for Sport Science." *Quest* 31, no. 1 (1979), 25–35.

Harper, William. "Textures." In *Undergraduate Physical Education Programs: Issues and Approaches.* Ed. Hal A. Lawson. Reston, Va.: AAHPERD, 1981, pp. 87–94.

Henry, Franklin M. "The Academic Discipline of Physical Education." *Quest* 29 (Winter 1978), 13–29.

Hoffman, Shirl J. "SPECIALIZATION + FRAGMENTATION = EXTERMINATION: A Formula for the Demise of Graduate Education." *JOPERD* 56 (August 1985), 19–22.

Hopper, Christopher. "Knowledge—Toward an Integration." *JOPERD* 55 (March 1984), 66–68.

Hutslar, Jack. "This Thing That We Do: A Model for Sport and Dance." *Quest* 33, no. 1 (1981), 87–95.

Kleinman, Seymour. "The Reunification of Health and Physical Education." *JOPERD* 53 (April 1982), 19–21.

Lawson, Hal A. "Paths Toward Professionalization." *Quest* 31, no. 2 (1979), 231–243.

——, and W. Robert Morford. "The Crossdisciplinary Structure of Kinesiology and Sports Studies." *Quest* 31, no. 2 (1979), 222–230.

Loy, John W., Jr. "The Nature of Sport: A Definitional Effort." *Quest* 10 (May 1968), 1–15.

Meier, Klaus V. "An Affair of Flutes: An Appreciation of Play." *Journal of the Philosophy of Sport* 7 (Fall 1980), 24–45.

"The Nature of a Discipline." *Quest* 9 (December 1967): entire issue.

O'Hanlon, James, and Thomas Wandzilak. "Physical Education: A Professional Field." *Quest* 32, no. 1 (1980), 52–59.

Ojeme, E. O. "Has the Name, Physical Education, Outlived Its Usefulness?" *The Physical Educator* 41 (December 1984), 190–194.

Pooley, John C. "Physical Education and Sport and the Quality of Life." JOPERD 55 (March 1984), 45–48.

Powell, Richard R. "Play as an Ideal: Toward a Biosocial Model." *Quest* 35, no. 2 (1983), 107–119.

Progen, J. L., and Joy T. DeSensi. "The Value of Theoretical Frameworks for Exploring the Subjective Dimensions of Sport." *Quest* 36, no. 1 (1984), 80–88.

Rose, David A. "Is There a Discipline of Physical Education?" *Quest* 38, no. 1 (1986), 1–21.

Sage, George H. "The Quest for Identity in College Physical Education." *Quest* 36, no. 2 (1984), 115–121.

"The Scholarly Enterprise." *Quest* 20 (June 1973): entire issue.

"Synthesizing and Transmitting Knowledge: Research and Its Application." *The Academy Papers,* 16 (1982): entire issue.

Watson, Scott B. "The Legitimization of Sport: Pindar and Weiss." *Quest* 35, no. 1 (1983), 37–45.

Williams, Jesse Feiring. "Education Through the Physical." *Chronicle of American Physical Education, 1855–1930*, ed. Aileene S. Lockhart and Betty Spears, pp. 1–5. Dubuque: Wm. C. Brown, 1972.

Zeigler, Earle F. "Physical Education—Dead, Quiescent, or Undergoing Modification?" *JOPERD* 53 (January 1982), 51.

——. "Relating a Proposed Taxonomy of Sport and Developmental Physical Activity to a Planned Inventory of Scientific Findings." *Quest* 35, no. 1 (1983), 54–65.

See also the following books listed in the Resource Readings at the end of this book:

Caillois; *HPER Omnibus*; Kroll; Metheny; Siedentop; Ulrich and Nixon; Zeigler, *Issues*.

PART II

OUR HERITAGE:
Physical Education and Sport Through the Past

Roper's gymnasium, an example of an early American gymnasium in Philadelphia around 1830. (Courtesy Print Collection, The New York Library, Astor, Lenox and Tilden Foundations)

INTRODUCTION: THE DISCIPLINE OF SPORT HISTORY

Sport history is the study of sport in the past. It can show us how things came to be as they are today, and it can direct us to problems that need to be solved. There are two types of historical research: descriptive and interpretive.[1] Descriptive historical research is the early groundwork for historical study, for it simply determines the facts of the matter—the what of history—and reports them. Early historical works are usually descriptive. The more advanced (and more difficult) level of historical research is interpretive, an attempt to tell or determine why something happened or what is important about an event or trend. Evidence must be not only analyzed but also interpreted; this injects the issue of values and value systems into the research process.

Sources for historical research are generally primary or secondary sources.[2] A primary source is any person who was a direct witness to the event being studied or the record kept by such a person. It may be the account of a person who was there, or it may be official records kept during the event. In short, a primary source is firsthand information. A secondary source is any source not actually there when the event happened, such as a report by a person who interviewed one of the participants.

Historical research involves three basic concepts: change, development, and progress.[3] Change is a simple concept—a difference from an earlier state of being or condition. Change can be documented easily because no values are involved. Either a rule did or did not change; the evidence is usually clear. Development is a series of changes in a direction; it, too, is not difficult to establish with evidence. The speed of change in a direction can range from slow (evolution) to fast (revolution), and if it is consistent in a single direction, it can be documented to show a trend. Again, no values are involved. Simple facts can establish direction.

The third concept of historical research is progress, which does require value judgements and is thus less grounded in facts. Change and development are descriptive ideas, but progress is always interpretive because it assumes improvement. One of the difficulties of historical research is that many ideas are based on the concept of progress, which Robert Nisbet says has been an accepted concept for three thousand years of Western history.[4] Yet, the validity of progress as a concept is beginning to be questioned because it is so value-laden. As Nisbet summarizes it, "The idea of progress holds that mankind has advanced in the past—from some aboriginal condition of primitiveness, barbarism, or even nullity—is now advancing, and will continue to advance through the foreseeable future."[5]

This idea, clearly, is a value judgment, for one must believe in the idea of progress to begin with. The concept is critical to sport, since modern sport is very concerned with records and their breaking; only the belief in the idea of progress makes those records worth keeping, for they are goals to be surpassed, which is only possible if there is a belief in progress.

Sport history, with its concern about the who, what, when, where, and how of sport, serves to complete the circle of studies covered in sport science. Obviously, not all of the discipline areas are sciences; for those areas of study not strictly considered science, the term *sport arts and sciences* has been suggested, as has the term *sport social sciences*. Sport history serves to show us where we have been, how we got where we are today, and perhaps where we may be going and what we should be looking for when we get there.

One of the early sport history books was Joseph Strutt's *Sports and Pastimes of the People of England* (1800 and many other editions). John A. Krout's *Annals of American Sport* (1929) was the first scholarly book on sport history in the United States, though earlier writings on the subject are available. Many of the sources on sport history are cited in a booklet produced in 1980 by the History of Sport and Physical Education Academy of the AAHPERD, *Getting Started in the History of Sport and Physical Education*, also available through the ERIC Clearinghouse. Many excellent works on historical research methods are also available, such as the one by Jacques Barzun and Henry A. Graaf[6] (though its view of word-processing reflects the age of the authors) and an excellent work with real-life example-topics treated in depth by James West Davidson and Mark Hamilton Lytle.[7] Other works, such as the one by Allen Guttmann,[8] serve as an introduction to the problems of sport history research itself.

The North American Society for Sport History (NASSH) was founded in 1973 and held its first convention at Ohio State University that same year. It meets annually and publishes the *Journal of Sport History* three times a year, along with an annual *Proceedings* with abstracts of the research papers presented at the convention. Its members are primarily from the United States and Canada. The History of Sport and Physical Education Academy was founded as a scholarly division within the National Association for Sport and Physical Education (NASPE) branch of AAHPERD when the first discipline-oriented academies were begun in the mid-1970s. Its beginnings, along with those of NASSH, were an outgrowth of the work by scholars who began presenting papers at annual meetings of the old College Physical Education Association in the late 1950s and early 1960s, though sport history was slow to be accepted as a scholarly discipline or subdiscipline in the field of sport studies.

The names of sport history publications have been cited at length by Ronald Smith,[9] with a shorter list in *JOPERD* by Darrell Crase.[10] The most commonly seen ones are the *Canadian Journal of History of Sport*, which first appeared in 1970 as the *Canadian Journal of History of Sport and Physical Education*, and NASSH's *Journal of Sport History*, which first appeared in 1974. Many sport historians are listed, along with their research interests, in a directory compiled for the NASSH.[11]

Now we need to study where we have been and how we got where we are today. For the next several chapters, we will examine the historical development of physical education and sport from the earliest times up to the present day. In recent years, interest has risen in studying sport as a separate topic from physical education. However, we do not wish to separate them entirely, for that is perhaps one cause of the problems that physical educators are now trying to resolve. After we have studied these chapters, you should understand more clearly how we arrived at our present systems of physical education and of sport, and you will have a better understanding of the sometimes delicate relationship between the two. In the minds of most people, physical education and sport cannot be separated, so a firm understanding of the historical development of the relationship is critical.

NOTES

1. J. Thomas Jable, "The Types of Historical Research for Studying Sport History," in *Getting Started in the History of Sport and Physical Education*, ed. William H. Freeman, History of Sport and Physical Education Academy, Washington, 1980, pp. 13–14.
2. Roxanne Albertson, "Working with Primary Sources," in *Getting Started*, ed. Freeman, pp. 20–21.
3. Robert Nisbet, *History of the Idea of Progress*, Basic Books, New York, 1980.
4. Ibid., p. 4.
5. Ibid., pp. 4–5.
6. Jacques Barzun and Henry F. Graaf, *The Modern Researcher*, 4th ed., Harcourt Brace Jovanovich, New York, 1985.
7. James West Davidson and Mark Hamilton Lytle, *After the Fact: The Art of Historical Detection*, Alfred A. Knopf, New York, 1982.
8. Allen Guttmann, *From Ritual to Record: The Nature of Modern Sports*, Columbia University Press, New York, 1978.
9. Ronald A. Smith, "Presenting and Publishing Sport History," in *Getting Started*, ed. Freeman, pp. 24–31.
10. Darrell Crase, "Current Periodicals in Physical Education and the Sport Sciences," *JOPERD* 56 (October 1985), 76–80.
11. Don Morrow, comp. and ed., *The Directory of Scholars Identifying with the History of Sport*, 3d ed., N.p., University of Western Ontario and NASSH, Spring 1984.

SUGGESTED READINGS

Barzun, Jacques, and Henry F. Graaf. *The Modern Researcher*, 4th ed. New York: Harcourt Brace Jovanovich, 1985.

Davidson, James West, and Mark Hamilton Lytle. *After the Fact: The Art of Historical Detection*. New York: Alfred A. Knopf, 1982.

Dewing, Rolland. "History of American Sports: Academic Featherbedding or Neglected Area?" *The Social Science Journal* 14 (October 1977), 73–82.

Freeman, William H., ed. *Getting Started in the History of Sport and Physical Education*. Washington: History of Sport and Physical Education Academy, 1980.

Guttmann, Allen. "Who's on First? or, Books on the History of American Sports." *Journal of American History* 66 (September 1979), 348–354.

Lucas, John. "A Critique of a Recent Doctoral Dissertation— Possible Watershed in Physical Education Research." *The Physical Educator* 40 (December 1983), 171–173.

Osterhoudt, Robert G. "The History and Philosophy of Sport: The Reunification of Once Separated Opposites." *Journal of Philosophy of Sport* 5 (Fall 1978), 71–76.

Overman, Steven J. "Work and Play in America: Three Centuries of Commentary." *The Physical Educator* 40 (December 1983), 184–190.

"The Promise of Sport History: Progress and Prospects." *Journal of Sport History* 10 (Spring 1983), 5–106. Special issue with articles reviewing research in ancient, European, British, Canadian, and American sport history.

Park, Roberta J. "Research and Scholarship in the History of Physical Education and Sport: The Current State of Affairs." *Research Quarterly of Exercise and Sport* 54 (June 1983), 93–103.

Rader, Benjamin G. "Modern Sports: In Search of Interpretation." *Journal of Social History* 13 (Winter 1979), 307–321.

Redmond, Gerald. "Sport History in Academe: Reflections on a Half-Century of Peculiar Progress." *British Journal of Sports History* 1 (May 1984), 5–13.

Struna, Nancy L. "In 'Glorious Disarray': The Literature of American Sport History." *Research Quarterly for Exercise and Sport* 56 (June 1985), 151–160.

Voigt, David Q. "Myths After Baseball: Notes on Myths in Sports." *Quest* 30 (Summer 1978), 46–57.

Walvin, James. "Sport, Social History and the Historian." *British Journal of Sports History* 1 (May 1984), 24–40.

Wheeler, Robert F. "Teaching Sport as History, History Through Sport." *History Teacher* 11, no. 3 (1978), 311–322.

Zeigler, Earle F. "Excellent Teaching of Sport and Physical Education History Demands Interpretive Criteria." *The Physical Educator* 38 (March 1982), 47–51.

chapter 2

Physical Education and Sport in the Ancient World

Scientists have difficulty determining where humans originated, that is whether life began in one single area of the world. Scholars have theorized that human beings gradually evolved from simpler forms of life, but researchers have been unable to find concrete examples of all stages of the evolutionary process. Traces of early humans have been found in Africa, Asia, and Europe, though current theory suggests that people most similar to modern people first appeared in eastern Africa, in the vicinity of the Great Rift Valley.

During prehistoric times, the world went through long periods of great changes in climate. In time, these changes, which varied from periods of tropical conditions to great ice ages and back to tropical conditions, forced prehistoric people to disperse gradually across the face of the earth in search of havens from nature's harshness. Primitive people eventually reached the major continents and appeared on many of the earth's islands. Because of the differences in the level of the seas, many areas that are now below water level were at one time dry land; those dry areas provided many land bridges to areas that are now separate islands or continents. A prominent example of an area where a land bridge may have existed is the Bering Strait, which might have been a dry land connection used by Asian people to move into North America.

PRIMITIVE TIMES AND SURVIVAL SPORT

Primitive people lived in a harsh environment. In order to survive constant battles with nature, they gradually developed crude tools, such as axes, knives, and bows and arrows, which elevated them above other forms of animal life. The primitive human's cranial capacity, which was larger than that of other creatures in relation to body size, permitted the full development of the human intellect and capacity to reason and thus improved the chances of human survival over that of the animals.

More advanced patterns of speech developed as people became able to differentiate among shades of meaning. This greater precision and refinement in communication skills was a necessary step toward civilization, for it allowed people to begin working together to improve their group situation. While only the toughest and fittest individuals could survive the harsh life in primitive times, the formation of increasingly larger groups eased the difficulties of survival for the individual members, who were then able to improve their defenses.

Primitive people gathered first into family groups; in later times, several family groups would band together into a tribe under a strong leader or chief. The tribe overcame the difficulties of providing food by learning to plant and harvest crops, and thus they led a more settled life than the migratory prehistoric people who constantly wandered, searching for food.

As farming developed and people were able to live and feed in one area for much longer periods of time, villages grew and society became more stable. People were no longer forced to move when game animals became scarce, for the sources of food had expanded. Living in settled villages sped up the process of civilization by leading to improvements in the crude standards of living and to a gradual elevation of the type of education provided for the young.

The basic aim of education within primitive society was survival—both individual survival and group survival. The education provided to young males was primarily physical education, for it was oriented strongly toward physical strength and cunning. Good hunting and fighting skills were necessary if early man was to feed himself and his family and provide protection from other forces.

Deobold Van Dalen and Bruce Bennett suggest that primitive education was concerned with learning in two areas: survival skills and conformity conduct.[1] Survival skills included the ability to defend oneself and others; the ability to provide food, clothing, and shelter; and the skills necessary to survive as an individual in the world. Conformity skills were designed to insure the survival of the group by putting the skills of the individual into the service of the group. People had to be able to work with others to fulfill the needs of the group or the group would not survive. If the group did not survive, then human life would eventually pass from existence.

The emphasis of education in primitive times was survival; prehistoric cave paintings often depict hunting and warfare. (Negative #336184, Courtesy Department Library Services, American Museum of Natural History)

Dance activities and other ceremonial forms had meaning in primitive societies as prayers or as means of communicating to forces that could not be explained. Primitive people both feared and revered the forces of nature, and in trying to influence what they could neither understand nor explain, they gradually developed religious beliefs and customs. Through dance, primitive people sought religious communication and experience.

Among the physical activities of primitive people were the hunting skills of archery, spear and rock throwing, and stalking animals. Survival skills included such activities as running, jumping, and swimming, while hand-to-hand combat—primarily wrestling—represented the fighting skills.

As societies grew more advanced and life became easier, recreational activities developed. These activities often grew from earlier survival skills such as archery and running contests, but they became more something that children did or that adults used as entertainment. As games and sports developed, ball games became popular activities in early societies. Despite differences caused by climate, local customs, and available natural materials, the games that developed around the world were basically similar, for they often served as training methods in skills the children would need as adults.

The character of this type of education changed with the development of more complex cultural patterns than those that existed in village societies. As civilizations grew, the world moved closer to the state concept. Large groups of people sharing many characteristics, such as racial group, language, customs, and mode of living, developed loose governmental forms and leaders. Rather than aiming education, which had been primarily physical education in primitive cultures, toward the survival of the individual and small groups, the new states oriented the educational process toward their own strength and survival and often toward their expansion.

Just as the essential characteristic of primitive physical activities was a base of survival skills, providing practice in the skills needed for survival and defense against their natural enemies, so was sport essentially "survival sports," or "natural sports," for many of the sporting activities had their source in the same basic skills as the physical activities.

The sporting activities of primitive people can be viewed in the categories of games and sports, but they also can include dance activities, which were important to primitive cultures. Hackensmith refers to three types of primitive games: games of chance, games of dexterity and skill, and children's games.[2] We will view sport primarily in the area of the games of dexterity and skill. These activities included ball games and games such as archery, hoop and pole, and snow snake. While the competitive sports were often between two or more people in a village or tribe, some competitions were held between different villages and tribes. Most often these were ball games similar to forms of today's lacrosse or soccer contests.

When we look at the early forms of sports used by primitive people in Western culture (European prehistory), we often see a warlike basis for the activities. The sports required adeptness in the basic skills of war if a contestant was to be successful. While we have traditionally considered this warlike basis of sport to be a common trait of primitive societies, evidence suggests that this idea is untrue.[3] However, even though primitive sport was not always warlike or war oriented, it was taken seriously.

BEFORE THE GREEKS

Ancient China

The Chinese civilization was not the earliest civilization, and while it had almost no effect on the development of Western civilization and patterns of education, it was the major civilization of the Far East. Chinese history extends more than 2000 years before the Christian era, and its civilization remained stable well into modern times, which makes it one of the longest lasting of history's civilizations.

Early China was a society of agrarian people governed by tradition. All persons fulfilled assigned tasks just as those tasks had been performed before their birth and would be performed long after their death. The strong societal organization was based on a strong family unit, which was controlled by its eldest member. Every individual had strong family ties and followed the tradition of ancestor worship, for individual obedience and subservience to the family or group rather than individuality were stressed.

The nation's feudal system was based on a group of major lords who had the allegiance of many vassals. The dominant interest of the government was the maintenance of the status quo, or keeping things as they had been in the past.

The educational process, which was primarily for the upper classes, gradually became book oriented and formal. The emphasis on memorizing ancient writings required oral tests in which entire passages would be recited from memory; the result was a widespread system of rigorous examinations that left no time for physical activities. Many of the ancient writings or teachings were based on the works of Confucius and Buddha, and an attempt was made to develop a student's intellectual, moral, and aesthetic senses. During the earlier period of China's history, the educational process had included physical training, but as the process became more ritualistic, less time was available for such activities.

In many societies the military needs of the nation provided a reason for developing a program of physical training, but this reason was not generally true for the ancient Chinese, as they had developed a policy of isolationism. Their country also was blessed with many natural barriers that made invasion by outside forces extremely difficult. The towering Himalaya Mountains, which were all but impossible to pass, blocked many of the southern approaches to the land, and further complications were presented by the Gobi Desert to the west. In answer to the few unprotected borders, the Great Wall (completed about 200 B.C.) was built to protect much of the northwest border of China.

Many social problems resulted from the static nature of Chinese society, for it could accept no innovations unless they were justified by ancient authorities. The system of respect for the past and honor of family elders was implemented and upheld, moreover, by the teachings of Confucianism, which stressed the self-restraint and moderation necessary to survival in such an unchanging society. As religions developed, they had the sort of teachings that emphasized a life of contemplation as the ideal.

The combined nature of the various aspects of Chinese life made vigorous physical exercise an idea of little interest to the society. However, such recreational games and sports as early versions of soccer, polo, chess, and competitions in archery and wrestling were practiced by the people. A program of mild physical exercises, similar to gymnastics-oriented calisthenics, was developed and called *Cong Fu*. These activities were designed to prevent disease, which the Chinese believed could result from a lack of physical activity. Dancing was also popular. It was used primarily for ceremonial purposes, though there were both religious and popular forms. The popular forms were informal dances that the people used for recreational purposes.

Ancient India

India was not a major influence on the development of Western civilization, but it represents an important civilization that is almost as ancient as China's.

踢鞠圖

Although vigorous physical activities were generally of little interest in ancient China, the Chinese did participate in early versions of modern sports. The ball game here is similar to modern-day soccer. (From H. A. Giles, Adversaria Sinica, I, 92. Courtesy Widener Library, Harvard University)

India was invaded and largely taken over by an Aryan people around 1500 to 1200 B.C. The primary religion was Hinduism, which was also a social system and thus a factor of importance in the development of Indian civilization. The caste system within this religion eventually became rigid and severely limited the flexibility of Indian society. The people were divided by the system into castes, or social classes. Because they could not move either upward or downward in caste, their position in life was unchanging.

The primary aim of a person under Hinduism was to be virtuous. Asceticism, which was also stressed by the religion, could take almost any form, from a simple moderation of the wants of the individual to self-torture (only occasionally), depending on the strength and direction of the person's religious views.

Education was based on a person's caste, for the castes dictated the type of occupation their members could follow, even though the occupation might not have any relationship to a person's talents or abilities. No stress was put on individuality; emphasis was placed on the future life. The Hindus believed in reincarnation, that is, in the soul of the person returning to earth after the body's death to inhabit another body, which might be human or animal depending on how well a person's previous life was lived.

Little interest was shown in physical education, though some recreational sports and games and some dances were used for ceremonies and religious observances. Some physical training was necessarily provided for members of the military, who entertained themselves with hunting activities when there was no war. Physical exercises were sometimes used to promote health, but the care and exercise of the body were not major concerns of Hinduism.

Ancient Egypt

The predecessors of Western civilization were found in the Middle East, an area that spread inland around the eastern end of the Mediterranean Sea into the area of the ancient Fertile Crescent along the valleys of the Tigris and Euphrates rivers. Egypt furnished a natural place for an ancient civilization to flourish. The annual floods of the Nile River provided rich soil for farming, and water was always available for irrigation.

Although the civilization of ancient Egypt arose thousands of years in the past, it reached its peak around 1500 B.C., when it controlled large areas of the Middle East. The Egyptian people had an advanced civilization for that period. They developed writing and paper, produced great feats of engineering, developed a 12-month calendar, and did much work in the sciences, farming, and the arts. Egyptian society was very religious, for the people believed in many gods and a life after death. It was also one of the earliest to give women a role and status roughly equal to that of men; women had many more rights and powers in Egypt than were available to them in other early societies.[4]

Much of the educational process in early Egypt was aimed at professional training, particularly for the position of scribe, which required the important skills of reading and writing. Education was primarily oriented toward the practical aspects of learning a trade, and students often served apprenticeships.

Little interest was shown in physical education. Since the Egyptians were not usually militarily oriented, little impetus for physical training came from that direction. Although physical education was not a major part of Egyptian life, physical activities were important to the Egyptians. Many games and sports were popular with them, and women frequently participated in physical activities. Swimming was popular—the civilization's life was based on the river—as were gymnastic activities, hunting, games using the skills of fighting and war, and many types of ball games. The Egyptians also had a great love for dance activities.

The Ancient Middle East

The Middle Eastern civilizations included those of the Sumerians, Babylonians, Assyrians, Persians, and Macedonians. Their area of the world spread eastward from the Mediterranean Sea across the Tigris and Euphrates valleys and ranged northward to present-day Turkey, southward to the Arabian Peninsula, and eastward to an area near today's India.

The Assyrian civilization began before 2000 B.C., and reached its peak of power about 1200 B.C. Thereafter, one civilization followed another until about 100 B.C., when the Macedonians faded from the scene.

Much of the emphasis within those successive civilizations was on military conquest. Because of their military orientation, physical education in the Middle Eastern civilizations consisted primarily of warring activities, such as handling weapons and developing the ability to engage in hand-to-hand combat. Much of the fighting of the Persians was done on horseback, so the skills needed for good horsemanship were emphasized in their culture. Also, strong emphasis was placed on swimming.

The physical education process for men began in early youth, lasted well into the adult years, and was rigorous. Since little emphasis was placed on intellectual development, the process was more training than true education. Dance, which was largely a part of ceremonial exhibitions, was discouraged as a recreational activity for the people.

ANCIENT GREECE: THE GOLDEN AGE OF "PURE" SPORT AND PHYSICAL EDUCATION

The first Greek-speaking people were the Achaeans—invaders who settled in the northern areas of the Greek peninsula about 1900 B.C. and replaced the society and culture of the Minoan civilization of Crete. By about 1500 B.C., the Achaeans controlled most of the peninsula and had established Mycenae as their capital. Their economy was based on trade, and they established a number of commercial alliances with other prominent cities and states of the eastern Mediterranean area, such as Troy, Cyprus, Palestine, and Egypt.

After several hundred years, however, prolonged warfare and a declining Mycenaean economy permitted another invasion of the Greek peninsula from the north. These invaders, the Dorians, referred to themselves as Hellenes and the area they had invaded (the peninsula of modern Greece) as Hellas.[5]

The period of the Achaean or Mycenaean culture, from about 1500 to 800 B.C., is often called the Age of Homer. Many descriptions of Greek life and customs at that time appear in the two epic writings attributed to Homer, the *Iliad* and the *Odyssey*. The *Iliad* includes the first written accounts of sports competition, along with the first coaching advice—from Nestor to his son.[6]

Political rule was by an oligarchy, that is, by a small group of male aristocrats. Women were not considered equal to men in this society, but were considered the property of the men, with a certain value in livestock.[7] The education of the men at this time was essentially military, for there was no formal education as we think of it today. The emphasis was on developing military skills by such activities as running, boxing, and wrestling.

The people developed rituals similar to the funeral customs of the Egyptians for the burial and entombment of their dead. Games had some religious functions, for the people also developed funeral games that were meant to honor the dead. Prizes were given to the winners of contests in footracing, boxing, wrestling, and chariot races. Most other contests and sports at this time were informal rather than regularly occurring, organized events.

As the Mycenaean influence declined, the Greek peninsula gradually split up into a number of small city-states, or independent political units. Within each city-state, a town controlled the territory in its immediate vicinity but had no ties or obligations to any other city-state. As the city-states grew in strength, the classical Greek civilization with which most people are familiar gradually began to appear. During the Hellenic time period, the major city-states were Sparta and Athens. Those two city-states, though similar in many respects, were in marked contrast in their methods of government and in their philosophies of education.

Spartan Education

The Spartans, located in the southern Peloponnesus, were a totalitarian society; the individual existed for and was controlled by the state. The state was oriented entirely toward the military life. Weak children were abandoned to die in the wilderness so that weak citizens would not threaten the strength of the state.

Education, which was controlled by the state, was a harsh process of training for the males. The educational process was almost entirely physical. The emphasis on preparing the male child for the military life included diligent programs of running and throwing activities (javelin and discus), swimming, wrestling, boxing, and gymnastic activities. Dance was popular in Sparta because, while it was used to imitate military movements, it was part of ceremonial and recreational occasions as well. Music also was important, for much of the exercise was performed to music.[8] Many songs were composed to honor dead heroes, and the laws of the state were set to music.

The male children went through three stages of military training. They left their homes to live in barracks at the age of 7 years, training in packs under an older youth until they were about 14. They then underwent more intensive military training until they were about 20 years old, at which time they became regular members of the military. As military men, they had to continue to live in the barracks until they were 30 years old. At that age they could marry and leave the barracks, though they still were required to eat with the other soldiers rather than in their own homes.

The education of the girls was not neglected, for it also was controlled by the state from the time a girl was 7 years old until she was about 18. The training emphasized weight control and conditioning to prepare the girls for motherhood, and it included many of the same activities used by the boys. The girls participated regularly in athletics, just as the boys did. Many memorial markers honoring the girls' athletic feats were put up by their proud fathers and brothers. Unlike a man, however, a woman ended her athletic activities when she married, and she was expected to stay in the home.

While the Spartans were important participants in the games and sports at the many festivals of the times, they discouraged boxing and the *pankration* (a sort of free-style, no-holds-barred fighting), because the fighter had to admit defeat to prevent death or severe injury. Spartans were taught never to admit defeat; they considered victory important. Indeed, the records of their victories provide many of our earliest clues to the nature of sport in Greece.

Because of their emphasis on military training, the Spartans developed the best war machine in Greece, but they did not develop the ability to rule well politically. The boundaries of the areas that they ruled successfully were never very large, even though they did defeat the Athenians in the Peloponnesian Wars.

The Spartans placed no real emphasis on intellectual forms of education. They were trained for war, but they were not equipped to survive a successful peace. Their inability to rule well in times of peace eventually led to the conquest of the Greek people, first by the Macedonians and then by the Romans. The Spartan failure points out the severe shortcomings of their unbalanced approach toward education.

Athenian Education

The Athens of classical times has long been our favorite model for the theoretical balance necessary in education, particularly so to physical educators because of its emphasis on physical education.

Athens contrasted strongly to Sparta in many ways. While Athens had begun as an oligarchy, it developed a democratic society oriented toward the individual rather than toward the state. Their concept of democracy, however, was basically one for the men rather than for the women.

Athenian education was the first system of education that we think of as modern. It was the first system to be concerned with the all-around development of the individual, both mentally and physically.[9] The old motto that stresses the goal of education as "a sound mind in a sound body" (*mens sana in sano corpore*) expresses the essential balance that was the best quality of Athenian education. The process stressed physical training, public worship (which included music), public speaking, and learning the traditions and customs of the state. Later, "book learning" was added to this list, as reading and writing came to be considered necessary skills.

Hermann Weimer speaks of Athenian education as stressing *paidia*, which means the "beautiful and the good."[10] This represented the ideal characteristics of the Athenian citizen: aesthetic sensibilities, knowledge, physical skills, and a strong sense of ethics.

The educational system in Athens, like its government, was primarily for the men; the women were educated in the home and had few rights. Plato had suggested that the educational process for boys should begin with physical education around the age of 6 years, with grammar added at the age of 10 and music added at the age of 13. In reality, however, all three portions of the process were begun about the same time and continued until a boy reached the age of 18 and entered the military.

The program of physical education for older males was concentrated at the *gymnasium*. The name for this type of training school came from the Greek word meaning "naked," for the Greek males exercised and performed in the nude. The gymnasium was relatively elaborate, and because much room was needed for running and throwing activities, it was built outside the city. A smaller version of the gymnasium, the *palestra*, or wrestling school, was located within the city and was used primarily for the training of schoolboys.

A teacher of physical exercise at the palestra was called a *paidotribe*, and was similar to today's physical education instructor. The men who coached or trained the athletes for competition were called *gymnastses*.[11] These instructors were often retired champion athletes, and their duties were similar to those of today's coaches.

The basic aim of the educational process at the gymnasium and at the palestra was not the development of the physical for its own sake; instead, it was designed to develop the qualities of the individual *through* the use of physical means.[12] The activities used by the Athenians at the palestra and the gymnasium were essentially the same as those used by the Spartans, but with the addition of exercises designed to improve movement skills, such as posture and the mechanics of graceful movement. The Spartans stressed the development of the man of action, while the Athenians sought a harmonious development of the individual across physical and intellectual lines. Because of this balance, physical activities were more fully integrated into the educational process than in any other civilization before or since Athens.

The Greeks and Modern Society

We feel close to the ancient Greeks for many reasons. We see the Greeks as the first people to express our modern concept of democracy, and we still think of their theoretical educational system as one of the best-balanced systems of all time. Their philosophy of the harmonious relationship between the mind and the body lies at the heart of most contemporary theories of physical education.

The Greeks were similar to modern societies in many respects, but one common link is the similarity of their strong interest in athletic competition. Sport was an important part of life for the Greeks. It was supported by most Athenians as an important part of the educational process in the sense that it assisted in their search for bodily perfection to accompany their training of the intellect. Sport also was supported by the government, as in Sparta, for it produced a population that would be prepared to serve in the army if the need arose.

Athletic Games and Contests

The religious games and festivals held by the Athenians and other Greeks during this period (1000 to 300 B.C.) were generally celebrated by athletic contests, dances, and music. Some of the festivals were celebrated within a single city-state and by only one sex, such as in the case of honoring local gods. Other festivals, however, were broader in appeal and sometimes were celebrated by all of the Greek people. Some of the major festivals appear to have grown from earlier funeral games. This funerary origin was not rare in ancient times, as can be seen in the similar *Aonach Tailteann*, the great Irish festival, which may be older than the Olympic Games. Indeed, the Irish claim that it was the inspiration for the Greek games.

The greatest of those festivals was the Olympic Games, celebrated in honor of Zeus, chief god of the Greeks.[13] The festival lasted for five days in late August and was held in every fourth year (which resulted in the term *Olympiad*, meaning a four-year period).

The first recorded Olympic Games took placed in 776 B.C., though there were undoubtedly contests prior to that date. The games took place near the village of Elis in western Greece. They may have been held originally in honor of Heracles, an early traditional hero, with the worship of Zeus appearing in the sixth century.[14] Women were banned, perhaps because Heracles was a warriors' hero, and the presence of women was thought to diminish the warriors' power.

Matthew Dickie argues that "winning was not everything in Greek athletics and that the spirit in which a man competed in the games was a matter of some importance." He suggests that cheating or valuing victory too highly was not respected.[15]

Manfred Lammer, however, presents a view of Greek sport that is different from our traditional beliefs. In writing of the Greek concept of *agon*, often translated as "contest" in the term *agon olympikoi*, he notes that the word can as easily mean "war" and "battle," that in fact the "games" translation comes to us from the Romans, who thought the Greek festivals *looked* like Roman *ludi*, or "games." He stresses that the early competitions were exercises by the upper classes in the skills of war, and that the gymnasium was "a military training centre for the heavily-armed sons of middle-class citizens who had acquired wealth and political influence during the period of colonization and expanding trade." He notes that the earlier champions were warrior-athletes; only later were there victors with no military ties.[16]

Each fourth year, a month-long peace (the *pax Olympica*) was declared around the time of the games. It required each city-state to cease any fighting with any other city-state and to allow all athletes passage through its territory. Lammer maintains that the Olympic "peace" was really more of a treaty of immunity during the games rather than a true declaration of peace. It was agreed to by the city-states so that no local war would interfere with the competition.[17] Until later years, no women were allowed to view or compete in the games, and as was the custom of the day, the athletes competed in the nude.

The games may have been the greatest cultural exchange among the various Greeks of that period. The multitudes of people who came to watch the games mingled during the week of competition, and all of the athletes were required to spend the last month of training prior to the games in a common training camp with all of the other Olympic competitors.

The games originally were held on a field beside a statue of Zeus, with the footraces starting at its base. Later, over a period of years, a stadium was constructed. The primary footrace of the games was the *stade*, which was a race for the length of the long, narrow stadium, or about 180 meters. Another race was twice that long, while other races of up to 5 kilometers in length were held in some festivals. However, the shortest race was the most important one. Starting places were carved into stone for the sprinters, and javelins, later replaced by stone pillars, were used to mark the turning points and finishing lines.

Other events in the Olympic Games included the discus throw, the javelin throw (in which a leather strap was used as a throwing aid), the long jump (with hand-weights to assist the takeoff), wrestling in several different styles, boxing, the very rough *pankration*, chariot and horse racing, and the pentathlon. The pentathlon consisted of five events: a short run, the long jump, the discus and javelin throws, and wrestling. The manner of determining the winner has not been settled by scholars,[18] though H. A. Harris suggests that it required victory in three of the five events.[19]

In addition to the Olympic Games, there were many other Greek festivals that included athletic competitions. The most prominent ones were the Pythian Games at Delphi (honoring Apollo and awarding a laurel wreath), the Isthmian Festival at Corinth (honoring Poseidon and awarding a pine wreath), and the Nemean Festival at Nemea (honoring Zeus and awarding a celery wreath). They were the other three members of the "Big Four" circuit.[20] Many lesser local festivals also took place.

Evidence is clear that separate athletic competitions for women also were held. Records indicate that a festival of Hera was held every four years at the Olympic stadium at a time separate from that of the Olympic Games.[21] In this competition the racing distance for women was shortened by one-sixth. Apparently, the women's competitions were expanding by the first century A.D., for their events were being recorded as a part of the other competitions we have mentioned.[22]

Women's competition may have appeared at least as early as men's competition in Greece, and the Heraea (games of Hera, the sister-wife of Zeus) at Olympia might have begun before the Olympic Games.[23] However, because so little evidence is available for women's sport in ancient Greece (though it was present very early, and occasionally had highly skilled participants), it probably was still insignificant, reflecting women's relative place in Greek society.[24] Games for women and for youths appeared in later years.

Although many of the competitions were at times of religious holidays, Harris suggests that this has little actual religious significance in terms of the origin of the various games. He theorizes that the holidays simply provided a convenient leisure time for the competitions, just as the American football bowl games were not founded as religious celebrations of Christmas and New Year's Day.[25] Indeed, later we shall see that a tie between religion and sport was very much the case during the late Middle Ages.

The Rise of Professionalism

Because the Greeks held many local games other than just the Olympic Games, interest in athletic competition became widespread. The presence of a coach's handbook on training, by Philostratus in the third century B.C., shows that the coaching profession was well established by the Golden Age of Greek sport.[26] The athletic games had developed from ceremonies to worship the gods and from games that were held to honor the dead at their funerals. During earlier times, the prizes were small, usually tokens representing the importance of the god or the person who had died. As time passed, however, the size and nature of the awards changed.

The prize for an Olympic victory was traditionally a wreath or crown formed from an olive branch and its leaves. It was primarily a symbolic prize rather than a valuable one. However, the city-states began to offer additional prizes to their natives who won Olympic victories. At the vale of Olympia, a man received only an olive wreath, but when he returned home, he might be given enough wealth to last a lifetime. The victorious athletes usually were feted by their city-states when they returned home. Triumphal parades were held, and many privileges were given to them. Often, statues of the Olympic champions were erected. Gifts of food, money, and civic honors were frequent and worth winning, so more competitors entered the games.

As the civic prizes grew, the level of Olympic competition gradually changed. Fewer true amateurs competed, for they could not match the skills of those who had no occupation other than athlete. As the athletes competed for larger prizes, professionalism grew. As the extent of professionalism spread, the Olympic Games began to die. The games faced heavy competition from city-state games that began to offer larger prizes. Men no longer competed for the honor of victory, but for the prizes that were offered.

Over a period of hundreds of years, interest in the Greek athletic competitions declined. The Olympic Games in particular fell gradually into disrepute with the rise of professional athletes. The athletes with more money were able to devote more time to training for the games, which gave them an advantage over the athletes who did not have similar training. This professionalism became more prevalent after the Romans conquered the Greeks. The games were finally abolished by the emperor of the Byzantines (the Eastern Roman Empire), Theodosius I, in A.D. 394. This was partly because Theodosius, as a Christian, considered the games (which were held to honor the Greek gods) to be pagan events, though their corruption by professionalism had also changed the character of the games considerably by then.[27]

Greek Sport and Physical Education Revisited

Although we think of the time of the ancient Greeks as a time of "pure" sport, genuinely amateur athletic competition was not the true state of affairs. Although the number of professionals grew slowly, amateurism was dying even during the Golden Age, for the amateurs had neither the time nor the money to compete on equal terms with the professional athletes. The problem of amateurism versus professionalism, with which we are so familiar, dates not to the Romans but to the Greeks. The Greeks developed a philosophy of "sport for sport's sake," but they were not able to live up to that philosophy. While the Olympic Games continued well into Roman times, they had long since lost most of their purity.

The decline of sport came when sport shifted its emphasis from participation to the winning of prizes and the amusement of spectators. The Greek athletes competed for prizes offered by the city-states, the city-states offered the prizes to attract the athletes, and the various games were staged to bring fame and business to the city-states. Sport became more of a business than an amusement, for both the organizers and the competitors.

Greek civilization, particularly as represented by the Athenians, was a high point in the history of education. This period marked the first time in Western civilization that the educational process had developed beyond simply meeting predominantly military or trade designs and needs. For the first time, education had a balanced goal: the development of a "whole" man, a person who was well and equally developed in mind and body, a man who was acceptable to the military needs of his day but who, unlike the Spartans, could also fulfill the civic or governmental needs of his time.

Philosophy had entered education during this period, for people such as Socrates, Plato, and Aristotle had sought to develop or discover an "ideal" educational process to produce the well-rounded product of education that they believed should be its goal. Such a balanced educational process as the Athenians had was not to be seen again until the Renaissance, and when it did appear, it was a deliberate attempt to copy the newly rediscovered Greeks. As Greek civilization declined and Roman civilization grew to replace it, much of the glory of Greek culture was lost to Western civilization. As the power of the Greek people declined (largely because of prolonged wars between the city-states), they were conquered by the Macedonian empire of Alexander the Great. When Alexander died around 320 B.C., his empire broke into smaller nations. Greek civilization went through a process of blending with the civilization of the Middle East over the next two centuries. The resulting diluted Greek culture was encountered by the Romans as they became powerful in the eastern Mediterranean between 200 to 100 B.C.

THE AGE OF PROFESSIONALISM AND UTILITY: THE ROMAN EMPIRE

Roman civilization grew at a hilly point on the Tiber River in the central part of the Italian Peninsula. Founded by shepherds and traders, Rome began as a republican society with the government of the state shared by its citizens. The small city-state gradually expanded its control of the surrounding territory until it had conquered the entire peninsula of Italy. It then looked to other parts of the Mediterranean, always with the excuse that Rome was only protecting herself against potential invaders.

The essential characteristic of Roman civilization was practicality—what would work in a given situation. While the Greeks had been thinkers and philosophers, the Romans were doers. The Greeks built philosophies, and the Romans built roads.

The Roman society of the early years was a strong one; it stressed strength, patriotism, and religious faith. Character, or morals, also was stressed strongly. Women were more important and equal in the Roman society than they had been in Greece.

Roman Education and Physical Education

The object of early Roman education was to produce children who would be true to the Roman ideals and religion. During this time their education was received at home.

Physical training for the boys was oriented almost entirely toward military goals. Unlike the Greeks, the Romans had no real interest in beauty, harmony, or the balanced development of the individual, though a strong sense of morals was considered important. Much of the contact with literature came from the memorization of the Twelve Tables, Rome's codification of the laws.

As the power and influence of the Romans grew and they gained control of more provinces in the eastern Mediterranean, they saw a greater need for the education that would enable them to administer their territories. The trend was also away from the military orientation of physical training as the old part-time army of citizens became more a full-time army of mercenaries, or noncitizens who were paid to serve in the army.

Education in the home had made early Rome strong, but as the empire grew, schools were developed outside the home. Much of the instruction was done by Greek slaves, who had a broader education than the Romans.[28] These Greeks provided the grammar part of the traditional Greek education, but since the Romans saw no practical use for the gymnastics or music, those studies were not included in the program. The educational program was unbalanced, for the Romans were interested primarily in education that had practical uses. Their contributions to civilization were notably in the practical areas of law and engineering.

The great wealth that came into the Roman Empire from the conquered nations, along with the many slaves who did much of the work previously done by the poorer Romans, led to a breakdown of the societal morals of the Roman people. A Roman did not have to work to survive, for the state provided free food. Political corruption grew with this luxury, and the old Roman ideals of patriotism and self-sacrifice died.

The later Romans saw little reason for physical training. Rome became a nation of spectators. The people would go to the circus or the amphitheater and watch chariot races or gladiatorial fights to the death. As they demanded more variety in the death struggles, they used fights between animals and men, between larger groups of men, and eventually even small sea battles made possible by flooding the arena.

This emphasis on spectatorship and the growing professionalism in athletics had a weakening effect on the strength of Roman society, just as it had eventually destroyed the Olympic Games of the Greeks. The moral and educational values of the Romans' games disappeared. The Romans were more interested in the violent sports—and only as spectators. They had little interest in personal competition or in personal excellence.

The Romans also were interested in baths. Ruins of old Roman baths, many of which were built and operated by the government, can be found in many areas of the Western world today. Some facilities were provided for exercise at the baths, but not on the scale of the Greek facilities. Exercise was only a minor part of the experience at the Roman baths, for the emphasis was on the sedentary pleasures of hot and cold baths and massage. The baths were more like health spas or social clubs today.

Roman Sport

A number of advantages aided the survival of sport, particularly track and field, in Greece. The Greeks had centuries of experience in sport. Sport had religious ties because of its ceremonial uses, it had been a pastime of the wealthy, and it was still a part of the educational experience for Greek youths.[29] Sport did not have the same advantages in the Roman world.

As was mentioned, the Greeks were more philosophical than the Romans, who were more practically minded. The Greeks had a philosophical basis for sport as a cultural activity, but the Romans saw sport only in two ways, both of which were basically practical: as military training and as entertainment. The Romans were not interested in the educational value of sport, except as preparation for war.

Two primary differences existed between the Greek and Roman approaches to sports: (1) the Romans were primarily spectators rather than participants as were the Greeks, and (2) the Romans were more wholehearted in their support of professionalism, which was in contrast to the Greek ideal of amateurism in sport. The Romans for the most part did not compete in sports; they watched others take part. Many questions have been raised concerning whether we should call the Roman spectacles athletics, or even entertainment, rather than sport. This change also would affect our calling the participants athletes as opposed to competitors or simply participants. The Romans did not want to see less skilled amateurs; they preferred highly skilled professionals. The Roman pattern of going to sporting events to be entertained is a trend that can be seen in contemporary athletics.

As William Baker notes, the difference between the Greek and Roman approaches to sport can be seen in their choice of words used to describe it. While the Greeks used *agon*, roughly translated as "contest," the Romans used *ludi*, which meant "games," but with the meaning of an entertainment or amusement. This difference could shift the emphasis from the competitors to the spectators, which the Romans did.[30]

The growth of professionalism under the Romans helped to destroy what strength remained in the Greek sports system. Few amateur athletes were interested in the Olympic Games, for they could not compete with the professional athletes. The concept of the mind-body balance was lost, as was the idea of all-around body development. The age of specialization had come to the ancient world, and we can still see the ill effects in modern sport.

The emphasis of sport originally had been the honor of victory and the joy of competition, but over a period of centuries it gradually changed until there was only one real emphasis: victory. The better it paid, the more pleasant it was. The athlete competed primarily for the prize, rather than for the honor or the joy.

This overemphasis on victory and professionalism carried into the early medieval period when it (and much of sport) lost favor in a Christian reaction against the pagan elements in sport. As the Roman Empire dissolved, the rich prizes were no longer available on a regular basis, and organized sports as the Greeks and Romans knew them gradually disappeared.

The wealth and sedentary decadence of the Romans eventually brought down the empire. When the barbarians began to try to take it over, the Romans no longer had the internal strength to oppose a strong outside force. Although the Romans had gained control over most of western Europe, the Mediterranean, and the Middle East, the conquests began to reverse as the barbarians nibbled at the edges of the empire. By A.D. 400, the Romans were in full flight; they withdrew their outlying garrisons to return home to defend Rome, but to no avail. Wealth and moral laxity had made Roman culture too weak for a successful defense. Although the last true Roman emperor passed from the scene in A.D. 476, the empire continued, controlled by the newcomers and split into two parts: the western empire, centered about Rome, and the eastern empire, centered at Constantinople. From that time, the Roman Empire had little influence. Most of its former territories had fallen to various barbarian groups who had hoped to get a piece of the rich Roman life for themselves.

NOTES

1. Deobold B. Van Dalen and Bruce L. Bennett, *A World History of Physical Education*, 2d ed., Prentice-Hall, Englewood Cliffs, N.J., 1971, p. 1.
2. C. W. Hackensmith, *History of Physical Education*, Harper & Row, New York, 1966, p. 7.
3. Maxwell L. Howell, Charles Dodge, and Reet A. Howell, "Generalizations on Play in 'Primitive' Societies," *1974 North American Society for Sport History Proceedings*, pp. 18–20.
4. Hackensmith, pp. 16–18.
5. Arthur Weston, *The Making of American Physical Education*, Appleton-Century-Crofts, New York, 1962, pp. 1–2.

6. Darwin Semotiuk, "Human Energy in Sport Coaching: Historical Perspectives from Ancient Greece," *Canadian Journal of History of Sport* 13 (December 1982), 20–21.
7. Emmett A. Rice, John L. Hutchinson, and Mabel Lee, *A Brief History of Physical Education*, 5th ed., Ronald Press, New York, 1969, pp. 11–14.
8. Hackensmith, pp. 26–31.
9. Hermann Weimer, *Concise History of Education*, Philosophical Library, New York, 1962, pp. 3–11.
10. Ibid., p. 8.
11. E. Norman Gardiner, *Greek Athletic Sports and Festivals*, Macmillan, London, 1910 (Wm. C. Brown Reprints, Dubuque, 1970), pp. 468, 503.
12. Van Dalen and Bennett, pp. 46–67.
13. Ibid., pp. 51–56.
14. John Mouratidis, "Heracles at Olympia and the Exclusion of Women from the Ancient Olympic Games," *Journal of Sport History* 11 (Summer 1984), 41–55.
15. Matthew W. Dickie, "Fair and Foul Play in the Funeral Games in the Iliad," *Journal of Sport History* 11 (Summer 1984), 8–17.
16. Manfred Lammer, "The Greek Agon—War or Game?" paper presented at the Olympic Scientific Congress, Eugene, Ore., 19–26 July 1984, pp. 5–6, 7–9.
17. Ibid., pp. 10–11.
18. Gardiner, pp. 359–371.
19. H. A. Harris, *Sport in Greece and Rome*, Cornell University Press, Ithaca, N.Y., 1972, pp. 34–35.
20. William J. Baker, *Sports in the Western World*, Rowman and Littlefield, Totowa, N.J., 1982, p. 14.
21. H. A. Harris, "The Greek Athletic Programme," *Proceedings of the First International Seminar on the History of Physical Education and Sport*, Wingate Institute for Physical Education and Sport, Nitanya, Israel, April 1968, p. 7-2.
22. Harris, *Sport*, pp. 40–41.
23. Thomas F. Scanlon, "The Origin of Women's Athletics in Greece," *1982 North American Society for Sport History Proceedings*, pp. 33–34.
24. Betty Spears, "A Perspective of the History of Women's Sport in Ancient Greece," *Journal of Sport History* 11 (Summer 1984), 32–47.
25. Harris, *Sport*, p. 17.
26. Semotiuk, 27–28.
27. Hackensmith, pp. 54–55.
28. Weimer, pp. 11–16.
29. Harris, *Sport*, pp. 72–74, 184–185.
30. Baker, p. 31.

SUGGESTED READINGS

Abrams, Harvey. "A Brief History of the Pankration." *Canadian Journal of History of Sport* 10 (December 1979), 36–51.

Bennett, Bruce L. "The Curious Relationship of Religion and Physical Education." *JOHPER* 41 (September 1970), 69–71.

Boe, Alfred F., and Lyle I. Olsen. "Beauty, Strength and Wisdom: Aidos in Athletics." *Arete: The Journal of Sport Literature* 1 (Fall 1983), 165–176.

Dickie, Matthew W. "Fair and Foul Play in the Funeral Games of the Iliad." *Journal of Sport History* 11 (Summer 1984), 8–17.

Fairs, John R. "The Influence of Plato and Platonism on the Development of Physical Education in Western Culture." *Quest* 11 (December 1968), 14–23.

Finley, M. I., and H. W. Pleket. *The Olympic Games: The First Thousand Years.* Toronto: Clarke, Irwin, 1976.

Forbes, Clarence A. "Ancient Athletic Guilds." *Classical Philology* 50 (October 1955), 238–252.

——. *Greek Physical Education.* New York: Century, 1929.

Gardiner, E. Norman. *Greek Athletic Sports and Festivals.* London: Macmillan, 1910 (Dubuque: Wm. C. Brown Reprints, 1970).

Guttmann, Allen. "Sports Spectators from Antiquity to the Renaissance." *Journal of Sport History* 8 (Summer 1981), 5–27.

Hardy, Stephen. "Politicians, Promoters and the Rise of Sport: The Case of Ancient Greece and Rome." *Canadian Journal of History of Sport and Physical Education* 8 (May 1977), 1–15.

Harris, H. A. *Greek Athletes and Athletics.* Bloomington: Indiana University Press, 1966.

——. *Sport in Greece and Rome.* Ithaca, N.Y.: Cornell University Press, 1972.

Kyle, Don. "Professionalism and Elitism in Athenian Athletics." In the *Proceedings: 5th Canadian Symposium on the History of Sport and Physical Education,* ed. Bruce Kidd, University of Toronto, 1982, pp. 42–51.

McKernan, Mary. *A Historical Account of the Three Phases of Aonach Tailteann.* M.S. thesis, Springfield College, 1981. Microfiche.

Martin, Dennis W. *A Biblical Doctrine of Physical Education.* Ed. D. dissertation, University of North Carolina at Greensboro, 1983. Microfiche.

Miller, Stephen G. *Ancient Writers, Papyri and Inscriptions on the History and Ideals of Greek Athletics and Games.* Chicago: Ares, 1979.

Moore, Sandra L. *The Ancient Olympic Games as a Culturally Unifying Force for Greek Nationalism.* M.S. thesis, Pennsylvania State University, 1977.

Mouratidis, John. *Greek Sports, Games and Festivals Before the Eighth Century B.C.* Ph.D. dissertation, Ohio State University, 1982.

——. "Heracles at Olympia and the Exclusion of Women from the Ancient Olympic Games." *Journal of Sport History* 11 (Summer 1984), 41–55.

Olivova, Vera. "Kalogathia—The Greek Ideal of the Harmonious Personality." *Canadian Journal of History of Sport* 14 (December 1983), 1–15.

Poole, Lynn, and Gray Poole. *History of Ancient Olympic Games.* New York: Ivan Obolensky, 1963.

Robinson, Rachel Sargent. *Sources for the History of Greek Athletics.* Privately published, Cincinnati, Ohio, 1955.

Roland, Auguet. *Cruelty and Civilization: The Roman Games.* New York: Humanities Press, 1972.

Scanlon, Thomas F. "The Vocabulary of Competition: *Agon* and *Aethlos,* Greek terms for Contest." *Arete: The Journal of Sport Literature* 1 (Fall 1983), 147–162.

Semotiuk, Darwin. "Human Energy in Sport Coaching: Historical Perspectives from Ancient Greece." *Canadian Journal of History of Sport* 13 (December 1982), 18–29.

Spears, Betty. "A Perspective of the History of Women's Sport in Ancient Greece." *Journal of Sport History* 11 (Summer 1984), 32–47.

Swaddling, Judith. *The Ancient Olympic Games.* London: British Museum, 1980.

Thurmond, Ray C. "Athletics and Physical Exercise as 'Evidence of Sensible Things' in Aristotle." *Canadian Journal of History of Sport and Physical Education* 8 (May 1977), 28–37.

Young, David C. *The Olympic Myth of Greek Amateur Athletics*. Chicago: Ares, 1984.

See also the following books listed in the Resource Readings at the end of the book:

Arlott; Baker; Gerber; Guttmann, *From Ritual to Record*; Howell; Huizinga; McIntosh et al.; Mandell, *Cultural History*; Spears and Swanson; Van Dalen and Bennett; and Zeigler, *History*.

chapter 3

Physical Education and Sport in Medieval and Early Modern Europe

The Roman Empire fell because most Romans made little effort to prevent its fall. While the incoming barbarians wished to share in the advantages of the empire and had considerable respect for Roman traditions, they did not understand the Roman culture and thus were unable to preserve it. The rapidly growing Christian church was the only stable institution in Europe after the fall of the Roman Empire. Its strength lay in its uncompromising dogmatism and its rigid organizational structure. Consequently, it was the strongest political force in Europe during the medieval period.

MEDIEVAL SOCIETY AND PHYSICAL EDUCATION

The Middle Ages are a period that many people misunderstand. It is often called the Dark Ages in the belief that little is known about the period or that the people of the times were uncivilized or unenlightened. Those beliefs, however, are incorrect. Essentially, the Middle Ages formed a transition period between a time when a large, unified nation or civilization (the Roman Empire) had disappeared and a later time when nations regained strength and stability (the Renaissance). However, the people of the Middle Ages did seem to be retreating from civilization.

The feudal system was the dominant form of social and political organization. Some scholars have suggested that the system had Germanic origins and had developed from a form of tribal organization that tied the fighting men to a single chieftain. In the pyramidic structure of feudalism, the greater partners (lords) furnished financial or political support to the monarch and protection or some manner of making a living to their many lesser partners (vassals), while the vassals provided military and political support for their lords and the monarch.

A vassal owed a stated period of military service for each land holding that he was given. The monarch owned all of the land and had the right to evict any person who broke his oath of fealty or loyalty. The land holdings were not hereditary, so the monarch could disown the heirs of a vassal (lords were considered vassals to the monarch). Within this system, the land was divided into large manors or farms. The lords possessed the domain and all its products, plus a share of the products of the tributary lands that were worked by their vassals (in this case, similar to tenant farmers).

The towns were decaying for economic reasons from the fifth to the eighth centuries, the early Middle Ages. Trade in the Mediterranean Sea area was hampered by the rising Moslem tide, for its converts at their peak of power had gained control of the sea from Turkey around the south shore across Africa and upward into Spain. Travel was risky because of pirates at sea and barbarians and highwaymen on land. No strong, protective governments existed to assist free trade.

As Moslem strength declined, however, trade became more open on the Mediterranean. Towns gradually began to grow in areas where they could find protection, such as beside castles and monasteries, and trade fairs sprang up across Europe as the barbarians began to settle down. Thus, during the 9th to 11th centuries, the signs of a stable civilization began to reappear, and the growing trade across the face of Europe led to the peak of medieval development around the 12th to 13th centuries.

During this time, the need for money to wage wars led many monarchs to sell charters for towns, along with the rights of a lord. Those towns, surrounded by walls for safety, became growing commercial and industrial areas. Traders and skilled artisans developed guilds, or trade unions, designed to ensure the quality of their products, to train apprentices in the skills of the trade, and to limit their competition in the field to maintain price levels.

Between 1096 and 1270, a series of eight Crusades, or military expeditions, were called for by the popes of the Catholic church. Those campaigns were in response to several recurring problems: the Holy Land around Jerusalem was captured by the Moslems, who hated the Christians; the Western world was threatened by the Turks; and the papal strength and control was challenged by the Holy Roman Emperor, whose territories were concentrated in the area of today's Germany.

People responded to the call for the Crusades for many different reasons. Some of those reasons were greedy. A fortune might be made in the booty of victory, fame could be gained, and adventure was available. Some of those reasons were religious. People went on the Crusades to protect the church, or they went simply to gain salvation. However, as more Crusades were called, their religious appeal diminished until they finally amounted to little more than self-seeking expeditions of greedy knights. A major effect of the Crusades on late medieval Europe was the reestablishment of contact with areas beyond Europe.

Perhaps the best-known tradition of the Middle Ages is chivalry, or the tradition of courtly love, which is based on heroic fancy and romantic notions. The fiction that chivalry ruled the world resulted primarily from a thirst for honor and glory and the nobility's desire for praise and lasting fame. It implied the qualities of compassion, piety, austerity, fidelity, heroism, and love.

The Catholic church frowned on chivalry because of its erotic elements; the romantic ideal was actually adulterous in that the knight was expected to pine away for a married woman. The church did approve of some of the other ideals of chivalry, such as the ascetic tendencies implied in suffering for one's faith.

Education during the Middle Ages usually was education of the nobility, for what little education was available for the common people was oriented toward learning a trade and surviving. The male nobility was educated for knighthood.

A noble youth was trained in the house of another noble rather than being trained by his own family. Around age 7 he became a page. Until age 14 he was trained by the women and household workers. Women were not usually rated very highly in the Middle Ages, although among the nobility they were expected to organize and administer large households and estates, particularly during the frequent absences of the men.

Following the page phase of training, in which emphasis was on learning to serve people, a boy became a squire, usually by serving a knight or group of knights until he was 21 years old. During this period he concentrated on learning the arts of war, developing his body, and performing acts of obligation to his lord.

Around age 21, perhaps earlier in cases of exceptional bravery, a young man became a knight. Knighthood was usually bestowed in a serious religious ceremony. A ceremonial bath, followed by an all-night religious vigil in the company of the young man's lord and a bishop, preceded the investitures, which often were held on major religious holidays and were accompanied by tournaments or other festivities. Physical education lay at the core of the training for knighthood at all stages, with the goals of acquiring military prowess and developing social graces and sport skills.

Much confusion surrounds the question of the beliefs about physical education held by the Catholic church in the late Middle Ages. No clear definition of its position has emerged from what is known about the trends within the church and the civilization at that time, but the traditional view is that the church was opposed to physical education for three particular reasons. First, the church was disturbed by what it considered the debased character of the Roman sports and games. Second, it closely associated the Roman games with pagan religions, and the church was extremely intolerant of other faiths.

Third, a growing belief in the evil nature of the body was developing in the church. The body and soul were viewed increasingly as two separate entities. The soul was to be preserved and strengthened, but the body should not be catered to in any way. It should not be given entertaining or beneficial physical exercises. The church attempted to suppress many games and sports at this time, for they were considered frivolous and perhaps tinged with sin. Dance was also strongly discouraged because of its sensual appeal.

A number of churchmen were advocates of physical education prior to the Middle Ages. Usually those men had been exposed to a classical education and thus viewed the body as a unity of parts, rather than as separated and perhaps antagonistic parts. In the first several centuries of the church's existence, and again after the Middle Ages, physical education was not opposed.

During the Middle Ages, however, the view of the church, and of much of society, was otherworldly. The primary concern of this life was in preparing for the afterlife; a future life of justice and peace was promised. Asceticism, or denial of the pleasures or needs of the body, was thus a popular concept among the more religious people.

At this time the church was the savior of education, for education as an intellectual process was generally connected to the church. Usually the educational process was purely intellectual and had no physical side. The common system consisted of the seven liberal arts, composed of the *trivium* (grammar, rhetoric, and logic) and the *quadrivium* (arithmetic, geometry, astronomy, and music). The monasteries preserved much of the learning that survived the Middle Ages and played a major role in education at that time.

In the 14th and 15th centuries, medieval civilization began to fade in the light of the new forces it had created. Europe was waking up and progressing rapidly. Its culture was flourishing; the towns were becoming strong; education and the arts were developing in new directions. Kings and queens began to consolidate their power and form nations similar to those we know today. This period of rebirth for civilization led to the term by which we know the era—the Renaissance.

MEDIEVAL SPORT: SOURCE OF THE SPORT DICHOTOMY?

The Sport Dichotomy—the growth or control of sport by the upper classes of a society—is a characteristic of sport that has been noted as far back as the ancient Greeks.[1] The Homeric games are referred to as involving primarily the upper classes, for the lower classes either were not permitted to compete or had too little time to train for competitive success. Some scholars suggest that this trait of the Greek games disappeared rather early, and they do not consider it a common characteristic of Greek games. We next see this dichotomy, or class split in sport, during the Middle Ages. As we mentioned, when we think of physical education or sport in the Middle Ages, we usually think of the activities of the upper classes. The age of chivalry, with its tournaments, was an upper-class age only; no chivalric tradition existed for the majority of the people. "Accepted" sports (i.e., sports that were considered "worthwhile") were always the sports of the upper classes. This tradition has continued to a marked degree to the present day. Even today the modern Olympic Games are completely controlled and dominated by a small group of wealthy men who are self-appointed custodians of the spirit of amateurism. Their requirements still reflect the upper-class prejudice against allowing the general populace a part in sport, a prejudice that was notable not only in the 19th century but also in the 14th century.

Knight Sports: The Haves

We have already discussed the tradition of chivalry. Most of what we think of as sport of the medieval upper classes falls into this area. We think commonly of the tournaments at which the knights would fight to prove their strength and prowess.[2] The tournaments are traced back to the tenth century, though elements of their activities go back to Roman times. They originated as military exercises, with some emphasis on the safety of the knights, but over a period of centuries they degenerated until they either were banned by the Catholic church or became pointless after gunpowder was invented.

The tournaments, like the tradition of chivalry, were strictly for the upper-class. Other segments of society could be spectators at a tournament, but only the upper classes could participate directly. As the Renaissance drew near, other activities developed that cut across such class boundaries. Also, the middle and lower classes began to develop their own sport activities separate from those of the upper classes.[3]

Middle-Class and Lower-Class Sport: The Have-Nots

The lower classes of the Middle Ages, the vassals and farmers, can be described as being almost outside of society. Although they might be lowly spectators at the tournaments, that was their only involvement in that type of sport. As a result, they had their own games, most of which had ancient origins. Their activities emphasized running, jumping, and throwing objects. The middle class, which began to develop with the rebirth of the cities after the tenth century, also was interested in sport activities. The people developed their own variations of the knights' tournaments as they trained themselves to defend their cities. They imitated upper-class sport in many respects, but they also were involved in adding democratic elements to sport.

One such influence was a French ball game, similar to rugby, called *soule*. Contests were held between many different competitive units, including cities, and the primary democratizing element was that people from every class—farmer, burgher, clergyman, and nobleman—might be on the same team. After the contest, both teams had a communal meal (which might not be a bad tradition to bring back to today's sport). People were beginning to discover that sports gave them opportunities in equality that were not available anywhere else.

In his struggle for recognition as an individual, man discovered in sports a meeting ground where he could prove himself under fair conditions. The respect for democratic practices and the self-esteem of the burgher, combined with the desire for fair play, may well be one of the most important contributions that the Middle Ages made to our heritage.[4]

We are now beginning to see more detailed research on medieval sport, particularly in the towns, which began to grow in size and importance during this period. Our discussion of medieval sport is largely of sport in England. In describing the sporting activities shown on the Bayeux Tapestry (which illustrates the Norman conquest of England in 1066), John Carter argues that the activities show that the distinction between the sporting activities of the nobles and peasants was less than we have believed in the past.[5] Discussing the accounts of sport in London written by William fitz Stephen, a 12th-century religious clerk, Carter notes that "it is the idea that play is ritualized aggression and that play is training for war which provides a consistent thread through his ludic [playing activities] tapestry."[6] William wrote of cockfighting, mock battles imitating the battles of the armored knights, archery, wrestling, stone and javelin throwing, bear and bull baiting, hunting, ice-skating, and football.

Indeed, Carter sees a precedent for the 19th-century Muscular Christianity movement during the medieval centuries, as the church accepted more worldly recruits into the newer religious orders.[7] Thomas Hendricks, in looking at the sports of the nobles in the later Middle Ages (the 14th and 15th centuries), suggests that the distinctions between the classes were then becoming more rather than less rigid, with more emphasis by the upper classes on maintaining class distinctions in sport.[8]

William Baker looks at the development of medieval sport in the context of the church, which he maintains did not discourage sport until the late Middle Ages.[9] He suggests that the church, in effect, followed the Roman policy of adopting or accepting many of the customs of the people in the new countries, Christianizing many pagan holidays and even many activities of worship or ritual. Unintentionally, the church popularized ballgames, taking on the ritualistic ball games, blending the Moslem spring ball games with Easter activities, and providing a natural time for ball games and other recreational activities by setting aside Sunday as a day of rest, with no work activities allowed.[10]

The growing number of religious holidays during the Middle Ages provided a large number of days with recreational potential. Indeed, there are accounts of clergy complaining of people playing early versions of three-wall handball against the outside walls of the churches, using the corners made by the buttresses to make their shots harder to return. One of the 19th century public school handball games required a room designed exactly like the space between two particular buttresses of the school's chapel, including a similar drop-off at the rear of the court.

Many of today's popular games have ancient origins, as this medieval drawing of bowling shows. (Courtesy Photo Vuillemin, Troyes, France)

In the later Middle Ages, both church and state began to make rules and laws against sporting activities. In part this was because of the civil disturbances (and occasional deaths) that resulted. Both church and state feared social unrest by the common people. At the same time, the government was concerned about national defense. The men needed to practice their archery regularly in case an army was needed, but they preferred other activities, such as playing football (soccer).

Times were changing, as indicated by the decline in some of the traditional chivalric activities. The tournament sports of the knights began to disappear (as did many of the knights) as the activities for which they were used became outmoded, largely a result of the changes in weaponry. The widespread use of the English longbow, which could drive an arrow through a knight's heavy armor, combined with the appearance of gunpowder and early forms of guns, had made the knight obsolete. The tournament as an upper-class activity had become too risky after its functional value as a training ground disappeared. Knights were sometimes killed in the tournament. By the early 1500s, the picture of armored knights at the tournament was largely gone, after a last spectacular gasp in 1520 at the Field of Cloth of Gold with Henry VIII.[11]

The church was developing a more negative view of the human body, a development that perhaps reached its peak with the Puritans in the 17th century. The church wanted a stricter observance of religious occasions and fewer activities that catered to the pleasure of the human body, regardless of the type of pleasure. All of the rules, laws, and threats made little difference. Though the church opposed play, many clerics themselves played as avidly as did the common people. A peasant had little freedom and few possessions in life, but sport was still free and there for the taking.

PHYSICAL EDUCATION AND SPORT IN THE RENAISSANCE AND REFORMATION

The Renaissance was a period of rebirth and transition in Europe. It began in Italy around the 13th century and spread gradually to the north and west across Europe for the next two centuries. It was a time of vast growth in learning and culture. Through contacts with the Arab world, the Western world was rediscovering many long-lost classical writings of the Greeks and Romans. Islamic scholars had preserved many of the ancient writings, and European scholars retranslated them from the Arabic and shared them across Europe. The classical writings became popular, and their writing style was imitated by the Europeans.

Universities, which were first established during the late Middle Ages, were growing into a potent intellectual force. Major centers of learning were located in Paris, Bologna, Salerno, Oxford, and Cambridge. Universities also were developing in other areas of Europe, especially in Germany, as the orientation toward church-controlled education weakened and secular education grew. Along with the growth of the universities came the growth of humanism, which emphasized the development of human capabilities or humanity. The humanist scholars studied the classics closely because the ancient writings expressed humanistic ideas about education. This study of ancient writings, which the church considered clearly pagan, created many problems for scholars in reconciling the humanities, or humanistic studies, to religion, which was still a dominant force in European life.

Europe also was making the transition to modern times. The political institutions were changing gradually from feudalism to more powerful monarchies, and a belief in the monarch's divine right to rule was growing. Europe was changing from a system of many small personal alliances between nobles to one in which the nation was the dominant unit. The governments were gradually being centralized, and the people were beginning to think of themselves as English or French or German, rather than as Londoners or Parisians or Hessians. The birth of nationalism changed the complexion of European affairs. Towns were becoming the new center of life as the economy began to edge away from its old feudalistic, agrarian orientation.

The invention of gunpowder changed the face of feudalistic military tactics. It helped to blow Europe into modern times, for with it a small force of men was vastly superior to a much larger force of bowmen.

The discovery and dissemination of knowledge was enhanced by Johannes Gutenberg's printing press. The availability of books allowed knowledge and information to spread rapidly across Europe and provided a great impetus to education, for the need to be literate increased immensely.

The Renaissance was a period of discovery of the outside world as well, for people began to question the old teachings about the nature of the world and what lay beyond Europe and northern Africa. They undertook voyages west across the Atlantic Ocean and south and east around Africa to India and beyond. The circumnavigation of the world showed how limited human knowledge had been.

The education of the period began to develop along the lines of the Greek ideal; it stressed a classical education combined with physical education. A major early leader was Vittorino da Feltre (1378–1446). His school for the children of nobility imitated the Athenian model of classical studies taught according to the model set by Quintilian.[12] The subjects included Greek and Latin literature, swimming, fencing, riding, and dancing. Education was primarily for the men, though women were treated as relative equals in Italy.

The Renaissance ideal was *l'uomo universale*, the "universal" or all-around man, who had many talents and interests in the arts and literature, politics, games and sports, and the social graces. He was supposed to be interested and moderately skilled in almost every aspect of contemporary life. The goal of Renaissance educators was to develop an all-around person with a balanced education.

Education was beginning to be seen as valuable for its own sake, regardless of whether it was immediately practical. The barriers between separate areas of learning were beginning to break down, for the Renaissance ideal stressed training across any narrow divisions between areas of learning. The ideal was similar to the current concept of interdisciplinary studies, where the student tries to avoid the hazards of overspecialization that might result in an educational imbalance. After the Renaissance, this trend reversed, and students moved back toward specialization.

The humanistic impulse was strongly tied to the Reformation, the Protestant struggle against the Catholic church in the 16th century. The humanists' retranslations of the Scriptures indicated numerous areas of disagreement with the church's teachings. Many of the humanists were very antagonistic toward the church, and some, who were convinced that the church had strayed from the early Christian teachings, began to break away and form new churches. Because they "protested" the actions of the Catholic church, those humanists were called Protestants. Martin Luther, founder of today's Lutheran church, was a major leader of the movement in Germany.

The Protestants often were more supportive of physical activities than the Catholic church was. The Protestants believed that such activities were of moral value because they would help prevent corruption of the body in word and deed. The Protestant belief that everyone had the right to read and interpret the Scriptures personally, which required some degree of literacy, increased interest in education for the general public. Most education under the Catholic church had been the education of its leaders and scholars. The idea that each person should have any say in his or her beliefs and actions was a new concept for the time; the church had previously told people what to believe and what to do. The Protestants were interested in education for both sexes, but women were not considered equal. Their status had been raised somewhat in the Catholic church by the emphasis on the Virgin Mary, but the emphasis was on woman in the home setting, rather than as an equal and a partner to man.

As the struggles over religion spread across Europe, they were used by some rulers as one more way to consolidate power. An example was Henry VIII, who made himself head of the Anglican church, the English national church that replaced the Catholic church. As the nations gradually became modern states, similar to the nations of today, the stage was being set across Europe for the gradual move into the modern era.

RENAISSANCE SPORT

As we move from the Middle Ages through the Renaissance period, we find no radical changes in sport. The Renaissance was a period of rebirth of learning and interest in the arts. The classics of the ancient Greeks were imitated, and many of their theories of physical education and sport also were tried. Evidence indicates that the Sport Dichotomy—the distinction between the upper classes and the common people in sporting activities—continued in Italy, where the Renaissance originated.[13]

The Renaissance was also the period of expansion of the universities, many of which were founded at the height of the Middle Ages. Much evidence suggests that university sports were just as popular in the Middle Ages and Renaissance as they are today.[14] However, sport was an area of student activity that the schools frequently tried to suppress or limit, for physical activities were thought to interfere with academic studies. We do not think of student sports of the Renaissance in the sense that we think of them today; the activities were more similar to today's intramurals.

The Renaissance concept of the all-around person, developed intellectually and physically, helped contribute to physical training and sport, for sporting skills were considered as important as intellectual skills for the well-rounded person. Team games were developed, and individual competitive activities, such as those in the military skills, were popular.

Sport, like education, was for the elite, the aristocrats, who engaged in such sporting activities as swimming, running, horseback riding, acrobatics, archery, swordsmanship, and wrestling. At the same time, more activities were learned for use in court and social activities, such as dancing, ball games, recreational hunting, singing, and playing musical instruments. Castiglione's *The Courtier* (1528), followed by Thomas Elyots's *The Boke Named the Governour* (1541), included chapters on physical education, promoting the physical activities mentioned in Greek and Roman literature, along with fencing, archery, tennis, and dancing, as good exercises.[15] By 1600, the idea of physical education as part of the education of young aristocrats at school was widely accepted.

As we move closer to the modern era, sport was still in a low-level, disorganized state. Games had general forms and rules, but they were not standardized. Many variations of the same basic game could be found across Europe. Although the concept of nationalism was growing, no such thing as national or international sport had emerged. No sporting contests on the scope of the early Greek Olympics had yet appeared in any nation. It is only in relatively recent times that we see the rise of sport as we know it today: a more formal activity with set, standardized rules of competition and with competition both within and between nations.

SEVENTEENTH-CENTURY EUROPEAN PHYSICAL EDUCATION AND SPORT

Education and Physical Education in the 1600s

The 17th and 18th centuries saw more progress toward our current educational practices than any previous age, except perhaps ancient Greece. To see this progress we must look not at the different nations at that time, for there were still no national programs of education, but at the people who were the most prominent educational theorists of their time.

The 17th century saw the rise of the realists, whose goal was to tie education to reality, or life as it really was. They questioned the humanists' total reliance on ancient languages and teachings for the contemporary educational process. They believed that education should teach more useful things to prepare the students for life. They also began to stress teaching in the student's native language, rather than in only the classical languages, such as Greek and Latin. They wanted to get away from imitating the past.

Three slightly different groups of realists can be defined according to the degree to which they wanted to break away from the theories of the humanists.[16] The first group, the humanist realists, wanted to retain classical education as the foundation for all education. Although similar to the humanists, this group wanted to modify the process of the classical studies by emphasizing the content of ancient works but no longer copying the style of the ancient writers. The humanist realists' ideas were heavily classical.

The second group, the social realists, wanted more modification of the classical tradition. This group believed that the goal of education should be preparation for a career, rather than the humanist aim of simply training scholars. The social realists wanted education to develop closer ties to contemporary needs and problems.

The third group, the sense realists, believed that knowledge was best obtained through the senses, that is, by observation and experience. This group wanted the schools not only to teach in the vernacular, the language that the students spoke every day (rather than in the classical languages), but also to teach useful arts and sciences. The sense realists tried to base their educational methods on scientifically proven principles.

These groups consisted of many different people. Their ideas are examples of the progress in educational thought and practice that evolved during this time. Education was still limited primarily to the upper classes and to males, but theorists were beginning to suggest that such a concept of education was far too limited. Physical education was still a minor part of the educational process, but as educational theory developed, so did the idea that physical education could be a valuable part of the curriculum. More theorists were beginning to call for the use of physical activities in education, though their primary reason was for improved health.

One of the earliest of the humanist realists was the Frenchman François Rabelais (1495–1553).[17] He wrote of the education of a boy named Gargantua, who studied the classics for their content but was not concerned with their style. His education included practical training as well as physical education activities. The emphasis of the physical activities was to prepare him for war, since he was being trained to become a scholar and a knight. In earlier times he would have been trained for one or the other, but never for both. The physical activities were to strengthen his body and to serve as recreation. Objects in nature were used in the educational process.

Another prominent humanist realist and also a forerunner of the Enlightenment period of the 18th century was John Milton (1608–1674), the English writer.[18] He believed that a classical education was useful, but he thought the eight years of study could be condensed to a single year. He wanted to include physical exercises in the studies and divide each day's activities into three parts: study, exercise, and meals. His exercises were basically war oriented. The humanist realists thought that play and games were good training for skill and alertness, but they had little interest in the potential of such activities for developing social or recreational values.

One of the great theorists among the social realists was the Frenchman Michel de Montaigne (1533–1592). His theories concerned the education of aristocratic boys. He believed that experience and reason were the roads to knowledge. He expressed strong opposition to rote memorization by saying, "To know by heart is not to know."[19] His use of physical activities to further a pupil's experiences was similar in manner to John Dewey's later theories of "learn by doing." Montaigne stressed the education of the mind and the body at the same time, but he was not interested in providing learning experiences through games. Much of modern educational theory can be traced to Montaigne's ideas.

An English social realist, John Locke (1632–1704), used the now-popular phrase of physical educators, "a sound mind in a sound body,"[20] which was originated by Juvenal, a Roman writer. Locke believed that mind and body were separate entities and that all ideas came from personal experiences, which might be better described as the experiences of the senses combined with mental reflection or thought based on the experiences. He stressed physical exercise as a way to health and also believed that dancing helped to develop grace. He thought of recreation as a useful and beneficial break in the normal pattern of activity, which is similar to Nash's 20th-century statement of recreation as the "re-creation" of the person through a change in the pattern of his or her activities. Locke's ideas not only were a major factor in the development of contemporary educational theory but also were widely used in the development of other educational theories during his time.

Despite such forward-looking ideas, education under the social realists remained oriented toward the aristocracy rather than toward the common people. For this reason, many of the ideas of physical activity were an attempt to overcome the tendency of the aristocrats to pamper their children, who usually became overweight, unhealthy students.

A leading sense realist was Richard Mulcaster (1521–1611), of England. He believed that students should be taught at a school with other students, rather than individually by a tutor at home. Mulcaster also was convinced that teachers should be trained professionally. He suggested that both men and women should receive some education, rather than only the males,[21] and he was one of the first to suggest coeducational activities among children. He was interested in physical and moral training through exercise and thought that mass education, unlike the more common tutorial system, could lead to the development of social values through physical activities. Mulcaster, who was one of the strongest early proponents of physical education, urged its use far more than any other person of his time. Although he did not have much influence during his time, his works were rediscovered during the late 1800s.

Wolfgang Ratke (1571–1635), of Germany, was another great theoretician of educational reform, though, like many of the other theorists, he was unable to translate his theories successfully into action.[22] The major points in his attempt to develop education as a science included such ideas as following nature in its teaching methods (teach the students what they need to learn, and teach it at an age when they are ready to learn it); going only one step at a time with new information, utilizing repetition to assist learning; not forcing learning or stressing memorization; learning through experience; and educating *all* children, without exception. Although Ratke was unable to translate his formulas into personal success, he is considered the father of modern educational theory.

John Comenius (1592–1670), a Czechoslovakian, became a Moravian minister in Bohemia.[23] For religious reasons, he was forced to move frequently; he lived at times in Poland, England, Sweden, Hungary, and finally Holland, where he died. He wrote education books that included illustrations to improve the teaching process. He wanted children to exercise to develop and preserve their health, but he also believed they could *learn* much through recreational activities, which was not a widespread idea at the time. Comenius believed in the importance of play in educating young children, and he believed that *all* children should be educated.

Sport and the Puritans

The Renaissance was combined with the Reformation in northern Europe and England, as its influence spread like ripples on a pond outward from Italy. Partly because of this mixing, and because the Reformation showed a stronger, more strictly moralistic side in the northern areas, less interest developed in balanced physical and mental development. Instead, with the strong influence of the severe views of John Calvin, the tendency was toward asceticism.[24]

In essence, the Puritans of the 1600s believed that the nature of mankind was sinful and vile; they wanted to put as many restrictions as possible on what people were allowed to do in their public and private lives. Consequently, they changed sports and recreations from simple leisure activities to political questions. Many sporting activities included informal gambling, which the Puritans opposed. Also, they were concerned about the possible wasting of time; they considered work more important than anything else except worship.

Great social changes were occuring during the 16th and 17th centuries. People were having to move into the towns or to new villages, while farmland was being enclosed by large estates, upsetting the stability of social life and limiting the places available for recreation.

One village games that became famous during the early 1600s was the Cotswold Olympick Games, revived by Robert Dover in the hills west of Oxford, along the flat top of a ridge overlooking the village of Chipping Campden. The games included wrestling, the quintain, fighting with cudgels (the quarterstaff) and pikestaffs, leaping, footraces, handball, pitching the bar and the hammer, and women's smock races.

To respond to Puritan complaints about people's recreations, James I (known for his support of the biblical translation called the King James Version) issued his *Declaration on Lawful Sports*, known as *The King's Book of Sports*, in 1618. It ordered that legal recreations should not be interfered with or discouraged, even on Sundays, so long as they did not interfere with or cause the neglect of Sunday church services.

The declaration was reissued by his son, Charles I, in 1633, but by 1641 the Puritans had gained enough strength to put the king to flight, eventually executing him. As Baker sums up the period:

> Even the public pastimes proved to be remarkably resilient. Although the Puritans controlled the government and the laws of the land, they were a minority whose rigorous views remained unacceptable to the bulk of the population. Rural laborers continued to live their lives in terms of seasonal cycles, with periodic festivals and games compensating for times of intense labor. Puritanism was too urban in character, too austere, ever to be fully acceptable to that preindustrial society. Puritan prohibitions against sports and games were doomed to fail. In the end, only the Puritan Sunday established itself firmly in the lives of Englishmen, to become sacrosanct, free of sports and public amusements, until the 20th century.[25]

EIGHTEENTH-CENTURY EUROPE
Education and Physical Education

The realism of the 17th century was followed by the Enlightenment of the 18th century, a movement to spread rationalism and knowledge to all people. The concurrent trend toward the belief in the essential equality of all men, however, still did not necessarily apply to women. The educational theorists were beginning to move away from the idea that only the aristocracy should be educated. Those theorists of the Enlightenment helped to reinforce the work begun in the 17th century; they used many of the realists' theories as the starting point for many of their own theories. Hermann Weimer writes of John Locke as the founder of the English Enlightenment, for Locke's stress on educating people through rational, natural means led to the later theories of Rousseau.[26]

Jean-Jacques Rousseau (1712–1788), of France, was one of the most important theorists of the Enlightenment.[27] In 1762 he published two extremely influential books, *Emile* and *Social Contract*. *Social Contract* expanded on his views that all humans are free and equal by nature and that inequality developed only after they had gotten away from nature and developed governments. Rousseau considered people good by nature but corrupted by so-called civilization.

In *Emile*, Rousseau wrote that the task of education was to develop all of a child's capabilities freely, as nature intended, and to avoid anything that would hamper this "natural" development. His book was considered a revolt against the education and society of the day and was first banned by the Catholic church, then condemned by governments.

Rousseau's plan of education for the imaginary Emile required a tutor, for the child was educated alone. Nature was the primary teacher, and the tutor was the guiding force. He believed that the child could not be taught by logic, as Locke had suggested, because as a youth, the child would not yet have developed common sense. He wanted to let children progress naturally, learning what they wanted to learn when they were interested in learning it.

They were given tasks that were considered appropriate to their ages and that were geared toward learning from nature and experience. When they became young adults, they would be introduced to languages and to the classical authors, who were considered closer to nature than the contemporary writers were.

Rousseau also discussed the education of Sophie, Emile's future wife. Sophie was educated in the manner that was traditional for girls. Her education took place in her parents' home, unlike Emile's education in the country. She was educated primarily to be a wife, so she could make her husband's life pleasant. While Rousseau had many liberal tendencies in his theories, he was not liberal where women were concerned. He said that all men are born equal before nature, and he did mean men.

Rousseau considered play to be both healthful and educational, but he did not think it should be forced. He was opposed to compulsion in any area of education; he believed it was contrary to the ways of nature. Although Rousseau stressed equality of men in his educational theories, his idea of a tutorial educational process required a 1:1 pupil/teacher ratio and thus was beyond the reach of all but the wealthy.

Rousseau's theories, which made the education of the mind and the body almost the same thing, were similar to contemporary educational thought, but the influence of his works cannot be estimated. The most visible immediate influence was on the Germans, who followed rapidly in developing his theories of "naturalism" into actual educational practice.

Johann Basedow (1724–1790), a German educator, had experimented with an educational system that was based on the theories of Locke and others and that involved physical activity.[28] His discovery of Rousseau's work *Emile*, however, was the basis for the development of his own version of an educational system. In 1774, with the help of a number of financial supporters, Basedow was able to start a coeducational school called the Philanthropinum, later known as the Dessau Educational Institute. He tried to educate the children free from the influence of any particular church, and he preferred to treat the children as children, rather than as small adults. Basedow published several illustrated books that explained his educational theories and gave examples of the methods and content to be used when teaching children.

He placed a heavy stress on physical activities. The ten-hour day in his school included five hours of classes, three hours of recreation (including fencing, riding, dancing, and music), and two hours of manual labor to teach a craft to the student. He also planned a camping experience that shared some charateristics with the later concept of outdoor education.

The school hired Johann Simon as its teacher of physical education. Simon can be considered the first modern physical education teacher. He taught fencing, dancing, and games, and some crude "gymnastics" activities that he developed. He held a contest similar to the ancient Greek Olympics. In 1778 Simon was succeeded by Johann Du Toit, who expanded on the gymnastic activities. The exercises were performed outdoors with apparatus built from natural materials.

Basedow was unable to make the school work under his direction and left in 1778, but the school, which reached its peak in the early 1780s, continued until 1793. Although the school did not survive, its experimental program, which recognized the importance of physical activities to the child, was influential throughout Europe. It had a strong influence on Christian Salzmann (1744–1811), who founded the Schnepfenthal Educational Institute in 1785 near Gotha, in present-day East Germany.

Salzmann's institute was a good copy of the Philanthropinum, only his version succeeded. One year after the founding of the school, Salzmann hired a new, young teacher, Johann Guts Muths (1759–1839), who taught there for 50 years and became one of the most influential of German physical educators.[29] Strongly influenced by the writings of Basedow, Guts Muths developed an outdoor gymnastics program that included many activities, with exercises in tumbling, climbing, jumping, vaulting, the horizontal bar, balance beam, and rope ladders. He organized his activities by age level and difficulty, and kept careful records of each student's progress. His book *Gymnastics for the Young* was published in 1793 and was reprinted in many countries; it was reprinted in the United States in 1802 with Salzmann listed as the author. Guts

An example of the outdoor gymnastic activities popularized by Guts Muths in Germany. (Reproduced from the English translation of Johann Guts Muths, *Gymnastics for Youth, or a Practical Guide to Healthful and Amusing Exercises*, Philadelphia, 1803. Courtesy Francis A. Countway Library of Medicine)

Muths' work set the pattern for German gymnastics, which was introduced into the United States around 1825 and which was a less formal system than the one that developed later in Germany.

The influence of Guts Muths was widespread across two continents both because of his writing skill and because of the interest of many prominent theorists and practitioners of the day. Friedrich Jahn, Adolph Spiess, and Immanuel Kant were among those who visited Schnepfenthal before 1835, when Guts Muths retired, to study the work done there. Many of his practices are similar to those suggested and followed in today's schools.

Johann Pestalozzi (1746–1827) was a Swiss teacher whose school at Yverdon in Germany was also extremely influential among the educational reformers of the early 1800s.[30] He taught at the school from 1804 to 1825 and wrote a number of books on his theories. His most important book, *How Gertrude Teaches Her Children*, was an expansion of the educational ideas he had introduced in an earlier novel, *Leonard and Gertrude*.

Pestalozzi stressed the early education in the family by writing of humans as social creatures. He tried to connect education with life and make it useful.

He believed that the learner had to be stimulated to *want* to learn and that the teacher should act as a guide rather than force the child to learn. He wanted learning to follow the natural process from easy to difficult activities according to a child's level of development. He saw education as having three aspects: intellectual, practical, and most important, moral. Physical education also was important to Pestalozzi for bringing the mind and body into full harmony.

His school provided many physical activities, including one hour of gymnastics five days a week. While the gymnastics program, which gradually became formalized as the influence of the formal German system spread, was not advanced, it did provide a great impetus for the development of physical education activities on the part of people from many nations who visited the famous school.

Philipp von Fellenberg (1771–1844) based many of his ideas on Pestalozzi's writings and began one of the first European schools for vocational education, sometimes referred to as schools of manual labor.[31] The one essential difference between Fellenberg and most of the educational theorists was that his ideas worked. Fellenberg's activities were a practical success throughout his life; his school, started in 1804 at Hofwyl, was an immediate success.

Fellenberg believed in the value of physical activity, though he believed that his vocational students received enough activity without having a planned program. He considered their manual work sufficient exercise. Also, it kept them outdoors, which he considered important. He encouraged outdoor activity, and allowed his students a free choice of activities in their leisure time.

Friedrich Ludwig Jahn (1778–1852), a German educator, is often considered the "Father of Gymnastics."[37] Jahn was an ardent Prussian patriot who was opposed to the provincialism that kept Germany separated into a multitude of small kingdoms. He began teaching in a Pestalozzian school, where he tried to use the ideas of Guts Muths in an outdoor gymnasium setting.

In 1837, his interest in the education of children and play activities led to his founding a school, which he called a *kindergarten*, for young children in Germany. His ideas on education, which his disciples implemented along with those on the kindergarten, became a major influence on early childhood education.

During the last part of the enlightenment period, the ideas of the European theorists were beginning to influence the development of education in the United States. From about 1800 onward, educational theories in Europe moved rapidly to the United States as immigrants brought many of the new ideas with them to the huge, growing land. While many educational developments were concurrent on both continents by 1850, the developing American educational practices were strongly based on the work of the 19th-century European theorists.

The Seeds of Modern Sport

The transition toward modern sport began during the 1700s, as some sporting activities began to develop higher-level organization and standardized rules.[33] In horse racing, the Jockey Club was formed about 1750 as an organization of rich owners and horse breeders. It began to write rules for racing, appointing officials and assessing penalties for the breaking of the rules. The club published the rules and the annual racing schedules in a new publication called the *Racing Calendar*, first published about 1770.

During roughly the same period of time, the Marylebone Cricket Club was founded (perhaps in 1787), soon to plan its important matches at Lord's Cricket Ground in northwest London. The MCC began writing and refining formal rules for cricket, quickly standardizing the play in that sport.

The Royal and Ancient Golf Club, founded in 1754 at St. Andrews, Scotland, began to write rules for golf, standardizing the game at 18 holes in 1764. Even the rough sport of pugilism (boxing) became more standardized with the appearance of written rules, first with Broughton's Rules in 1741, which laid the basis of the London Prize-ring Rules of 1838 and the Queensbury Rules of 1867.

Dennis Brailsford suggests that spectator sports had developed enough during the 1700s to be a significant part of popular recreation.[34] Such events were planned to be convenient to the working week, with most events held in the early part of the week, such as Monday or Tuesday. No events were held on Sunday because of attempts to make sports more "respectable."

The tempo of work increased as the week progressed. Brailsford refers to

the phenomenon of St. Monday and of a weekend which covered Sunday and Monday....Monday was the nearest day to the last wage and the work day furthest from the wage yet to come. It was the day on which freedom from work was easiest to envisage and one which, for large groups of workers, was regarded as a more or less regular holiday.[35]

During the 1700s and on into the 1800s, England was

a nation rapidly changing from rural to urban, a shift of far-reaching consequences. The rural sporting ethos was passing away as the villages dwindled and the economic importance of the landed gentry decreased; the traditional sporting activities were coming to be more nostalgic than consequential in local life. Religious and civil influences were changing accepted practices from the old 'bloody sports' to a taste for less cruel activities more fitting to the sensitivities of city-dwellers affected by growing straitlaced ideals. A new urban sporting ethos was developing, leading gradually to mass spectator sports and highly organized activities. A shift came about from taking the people to the event, as in the early seat of English sporting activities in the villages and fields, to taking the event to the people, moving the activities to large urban centers for the convenience of masses of paying customers.[36]

NINETEENTH-CENTURY EUROPE

We cannot draw a line separating the 18th century from the 19th century when we study the development of physical education and sport, for the philosophies and experimental schools of the late 1700s in Europe produced the progress of the 1800s. We have already mentioned several of the educators who were more a part of the 19th century; others who were equally influential during the 19th century had their foundations in the events of the 18th.

During the late 18th century, revolution was in the wind. The young United States had rebelled against Great Britain, and Rousseau's ideas still had much of Europe in shock. The educational theories that leaned toward Rousseau's views on the equality of men were given a popular boost by the French Revolution. As the year 1800 came and went, Napoleon had gained power in France and was trying to gain control of all Europe. As nations allied to block him, the feelings of national consciousness rose to an all-time high.

After Napoleon was put to rest and the Congress of Vienna had tried to reestablish the old Europe, many differences became obvious. The people were less content, as the numerous rebellions between 1815 and 1850 demonstrated. The people also were beginning to clamor for national systems of education. At the same time, they were fleeing the Old World in large numbers, taking a chance on finding a better life in the United States. Those who remained behind sought systems of education that would strengthen their nations and have a positive effect on national pride.

Friedrich Ludwig Jahn (1778–1852), a German educator, is often considered the "Father of Gymnastics."[37] Jahn was an ardent Prussian patriot who was opposed to the provincialism that kept Germany separated into a multitude of small kingdoms. He began teaching in a Pestalozzian school, where he tried to use the ideas of Guts Muths in an outdoor gymnasium setting.

In 1810 he began using an open area that he named the *turnplatz*, or "exercise area" which was basically a playground with apparatus for exercises. The formal organization of his program gradually became the "Turner" movement (for *turnverein*). Some people have considered Jahn's system too formal. However, he did oppose artificial activities in the early development of his system and sought to use natural activities instead. A book by one of his followers described Jahn's work in 1816, the same year Jahn wrote *German Gymnastics* to explain his system.

Jahn's emphasis on German nationalism eventually put him in prison. The rulers of the separate states considered his views on a unified Germany a threat to their rule, and he was out of favor until the 1840s, when the political climate changed. The success of the Turner movement depended on other men during that interval.

Adolf Spiess (1810–1858) was the man who had the greatest impact on educational gymnastics in Germany.[38] Having met both Guts Muths and Jahn, he experimented as a teacher with gymnastics by applying the movement to the formal classroom situation. He also worked with Froebel in Switzerland, where he was strongly influenced by Froebel's views on the function of play in education. Spiess's later writings, especially his *Gymnastics Manual for Schools*, strongly influenced the schools, as it had the exercises classified by difficulty and by appropriate age and sex.

Spiess devised a system of "free exercises" that required almost no apparatus. He also used musical accompaniment for those activities. He stressed the idea of having professionally trained specialists to teach the gymnastics classes. Spiess wanted indoor exercise areas in addition to the traditional outdoor areas so that the winter weather would not limit the program. He also stressed gymnastics for girls, and his free exercises were a great benefit for them because those exercises required less strength than the apparatus activities. Although Spiess considered the existing formal systems of gymnastics inappropriate for the schools, his own system also included much marching and stressed discipline and obedience. Traces of his system, which served as a model for the later German system of school gymnastics, can still be seen in use today.

Franz Nachtegall (1777–1847) is considered the father of physical education in Denmark.[39] Inspired by the writing of Guts Muths, he gradually became known as a leader in Danish gymnastics and physical training. In 1804 he was made director of the newly established Military Gymnastic Institute, which had the task of preparing teachers of gymnastics first for the military, and later for the schools. Today, the Military Gymnastic Institute is the oldest institution training gymnastics instructors in Europe. Although Nachtegall did not design his own system, he was instrumental in the development of school gymnastics and physical programs in Denmark. He was also an influential factor in the development of Per Henrik Ling's Swedish system of gymnastics.

Per Henrik Ling (1776–1839) was the founder of Swedish gymnastics,[40] though he also was well known for his literary works. While living in Denmark, Ling was influenced by the work of Franz Nachtegall. He later decided to train teachers of fencing and gymnastics to strengthen Sweden's army. A fierce Swedish nationalist, he became the director of the new Royal Central Institute of Gymnastics in 1814, where he later developed his program of gymnastics which is called either the Swedish system or Ling gymnastics. His emphasis on simple, fundamental movements and exercises was a change from Jahn's complicated exercises.

Although the Ling exercises were developed for both educational and military purposes, they worked better as military training. Per Henrik Ling's medical and military gymnastics were successful, but his son, Hjalmar Ling, did the major work in developing the educational aspect of the Swedish system.

Archibald Maclaren (c. 1820–1884) was a major early influence on physical education in England.[41] Asked to design a physical training program for the military, he stressed a gymnastics program, similar to Jahn's, that made

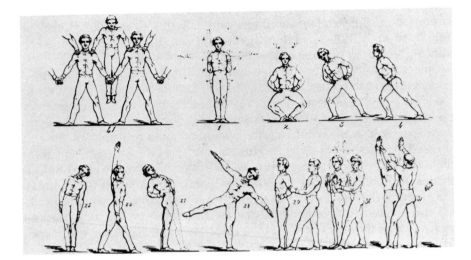

These examples of the Swedish system, or Ling gymnastics, show the simple, fundamental movements involved. (Reprinted from *The Gymnastic Free Exercises of P. H. Ling,* arranged by H. Rothstein and translated by M. Roth, M.D., Groombridge & Sons, London, 1853. Courtesy Francis A. Countway Library of Medicine)

heavy use of apparatus activities. Above all, Maclaren stressed a balance between recreational activities (physical play) and educational physical activities, which he wanted to use in a regular class (in addition to the noneducational play time) as a part of the educational process. Although Maclaren's ideas on gymnastics never really took hold in England, his writings were a major influence on the development of physical education in England in the late 1800s. His military system of physical education also spread across England as the instructors whom he had trained for the military left military service but continued to teach as civilians.

During the first half of the 19th century, the European theorists and their systems were a powerful influence on the development of physical education in the United States. After the Civil War in the United States, the European influence declined rapidly, for American physical educators were passing beyond the point at which they needed the European ideas as an impetus for developing their own programs and systems. By the end of the century, leaders in the United States were calling on their fellow teachers to work together to develop an "American System," instead of continuing their reliance on the European systems, which were (after all) designed for Europeans. The turn of the century saw the beginnings of that distinctly American system, though it was not stressed in writing for several more decades.

NOTES

1. E. Norman Gardiner, *Greek Athletic Sports and Festivals*, Macmillan, London, 1910, p. 25.
2. Jan Broekhoff, "Chivalric Education in the Middle Ages," *Quest* 11 (December 1968), 24–31.
3. Nicolaas J. Moolenijzer, "Our Legacy from the Middle Ages," *Quest* 11 (December 1968), 32–43.
4. Ibid., 42.
5. John Marshall Carter, "The Bayeux Tapestry, Bishop Odo of Bayeux, and the Pastimes of the Medieval Silent Majority," *Canadian Journal of History of Sport* 16 (May 1985), 14–26.
6. Carter, "Perspectives on Medieval Sport in Twelfth and Thirteenth Century England," *Canadian Journal of History of Sport* 12 (May 1981), 12.
7. Carter, "Muscular Christianity and Its Makers: Sporting Monks and Churchmen in Anglo-Norman Society, 1000–1300," *The British Journal of Sports History* 1 (September 1984), 109–124.
8. Thomas S. Hendricks, "Sport and Social Hierarchy in Medieval England," *Journal of Sport History* 9 (Summer 1982), 20–37.
9. William J. Baker, *Sports in the Western World*, Rowman and Littlefield, Totowa, N.J., 1982, p. 42.
10. Ibid., pp. 44–45.
11. William H. Freeman, "Henry VIII and Francis I at the Field of Cloth of Gold: The Last Gasp of Chivalric Sports?" in *Proceedings: 5th Canadian Symposium on the History of Sport and Physical Education*, ed. Bruce Kidd, University of Toronto, 1982, pp. 94–103.
12. Hermann Weimer, *Concise History of Education*, Philosophical Library, New York, 1962, pp. 38–42.
13. Peter C. McIntosh, "Physical Education in Renaissance Italy and Tudor England," in *A History of Sport and Physical Education to 1900*, ed. Earle F. Zeigler, Stipes Publishing, Champaign, Il., 1973, pp. 249–266.
14. Ray C. Thurmond, "Student Sports in the First Five Centuries of Universities (1150–1650)," *1974 North American Society for Sport History Proceedings*, pp. 9–10.
15. Baker, pp. 59–65.
16. C.W. Hackensmith, *History of Physical Education*, Harper & Row, New York, 1966, pp. 98–107.
17. Ellen W. Gerber, *Innovations and Institutions in Physical Education*, Lea & Febiger, Philadelphia, 1971, pp. 54–56.
18. Hackensmith, pp. 99–100.
19. Quoted in Gerber, p. 57.
20. Ibid., p. 70.
21. Ibid., pp. 61–64.
22. Weimer, pp. 73–77.
23. Gerber, pp. 65–69.
24. Baker, pp. 72–84.
25. Ibid., pp. 81–82.
26. Weimer, pp. 98–103.
27. Ibid., pp. 104–110.

28. Gerber, pp. 83–86.
29. Ibid., pp. 115–121.
30. Ibid., pp. 87–92.
31. Hackensmith, pp. 124–126.
32. Gerber, pp. 93–99.
33. Baker, pp. 88–94.
34. Dennis Brailsford, "Sporting Days in Eighteenth Century England," *Journal of Sport History* 9 (Winter 1982), 41–54.
35. Ibid., 52.
36. Freeman, "Book Review," *Journal of Sport History* 9 (Winter 1982), 81–82.
37. Hackensmith, pp. 133–134; Gerber, pp. 126–133.
38. Gerber, pp. 139–144.
39. Gerber, pp. 177–180.
40. Hackensmith, pp. 142–144.
41. Ibid., pp. 215–219.

SUGGESTED READINGS

Bailey, Peter. *Leisure and Class in Victorian England: Rational Recreation and the Contest for Control, 1830–1885.* London: Routledge & Kegan Paul, 1978.

Bennett, Bruce L. "The Curious Relationship of Religion and Physical Education." *JOHPER* 41 (September 1970), 69–71.

Brailsford, Dennis. "Religion and Sport in Eighteenth-Century England: 'For the Encouragement of Piety and Virtue, and for the Preventing or Punishing of Vice, Profaneness and Immorality.'" *The British Journal of Sports History,* 1 (September 1984), 166–183.

———. *Sport and Society: Elizabeth to Anne.* London: Routledge & Kegan Paul, 1969.

Broekhoff, Jan. "Physical Education, Sport, and the Ideals of Chivalry," *Proceedings of the Big Ten Symposium on the History of Physical Education and Sport,* ed. Bruce L. Bennett, pp. 9–13. Chicago: Athletic Institute, 1972.

Carter, John Marshall. *Sports and Pastimes of the Middle Ages.* Columbus, Ga.: Brentwood University Edition, 1984.

Cone, Carl B., ed. *Hounds in the Morning: the Sundry Sports of Merry England.* Lexington: University of Kentucky Press, 1981.

Cunningham, Hugh. *Leisure in the Industrial Revolution, c. 1780–c. 1880.* New York: St. Martin's, 1980.

Golby, J. M., and A. W. Purdue. *The Civilization of the Crowd: Popular Culture in England, 1750–1900.* New York: Schocken, 1985.

Hardy, Stephen T. "The Medieval Tournament: A Functional Sport of the Upper Class," *Journal of Sport History* 1 (Fall 1974), 91–105.

Harris, Harold A. *Sport in Britain: Its Origin and Development.* London: Stanley Paul, 1975.

Hendricks, Thomas S. "Sport and Social Hierarchy in Medieval England." *Journal of Sport History* 9 (Summer 1982), 20–37.

Jable, J. Thomas. "The English Puritans: Suppressors of Sport and Amusement?" *Canadian Journal of History of Sport and Physical Education* 7 (May 1976), 33–40.

Lee, Frieda. "Continuity? The Palaestra, La Giocosa, The Philanthropinum." *Canadian Journal of History of Sport and Physical Education* 7 (December 1976), 58–69.

Longrigg, Roger. *The English Squire and His Sport*. London: Michael Joseph, 1977.

McConahey, Michael William. *Sports and Recreations in Later Medieval France and England*. Ph.D. dissertation, University of Southern California, 1974. Microfiche.

McIntosh, Peter C. "Hieronymus Mercurialis 'De Arte Gymnastica': Classification and Dogma in Physical Education in the Sixteenth Century." *British Journal of Sports History* 1 (May 1984), 73–84.

McKernan, Mary. *A Historical Account of the Three Phases of Aonach Tailteann*. M.S. thesis, Springfield College, 1981. Microfiche.

McLean, Teresa. *The English at Play in the Middle Ages*. Windsor Forest, Eng.: Kensal Press, 1983.

Malcolmson, Robert W. *Popular Recreations in English Society, 1700–1850*. London: Cambridge University Press, 1973.

———. "Sports in Society: A Historical Perspective." *British Journal of Sports History* 1 (May 1984), 60–72.

Martin, Dennis W. *A Biblical Doctrine of Physical Education*. Ed.D. dissertation, University of North Carolina at Greensboro, 1983. Microfiche.

Medlin, William K. *The History of Educational Ideas in the West*. New York: The Center for Applied Research in Education, 1964.

Ruhl, Joachim K. "Religion and Amusements in Sixteenth- and Seventeenth-Century England: 'Time Might Be Better Bestowed, and Besides Wee See Sin Acted.'" *The British Journal of Sports History* 1 (September 1984), 125–165.

Ueberhorst, Horst. "Jahn's Historical Significance." *Canadian Journal of History of Sport and Physical Education* 10 (May 1979), 7–14.

Vale, Marcia. *The Gentleman's Recreations: Accomplishments and Pastimes of the English Gentleman, 1580–1630*. Totowa, N.J.: Rowman and Littlefield, 1977.

Walvin, James. *Leisure and Society, 1830–1950*. London: Longman, 1978.

See also the following books listed in the Resource Readings at the end of the book:

Arlott; Baker; Gerber; Guttman, *From Ritual to Record*; Howell; Huizinga; McIntosh et al.; Mandell *Cultural History*; Spears and Swanson; Van Dalen and Bennett; and Zeigler, *History*.

chapter 4

The Early Development of American Physical Education and Sport

We have discussed the evolution of physical education and sport in the ancient world and in Europe to the mid-1800s, so we now turn our attention to the development of physical education and sport in colonial America and the United States prior to the Civil War. To understand the development of physical education and sport in the United States, we also must look at the developmental period of the nation itself and the ways in which it was influenced by the European ideas of the 19th century. After the mid-1800s, however, Europe began to lose its influence in the United States, and we need to see how this period of declining influence affected the later directions that American physical education and sport took.

As sport and physical education had little, if any, relationship to each other at this time, we will consider the development of each separately. We will look first at the growth of the idea of physical education as part of the education of American youths and then at the evolution of popular sporting activities during this period.

COLONIAL AMERICAN PHYSICAL EDUCATION (1607–1783)

In colonial America there was no physical education as we think of it. The colonies made attempts to start schools, but their primary concern was to provide the rudiments of a practical education—learning to read, write, and handle basic mathematics. Physical education activities such as those being developed in Europe would have been considered a frill at that time. The colonies of the New World were expanding into wilderness areas, and the pioneers, who frequently faced the threat of attack by the Indians whom they were displacing, usually got more outdoor exercise than a European would receive in the most educationally advanced school of the day. During this period the nonworking physical activities of the people were primarily recreational activities.

The developing colonies were a diverse culture—a mixture of many nationalities and religious groups. The Puritans in New England were opposed to many activities that might be thought of as pleasurable; they considered such activities to be either distractions from more serious concerns or questionable because they might lead eventually to sin. While the Puritans were the most negative group of the colonial settlers regarding the pursuit of physical pleasures, the Quakers, who settled in Pennsylvania, were also strict in their outlook on this matter. The Virginia colony, predominantly Anglican, was officially opposed to many recreational activities in its early days, too. Other groups in the New World, such as the Dutch in today's New York City and Hudson River valley areas, were more inclined to allow and enjoy such activities.

The colonies, which were widely separated in their early days, might be compared with ancient Greek city-states—all were of the same "nation," but they were more competitive than cooperative. The spirit of cooperation among them was noticeably thin even during the Revolutionary War. After the Revolutionary War, the nation was still very spread out, so there was little spirit of nationalism. People were from Massachusetts or Virginia or Pennsylvania rather than from the United States.

The hard nature of the settlers' life led to the gradual development of a society far more tolerant of differences among people than European societies had been. Ancestors had little to do with a settler's ultimate survival or value to colonial society. As the political development of the colonies proceeded, strong regional antagonism developed among three groups of people that were established in many states.

In colonial society the new elite were the residents of the coastal areas that had been settled earliest. Many of these people were well-to-do traders. They were better educated than the other groups, and they had regular contact with Europe. The second social group included the people of the piedmont and foothill areas, who were primarily farmers. They lived in less settled areas than did the coastal dwellers and had little in common with them, either in wealth or in politics. The third group—the settlers of the still-unopened areas—gradually moved into the mountains and beyond and were far out of touch with the coast, let alone Europe. They had some ties with the piedmont farmers, for often they were farmers themselves, but they had nothing in common with the coastal people. The result of the differences among these three groups of people was a long period of political struggle in almost every state legislature between the people in the east, who had the power, and those in the west, who did not.

The schools in the colonies were copies of the European schools of the time. The first schools were Latin grammar schools, which proved to be of little value and were gradually replaced by academies that were concerned primarily with basic instruction, as mentioned previously. Advanced educational institutions, also modeled after European schools, were primarily for those people who were going into the ministry. An example is Harvard University, which was founded in Massachusetts in 1636.

Physical activities served almost no official function in colonial education, but many unorganized recreational games and sports were carried on for entertainment. The daily activities of the pioneers involved the survival skills used in hunting, fishing, and swimming and required such physical activities as running, jumping, lifting heavy objects, and fighting. Dance also gradually became more acceptable as the Puritans became more affluent.

Although no real education of the physical existed in colonial times, the idea was supported by some prominent men. Thomas Jefferson wrote in support of physical education, and Benjamin Franklin was a swimming enthusiast, though swimming was considered a quaint but questionable custom in his time. One of the few educators who supported physical activities in the schools was Samuel Moody, headmaster of one of the first private boarding schools in America.[1] He promoted physical activities as vital to the health of the students, but most activities were the strictly traditional ones inherited from European backgrounds.

Little real spirit of nationalism appeared in the United States until after the War of 1812. The people shared a basic reluctance to submit to any centralized form of government. Thus nationalism was not the strong impetus toward physical education that it was in the European nations in the late 1700s and early 1800s. The second impetus in Europe, pursuing physical training to help serve the military needs of the country, was also weaker in the United States. The Americans usually were concerned with the strength and fitness of the military only in times of war, so physical training was not a major concern during this period of rapid expansion across the Appalachian Mountains and on toward the great American Midwest. While some military schools were being formed during the early 1800s, the idea of military instruction did not become popular until the time of the Civil War in the 1860s.

SOCIAL SPORT IN COLONIAL AND EARLY NATIONAL AMERICA (1607–1860)

We now need to look at the sporting side of early American history. This period of sport can be considered premodern by the characteristics we shall discuss in the next chapter. Sport in colonial and early national America was essentially recreational and not highly organized. The primary emphasis of sport in the American colonies and the early United States was largely social.

Life was not easy for the early settlers, who had few chances to relax and enjoy themselves. On the frontier, unlike in the early coastal colonies, people often were widely separated and had few opportunities to meet other people. They welcomed the chance to get together socially on such occasions as holidays, militia training days, election days, court meeting days, and church meetings and revivals.

The religiously oriented colonies usually were opposed to recreational activities as wasteful idleness. They passed "blue laws" designed to prevent any irreligious activities on Sundays. They passed other laws against many sporting activities, but they were not very successful in preventing such activities. Our conception of the Puritans in New England as being stern people opposed to any sport or recreation is incorrect. The Puritans came to America seeking religious freedom, as they interpreted it. They interpreted it to mean that instead of someone else telling the Puritans how to worship, the Puritans would tell everyone else how to worship. They believed in a hard-working, serious life, yet it was not one that ruled out laughter or sport.

The Puritans held to a strong work ethic, and they passed laws to see that the citizens worked hard and adhered to the Puritan religious doctrine. They observed no religious holidays, other than the Sabbath, not even Christmas. They objected to anyone either feasting or fasting on the Sabbath, and their rules against Sunday sport were rules to see that the religious nature of the Sabbath was observed. They were not rules against sport, but against anyone forgetting that Sunday was primarily a day with religious meaning.

Indeed, early accounts note the streets of Boston "full of Girles and Boys sporting up and down."[2] For the most part, the Puritans recognized a value for recreational and sporting activities in the sense of re-creation or change-of-pace activities that refreshed people and permitted them to work with renewed energy and zeal. At the same time, as their colony grew in size, stability, and wealth, they were fighting a losing battle against the outside world's influence. People with a stable, prosperous life were less interested in a relatively ascetic way of living when it was no longer necessary for survival.

As the colonies became more solidly based and the citizens had more free time, more recreational activities appeared. Sports were not highly organized at that time; people played games they had learned as children, or they followed the directions for games given in the English sporting magazines and game books. Since most of the early settlers were English, most of the early games were of English origin. English publications, which became widely spread in America during the late 1700s and early 1800s, helped make the development of English sport a major influence on the later organization of sport in the United States.

As the settlers moved westward, life again became difficult, and the competitions also became much tougher. The most popular competitive activities during early national times were contests such as horseracing, cockfighting, gambling activities, rowing, and baseball. Indeed, one of the major objections of religious groups to many sporting activities, if not the very idea of sport, was the heavy use of such activities as an excuse for gambling. For the colonial aristocracy, just as for the English aristocrats, gambling lay at the heart of most sporting activities.[3] Horseracing, with both open races and match races, was always popular throughout the colonies. While aspects of modern organization appear in other activities, Melvin Adelman argues that harness racing was the first modern sport in the United States.[4] Cockfighting (matches between specially trained fighting roosters) also was popular, particularly in the southern states. Rowing developed in the mid-1800s as one of the first collegiate sports. Baseball gradually evolved from English ball games, until it was considered a native American game. One reason for baseball's popularity was that it was one of the few sporting activities that showed no distinction between the social classes.

Although many sporting activities were popular in early times, the real growth of sport in the United States came only after the nation had become more settled and urbanized. Some stability and a certain level of wealth and leisure time are needed before sport can become highly organized in a society. Those conditions did not become noticeable until after the middle of the 19th century. As the young nation moved into the mid-19th century, we see the growth of sporting events that were more commercial, planned for urban areas to attract a large audience of paying customers. Reflecting similar developments in England, races were early mass-leisure events. Horse races were popular as, for a time, were footraces (or "pedestrianism"). Boat races, involving craft that ranged from sculls similar to those in today's Olympic races through larger manned boats to yachts also drew quite a few spectators.[5] The rise of improved transportation, such as steamboats and railways, resulted in attempts to organize large spectator sporting events that would draw passengers traveling to the heavily promoted events.

Despite an English influence toward Muscular Christianity (see Chapter 5), which was inspired by writings such as *Tom Brown's Schooldays*, and despite the diligent work of exercise and health enthusiasts such as Oliver Wendell Holmes and Thomas Wentworth Higginson, most Americans were not physically vigorous or healthy, nor were they as inclined to take part in vigorous sports as Europeans were.[6] In part, this was the influence of the growth of an urban, industrial nation, for city dwellers had only limited opportunities for recreational exercise. At the same time, Americans still showed little interest in devoting themselves to exercising and spending their money as wealthier Europeans did. Yet another generation was required for that development.

By the time of the Civil War, however, the stage had been set for the United States to develop a modern system of sport. It was rapidly becoming a wealthy nation with an advanced technology, particularly in transportation and communications.[7] Once the bloody bitterness of the Civil War had passed, the United States shifted from a nation on the move to one on the run. Sport was part of its leap toward the future.

PHYSICAL EDUCATION IN THE EARLY NATIONAL PERIOD (1783–1820)

In colonial America and during the early national period, educational theory was not of great concern. The major concerns before 1800 were survival and politics, in that order. As the nation became more settled and the larger population centers became more stable in their life-styles, the interest in education beyond the lowest level grew. The first real attempts to put physical education into the educational curriculum were just developing in the 1820s and 1830s, as experimental schools and academies began to open under the direction of men and women who had been influenced by the growing interest in physical education within the new European schools.

Much of the impetus for the improvement of programs of physical activity before the Civil War came from Europe.[8] However, three movements within the United States enhanced the effects of these pre-Civil War influences from Europe. The first was the women's education movement, seen particularly in the growth of female seminaries. The second was the move of religious groups into education and later into physical education. The third was the growth of sport in the United States during the years before 1860.

The major European influences in the United States at this time were the ideas of Johann Pestalozzi, Joseph Lancaster, Philipp von Fellenberg, and the German gymnastics system. Pestalozzi's ideas have already been discussed. His internationally famous school was visited by people from many nations. One of his visitors from the United States was William McClure (1763–1840), who also visited Fellenberg's school. McClure, who wanted to open a Philadelphia school that would follow Pestalozzi's methods, hired Joseph Neef (1770–1854), an instructor at Pestalozzi's school. The Philadelphia school, which opened in 1809 and offered many physical activities and much military exercise, was among the early American schools that were beginning to follow Pestalozzi's example by the 1820s.

Joseph Lancaster (1778–1838), an Englishman, developed a system of instruction that used student assistants to share the teachers' duties, much as contemporary theory has suggested that teacher's aides or paraprofessionals be used. Lancaster's assistants were called monitors. After they had learned a lesson, they would teach the same lesson to another group of students.

His ideas, published in 1803, included a recommendation for the use of playgrounds and play activities as part of the educational process. Most of the American schools of this type, which developed later in New England, followed Lancaster's teaching handbook, which was reprinted in Philadelphia in 1820. As free public education gradually developed, the Lancastrian schools dwindled in number.

Fellenberg, whose methods and views on physical activity have already been discussed, also influenced the development of United States schools. His model was considered a good combination of the academic and the useful in an education that included physical activity as an important part of the process. Schools following Fellenberg's ideas became popular in the 1830s, though many teachers thought the manual labor requirements removed the need for any other physical activities. Those manual labor schools gradually lost popularity about the time of the Civil War, though after the war their basic plan reappeared in the manual arts schools.

The German gymnastics system, which was based on the work of a number of men (notably Friedrich Jahn), was brought to the United States during the early years of the 19th century by German immigrants. Three prominent leaders appeared in the United States to do much of the work toward making German gymnastics popular in this country. Two of them were Charles Beck (1798–1866), who taught at Round Hill School in Massachusetts,[9] and Charles Follen (1796–1840), who taught at Harvard University; both arrived in the United States from Germany in 1824. Francis Lieber (1800–1872), who also taught at Harvard, came from Germany in 1827. All three generally followed Jahn's teachings in their programs and helped to spread his system, which played a part in the development of American physical education programs prior to 1900.

During the late 1700s and early 1800s, women's education grew in popularity, though the growth was not rapid. First supported strongly by Dr. Benjamin Rush (1745–1813), female seminaries or academies were founded in many communities during this period. Tuition was required at the private institutions, for providing free public education to women was not yet considered worth the expense. Attempts to open public high schools for women in Boston and New York City in the 1820s were failures, because too many women wanted to attend, and the citizens thought the cost was too high.

During the first half of the 19th century, interest in sports began to grow rapidly. Most of the Puritan-based objections to games and sports had gradually disappeared as the nation grew larger and more stable. Groups of various nationalities had brought their own favorite games to the United States, and the melting pot of peoples became a melting pot of sports. The time when sports would begin to organize had not yet come, however.

ANTEBELLUM PHYSICAL EDUCATION IN THE UNITED STATES (1820–1860)

The period from 1820 to 1860 saw many new developments in both education and physical education. The Round Hill School was opened in Northampton, Massachusetts, in 1823 by Joseph Cogswell (1786–1871) and George Bancroft (1800–1891).[10] This college preparatory school was the only school in the nation that was concerned with the idea of individualized instruction. It also recognized the importance of physical activity as part of the educational program. The founders had observed the programs of the German gymnasiums and of Fellenberg, and had decided to try an experimental school based on those ideas.

The Round Hill School provided a classical education, but it also included dancing, riding, and gymnastics. The classes were small, usually about six persons each, and the instruction was individualized at the level of each student. Cogswell, who ran the school, tried to be like a father to the students. He abolished most systems of punishment and rewards, and led much of the exercise himself, for he especially liked long hikes and running.

Charles Beck taught Latin and gymnastics at the Round Hill School from 1825 to 1830. Beck had translated a gymnastics book of Friedrich Jahn's into English, and following Jahn's system, he started the first outdoor school gymnasium as well as the first school gymnastics program in the United States at Round Hill. His program served as the introduction of German gymnastics into the United States. As Roxanne Albertson has noted:

> During the late 1820s many academies and colleges provided German gymnastic apparatus for students to use during recess or idle time. A small number of academies followed the example of Round Hill and included gymnastics in their regular curriculum.[11]

The Round Hill School closed in 1834. Although the school had some financial problems, the primary reason for its closure was that the school was so different from other American schools. Its educational work had been of superior quality, and its graduates were ready for the last year or so of work at most colleges. However, many colleges required their students to pay for the full four years of college work even if they entered the college as advanced students. This practice made the Round Hill School a financial hardship for many of its graduates.

During this period before the Civil War, the number of school gymnastics programs and the construction of gymnasiums gradually increased. The first college gymnasium, which was furnished with the types of equipment generally used in German gymnasiums, opened at Harvard in 1820. By the 1850s, many colleges had begun providing gymnasiums for their students, and the gymnasium construction boom was under way.

This period also saw an increased interest in swimming, and this led to the building of many new swimming pools. Benjamin Franklin, who had long been a proponent of swimming, was quoted liberally in William Turner's *The Art of Swimming* in 1821. In 1827, Francis Lieber opened the first public swimming pool under the control of the Boston gymnasium. The first college to construct a swimming pool was Girard College, which opened in 1848. The college's four indoor pools in its dormitory basements, as well as its outdoor pool, were all planned by Lieber.

Public education also began to develop during this time. Although many public schools for elementary education were being opened, most opportunities for secondary education remained in the private academies, or schools that charged tuition. The academies, which were frequently coeducational, stressed terminal education. That is, they were not college preparatory, and they were more practical than classical in their curricula. Because of the large number of private academies, the first public schools were often ridiculed as schools for the poor.

By the 1830s, the aristocratic tendencies of the rapidly growing nation and its educational system were beginning to disappear. With the example of President Andrew Jackson, more democratic feelings began to emerge. The people wanted more useful education than that being offered at the classically oriented private schools. By the middle 1800s, people were beginning to believe that education should be free and that it should be provided for both sexes.

In 1818, the first public high school for boys opened in Boston, while in 1852, Massachusetts became the first state to pass legislation requiring all children to attend school. The problems of public education for girls have already been mentioned, but a similar lack of interest in forming colleges for women was overcome in 1853 when the first four-year college for women, Elmira (New York) College, was established.

In 1832, John Warren (1778–1856), a Harvard professor of anatomy, published a book supporting physical education in education. This work, *The Importance of Physical Education*, can be considered the first theoretical book on physical education, for it was philosophical in nature. However, most colleges were not very interested in physical education. Although they had begun to provide gymnasiums and other facilities for physical activities, the improvements were primarily the result of student agitation for the facilities, not of any administrative or scholarly interest in the value of exercise for students. The outdoor gymnasiums that developed in many schools in New England followed the leadership of the German gymnastics model set up by Charles Follen at Harvard in 1826. Those gymnasiums were not recognized as a part of the official school programs, however.

A prominent leader in physical education for women in the antebellum period was Catharine Beecher (1800–1878).[12] She was conservative in most areas concerning women, for she basically believed that a woman's place was in the home, a popular idea with the men. Unlike other women of her time, however, Beecher thought that women should be educated for that position. She viewed the mother as the core of the family, and she believed that mothers needed to be educated if they hoped to do well at their difficult task. Beecher objected to the clothing styles of her time as too restrictive and heavy to permit good health. She emphasized the idea of exercising to improve health. For her students, both women and children, she prescribed exercises similar to Per Henrik Ling's Swedish gymnastics, which were not widely used in the United States until the 1860s.

Although Beecher was in favor of sports and games as good exercises and considered them useful in promoting family unity, she was puritanical in her opposition to other activities. She considered hunting for recreational purposes to be sinful and was suspicious of the directions in which dance might lead people. She was more interested in women's role in the home than in their intellectual role. Because women were beginning to struggle for their rights at this time, Beecher's ideas were not extremely popular with many women. Even so, they were refined and spread by Dio Lewis after the Civil War.

Colleges began to grow rapidly in number before the Civil War. The government had set aside land in each state to be used in providing education for the people, and this impetus led to the founding of many state colleges, sometimes called land grant colleges. The earlier colleges had been formed by religious groups, except for Benjamin Franklin's school, which later became the University of Pennsylvania.

Religious groups also began to get involved in physical education and recreational activities during this period. The recreational life of many people centered on the church, which was a common gathering point in rural areas.

The Young Men's Christian Association (YMCA), founded in London in 1844 by George Williams to help young men to lead moral lives, was first brought to the United States in 1851. The YMCA programs in the United States moved into physical education when interest grew in gymnastics and other health-oriented activities after the Civil War. A women's version, the Young Women's Christian Association (YWCA), was organized in Boston in 1866. Meanwhile the Young Men's Hebrew Association (YMHA), which had been founded in 1854 as a literary society, also began moving into physical education activities.

During the 1830s and 1840s, a developing trend in the heavily populated cities concerned public health.[13] Doctors began to notice the large number of unhealthy citizens, particularly children, and assessed the problem as one caused primarily by a lack of exercise. In most cities, people had no place to get any "country-type" exercise away from the city's crowded, dirty environs. Boston was fortunate in having its large common, which had been used as a pasture, but it was an exception among the cities. Gradually other cities in the United States began to try to provide public parks for their citizens' exercise. European parks were studied by people who began to develop the architecture of public parks. This civic concern for low-level recreation was the start of a long period of gradual growth toward the important field of recreation.

The United States was gradually becoming a land of large cities complete with slums, and it was beginning to face for the first time some of the problems that the European cities had been facing for centuries. Fortunately, most American cities were young enough or small enough to be able to set aside land for parks in their interiors, which was an impossibility for most European cities. This period of interest in public health and public parks continued until the Civil War, and it progressed with increased vigor after the war.

Perhaps the most influential factor in the development of physical education in the United States in the last decade or so before the Civil War was the example of the *turnvereins*, or German gymnastic societies. The turnverein, or Turner, movement grew in the United States, as the unsettled political situation in the many states that later became Germany caused increasing numbers of Germans to immigrate to the United States. Those immigrants brought many of their customs with them, and by 1848, the Turners had established their first group in the United States, probably in Louisville, Kentucky, followed quickly by Cincinnati, Ohio, and New York City.[14] (The first national turnfest, a large, organized, outdoor gymnastics meeting, was held in Philadelphia in 1851.)

The popular Turner groups might be called family physical and social clubs, for they were as much social organizations (for entire families) as they were groups oriented to physical activity. The goals of the Turners in this country were to promote physical education, to improve the individual's intellect, and to provide opportunities for socializing with other members.

The demarcation point in the 19th-century development of physical education might be set at 1861. In that year, Dr. Edward Hitchcock (1828–1911), recently graduated from Harvard's medical school, was hired by Amherst College as a professor of hygiene and physical education, the first such recognized position in the United States. He was asked to develop a program to contribute to the health of the students at Amherst. Hitchcock's program began as heavy gymnastics, using large, fixed apparatus in the German manner. Later, he modified it to light gymnastics, using light hand apparatus and exercising to music, which he thought was more beneficial to the students. He began to record measures of the students' body dimensions and gradually developed a large pool of anthropometric measurements that were useful to later physical educators. He also started one of the nation's first intramural school sports programs.

Hitchcock headed the Amherst physical education program for 50 years, until his death in 1911. His hiring represented a turning point in United States physical education, for it was the first recognition by a college of the value of physical education in its students' educational program. The Amherst program served as a major example to other United States schools for many decades.

Another major factor in the development of physical education in the year 1861 was the start of the Civil War, which marked the beginning of a period of drastic change in the United States. The country was changing from a heavily agricultural nation toward a highly industrialized one. Over the next half-century, radical changes in the complexion of the nation led to an increased demand for physical education activities and gymnastics.

THE PROFESSIONALIZATION OF AMERICAN PHYSICAL EDUCATION (1860–1900)

By the close of the Civil War, many changes had taken place in the country. The teaching of physical education was beginning to expand more rapidly. Dio Lewis (1823–1886) was a major influence on the development of American physical education at this time.[15] Although Lewis's only degrees were honorary, he practiced medicine. He had some academic learning and practical experience in the medical field, and he was an enthusiastic supporter of health-related activities, particularly physical education pursuits and temperance campaigns against the use of alcohol.

Lewis developed his own system of gymnastics, which he referred to as the "New Gymnastics."[16] He was especially concerned with the development of the upper body, and he tried to develop a system of exercises that would be applicable to men, women, and children. He used no large or fixed equipment, preferring free exercises and activities using wands, Indian clubs, rings, and even beanbags. In his program the students performed the activities to music.

Lewis started the Normal Institute for Physical Education in Boston in 1861 to instruct teachers in his system of gymnastics. The course was a ten-week training session with classes in anatomy, physiology, hygiene, and gymnastics. This first teacher-training institution for physical education in the United States remained open until 1868 and graduated between 250 and 400 teachers during its existence.

Lewis was something of a charlatan-salesman. Although he practiced medicine without a degree, gave many lectures based on little experience, and made many unscientific claims that could not be supported, he was an excellent salesman of physical education. He did more to popularize gymnastics than anyone in his time. His system became a major influence in the use of gymnastics in the schools, for it required minimal equipment and expense. His book of instructions for the system, first published in 1862, went through ten editions in six years. Lewis also devoted much of his life to the work of the Women's Christian Temperance Union (WCTU), which he founded and which became an avid supporter of physical education in the schools.

The Turner School

The German Turners also formed a school to train teachers of their system, though their school had many early difficulties.[17] The school, which opened in New York City in 1866, was called the Normal School of the North American Gymnastic Union. (The Turners had been split by politics before the Civil War, but they dropped all political concerns afterward and changed their name to the North American Gymnastic Union.) Their primary objective of physical training was evident in the new school. The one-year course included the history and aims of physical education, anatomy, first aid, dancing, and gymnastics instruction, combined with work in teaching methods. The classes met during the evenings, so the students could have jobs during the day. The first class began with 19 students, 5 of whom graduated.

In the years that followed, the teacher's course varied in length from four to ten months. The site of the school shifted from New York to Chicago and back, then to Milwaukee (for 13 years), to Indianapolis, and then back to Milwaukee, where the course was a 2-year program from 1895 to 1899. The curriculum gradually became diversified and similar to a junior or senior college

The popularity of Friedrich Jahn's *turnplatz* reached the United States in the early 19th century; this Turner gymnasium in the United States shows activities typical of about 1890. (Courtesy The Bettmann Archive)

program as the Turners discovered that they needed to broaden their program if they wanted their influence to reach beyond the German community. By 1907 the school was in Indianapolis to stay; it offered a four-year degree program, which resulted in a Bachelor of Science in Gymnastics (B.S.G.) degree, and later became affiliated with Indiana University.

Development of Other Schools and Systems

Dr. Dudley Sargent (1849–1924) was named director of the Hemenway Gymnasium at Harvard University in 1879.[18] He had received an M.D. degree at Yale and had taught there and at Bowdoin College. He developed a gymnastics program based on the German and Swedish systems, constructed many types of apparatus to be used in his program, and also did much experimentation in anthropometric measurements. He referred to his system as the Sargent System, an eclectic system that drew from many others. He used a thorough medical examination as the basic preliminary to any program of physical activity.

The school that Sargent founded in 1881 to prepare teachers of physical education was originally called the Sanatory Gymnasium. It later became the Sargent School for Physical Education, which eventually merged with Boston University. In 1887 Sargent introduced a summer session, which met at Harvard, to prepare physical education teachers. Sargent became a key figure in the development of modern American physical education, along with Dr. Edward Hitchcock, of Amherst, and Dr. Edward Hartwell, of Johns Hopkins University, who also directed influential American programs of gymnastics and physical education.

Other plans and systems of physical education introduced into the United States in the 1880s included the Swedish system of gymnastics based on Ling's work. This system was first taught by Hartwig Nissen (1855–1924) in Washington, D.C., then at Johns Hopkins University, and later in Boston. Nils Posse (1862–1895) also taught the Swedish system in Boston. A graduate of Sweden's Royal Central Institute of Gymnastics, Posse came to Boston in 1885.[19] He was hired by Mary Hemenway to teach the Swedish system to 25 women teachers. Later he became director of the Boston Normal School of Gymnastics when it was founded in 1889.

The Swedish system, which began to replace the German system in popularity, used no apparatus and was more free and less rigid than the German system. This flexibility was the strongest point of the Swedish system, for it allowed the program to adapt more easily to local conditions than the German system could. Posse added exercises with Indian clubs and other objects because they were popular in America. His primary concern was to achieve the desired health benefits rather than to maintain the "purity" of the Swedish gymnastics.

Posse wrote three popular books on his version of the Swedish system and published a journal that rapidly spread word of the system throughout the United States before his death at the age of 33. He had formed his own school of teacher training in 1890, and he was succeeded as its director by Nissen. Posse's influence was great in developing the popularity of Swedish gymnastics.

The "system" of François Delsarte (1811–1871) of France also enjoyed some popularity in the late 1800s. Delsarte had worked with the use of body movements to express feelings. His exercises were aimed at training actors, singers, and public speakers, but since he left no writings about his ideas, his followers interpreted his work into a program of physical exercise that they called the "Delsartean system of physical culture." His system of expressive exercises was used as a counter to the German and Swedish systems, though its influence was much smaller. The system was later absorbed by dance, to which it was more applicable.

The Physical Education Requirement

After the Civil War, the first moves were made toward requiring physical education activities and instruction in the public schools. Under the leadership of John Swett, California's superintendent of public instruction, the California state legislature passed the first law requiring physical education in the public schools in 1866.[20] This first law did not signal a dramatic surge in the number of such laws, however. The second law requiring physical education was not passed until 1892, when Ohio required such instruction, but only in the larger schools in the state. Much of the work leading to the passage of such state laws around the turn of the century was done by the Turners and the WCTU. The WCTU, in seeking to gain more public recognition of the place of physical education in the educational process, was also instrumental in having a physical education division organized within the National Education Association in 1895.

The Move Toward Professional Organization

A focal point in the history of physical education in the United States was the 1885 formation of the Association for the Advancement of Physical Education (AAPE). Most teachers of physical education were then called gymnasium teachers or directors of gymnasiums. At this time there were few leaders in physical education, and not many of the better-known teachers had received formal training in the work they were doing. Most teachers had learned more through trial and error, plus reading, than they had learned through teacher-training programs.

William Anderson, M.D., a teacher of physical training at Adelphi College in Brooklyn, wanted to learn what other teachers were doing, so he called for a meeting in Brooklyn of people interested in gymnastics. The group met on 27 November, 1885, with 60 persons present. Dr. Edward Hitchcock was appointed chairman and later elected the first president as 49 people joined the new AAPE. Most of the leaders in the new organization held M.D. degrees and were interested in physical education for the health benefits that they believed it provided.

The group met in the same place during the following year, but changed its name to the American Association for the Advancement of Physical Education (AAAPE). The members stated that their objectives were "to disseminate knowledge concerning physical education, to improve the methods, and by meetings of the members to bring those interested in the subject into closer relation to each other." A new member was Edward Hartwell, M.D. and Ph.D., who had helped to define the field of physical education and show the extent of its practice with the publication of his 1885 report to the government called *Physical Training in American Colleges and Universities*.

The Boston Conference of 1889 might be considered an outgrowth of the AAAPE. Whether this is true, the AAAPE did cancel its convention that year so its members could go to the Boston meeting, and most of them did go to Boston.[21] The meeting was called by Mary Hemenway, assisted by Amy Morris Homans. The two women were advocates of the Swedish system, but the conference was designed to discuss all of the systems. While many prominent leaders of physical education spoke on the German, Swedish, and Sargent systems, it is interesting to note that no spokesperson was called on for games and sports, probably because those activities were not included in the curriculum used by the schools and colleges at that time. The 1889 conference is significant, for it was the first meeting to bring together the leaders in the field of American physical education specifically to discuss the various sys-

The exercise gymnasium has changed in many ways since the 1800s. (Courtesy DUPAC, Duke University Preventive Approach to Cardiology)

tems of physical education and which program might provide the best help to the American people.

By this time the "Battle of the Systems" between the German and Swedish systems of gymnastics was growing to fever pitch. During the 1892 convention of the AAAPE, many arguments were presented on both sides, with Nils Posse, champion of the Swedish system, suggesting that the greatest need was to develop an "American system" based on the needs of the American people, rather than to adopt totally either the German or Swedish system.

Another speaker at the 1892 convention was George Fitz (1860–1934), who pushed hard for physiological research into the benefits of physical activity to provide proof of such benefits and, at the same time, to help determine which activities were actually beneficial to the body.[22] An M.D. who taught physical education in Harvard's short-lived (1891–1899) bachelor's-degree program in physical education, Fitz was the impetus behind the formation of the *American Physical Education Review*, as well as its first editor. He also founded the first American physical education research laboratory at Harvard in 1892.

American Physical Education at the Turn of the Century

By 1900 there were 1076 members in the AAAPE, though none were from west of Nebraska.[23] The association was playing an increasingly important role in providing channels of communication among physical educators as physical education continued to spread and evolve. By the turn of the century, the Battle of the Systems was being decided in favor of the Swedish system, but this issue was becoming less important. As the new century dawned, the influence of sports, including games and play activities, moved irresistibly into programs of physical education, to the point of almost replacing the traditional activities.

Thus, at the close of the 19th century, physical education was becoming recognized for its value in the educational process. States were beginning to require its inclusion in public school programs (though most states did not do so until after 1900), and in turn, the increasing use of physical education in the schools was beginning to require more physical education teachers.

Although regular four-year degree programs to prepare teachers of physical education had not yet emerged, several institutions had begun training physical education teachers. The list of those schools begins with Dio Lewis' school and includes the Turner school, Sargent's regular school and his Harvard summer session, the Boston Normal School of Gymnastics, the Posse–Nissen School, and the newly expanding International YMCA School (later Springfield College) at Springfield, Massachusetts. The first graduates of such programs were appearing at the close of the century. The most recent research indicates that Harvard awarded the first baccalaureate degree in physical education to James F. Jones in June 1893. He became an instructor at Marietta (Ohio) College that fall, which was the first college in the United States to hire an academically trained physical educator.[24]

Another early four-year degree program was offered by Stanford University, which awarded a degree to Walter Davis in 1897 and a degree to the first female physical education graduate in the United States, Stella Rose, in 1899.[25] The first state university degree was awarded by the University of Nebraska to a woman, Alberta Spurk, in 1900. The big boom in four-year physical education degree programs was to come in the next 30 years, from 1900 to 1930, which we shall discuss later.

NOTES

1. Emmett A. Rice, John L. Hutchinson, and Mabel Lee, *A Brief History of Physical Education*, 5th ed., Ronald Press Company, New York, 1969, p. 146.
2. Cited in Nancy L. Struna, "Puritans and Sport: The Irretrievable Tide of Change," *Journal of Sport History* 4 (Spring 1977), 7.
3. T. H. Breen, "Horses and Gentlemen: The Cultural Significance of Gambling Among the Gentry of Virginia," *William and Mary Quarterly* 34 (April 1977),' 329–347.

4. Melvin L. Adelman, "The First Modern Sport in America: Harness Racing in New York City, 1825–1870," *Journal of Sport History* 8 (Spring 1981), 5–32.

5. William J. Baker, *Sports in the Western World*, Rowman and Littlefield, Totowa, N.J., 1982, pp. 107–111.

6. John A. Lucas and Ronald A. Smith, *Saga of American Sport*, Lea & Febiger, Philadelphia, 1978, pp. 108–118.

7. Benjamin G. Rader, *American Sports: From the Age of Folk Games to the Age of Spectators*, Prentice-Hall, Englewood Cliffs, N.J., 1983, pp. 42–43.

8. C. W. Hackensmith, *History of Physical Education*, Harper & Row, New York, 1966, pp. 332–345.

9. Ellen W. Gerber, *Innovators and Institutions in Physical Education*, Lea & Febiger, Philadelphia, 1971, pp. 245–251.

10. Ibid.

11. Roxanne Albertson, *Physical Education in New England Schools and Academies From 1789 to 1860: Concepts and Practices*, Ph.D. dissertation, University of Oregon, 1974, pp. 90–91. Microfiche.

12. Gerber, pp. 252–258.

13. John Rickards Betts, "Public Recreation, Public Parks, and Public Health Before the Civil War," in *Proceedings of the Big Ten Symposium on the History of Physical Education and Sport*, ed. Bruce L. Bennett, The Athletic Institute, Chicago, 1972, pp. 33–52.

14. Robert K. Barney, "America's First Turnverein: Commentary in Favor of Louisville, Kentucky," *Journal of Sport History* 11 (Spring 1984), 134–137.

15. Fred E. Leonard, *Pioneers of Modern Physical Training*, 2d ed., rev., Associated Press, New York, 1922, pp. 83–88.

16. Gerber, pp. 259–266.

17. Ibid., pp. 267–275.

18. Arthur Weston, *The Making of American Physical Education*, Appleton-Century-Crofts, New York, 1962, p. 34.

19. Gerber, pp. 314–318.

20. Ibid., pp. 100–105.

21. Weston, pp. 37–39.

22. Gerber, pp. 302–307.

23. *JOHPER* 31 (April 1960), 33.

24. Walter Kroll, *Graduate Study and Research in Physical Education*, Human Kinetics, Champaign, Ill., 1982, pp. 58–59.

25. Mabel Lee, "Further Discussion of the First Academic Degree in Physical Education," *JOHPER* 44 (April 1973), 89.

SUGGESTED READINGS

"AAHPERD Centennial Issue." *JOPERD* 56 (April 1985): entire issue. A historical overview of AAHPERD and its leading figures, by Bruce L. Bennett and Mabel Lee, with articles on divisions within AAHPERD by other professional leaders.

Adelman, Melvin L. "The First Modern Sport in America: Harness Racing in New York City, 1825–1870." *Journal of Sport History* 8 (Spring 1981), 5–32.

Barney, Robert K. "Knights of Cause and Exercise: German Forty-Eighters and Turnvereine in the United States During the Ante-Bellum Period." *Canadian Journal of History of Sport* 13 (December 1982), 62–79.

Bennett, Bruce L. "Sports in the South Up to 1865." *Quest* 27 (Winter 1977), 4–18.

Berryman, Jack W. "The Tenuous Attempts of Americans to 'Catch-Up with John Bull': Specialty Magazines and Sporting Journalism, 1800–1835." *Canadian Journal of History of Sport and Physical Education* 10 (May 1979), 33–61.

Betts, John Rickards. "Public Recreation, Public Parks, and Public Health Before the Civil War," in *Proceedings of the Big Ten Symposium on the History of Physical Education and Sport*. Ed. Bruce L. Bennett. Chicago: The Athletic Institute, 1972, pp. 33–52.

Cantwell, Robert. "'America Is Formed for Happiness.'" *Sports Illustrated*, December 22–29, 1975, pp. 54+.

Gelber, Steven M. "'Their Hands Are All Out Playing': Business and American Baseball, 1845–1917." *Journal of Sport History* 11 (Spring 1984), 5–27.

Geldbach, Eric. "The Beginnings of German Gymnastics in America." *Journal of Sport History* 3 (Winter 1976), 236–272.

Hardy, Stephen. "The City and the Rise of American Sport, 1820–1920." *Exercise and Sport Sciences Reviews* 9 (1981), 183–219.

Holliman, Jennie. *American Sports (1785–1835)*. Philadelphia: Porcupine Press, 1975. (Reprint of 1931 ed.)

Hyde, William J. *The Round Hill School, 1823 to 1834: An Early Experiment in American Physical Education*. M.S. thesis, University of Massachusetts, 1970. Microfiche.

Jable, J. Thomas. "The English Puritans: Suppressors of Sport and Amusement?" *Canadian Journal of History of Sport and Physical Education* 7 (May 1976), 33–40.

———. "Pennsylvania's Early Blue Laws: A Quaker Experiment in the Suppression of Sport and Amusements, 1682–1740." *Journal of Sport History* 1 (Fall 1974), 107–121.

Kirsch, George B. "American Cricket: Players and Clubs Before the Civil War." *Journal of Sport History* 11 (Summer 1984), 28–50.

Ledbetter, Bonnie S. "Sports and Games of the American Revolution." *Journal of Sport History* 6 (Winter 1979), 29–40.

Osbourne, Barbara J. *An Historical Study of Physical Education in Germany and Its Influence in the United States*. M.Ed. thesis, Woman's College, University of North Carolina, 1961. Microfiche.

Park, Roberta J. "'Embodied Selves': The Rise and Development of Concern for Physical Education, Active Games and Recreation for American Women, 1776–1865." *Journal of Sport History* 5 (Summer 1978), 5–41.

Paul, Joan. "The Health Reformers: George Baker Winship and Boston's Strength Seekers." *Journal of Sport History* 10 (Winter 1983), 41–57.

Rotundo, E. Anthony. "Body and Soul: Changing Ideals of American Middle-Class Manhood, 1770–1920." *Journal of Social History* 17 (Summer 1983), 23–38.

"Sport in America." *Quest* 27 (Winter 1977): entire issue.

Struna, Nancy L. *The Cultural Significance of Sport in the Colonial Chesapeake and Massachusetts*. Ph.D. dissertation, University of Maryland, 1979. Microfiche.

———. "Puritans and Sports: The Irretrievable Tide of Change." *Journal of Sport History* 4 (Spring 1977), 1–21.

———. "Sport and Colonial Education: A Cultural Perspective." *Research Quarterly for Exercise and Sport* 52 (March 1981), 117–135.

Swanson, Richard A. "The Acceptance and Influence of Play in American Protestantism." *Quest* 11 (December 1968), 58–70.

Vertinsky, Patricia A. "Sexual Equality and the Legacy of Catharine Beecher." *Journal of Sport History* 6 (Spring 1979), 38–49.

Wagner, Peter. "Puritan Attitudes Toward Physical Recreation in 17th Century New England." *Journal of Sport History* 3 (Summer 1976), 139–151.

Wiggins, David K. "Sport and Popular Pastimes: Shadow of the Slavequarter." *Canadian Journal of History of Sport* 11 (May 1980), 61–88.

——. "Work, Leisure and Sport in America: The British Travelers' Image, 1839–1869." *Canadian Journal of History of Sport* 13 (May 1982), 28–60.

Wosh, Peter J. "Sound Minds and Unsound Bodies: Massachusetts Schools and Mandatory Physical Training." *New England Quarterly* 55 (March 1982), 39–60.

See also the following books listed in the Resource Readings at the end of the book:

Baker; Baker and Carroll; Betts; Dulles; Gerber; Howell; Lee; Lockhart and Spears; Lucas and Smith; Noverr and Ziewacz; Rader; Riess; Spears and Swanson; Van Dalen and Bennett; Welch and Lerch; and Zeigler, *History*.

chapter 5

The Rise of Modern Sport in the United States and England (ca. 1860–1930)

THE CHARACTERISTICS OF MODERN SPORT

While sport was defined in the first chapter, the term *modern sport* needs to be explained. While many scholars have suggested definitions or characteristics of modern sport, the work of Allen Guttmann will be used as our model. He has suggested seven characteristics as distinguishing modern sport.[1] We will look at each of those seven characteristics briefly.

Secularism

By secularism, Guttmann means that sport has lost any religious meaning that it had in earlier times. Early sporting activities had religious overtones, if not actual religious functions. Even during the Middle Ages, some of those meanings lay close beneath the surface.

Guttman notes that modern sports are more like Roman sport than that of Greece, and that the new secular nature of sport was one of the factors that caused opposition to sport by religious leaders from the 1600s to the 1800s. He notes that "modern sports are activities partly pursued for their own sake, partly for other ends which are equally secular. We do not run in order that the earth be more fertile. We till the earth, or work in our factories and offices, so that we can have time to play."[2]

Equality

Equality refers to two provisions: (1) any person may compete, if he wishes, and (2) the conditions under which he competes will be the same as those for all other competitors.[3] Equality may be the most difficult characteristic to produce, for it is as difficult to define in sport as it is in education and in law. The meaning is that each person is treated the same under the rules, and that each person has an equal opportunity to participate. It does not mean that each person is guaranteed the right to perform regardless of ability, nor does it mean that the results are equal.

Sport is competitive, and the less skilled performers will lose. We see people as created equal to each other before the law and in their freedoms, but that does not mean that their talents, abilities or skills are equal, for they are not. Just as in other areas of life, the people with greater inherited and developed talents will rise higher than those who are less talented. Equality of access and competitive conditions does not give a person of limited ability the right to compete in an Olympic contest. As Guttman notes:

> Equality of opportunity is not the same as equality of results.... The more equal the chance to participate, the more unequal the results will be. For men and for women, the distance between the ordinary athlete and the international champion is greater every year.... Inequality of results is an essential characteristic of modern sports.[4]

Nevertheless, even in modern times sport has fallen short of equal access to competition. Guttmann points to the code of amateurism, developed during the 1800s and based on medieval ideas about separation of the social classes. Our current rules defining the "amateur" have evolved from Victorian and Edwardian England, where sport was controlled by an upper class as concerned with keeping the social classes separated as with providing competition at a high level. Indeed, under the early rules, certain occupations (those of laborers) were declared automatically professional if a person wanted to compete. Social inferiors were not to compete against (and certainly not to defeat) their "betters."

A clearer understanding of the current amateurism controversy can be had by looking closely at the people who form the rulemaking bodies. The members of the International Olympic Committee (IOC) are almost entirely wealthy (and often titled) white males. Their sympathy has never been great for the athlete who has to work to earn a living while training on the side.

Guttmann describes the code of amateurism as "an instrument of class warfare...[designed] to limit sports to gentlemen of means."[5] The basis of the rules often is difficult to understand. In part, the amateur code was an attempt to protect people who only participated for the enjoyment of sport from having to compete against people who considered sport a way of life or an occupation. We still face that difficulty today: How does an athlete working 40 hours a week compete to make an Olympic team against an athlete who makes a living at the sport and has no other task in life except to train?

Other rules have equally complicated bases. The objection to women athletes was the result of the Victorian view of women as weak creatures who needed to be protected against harm. Objections to their sports were as much for their protection (the rulemakers believed) as from any objection to the idea of women competing. Because of this protective attitude, coupled with a profound ignorance of the capabilities of women, women's sporting opportunities were severely limited until the last few decades. Only in the 1980s did the IOC decide that women were physically capable of endurance events, such as running a marathon, without severe harm.

Specialization

Specialization is a result of an emphasis on success. Instead of having a dozen or so men on a football team, each playing the entire game on both offense and defense, we have a team of over 100 athletes, some of whom may have no function other than that of substitute kicker or opposition player for practice sessions.

It includes the development of specialists who handle the off-the-field details, such as field maintenance, equipment upkeep, business details, scouting, recruiting, coaching, and such. Guttmann suggests that specialization is an inevitable development, along with professionalism, saying that "to an extent, they are the same thing.... The plain fact is that world-class competition is usually incompatible with an ordinary vocation."[6]

Rationalization

Rationalization refers primarily to the development of standard rules of the conditions and procedures of competition. Greek sports are an example of earlier developments, for while the discoi at Olympia were all the same size, for example, they were not the same size as those at Nemea or those at Delphi. While some rationalization was there, it was not complete.

At the same time, the Greeks apparently were the first to try to study sports performance and how it could be improved. As Guttman says,

> The Greeks did more than practice. They trained. The distinction is important. Training implies a rationalization of the whole enterprise, a willingness to experiment, a constant testing of results achieved.... There was a whole way of life concentrated on the single goal of athletic excellence.[7]

Bureaucracy

A bureaucracy is necessary to set and administer the rules that are developed for a sport. As we shall see, modern sport began to develop in England with the rise of organizations devoted to a single sport. Each would write the rules, standardizing the equipment, the site, and the procedures for competitions. The first organizations were usually local clubs, but the real progress came with the appearance of national bodies, which provided more widely standardized rules and arranged for national championships. International groups later provided for world championships.

The bureaucratic structure can be seen today in the Olympic movement. The IOC oversees the Olympic Games, but under it is an international group for each Olympic sport, setting the rules for that sport. Each nation has its own national body for each sport, as well as a national Olympic committee that is below the IOC. According to Guttman,

> One of the most important functions of the bureaucracy is to see that the rules and regulations are universal. Another is to facilitate a network of competitions that usually progress from local contests through national to world championships...[and] another function of sports associations [is]...the ratification of records.[8]

Quantification

Quantification, or the measurement and keeping of records of performance, is a critical characteristic of modern sport. We view almost every modern sport in terms of some measurable standard of perfection. A bowler wants a 300-pin game, a baseball player wants more hits (or more home runs or a higher batting average), and a team wants more victories than other teams. Some people consider the stopwatch, invented 250 years ago to time races, to be a symbol of modern sport.

Guttmann notes that "at least one theorist suggests that sport be defined as that physical activity which can be measured in points or in the c-g-s system (centimeters-gram-second)."[9] As he points out, even sports in which performance cannot be easily measured are changed to make performances measurable. In gymnastics and in diving, for example, we have points subjectively awarded against a "perfect" performance and its supposed difficulty, leading Guttman to refer to *Homo mensor*, or "measuring man."[10]

Records

The concept of the record is a modern one, based on the idea of progress, the idea that we shall always be able to improve, that performances can always become greater or faster. It requires quantification, for counting and recording are combined with the desire to win. The result is the desire to be the best ever—the record-holder. Guttman states that the Greeks had no word meaning "record." In fact, the use of that term in English dates only from the 1880s.[11] He speculates that with secularization of society, people no longer run "to appease [the gods] or to save our souls, but we can set a new record. It is a uniquely modern form of immortality."[12]

Guttmann summarizes the development of modern sport by citing Hans Lenk, who said that "achievement sport, i.e., sport whose achievements are extended beyond the here and now through measured comparisons, is closely connected to the scientific-experimental attitudes of the modern West."[13] Guttmann expands the explanation by noting:

> The mathematical discoveries of the seventeenth century were popularized in the eighteenth century, at which time we can observe the beginnings of our modern obsession with quantification in sport....The emergence of modern sports represents neither the triumph of capitalism nor the rise of Protestantism but rather the slow development of an empirical, experimental, mathematical [world-view]. England's early leadership had less to do with the Protestant ethic and the spirit of capitalism than with the intellectual revolution symbolized by the names of Isaac Newton and John Locke and institutionalized in the Royal Society, founded during the Restoration, in 1662, for the advancement of science.[14]

Melvin Adelman has taken Guttmann's model and modified it further to show the difference between what he calls "premodern sport" and modern sport (Table 5.1). It provides a simpler model for deciding how far sporting activity had progressed toward what we call modern.[15]

THE BIRTH OF MODERN SPORT IN ENGLAND AND EUROPE

To study early modern sport in England and Europe, we must look at 19th-century Europe, for most of what we have come to know as modern sport has developed from the growth of sport in that century, primarily in Europe. In studying European sport between 1850 and 1900, we shall look at three particular trends or developments: the continuation of the class dichotomy in sport, the origins of organized competitive sport as opposed to informal or internal sport activities, and the revival of the Olympic Games under Baron Pierre de Coubertin in 1896.

The Dichotomy Continues

Our best example of the dichotomy in the sports world comes from the British public (private) schools, for they preserved their traditional educational patterns for centuries, until the mid-19th century. The British public schools had a strong sporting tradition, because sport was considered an activity of the leisured gentleman. The school system that promoted sports was also strongly class conscious. England had clearly defined social classes, and the upper classes were hesitant to associate with the other classes.

The graduates of the British public schools were perhaps the major influence on the development of organized sport. Not only were they the primary leaders in organizing sport, but also they organized it within the framework of the public school philosophy: Sport was purely for the sake of the competition and pleasure; winning was at best a secondary interest. This philosophi-

TABLE 5.1
THE CHARACTERISTICS OF PREMODERN AND MODERN SPORT TYPES

Premodern sport	Modern sport
1. *Organization*	
Either nonexistent or, at best, informal and sporadic; contests are arranged by individuals directly or indirectly (e.g., tavern owners, bettors) involved	Formal; institutionally differentiated at the local, regional, and national levels
2. *Rules*	
Simple, unwritten, and based on local customs and traditions; variations exist from one locale to another	Formal, standardized, and written; rationally and pragmatically worked out and legitimated by organizational means
3. *Competition*	
Locally meaningful only; no chance for national reputation	National and international, superimposed on local contests; chance to establish national and international reputations
4. *Role differentiation*	
Low among participants; loose distinction between playing and spectating	High; emergence of specialists (professionals) and strict distinctions between playing and spectating
5. *Public information*	
Limited, local, and oral	Reported on a regular basis in local newspapers, as well as national sports journals; appearance of specialized magazines, guidebooks, etc.
6. *Statistics and records*	
Nonexistent	Kept and published on a regular basis; considered important measures of achievement; records sanctioned by national associations

Adapted from Melvin L. Adelman, *A Sporting Time* (University of Illinois Press, Champaign, 1986), p. 6. Copyright 1986 by the Board of Trustees of the University of Illinois. Used by permission of the University of Illinois Press.

cal direction was probably one of the most fortunate aspects of the early development of organized sport, though it created problems then and still does now.

Another notable aspect of the British public school influence at this time was the definition of amateurism. The requirements for amateur status, which enabled the athlete to enter organized competition, made participation difficult for the lower classes, because their jobs did not allow them time to train. The lower classes were discouraged, if not barred outright, from competing with the leisured gentlemen who made the rules. The "accepted" sports were still largely a domain of the upper classes.

Muscular Christianity

The traditional philosophical leader in the sport movement in the British public schools was Rugby School, with its famed headmaster Thomas Arnold. Actually, Arnold is an English version of the American Abner Doubleday. Just as many people believe Doubleday invented baseball (a game played before his birth), many people believe Arnold was the developer of public school sports as a vital part of the curriculum. The reality is explained by J. A. Mangan:

> From 1850 onwards, games were purposefully and deliberately assimilated into the formal curriculum of the public schools....It must be made quite clear that the conviction that Arnold was responsible for the "athletic sports system" of the public schools...does not accord with the evidence and should be firmly rejected....Arnold appears to have been insensitive to the possibilities of an athletic ethos with team games as the instrument of moral conditioning, as a mechanism of control, as a desirable antidote to vandalism and even as a measure of personal enjoyment. In plain fact, at no time in his life did Arnold appear to be much interested in such activities....in Arnold's own contributions to educational theory there is not a single reference to physical activities.[16]

Instead, the leadership role went to headmasters at Marlborough, Harrow, Uppingham, and other schools. It was they who "took the then novel step of encouraging pupils and staff to consider games as part of the formal curriculum."[17] Thomas Hughes popularized the changes with his novel *Tom Brown's Schooldays*, published in the 1850s to a wide British and American audience. The real influence at Rugby, and in the novel, was G.E.L. Cotton, a master who promoted sports at Rugby in Arnold's time, then became an influential headmaster at Marlborough, where he continued to preach the gospel of sports.[18]

The term *Muscular Christianity* was probably coined by T.C. Sandars in 1857, though that "ideal of manliness and the association of physical prowess with moral virtue" was promoted widely by the writings of Charles Kingsley.[19] Sports participation was promoted as moral education, a character-building experience. The goal was not victory; indeed, "the educational value of defeat and failure...was a recurrent theme in Victorian England."[20]

The value of sports in education was its encouragement of youths to learn to cope with defeat, with losing or falling short, as most people will do in competition and life. The value was in the taking part, in the striving for, rather than the achievement of a victory.

Victory was valued just as highly then as it is now. Practice time was probably as extensive as with today's athletes. Even so, it was the *struggle* to succeed that was seen to have the true value in education. Winning was all very well, but most people will not win, and they must learn to accept defeat, yet not give up.

Competition was encouraged "on the moral grounds that games were a preparation for the battle of life and that they trained moral qualities, mainly respect for others, patient endurance, unflagging courage, self-reliance and self-control, vigour and decision of character."[21] Sport was used to help in developing an attitude, a philosophy of striving to do better, regardless of the conditions faced. This idea, called Muscular Christianity, became popular in both England and the United States during the second half of the 19th century, the formative period of modern sport.

The Birth of Modern Organized Sport

Organized sport really dates from late in the 19th century. During much of the first half of the century, wars and national revolutions in Europe created unstable conditions that were not conducive to the development of sport. In the second half of the century, times were more peaceful and nationalism was growing. Sporting organizations were beginning to develop, along with a consciousness of national pride.

Sports clubs are an easily noticed development of that period. Although there was some mixing of the classes in the membership of the clubs, their policies and practices were dominated by the public (private) school graduates. Local championships were started, playing fields were constructed, and eventually steps were taken to form national sporting bodies.

We can see six rough stages of development during the rise of organized sport. The first stage was the growth of university sports, for the early organizing moves were born in the universities. The second stage was the growth in popularity of sport, as people first became interested as spectators, then as participants. This popularity led to the third stage, the development of sports clubs, as the participants banded together with other people interested in the sport to provide competition and playing facilities that would permit them to follow their sporting interests. (Some sports clubs were oriented toward several sports, while others concentrated on a single sport.) In the fourth stage, national organizations and national championships were developed for each sport. The fifth stage, the development of common national and international rules for each sport, was followed by the sixth stage (where it was applicable)—the keeping of national and international records. Most of these stages were completed during the 19th century, when the emphasis on informal sport ended and the move toward standardized national and international sports competition started. Most of the international organizations were formed in the 20th century, for the primary emphasis before 1900 was national.

An example of these developmental stages may be seen in the changes in English track and field during this period. Competition within the universities began appearing in the 1850s, though the events were highly variable from one competition to the next. The first intercollegiate meet was between

Oxford and Cambridge in 1864. Multitudes of sports clubs began forming, and the first English championship meet was held in 1866.

The time and place of the meets, which kept most nonuniversity students and citizens who lived any distance from London out of the championships, caused considerable conflict among the sports clubs. After the Amateur Athletic Association, a national track and field body, was formed in 1880, the national meet was changed to a time of year when all athletes could compete, and the site of the meet was changed from year to year as well. The move to develop international rules and records came in the next century with the formation of the International Amateur Athletic Federation in 1912, whose task was revising the international rules and approving world records.

As the 19th century came to a close, many changes had taken place in European sport. Sporting organizations had developed to make the rules more consistent. National championships had been started for many sports. The upper class's influence on sport was beginning to weaken as multitudes of "the common people" became sports competitors and spectators. The last stage in the move toward organized sport was coming closer: the development of international sport. This stage appeared as the brainchild of Baron Pierre de Coubertin, of France, who worked for years to revive the ancient Olympic Games.

THE PHOENIX ARISES: THE REBIRTH OF THE OLYMPIC GAMES

Baron de Coubertin is called the father of the modern Olympics, for the games probably would not have been revived without his long years of work to promote their rebirth. John A. Lucas has studied the work of Coubertin at length, particularly as it relates to the Olympic movement.[22] Born in France in 1863, Coubertin was a well-educated nobleman. He was an ardent supporter of the tradition of the British public schools, especially the tradition of the Rugby School. This tradition of the English schools, which was considered by Coubertin to be a major reason for the strength of England, stressed character, intellect, and the development of the body. Organized games were required of all students, and sport was thus as important a part of the educational process as intellectual training.

Coubertin was motivated by a desire to help France. Because he believed that lack of exercise had made France a weak nation, he was a major supporter of physical education in the schools. He hoped to develop sport with an international outlook. In 1892 he called for a revival of the Olympic Games, but he discovered that no one was really interested. He spent the next three years trying to make people conscious of what he called Olympism.

At an 1894 congress at the Sorbonne, Coubertin formed the International Olympic Committee, with the purpose of reviving the Olympic Games in 1896. One man was elected to represent each nation on the committee. The committee members were required to value internationalism above nationalism. They also set the standards of amateurism. The formation of the committee continued, if it did not magnify, the class dichotomy in sport, for only wealthy men were on the committee. The choice of wealthy men was intentional. They formed as independent a body as Coubertin could devise, and they were thus more likely to be unaffected by political or nationalistic influence. Unfortunately, they also were unlikely to understand the views of the common people and the athletes.

Olympism, as Coubertin called it, was characterized by religion, peace, and beauty. The strong element of character has always been a notable part of the Olympic tradition. The love of beauty, especially as expressed in the beauty of movement, is also still notable. Today we often forget the religious part of the emphasis, but the early games were held to honor the gods; there was a strong religious element in the traditional Olympic Games.

Coubertin's experiment was an attempt to blend academic training with moral and physical education. It was designed to promote peace and to contribute to international understanding. He hoped to make the competition as close to "pure" amateur athletic competition as was possible. He did not visualize women taking part in the games for two particular reasons: They had not taken part in the original Olympic Games, and in his view, competing in sports was undignified for women. His views on sport for women, which were those shared by most men at that time, were not an example of the Olympic ideal carried to its logical conclusion.[23]

Coubertin succeeded in reviving the Olympic Games. The first modern Olympic Games, held in Athens, began on Easter Sunday, 5 April 1896. The rebirth of the games was the result of Coubertin's dream, and was one of the greatest influences on modern sport. Although sport has changed vastly from what it was in 19th-century Europe, most of our practices and problems can be seen even at that early time.

THE RISE OF ORGANIZED SPORT IN THE UNITED STATES (1850–1906)

The early transition to modern sport was visible in the New York City area by the 1820s. Adelman argues:

Between 1820 and 1870 American athletics became increasingly organized and commercialized, marked by the emergence of national standards and competition, specialized player roles, a burgeoning sports information system, and ideological sanctions promoting the moral and social benefits of sports. The transformation of American athletics from its premodern to modern form was nowhere more evident than in New York City—the nation's largest, wealthiest, and most dynamic city. It was there that sport—paralleling the rise of the modern city—first assumed its modern shape and set the tone and direction for the development of sport nationally.[24]

During the second half of the 19th century, a dual development occurred in the trend toward the organization of sport: Not only were teams being formed in the schools (beginning with the colleges in the northeastern United States) but also athletic clubs were being formed simultaneously, working to organize sport. Both played important roles in the organization of sport before 1900.

Betts refers to the period from 1860 to 1890 as "the age of the athletic club."[25] Many athletic clubs were formed in the larger cities. Some clubs concentrated on specific sports, while others emphasized a number of sports. Many of the clubs were sponsored by college students until the colleges permitted them to have school teams. One leading club was the New York Athletic Club. This club, which was oriented to track-and-field events, introduced such new developments as the spiked shoe, the cinder track, and standardized track-and-field rules. It also did much to promote the sport in general.[26]

The athletic clubs promoted the growth of some professional sports, particularly baseball. Eventually they worked to form national organizations and to hold national championship competitions. An example is the Amateur Athletic Union, formed in 1888 from an earlier track-and-field group started by the New York Athletic Club.

Sport also was growing rapidly in the colleges. The earlier school teams were similar to today's extramural or club sports programs, for they were organized and directed by the students themselves.[27] For the most part, the schools made no attempt to control these sporting activities, beyond occasionally banning an activity that was considered dangerous or was interfering with academic interests. The first competition between two colleges was a rowing match between Harvard and Yale in 1852, and by 1875, intercollegiate contests were held in baseball, football, and track and field.[28]

Although no more than two dozen schools had school teams by 1875, the popularity of such teams was increasing rapidly. The faculties of the colleges usually permitted the sports for two reasons: The idea of letting the students direct some of their own activities was coming into fashion, and the school teams made student life more attractive to prospective students.

Gymnasiums were being constructed in many areas by cities, by athletic clubs, and by schools. The addition of year-round athletic facilities helped to promote sports all the more, for activities became less limited by the weather and seasons. Gymnasiums also were being built because of a growing acceptance by schools of the value of physical education activities for the students. At this time, however, physical education and sport had no real connection. The 1889 conference on physical education included practically no mention of sports activities, for physical education was more ritual and calisthenics at that time.

By late in the 1800s many new developments were taking place in collegiate sports. The rowing enthusiasts became the first to use hired coaches.[29] The secondary schools developed sports teams in imitation of the collegiate teams, often for competition against the college teams. Collegiate athletic as-

Baseball has been called the American pastime. An American business-oriented group falsely attributed the game's invention to Abner Doubleday in Cooperstown, New York, but it really seems to have developed from an English game called "rounders," which was popular in the 1700s. This Currier & Ives lithography shows an early form of the American game. (Courtesy The Harry T. Peters Collection, Museum of the City of New York)

sociations and conferences also were formed to organize and regulate competition, such as the Intercollegiate Association of Amateur Athletes of America (IC4A) for track-and-field competition in the eastern United States and the American Intercollegiate Football Association, which was founded in 1876.[30]

Another reason for the growing popularity of sports programs in colleges came from the schools' belief that sports reflected the interests and values of leading businessmen, who often gave financial support as alumni. Many of the problems common to school sports—such as professionalization and excessive outside influence, especially by alumni—date from this era during which the schools did not wish to have any official part in sports. By the late 1800s, football had become one of the most popular school sports. It was particularly influential, for many of the problems created by college football led to the start of a struggle in the schools to control school sports and to eliminate what schools considered harmful outside influences.

American Sport at the Turn of the Century

We shall consider briefly four areas of sport as of 1900. The first area is the status of groups other than white males, notably women and blacks, in sport. The second area is the abuses of sport at that time. The third area we shall consider is the progress toward organized sport. Finally, we shall look at the relationship between sport and education.

Little time is needed to discuss the part women played, or more correctly, were permitted to play, in sporting activities. Women's sporting activities included those that did not require the lady (that was the point of it all) to perspire or to display her body.[31] The activities were those that could be played while fully dressed, which at that time was full indeed. Sports were used primarily for respectable social encounters and were usually individual sports, such as archery and croquet. Women's physical education was becoming accepted in the schools, and interest in sports was also growing. Team sports, particularly basketball, were coming to be more acceptable as women's activities by 1900, but much suspicion still surrounded the idea of women's activities. The women were often quite interested in sports, but the schools and the public tended to disapprove and discourage their competition as unladylike or unsafe.

Blacks had become involved in sport by 1900, but they were handicapped by a number of developments. During the slavery years, blacks were allowed to participate in boxing, horseracing, foot racing, and boat racing. After they had been freed from slavery, they began to imitate many of the "white" sports, just as the middle and lower classes of the Middle Ages had imitated the tournaments of the nobility. Although blacks were involved in many areas of sport in the late 1800s, they were most active and successful in baseball (some blacks were major league players in the late 1800s), horseracing (most of the top jockeys before 1900 were black), and boxing.

When women were permitted to participate in sports before 1900, they were usually required to hide their body much more than male athletes; they were to remain "ladylike" by not revealing their body in any way. (Courtesy State Historical Society of Wisconsin)

During the 1880s and early 1890s a rising tide of racism in the United States resulted in the Jim Crow laws, which called for the separation of blacks and whites in many areas of life. The laws, which were upheld by the Supreme Court's "separate but equal" decision in 1896, removed blacks from many previously integrated activities. Baseball barred black players in the 1880s; white players were pressured to refuse to play if a black was on the team. (This segregation in baseball lasted until 1946 in the major leagues.) Efforts to bar black jockeys from horseracing were largely successful by 1900. Numerous other sports were pressured to ban blacks, because they were considered "uncivilized" and thus should not be allowed to compete with whites. The racism of the late 1800s was reflected most vividly in the "great white hope" of boxing, the long-sought "savior" of the whites who would defeat the black boxing champion Jack Johnson. Johnson was an object of white hatred for several years after 1900 during which he was the world's best boxer.

By 1900, black athletes usually were barred from nonblack competitions. Black major leagues were formed in baseball, which was perhaps the most popular sport among blacks at that time, and the formation of black college athletic conferences provided segregated competition at the college level. In 1900 few sports were integrated, though occasionally (but not often) black competitors participated in mixed sporting events. Some colleges, notably Harvard, had some blacks on teams, particularly football and baseball, but those schools encountered difficulties in arranging competitions with other colleges. Many schools would not permit a black to compete against their teams, which forced the integrated school team to bench a black athlete. The breakthrough for integrated sport did not occur until the Depression, and most sports were not affected until after World War II.

Sport contained many abuses in its common practices by 1900, some of which we have already discussed. Other abuses involved the recruitment of athletes by offering them excessive inducements, the methods of recruiting athletes from one college by another college, and the lack of concern for safety procedures. Concern about the number of football deaths was growing, as were indications that a class system was present in American sport, just as it was in English sport.[32] The primary difference in American sport was that the upper class was based on wealth, much of which was recent, rather than traditional social standing and noble origins.

Considerable progress had been made toward modern organization in sport, however. The colleges had begun forming competitive conferences as well as associations to develop rules of competition and eligibility standards. The colleges began to take control of collegiate sport, which until that time had been in the hands of the students or outsiders. The steps the colleges were taking to control college sports were imitated at the high school level, as state athletic associations began to form for essentially the same purpose (the first of those associations was formed in New York in 1903).[33]

The colleges developed internal athletic associations to control sports in their schools. As physical education became accepted as having value in the educational program, the faculties added control of athletics as one more area of educational physical activity. National rules were written, and open (non-collegiate) national championships were held. By 1900 the organizational level of sport was radically different from what it had been in 1850.

The conflict between education and sport was growing rapidly. The formation of the National Collegiate Athletic Association (NCAA) under an earlier name in 1906 was the first step toward national control of school sports by the schools. The association was formed in reaction to the outcry over the growing number of deaths in college football. The NCAA had three basic goals: to establish high ethical standards for college sports, to develop physical education in the schools, and to promote intramural athletics.[34] Those goals were clearly those of a group of people more concerned with the broad goals of education than with narrower sporting goals.

CHANGES IN AMERICAN PHYSICAL EDUCATION AT THE TURN OF THE CENTURY

Before 1900, American physical education was more narrowly defined than today. To most teachers it meant gymnastics or physical training or physical culture. Its primary orientation was toward developing good health for the student, rather than toward looking at the total educational program. A philosophy of dualism was present—educating the mind and training the body— and educators viewed them as two separate processes, related but not very similar. Thus, most of the ideas for unified programs of instruction had come from foreign sources instead of from within the United States.

The Move Toward a Unified American System

At the 1892 convention of the AAAPE, Nils Posse had stated the need for American leaders to quit using foreign systems of training and to develop an American system based on the characteristics and needs of the American people. Such efforts actually began to occur around the turn of the century as new leaders moved into prominence in education and physical education.

A major leader in the "progressive movement" in education was John Dewey (1859–1952), who was teaching at the University of Chicago when his ideas on education first became known.[35] Later a professor of philosophy at Columbia University, Dewey sought social changes through an experimental form of education that was centered on the child. He was best known for a work on education called *Democracy and Education*, published in 1916.

Dewey, who strongly believed in the unity of mind and body, suggested that a major reason why the system of Greek education had worked so well was that the Greeks never tried to separate the mind from the body in the educational process. His teachings included the concept of the "whole child," and combined the mental and the physical as areas that could not be separated in education. This concept led to a gradual shift in the aim of physical education in the United States from a health-centered concern for the student's body to a concern for *all* educational values, that is, to a unified view of the child and of education.

Because Dewey considered the school a social institution, he believed that education had social goals and outcomes. He included physical education in this role and followed a philosophy sometimes referred to as the "learn by doing" method of education. He considered play quite important in education, because children were interested in play activities. If children were interested in an activity, he believed they would become more involved, which would result in greater accomplishments. Dewey's was a pragmatic approach, for the teacher could take useful things from many activities to form a better activity or group of activities.

The New Physical Education

Thomas Wood, Clark Hetherington, and Luther Gulick applied Dewey's ideas in physical education. Wood developed the "New Physical Education" during the first several decades of the 20th century. He referred to it as "a program of naturalized activities for education toward citizenship."[36] He included games and sports as well as other nongymnastic activities in his program, which was aimed at meeting the needs and interests of his students. Hetherington emphasized in turn that the physical education program must be a product of American society if it is to contribute to the total education of the American child. Gulick's work in the area of recreational activities included camping and outdoor education, and stressed the social values of education.

Although the trend away from the older, more rigid systems of physical education was beginning, the move toward the New Physical Education was delayed by a lack of teachers of physical education who were trained to teach the new program. After World War I, however, the new system began to catch on in the schools. Wood's textbook led the work of spreading the New Physical Education between World War I and World War II, as did the efforts of Jesse Feiring Williams, known for his work in the philosophy and principles of physical education, and Jay B. Nash, whose major work was in the field of recreation.

During the period from about 1900 to 1930, sports were gradually included in the school curriculum, partly in response to the problems out-of-school sports had created for the schools and partly because of a strong student interest in sports. This student interest showed itself not only in the changes in the physical education curriculum but also in the rapid growth of intramural sports as many colleges began responding to the student interest in sports participation.

A Growth in Programs

At the same time sports were moving into the school program as a result of their popularity with the students, another activity was moving into the program with equal vigor: dance. Dance, particularly folk dance, had been presented in depth at the 1905 convention of the renamed American Physical Education Association (APEA, formerly the AAAPE). This convention might in fact be called the "Dancing Convention," for the bulk of the program was devoted to explanations and demonstrations of various dancing programs and their educational benefits. Some educators feared that the rapid growth in popularity of dancing programs would push gymnastics from the school curriculum.

During the early years of the 20th century, many new programs of professional preparation were being developed—first at the undergraduate level, then at the graduate level. The need for trained teachers of physical education was great at this time, for more schools began to require that their teachers hold bachelor's degrees and few such programs were available in physical education. Many state normal schools (colleges for teacher training) were built at this time, while existing state schools expanded their programs and many universities and private schools added physical education majors to their programs. Teachers College of Columbia University in New York City awarded the first master's degree in physical education in 1910, and along with New York University, offered the first Ph.D. program in physical education in 1924.[37]

The recreation movement, led by people like Luther Gulick, also was beginning to grow at the turn of the century. The larger cities in the United States were beginning to expand their recreational facilities, and programs of recreation and play were receiving more attention from the federal government. After World War I, great interest in recreation was evident, and during the Depression, the government provided jobs for out-of-work citizens in constructing recreational facilities.

The National Park Service, formed by the federal government in 1911, led to an increased public interest in parks and recreational opportunities, and camping and outdoor education became part of a large movement. Many schools began camp programs, the most prominent being the program in New York City. Many other interested groups, especially the new youth groups such as the Boy Scouts, the Girl Scouts, and the Camp Fire Girls, moved into the area of camping.

The physical educators also began to form new professional groups according to their more specialized interests. The Academy of Physical Education was formed in 1904 (no relation to the later group), and other groups were formed for people interested in men's college physical education, women's college physical education, camping activities and recreation, and school health activities. The old AAAPE, which had become the APEA in 1903, changed its name twice in the next 30-odd years, first to the American Association for Health and Physical Education (AAHPE) in 1937 and then to the American Association for Health, Physical Education and Recreation (AAHPER) in 1938. The name was changed again in 1974 to the American *Alliance* for Health, Physical Education and Recreation. Then in 1979 *dance* was added to the name, forming the current American Alliance for Health, Physical Education, Recreation and Dance (AAHPERD).

On an organizational level across the country, new groups of physical educators united to form smaller versions of AAHPERD on the state and district levels and eventually established six districts (each containing several states), as well as the state associations. On the national level, many of the older divisions of interests became associations; for example, the Division of Physical Education and the Division of Men's Athletics combined into the National Association for Sport and Physical Education (NASPE).

SPORT AND PHYSICAL EDUCATION MEET IN THE TWENTIETH CENTURY

We see the first real meeting of sport (especially as competitive athletics) and physical education during the early years of the 20th century, particularly from 1900 to 1930. Two aspects of this growing relationship (and conflict) are noticeable: (1) the gradual addition of competitive athletics, including intramurals, to the school programs, followed by a boom in popularity after World War I, and (2) the addition of sports and games to the school physical education curricula, the "American system" or "New Physical Education" discussed earlier.

Those two developments were separate during the early years of the century, yet they were gradually drawing the areas of athletics and physical education closer together because of their common interest in movement activities. The resulting conflict between athletics and physical education can be seen even today. Part of the reason for the conflict was the fear that athletics would be overemphasized, which happened many times, and part of the reason for the conflict was the physical educators' fear that athletics might gain control of the entire program and subvert its goals and objectives. We can see those fears reflected in the conflicts related to women's sports in the 1930s and again in the 1960s and 1970s.

Today, physical educators have to work out differences of opinion as school programs are increasingly combined into physical education and sport programs. As we work to solve the problems and smooth the relationships, we need to understand how the shaky relationship between physical education and athletics developed.

SPORT COMES INTO THE SCHOOL PROGRAM (1900–1930)

As we look at the history of American physical education and sport in the first third of the 20th century, we can see three rough stages of development. The first stage was the period of student control of the sports programs in the schools, which lasted until about 1906, when the NCAA was formed. The second stage was the period of increasing control of sports by the schools, roughly from 1906 to 1922, when a national federation was formed for high school sports. The third stage, the New Physical Education, lasted from 1922 to 1930 and was the time of the greatest progress in drawing sports into the physical education program.

The Period of Student Control

As the 20th century began, school sport was still controlled by the students. The common practice was for a group of students to form a team and then choose a team captain and a manager. Selecting a manager was a critical decision, for the manager was responsible for the organizational success of a team. The manager arranged the schedule of contests, arranged for practice facilities and team equipment, raised money from alumni and local supporters, handled the business of the team, and hired a coach if one was necessary. This arrangement was the ultimate in student administrative control, for the school had no connection with the team other than usually having the members of the team as its students.

School administrators were gradually accepting the idea of the value of exercise as a part of the educational process. They were learning that healthier students were more successful students, and they were adding required physical education classes to the school curriculum. The faculty members were beginning to agree that sports could be a valuable part of the educational experience, and they were working to bring the control of sports under the protective wing of the schools. This move to control sports also was a reaction to the many abuses of sports at that time, since sports were not really controlled well by any organization. Football, because it had annual fatalities, was the most conspicuous example, but basketball was rapidly becoming a popular school sport.

Basketball had been invented by James Naismith at Springfield College in 1891, with the first official game played there on 20 January 1892.[38] The game spread rapidly across the country among both men and women students. The women adopted the game so enthusiastically that in some parts of the country it was considered exclusively a women's sport.

Women were becoming involved in many sports by this time, especially in the colleges, with participation in sports such as basketball, baseball, rowing, golf, bicycling, aquatics, and winter sports.[39] They were beginning to get away from the "delicate flower" concept of womanhood, though decades would be required to complete the change. The women were making their own basketball rules because no national organizations had been formed for women's sports.

Concern over abuses and serious injuries in competitive sports was leading to school interference in the student control of sports as the century began. Student control began to pass from the scene with the March 1906 founding of the Intercollegiate Athletic Association, which changed its name to the National Collegiate Athletic Association (NCAA) in 1910. The schools had decided to take control of school sports and were trying to put sports to some educational use.

Increasing Control by the Schools

During the years from 1906 to 1922, the schools were actively taking control of interscholastic sports programs. Six trends can be seen in sport and physical education during this time.[40] The first trend was the gradual assumption of control over intercollegiate sports by the NCAA and by college athletic conferences. The NCAA, whose purposes have already been discussed, began to develop rule books to standardize the rules of sports competition. Athletic conferences and associations were springing up and working to standardize sports procedures. They wanted to develop consistent rules, set standards of eligibility for competition, and make fairer competitive matches in their sporting events. Much progress was made in bringing the athletic programs into the schools, though problems continued to develop.

A second, parallel trend was the work by the high schools to control their sports programs. The high school athletic programs were imitative of the collegiate sports programs, just as the high school academic programs were largely patterned to meet college needs and practices. State associations, followed by some regional associations, were being formed in the hope of equalizing competition, standardizing rules, and setting consistent eligibility requirements. In 1922, a national body was formed, the National Federation of State High School Athletic Associations,[41] which has since broadened its scope of extracurricular activities beyond athletics and changed its title to the National Federation of State High School Associations.

A third trend of the period was the rapid growth of interest in women's athletics. Between 1906 and the end of World War I (1918), supervised women's athletic programs were added in many colleges.[42] The women students wanted sports competition. Ellen Gerber notes that the magazine *Review of Reviews* had a written symposium on women's sports in 1900.[43] Although many women wanted sports, their participation was controversial. During the 1920s many arguments were expressed both for and against women's sports. Many female physical educators spoke out in opposition.[44] The basic reason for opposition to sports for women was a combination of Victorian standards (women must be feminine and delicate)[45] and fear that women's athletics would end up as corrupt or uneducational as men's college athletics seemed to be. For this reason, the period of rapid growth was followed by another period of shrinking away from the concept of competitive school sports for women.

A fourth trend was the boom in intramural sports, or sports involving only the students within a single school. The school intramural program was an offshoot of the earlier student-run sports programs.[46] Intramurals had been gaining in popularity in the colleges, and in 1913, the University of Michigan became the first university to form a department of intramurals (led by Elmer Mitchell) to run programs for the student body.[47] The great boom in intramural sports that came after World War I is evident in a slogan of the times: "A sport for every student and every student in a sport." The emphasis was on numbers of participants rather than on how much they participated, which created a temporary sidetracking of the intramural program goals.[48] Intramurals were to become an important part of the goals of the total physical education program as it evolved toward its present state.

A fifth trend was the addition of games and sports to the physical education curriculum. Although the change was gradually accomplished over three decades, the new programs were a radical departure from the older, formal systems of gymnastics that had been at the heart of American physical education since its early days.[49] Games and sports were more popular with the students, and the acceptance of and enthusiasm for physical education improved considerably.

A sixth trend was also visible during this time: The emphasis of physical education gradually changed from health to education. This important trend signaled the acceptance of a much broader concept of physical education—one that was more in line with the developing philosophy of the American school system—and permitted the use of games and sports in the curriculum, which increased student acceptance of the physical education requirement. It also marked a gradual change in the professional preparation of physical educators. Rather than being products of medical schools and formal gymnastics training courses, they increasingly became graduates of regular college training programs in education and physical education. The eventual results of this trend were a more widely accepted physical education program and more and better-trained teachers of physical education.

The New Physical Education and the Golden Age of Sport

The period from 1922 to 1930 can be summarized from the viewpoint of either physical education or sport. For physical education advocates, it was the time of the New Physical Education, while for sports-minded people, it was the Golden Age of Sport. Athletics had a great boom period in the United States for a decade after World War I. Postwar prosperity strongly affected the country. The standard of living was higher, the cities were growing, and the people had more leisure time available.[50]

World War I provided a great impetus to sports, though we are not sure exactly why it had such an effect. Perhaps it was because sports activities had been pushed heavily as a part of the military training, and after the war many men continued to play the new sports they had learned, just as had happened with baseball after the Civil War.

The boom in sports may have been primarily a relieved reaction to the end of the war. Betts refers to this time as "a decade dedicated to escapism,"[51] and thus sport, which is a popular form of escapism, grew rapidly. In fact, football reached a pinnacle of popularity. Football games were followed widely on every level of competition, and the sport created much controversy. Just after this peak of "football mania," a city championship high school game in Chicago drew over 120,000 spectators.[52]

The abuses of sports during this decade were being attacked, and the colleges called for an examination of the college sports scene by the Carnegie Foundation. The year of 1929 was a difficult year for sports, since college sports took two hard blows. The economic collapse of Wall Street started the slide into the Great Depression, and the Carnegie Report on college athletics was released.[53] This detailed report of the abuses of college athletics showed the problems of professionalism, commercialism, and lack of academic integrity that affected many college athletic programs. It suggested that many colleges were losing sight of their primary purpose.[54] It was used as a weapon to make many changes in college sports programs.

Physical education and sport were beginning to be forced together by the schools during this time. One sign of the growing integration of physical education and sport was the founding of the nation's first School of Physical Education at the University of Oregon in 1920.[55] Led by Dean John F. Bovard, the school organized a unit of four departments that previously had been separate: the Department of Men's Physical Education, the Department of Women's Physical Education, the University Health Service, and the Department of Intercollegiate Athletics. The interest in this unified organization of different departments that were considered related to physical education spread across the country and was adopted by many other schools.

The rise of the New Physical Education has already been discussed. It was simply the acceptance of games and sports activities as a legitimate part of the school physical education curriculum. Clark W. Hetherington had been calling for a particularly "American" form of physical education, and Jesse Feiring Williams had been popularizing a broader concept of physical education. Sports activities were creeping slowly into the curriculum until the writings of Thomas D. Wood popularized their use in a well-planned program of physical education activities.[56]

NOTES

1. Allen Guttman, *From Ritual to Record: The Nature of Modern Sports*, Columbia University Press, New York, 1978, pp. 15–55.
2. Ibid., p. 26.
3. Ibid., p. 26.
4. Ibid., pp. 35–36.
5. Ibid., p. 31.
6. Ibid., p. 39.
7. Ibid., pp. 43–44.
8. Ibid., p. 47.
9. Ibid., pp. 47–48.
10. Ibid., pp. 50–51.
11. Ibid., p. 51.

12. Ibid., p. 55.
13. Ibid., p. 85.
14. Ibid.
15. Melvin L. Adelman, *A Sporting Time*, University of Illinois Press, Urbana, 1986, pp. 3–10.
16. J.A. Mangan, *Athleticism in the Victorian and Edwardian Public School*, Cambridge University Press, Cambridge, 1981, pp. 16–17.
17. Ibid., p. 18.
18. Peter McIntosh, *Fair Play: Ethics in Sport and Education*, Heinemann, London, 1979, pp. 27–29.
19. Ibid., p. 28.
20. Ibid., p. 30.
21. Ibid., p. 29.
22. John A. Lucas, "The Genesis of the Modern Olympic Games," in *A History of Sport and Physical Education to 1900*, ed. Earle F. Zeigler, Stipes Publishing, Champaign, Ill., 1973, pp. 331–340.
23. Mary Leigh, "Pierre de Coubertin: A Man of His Time," *Quest* 22 (June 1974) 19–24.
24. Adelman, vii.
25. John Rickards Betts, *America's Sporting Heritage: 1850–1950*, Addison-Wesley, Reading, Mass., 1974, p. 98.
26. Harry A. Scott, *Competitive Sports in Schools and Colleges*, Harper Brothers, New York, 1951, p. 19.
27. Charles A. Bucher and Ralph K. Dupee, Jr., *Athletics in Schools and Colleges*, Center for Applied Research in Education, New York, 1965, p. 5.
28. Guy Lewis, "Enterprise on the Campus: Developments in Intercollegiate Sport and Higher Education, 1875–1939," in *Proceedings of the Big Ten Symposium on the History of Physical Education and Sport*, ed. Bruce L. Bennett, Athletic Institute, Chicago, 1972, pp.53–66.
29. Betts, p. 102.
30. Scott, p. 17.
31. Ellen W. Gerber, *The American Woman in Sport*, Addison-Wesley, Reading, Mass., 1974, p. 4.
32. Richard Wettan, "Sport and Social Stratification in the U.S. 1865–1900," *1974 North American Society for Sport History Proceedings*, pp. 29–30.
33. Bucher and Dupee, pp. 6–7.
34. Ibid.
35. Gerber, pp. 106–111.
36. Thomas Denison Wood and Rosalind Frances Cassidy, *The New Physical Education*, Macmillan, New York, 1927.
37. Deobold B. Van Dalen and Bruce L. Bennett, *A World History of Physical Education*, 2nd ed., Prentice-Hall, Englewood Cliffs, N.J., 1971, pp. 441–443.
38. Scott, p. 25.
39. Betts, pp. 219–220.
40. Bucher and Dupee, p. 8.
41. Scott, p. 36.
42. Betts, p. 136.
43. Gerber, p. 12.

44. For the views of those who favored athletics for women, see Harriet I. Ballintine, "The Value of Athletics to College Girls," in *Chronicle of American Physical Education*, ed. Aileene S. Lockhart and Betty Spears, Wm. C. Brown, Dubuque, 1972, pp. 196–198; and Celia Duel Mosher, "The Means to the End," in the same book, pp. 402–409. For the opposing view, see Ethel Perrin, "A Crisis in Girls' Athletics," in the same book, pp. 440–443.
45. Gerber, p. 13.
46. Scott, p. 419.
47. Ibid., p. 51.
48. Ibid., p. 420.
49. Ibid., pp. 43–44.
50. Betts, pp. 136–139.
51. Ibid., p. 250.
52. Ibid., p. 257.
53. Howard J. Savage, *American College Athletics*, Bulletin No. 23, Carnegie Foundation for the Advancement of Teaching, New York, 1929.
54. Betts, p. 255.
55. Scott, p. 52.
56. C.W. Hackensmith, *History of Physical Education*, Harper & Row, New York, 1966, pp. 415–418.

SUGGESTED READINGS

AAHPERD Centennial Issue. *JOPERD* 56 (April 1985): entire issue. A historical overview of AAHPERD and its leading figures, by Bruce L. Bennett and Mabel Lee, with articles on divisions within AAHPERD by other professional leaders.

Adelman, Melvin L. *A Sporting Time: New York City and the Rise of Modern Athletics, 1820–70.* Champaign: University of Illinois Press, 1986.

Beezley, William H., and Joseph Hobbs. " 'Nice Girls Don't Sweat' —Women in American Sport." *Journal of Popular Culture* 16 (Spring 1983), 42–53.

Brown, D. "Sport, Darwinism and Canadian Private Schooling to 1918." *Canadian Journal of Sport History* 16 (May 1985), 27–37.

Chinn, Neil Richard. *The Development of Organized Sports in England, 1860–1890.* M.S. thesis, University of Oregon, 1979. Microfiche.

Chu, Donald. "Origins of the Connections of Physical Education and Athletics at the American University: An Organizational Interpretation." *Journal of Sport and Social Issues* 3 (Spring/Summer 1979), 22–32.

Cohen, Steven David. *More Than Fun and Games: A Comparative Study of the Role of Sport in English and American Society at the Turn of the Century.* Ph.D. dissertation, Brandeis University, 1980.

Fairs, John R. "The Athletics–Physical Education Dichotomy: The Genesis of the Intercollegiate Athletic Movement." *Canadian Journal of History of Sport and Physical Education* 2 (May 1971), 44–69.

Fletcher, Sheila. *Women First: The Female Tradition in English Physical Education 1880–1980.* London: Athlone Press, 1984.

Furst, Terry R. "Mass Media and the Transformation of Spectator Team Sports." *Canadian Journal of History of Sport and Physical Education* 3 (December 1972), 27–41.

Graham, Peter J., and Horst Ueberhorst, eds. *The Modern Olympics*. Cornwall, N.Y.: Leisure Press, 1976.

Hardy, Stephen. "The City and the Rise of American Sport, 1820–1920." *Exercise and Sport Sciences Reviews* 9 (1981), 183–219.

Hargreaves, Jennifer A. " 'Playing Like Gentlemen While Behaving Like Ladies': Contradictory Features of the Formative Years of Women's Sport." *The British Journal of Sports History* 2 (May 1985), 40–52.

Henderson, Edwin B. *The Negro in Sports*. Rev. ed. Washington: Associated Publishers, 1949.

Jable, J. Thomas. "High School Athletics: History Justifies Extracurricular Status." *JOPERD* 57 (February 1986), 61–68.

Johnson, William. "The Olympic Games." 3-part series. *Sports Illustrated*, 10 July 1972, pp. 36–44; 17 July 1972, pp. 28+; 24 July 1972, pp. 32–43.

Lewis, Guy M. "Adoption of the Sports Program, 1903–39: The Role of Accommodation in the Transformation of Physical Education." *Quest* 12 (May 1969), 34–46.

——. "Canadian Influence on American Collegiate Sports." *Canadian Journal of History of Sport and Physical Education* 1 (December 1970), 7–17.

Lipping, Alar. "Harvard University and the Emergence of International Collegiate Athletics, 1869–1874." *The Physical Educator* 41 (December 1984), 176–178.

McClelland, John. "The Beginnings of Quantification in Sport." *Proceedings: 5th Canadian Symposium on the History of Sport and Physical Education*, ed. Bruce Kidd, University of Toronto, 1982, pp. 104–110.

Mangan, J.A. *The Games Ethic and Imperialism*. London: Viking, 1986.

Mason, Tony. *Associated Football and English Society, 1863–1915*. Atlantic Highlands, N.J.: Humanities Press, 1980.

Massengale, John D. "The Americanization of School Sports: Historical and Social Consequences." *The Physical Educator* 36 (May 1979), 56–69.

Mitchell, Sheila. "Women's Participation in the Olympic Games, 1900–1926." *Journal of Sport History* 4 (Summer 1977), 208–228.

Nixon, Howard L. "The Commercial and Organizational Development of Modern Sport." *International Review of Sport Sociology* 9, no. 2 (1974), 107–131.

Powell, Roberta B. *Women and Sport in Victorian America*. Ph.D. dissertation, University of Utah, 1981. Microfiche.

Riess, Steven A. *Touching Base: Professional Baseball and American Culture in the Progressive Era*. Westport, Conn.: Greenwood, 1980.

Robicheaux, Laura. "An Analysis of Attitudes Towards Women's Athletics in the U.S. in the Early Twentieth Century." *Canadian Journal of History of Sport and Physical Education* 6 (May 1975), 12–22.

Savage, Howard J. *American College Athletics*, Bulletin 23. New York: Carnegie Foundation for Advancement of Teaching, 1929. Microcard.

Shapiro, Beth J. "John Hannah and the Growth of Big-Time Intercollegiate Athletics at Michigan State University." *Journal of Sport History* 10 (Winter 1983), 26–40.

Smith, Ronald A. "Harvard and Columbia and a Reconsideration of the 1905–06 Football Crisis." *Journal of Sport History* 8 (Winter 1981), 5–19.

——. "The Historic Amateur–Professional Dilemma in College Sport." *The British Journal of Sports History* 2 (December 1985), 221–231.

Sojka, Gregory S. "Evolution of the Student Athlete in America." *Journal of Popular Culture* 16 (Spring 1983), 54–67.

Spring, Joel H. "Mass Culture and School Sports." *History of Education Quarterly* 14 (Winter 1974), 483–500.

Uminowicz, Glenn. "Sport in a Middle-Class Utopia: Asbury Park, New Jersey, 1871–1895." *Journal of Sport History* 11 (Spring 1984), 51–73.

Vamplew, Wray. "Sports Crowd Disorder in Britain, 1870–1914." *Journal of Sport History* 7 (Spring 1980), 5–20.

Walvin, James. *Leisure and Society, 1830–1950*. London: Longman, 1978.

Westby, David L., and Allen Sack. "The Commercialization and Functional Rationalization of College Football: Its Origins." *Journal of Higher Education* 47 (November–December 1976), 625–647.

Wettan, Richard, and Joe Willis. "Effect of New York's Elite Athletic Clubs on American Amateur Athletic Governance—Governance—1870–1915." *Research Quarterly* 47 (October 1976), 499–505.

Whorton, James C. " 'Athlete's Heart': The Medical Debate Over Athleticism, 1870–1920." *Journal of Sport History* 9 (Spring 1982), 30–52.

Wiggins, David K. "Isaac Murphy: Black Hero in Nineteenth Century American Sport, 1861–1896." *Canadian Journal of History of Sport* 10 (May 1979), 15–32.

Williams, Trevor. "Cheap Rates, Special Trains and Canadian Sport in the 1850s." *Canadian Journal of History of Sport* 12 (December 1981), 84–93.

See also the following books listed in the Resource Readings at the end of the book:

Baker; Baker and Carroll; Betts; Cavallo; Dulles; Espy; Gerber; Guttmann; Howell; Kanin; Lee; Lockhart and Spears; Lucas; Lucas and Smith; MacAloon; Mandell; Mangan; Mrozek; Noverr and Ziewacz; Rader; Riess; Spears and Swanson; Van Dalen and Bennett; Welch and Lerch; and Zeigler, *History*.

chapter 6

The Last 50 Years: Sport and Physical Education in the United States

THE GREAT DEPRESSION AND THE SCHOOL SPORTS AND PHYSICAL EDUCATION PROGRAM (1930–1941)

The Depression, which took time to develop fully and affect the entire country, lasted from 1929 into the start of World War II (1941). The lack of money in communities hit physical education and sports hard. Many physical education programs were dropped from the school curriculum, based on the claim that it was a "frill" course.[1] This attack on the place of physical education in the school program came as a surprise to physical educators. For the first time they became aware of the need for a good program of public relations; they realized that people simply did not understand what the purposes of physical education were and how it contributed to the education of students.

School athletic programs also were hurt, for the combination of the embarrassing revelations of the Carnegie Report and the decline in the number of sports fans with spending money was a difficult blow. The programs depended heavily on gate receipts, which were dwindling; they also needed public support, which had been hurt by the Carnegie Report. Interscholastic sports extended to the junior high schools by this time, but were receiving much criticism. The suggestion that intramurals be used instead of interschool competition at that level (since intramurals would involve more students, yet cost less money) led to an increase in the number of junior high school intramural programs.

Small colleges, which were hurt more by the Depression than the larger schools, were forced to drop sports in many cases. The small colleges were becoming increasingly critical of the NCAA, for they thought that it had been founded by and thus favored the larger schools. During the late 1930s and early 1940s, moves were made to form national organizations similar to the NCAA for small senior colleges and for junior colleges.[2]

The big boom during the Depression was in recreation, for two reasons. First, unemployment gave many people much more leisure time for recreational activities. Second, the government tried to fight unemployment by creating jobs. Many workers were hired to build recreational facilities—playing fields, hiking trails, park areas, and so forth. The large growth in available recreational facilities also acted to increase the extent of public recreation.

Women's sports during the 1920s were being held back primarily by the efforts of the leading women physical educators.[3] One reason for their opposition had been an effort by the Amateur Athletic Union (AAU) to take control of women's track and field in the United States. Women educators believed that women should control and direct women's sports. They were irritated as much by the administrative procedures of the AAU as by its ambition to control women's track and field. Until that time the women had made no effort to organize sport.

The women created a Women's Division of the National Amateur Athletic Federation to control women's sports. It was a well-organized body of women who not only ran the college programs for women but also trained the teachers, which extended their influence over both the present and future practices in women's sports.

As mentioned before, the women leaders had several fears that limited their support for higher-level women's competitive sports. While they continued to hold the Victorian image of women as frail creatures who might suffer serious physiological and psychological harm from competing in sports, they also had a far more legitimate concern: They feared that a fully developed program of interschool athletics for women would end up suffering from the same excesses that plagued men's athletics. The poor example created by men's sports may have done more to hold back women's athletics during the 1930s than any other factor, though this would be difficult to substantiate.

Some of the arguments that appeared against sports for women during the 1920s and 1930s were merely old-fashioned, while others bordered on the ridiculous. As the 1930s drew to a close, the emphasis in women's sports was moving away from the idea of interscholastic athletic competition; the programs were becoming centered on a "playday" emphasis more similar to intramurals. These playdays were low-key sporting activities, with large numbers of people involved and with teams formed by mixing players in attendance from the various schools. Playdays were organized with the basic concept of "education for all," with the education coming through physical activities and an attempt made to reach as many people as possible with those activities.

As the 1940s drew closer, both physical education and athletics had come through a difficult decade. The Depression had forced both to give up ground in terms of the scope of their programs as well as public acceptance. The next decade would bring a radical reversal of that trend, as war once again clarified a need for both in the school program.

The onset of the Depression, which became a powerful factor in the nation's life during the early 1930s, created great social changes in the country. The United States gradually shifted from its old idea of "rugged individualism" to a new concern for equality of opportunity and a concern for society. It was a difficult time for physical education in the schools; the money shortage led to the belief that many physical education programs were expensive "frills" that cost money that could be put to better use elsewhere in the schools. The move to drop physical education as a requirement in many states forced physical educators into having to defend their programs vigorously.

The trend toward social and recreational goals in physical education programs continued through the Depression but began to slow down in the years just prior to World War II. The new programs in many European nations, which showed their aims to be fitness for war and the development of a stronger sense of nationalism, resulted in a gradual shift of the American programs back to emphasis on physical fitness.

THE EFFECTS OF WAR AND COLD WAR ON AMERICAN PHYSICAL EDUCATION (1941–1973)

The coming of World War II ended the arguments over whether physical education and sport belonged in the educational program. Of the first two million men examined for military service at the start of the war, 45 percent were rejected for mental or physical reasons. Only part of this high failure rate could be blamed on the school programs, but extensive publicity began to make the public aware of the fitness problem.[4] The government saw a great need to improve the health and fitness of all the people.

During World War II, the government formed a series of organizations to improve the health and fitness level of the citizens. A Division of Physical Fitness was formed to work first under the Office of Civilian Defense and later under the Office of Defense. It had an advisory board to help develop community fitness programs, as well as a sports board of celebrities and sports authorities to try to reach the public with a message about the importance of fitness.

Physical education programs were struggling to keep from having to return to the old concept of physical training, for the war-need emphasis was for fitness only, with little interest in any broader goals. Many physical educators became involved in creating fitness tests to assess the results of the armed forces training programs. Fitness tests, which had been available for boys, were also constructed for schoolgirls. One wartime gain for physical education was that many states replaced their laws recommending physical education in the school program with laws that required it.

During the war, sports activities continued with few limitations. Although many young athletes were in the armed forces and gasoline rationing hampered travel, sports were considered a positive influence on national spirit and thus were highly encouraged. Many of the sports teams that were formed on military bases competed against college teams. Intramural sports were encouraged in the armed forces, and sports activities were used as a part of basic training. An unfortunate but natural side effect was the tendency to limit the objectives of physical education to fitness for military needs alone.

During World War II, the physical education programs in the United States basically became programs of physical fitness oriented toward the military needs of the nation. Sports were strongly promoted as instruments of fitness, and many prominent physical educators became involved not only in developing programs of physical training for the armed forces but also in developing intramural sports programs for the military. The tendency for the school programs to adopt the physical training programs of the military and thus change from programs of physical *education* to physical *training* was the greatest problem created for physical education by World War II.

The end of the war started another sports boom similar to the one in the 1920s, as competition and sports facilities underwent great expansion.[5] The American people developed a greater feeling of world unity, as seen in the formation of the United Nations, and they became more conscious of international competition as the postwar Olympic Games were revived in London in 1948. Many international cooperative sports programs were founded to foster peaceful competitions and to help nations meet and come to know each other on the field of sport.

The period from World War II to the present exhibits several notable features. The first feature was the work done toward improving the standards of teacher preparation in the United States on both the undergraduate and graduate levels. Major conferences concerned with developing the undergraduate professional preparation curriculum were held at Jackson's Mill (1948), Washington, D.C. (1962), and New Orleans (1973); written reports on curriculum suggestions were published after each conference. Other conferences on graduate study in physical education were held at Pere Marquette, near Chicago (1950), Washington, D.C. (1967), and in Cincinnati (1986).

Physical education also began to split into a number of separate areas of concentrated interest in the decades following World War II. Major interest groups whose concerns were health education, safety education, recreation (including park activities), and dance grew rapidly during this period. Fitness became a major concern several times after World War II, first during the

Korean War and then soon afterward when the results of the widely publicized Kraus-Weber Tests implied that American youngsters were much less fit than their counterparts in other nations.

The results of the Kraus-Weber Test of minimal fitness of elementary school children appeared in the United States late in 1953. Those results hit the American public with explosive force. The test found that American children were far less fit than European children. President Eisenhower reacted to this blow to the American ego by forming the Council on Youth Fitness in 1955.[6] The purpose of the council was to promote fitness on the local level, but it primarily served as publicity for the administration. The programs never really got off the ground.

AAHPERD reacted to the study by working to develop fitness tests that could be used in the public schools. The battery of tests forming the AAHPERD Youth Fitness Test was published in 1958. Despite complaints that the Kraus-Weber Test was not a genuine fitness test, the Youth Fitness Test gave essentially the same results: American children were less fit than their European counterparts.

Although the Council on Youth Fitness was allowed to fade from the public eye during the late 1950s and early 1960s, AAHPERD worked to develop a program of physical fitness tests with norms for American schoolchildren. The Eisenhower-era Council on Youth Fitness was revived in 1961 by President Kennedy as the President's Council on Youth Fitness. Kennedy was a sports enthusiast who was concerned with the fitness of the country's youth. His influence and example brought on a rash of fitness-oriented activities, such as the fads of touch football and 50-mile hikes. He started a concentrated push toward more fitness activities in schools, a drive that was the first nonwar effort to come from the upper levels of the government. This action was an example of the increasing governmental concern for the state of fitness not just of children but of all citizens. The United States was becoming much more sports conscious as the decade passed.

In 1957, physical educators discovered that the required program of physical education had to be defended once again. When Russia orbited the first Sputnik satellite, the United States went into educational shock and for the first time became convinced that its schools were "behind." The result was a concentrated push toward the sciences and "bread-and-butter" education. Many educators began accepting the old dualistic concept of the mind and body as separate entities. The problem of dualism reappeared in the late 1960s as opposition to specific requirements in the educational process grew. The net result was to show physical educators that they had sadly neglected public relations in their dealings with the public as well as with their fellow educators.

The rapid growth of professional sports activities also was having an impact on the nation. Sporting activities as public entertainment had begun to team with television to start the nation on its way to becoming a society of spectators. The efforts of professional sports to gain imitators among the amateur sports affected football and basketball practices most heavily. Amateur sports at the grass roots were threatened with losing their local fans to television, which was sure to have a contest featuring more talented athletes. The professional "sport ethic," which seemed to be reaching down to the level of amateur athletics, promised many changes in sports in the years to come.

Sport was becoming a major international concern in a world shrunk by communications satellites. Nations were sending sports teams to other nations for friendly competitions as a sign of mutual trust and friendship and, increasingly, as a means to open the way to more political cooperation. Sport was becoming a political tool, a medium for political propaganda, to a greater degree than ever before. A time of rapid, radical change was beginning.

CHANGING EMPHASES IN PHYSICAL EDUCATION AND SPORT SINCE 1973

The late 1960s and early 1970s were a time of attack on many traditions in many nations. American involvement in the war in Southeast Asia carried over into many areas of life in the United States. Many people believed that the country had lost its ideals, while others thought that the traditional ideals were under attack. During this period of confrontation, many things seemed to be argued in purely political terms. Sport and physical education were attacked from numerous directions.

The attack on the physical education requirement as a part of the curriculum was renewed at many levels. The basic argument was that while physical activity is beneficial, the student should be allowed more freedom in deciding what activities to take, or even if such activities would be taken. The attack on the physical education requirement was a small part of a larger educational movement of the time, which was a general attack on all course requirements in the schools. Many opponents of school structure considered physical education to be the weak link in the requirement system and thus the most logical place for an initial attack. Because of this movement, some required programs of physical education at the college level were changed to elective programs.

By the late 1970s, the movement away from school course requirements had lost most of its force. A decade of experimentation had resulted primarily in young people who were less capable of communicating and of using abstract reasoning skills. Standardized tests showed consistent drops in student scores during the time of weakened school requirements. As the stress on school accountability grew, public interest in more traditional educational structures and standards increased. By 1980, the schools were beginning to provide more direction for students, rather than letting the students decide for themselves whether they would make any effort to become educated.

At the time course requirements were being dropped, a concurrent trend was toward a recreational emphasis in the program of physical education activities, or what were called "lifetime sports." This trend has continued through the 1980s as more students choose electives such as tennis, racquetball, and backpacking instead of the traditional fitness courses and activities oriented to competitive sports. In 1986, national surveys showed that the fitness level of young Americans had dropped over the last decade or so, which may provoke more emphasis on traditional fitness activities again.

The wellness movement has grown rapidly. It may indicate that many physical education programs are moving back toward the earlier strong health emphasis of physical educators. Physical education also has begun to increase its work with special populations, such as the handicapped and the elderly. Though much of the interest came only after federal laws were passed to promote such activities, many new programs were developed to work with the physically and mentally handicapped. Programs of recreation and fitness are being expanded for the elderly, a group that previously received little attention from physical educators.

The idea of the New Games has grown in popularity, especially with younger students. The New Games are activities that stress the cooperative aspects of physical education rather than the competitive aspects. Technically speaking, the New Games are not sport since they are not competitive, yet they might be termed "sport for the future." This designation is possible because the New Games are partially a reaction to the overemphasis on competitive activities and because they are most meaningful as an acknowledgment that the sporting individual of the past may have difficulty fitting into the world of the future. As overpopulation increases, the "rugged individualist" is considered less acceptable in a mass society. That individual may be forced to give way to being a more cooperative, group-oriented individual to survive. The New Games might be considered physical activities for the mass cooperation-oriented society instead of for the smaller competition-oriented one.

Like the Great Depression, the 1980s were a time of rapid growth of school costs beyond the ability of many communities to pay. A consistent result was the threat of terminating school sports programs and limiting, if not eliminating, physical education programs as unnecessary "frills." The popularity of school sports helped to defend those programs, but a public facing the problems of inflation lost much of its sympathy in the face of rising costs. Though the economy was improving in the late 1980s, the financial picture for local schools was no brighter. At the same time, a more stable population level ended the growing job market for most teachers, making the opportunities for full-time physical education teachers and coaches limited. Colleges have had to give far more attention to nonschool job possibilities for their students during the 1980s. The result was a drop in the number of physical education majors over the last decade, though the job market may improve within a few years.

Athletics, like physical education, faced many problems during the late 1960s and early 1970s. As a well-publicized area of American life, athletics was an excellent target for publicity seekers. Athletics became increasingly politicized and brought many of its problems on itself. Coaches claimed sports were what kept America a democracy, while Russians argued that sports helped keep their nation socialist. Sports leaders tried to wrap themselves in the cloaks of patriotism and religion by staging militaristic shows at football games and adding religiously oriented shows at the beginning of the festivities. The unfortunate result of those excesses was to widen the split between those who thought politics and religion were compatible with athletics and those who did not think so. Both sides were convinced that they were morally right.

One result of those excesses in sport may be seen in the riots and demonstrations at the 1968 Olympic Games in Mexico City and the murder of the Israeli athletes by Arab extremists at the 1972 Olympic Games in Munich. The games themselves have become a political symbol, and because of the intense worldwide publicity they generate, they are a perfect target for any group wanting instant, worldwide publicity. The heavily promotional aspects of the 1980 games in Moscow and the 1984 games in Los Angeles are cases in point, as each was used to promote the home country, while the political opponents boycotted and criticized.

The "big-time" college sports programs were attacked as an example of highly financed programs of "sports for the few." Student groups worked to

Steeplechasers show how sport has changed in facilities, organization, and the number of participants. (W. H. Freeman)

limit student funds allocated to athletic departments. The students preferred to have their money put into programs of intramurals, extramurals, and club sports that would reach more of the students. The students put increasing emphasis on a program with more sports for all, rather than the existing system of limiting competition to a narrow segment of the student population.

At the same time, there was a move to return sports more closely to the original traditions of student control. Students were agitating to run their own intramural and extramural programs, and they were increasingly starting club sports programs. Students were showing an increased interest in more informal types of intramurals, such as drop-in, coeducational intramurals in which the competitive units are always changing. They wanted sports competition for the fun, not for the honor.

Women's athletics underwent radical changes, starting in the early 1970s. The women's liberation movement gained strength and pushed for fairer treatment of women in all areas of life, including sport, for women had been given few opportunities for competition. Although women have competed in some sports to some degree since at least the 1860s, women's sports programs had been relatively unpopular with administrators and had only marginal educational support.

Women's school sports had been controlled by the Women's Division of the NAAF and later by the Division of Girls' and Women's Sports (DGWS) of AAHPERD, which did not accept the idea of intercollegiate sport until 1963.[7] Control of women's sports in the colleges eventually was passed to the Association of Intercollegiate Athletics for Women (AIAW), which was begun in 1972.[8] It promoted sport on the national and international levels. The National Federation of State High School Associations also became more active in girls' sports and developed rule books and statewide competitions at the high school level.

Unfortunately, even with those changes, most of the opportunities for women were as competitors or chaperones, for on the higher levels of administration and coaching, men continued to run the women's programs. The basic argument for this practice was that the women lacked experience, but they were given few opportunities to gain the necessary experience.[9] That situation is changing slowly.

The last decade has seen massive changes in women's athletics, both in practice and in public attitudes toward the programs. Most arguments against the programs are no longer based on whether sport is safe for women or whether they have a right to equal competition. Instead, many opponents now are concerned primarily with the economic aspects of women's sports. When Title IX appeared in the early 1970s, it led to a decade of upheaval in American school athletics. Challenges in the schools, the media, and the courts resulted in a massive growth of women's teams at the high school and college levels, a growth that began to level out only in the mid-1980s, a time of inflation and declining school revenues.

Women are participating in sports more and more, including sports that were once considered "male" sports because of the intense training and strenuous physical activity involved. (Courtesy Duke University Sports Information)

Experience has proven that while the increase in women's funding has created financial and administrative problems, the real worries of the early 1970s did not come true. Men's athletics did not collapse; the colleges did not suddenly lose their sources of funding. Instead, public interest in women's athletics mushroomed. Generally, the schools that wanted to be powers in men's sports have shown the same interest (and success) in women's sports. The challenges and benefits of the expansion have far outweighed the drawbacks or difficulties. Indeed, by the early 1980s the success of college athletics for women was great enough that the NCAA launched a successful effort to take over the programs (which they had opposed) from the AIAW, which had made them a success.

Many changes have also taken place to promote racial integration in sports. The segregation of black athletes was largely continued until after World War II. Some exceptions were: The first black American competed in the Olympics shortly after 1900, many blacks began to appear in the Olympics in track-and-field competition after World War I, and whites began to notice the abilities of the top black athletes in the late 1930s. Even as Hitler proclaimed his doctrine of the Aryan's racial superiority, a black American, J. C. "Jesse" Owens, won four gold medals in the 1936 Berlin Olympics, and Joe Louis, the "Brown Bomber," defeated the German world boxing champion. Finally, in 1946, Jackie Robinson became the first black athlete in professional baseball in over 60 years as a result of Branch Rickey's deliberate attempt to integrate baseball. Robinson's obvious athletic skills, combined with his ability to withstand considerable hostility from players and fans, were convincing enough to lead to the integration of other professional sports. Those achievements helped to pave the way for the integration of college sports in the 1960s, as did the early leadership of a small number of collegiate teams such as those at Harvard, which insisted on playing with integrated teams. The Supreme Court decision in 1954 that reversed the tradition of "separate but equal" schooling led to integrated sports in the public schools over the next two decades. Although many misuses of the athletes occurred in the schools, American sports were for the most part integrated by the 1970s.

Perhaps the most noticeable development in athletics since 1973, other than the expansion of women's sports, has been the trend toward accepting the international view of amateur athletics in the United States. The distinctions between the amateur and the professional have been rapidly disappear-

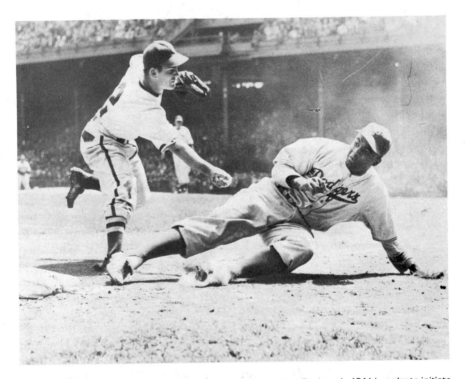

Branch Rickey hired Jackie Robinson as a member of the Brooklyn Dodgers in 1946 in order to initiate the integration of major-league professional baseball. Though black athletes had played in the major leagues in the 1800s, since about 1900 they had been forced to form their own segregated baseball leagues. (Courtesy AP/Wide World Photos, Inc.)

ing. More sporting bodies have begun to accept the idea of corporate support of athletes, with an annual salary that continues when the athlete is away from training or competition. This idea has been used in Europe for many years and is the Western version of the socialist state-supported athletics. It has been accompanied by a continuing downward trend of the age at which youths become involved in highly organized and highly competitive sporting programs. Where the schools have not provided these programs for the young, private clubs and competitive teams have more than filled the gap, especially in the individual sports such as swimming, ice-skating, gymnastics, skiing and boxing. Whether this trend is beneficial remains to be seen, though it largely depends on the viewpoint of the individual.

There is much concern about the rapid expansion of highly organized youth sports, with untrained coaches attempting to use the approach of professional athletes for children who, in some cases, have not yet begun school. The impact is most noticeable in the middle and upper elementary school grades.

THE CHARACTERISTICS OF TWENTIETH-CENTURY AMERICAN PHYSICAL EDUCATION

In reviewing the history of physical education in the United States, Daryl Siedentop suggested seven important characteristics visible during its development:[10]

1. The interpretation of physical education as an "umbrella" concept, with a multitude of activities such as sports, games, dance, recreation, and health education. (This is the "broad field of interests" interpretation of physical education this text has suggested.)
2. The downward movement of innovation from the college level to the high school level and, finally, to the elementary level. (Siedentop suggests that this is the normal direction for most new programs to take, since future teachers learn them at the college level.)
3. The development of sports and games through sources outside the schools.
4. The selection of physical education activities dictated by the trends in adult leisure. (This was a major direction of many required programs during the 1970s in response to the concept of "lifetime sports"—activities that could be practiced throughout an individual's life—as opposed to strenuous fitness activities that older persons could not engage in so well.)
5. The unclear relationship between physical education and athletics. (This has been a continuing problem in American physical education since the late 19th century when students began organizing their own sports programs.)
6. Periodic returns to a major emphasis on fitness. (This was the direction of the physical programs not only in times of war but also at other irregular

intervals such as when the negative results of the Kraus-Weber Tests were made known.)

7. Increased specialization in professional training. (This can be seen today even at the undergraduate level, as some students are asked to specialize in either elementary or secondary physical education, while larger schools have undergraduate majors in other areas, such as health education or recreation.) This trend may cause increasing problems for physical educators, for while such programs require longer periods of study and more money, the public is calling for programs that are shorter and less expensive.

American physical education has been through many changes during the 150 years since the start of the earliest programs that we think of as physical education. It has moved from an emphasis that was purely on the health of the student to a concept of concern for the education and state of the "whole" person—mind and body unified. It has come from a system promoted by self-taught "amateurs" to one supported by science and the medical profession, from one with teachers with ten weeks or less of professional training to one with trained teachers who hold degrees up through the doctorate. It has come from a field interested in a small area of physical concern to a diverse body of people who might at first glance seem to have little connection with each other; they are, however, united in physical education as a broad field, even though individually they may be health educators, park administrators, recreational program directors, or teachers of dance. Physical education has become a broad and complex field, but it has become no less a satisfying field for the practitioner.

The problem of what the relationship of physical education and sport should be has not been settled. This topic is worthy of volumes, for to many people, sport and physical education are the same and inseparable, and many people consider sport to lie at the heart of the study of physical education. Although many problems are to be overcome, sport and physical education have gradually been blended together to form a broad area of interest. As they have blended together, each has benefited—sport from the educational aims of physical education, physical education from the activity and application opportunities of sport. Both sport and physical education are stronger as a result of the relationship, but much work is needed to realize the full benefits of the combination and to make the relationship a harmonious one.

Who has won the battle between physical education and sports? The question is still open to debate. The need to share facilities, equipment, and even budgets causes conflict. Physical educators and athletic coaches are slowly coming to understand that they are closer together than they had realized. Each area is affected by the public reputation of the other. In the eyes of the public, the two areas are one. Whether physical education and athletics wish to be a single area, they are being forced together by the public. The question of which area will carry the greater influence, if either one, has not yet been settled.

NOTES

1. C. W. Hackensmith, *History of Physical Education*, Harper & Row, New York, pp. 439–442.
2. Ibid., pp. 455–456.
3. Ellen W. Gerber, "The Controlled Development of Collegiate Sport for Women, 1923–1936," *Journal of Sport History* 2 (Spring 1975), 1–28.
4. Hackensmith, pp. 467–474.
5. Harry A. Scott, *Competitive Sports in Schools and Colleges,* Harper Brothers, New York, 1950, pp. 76, 78–82.
6. Hackensmith, pp. 485–505.
7. Ellen W. Gerber, *The American Woman in Sport*, Addison-Wesley, Reading, Mass., p. 75.
8. Ibid., p. 84.
9. Ibid., pp. 43–47.
10. Daryl Siedentop, *Physical Education: Introductory Analysis,* 2d ed., Wm. C. Brown, Dubuque, 1976, pp. 38–44.

SUGGESTED READINGS

AAHPERD Centennial Issue. *JOPERD* 56 (April 1985): entire issue. A historical overview of AAHPERD and its leading figures, by Bruce L. Bennet and Mabel Lee, with articles on divisions within AAHPERD by other professional leaders.

Baker, William J. "New Light on the Nazi Olympics." *Journal of Sport History* 8 (Summer 1981), 118–120.

Berryman, Jack W. "Historical Roots of the Collegiate Dilemma." *Proceedings, 79th Annual Meeting of the National Collegiate Physical Education Association for Men,* 1976, 141–154.

Bruce, Janet. *The Kansas City Monarchs: Champions of Black Baseball.* Lawrence: University Press of Kansas, 1985.

Capeci, Dominic J., Jr., and Martha Wilkerson. "Multifarious Hero: Joe Louis, American Society and Race Relations During World Crisis, 1935–1945." *Journal of Sport History* 10 (Winter 1983), 5–25.

Chu, Donald. "The American Conception of Higher Education and the Formal Incorporation of Intercollegiate Sport." *Quest* 34, no. 1 (1982), 53–71.

———, Jeffrey O. Seagrave, and Beverly J. Becker, eds. *Sport and Higher Education.* Champaign, Ill.: Human Kinetics, 1985.

Davis, Howard. *Contributions of Blacks to the Physical Education Profession.* Birmingham: Alabama Center for Higher Education, 1978.

DeFord, Frank. "No Longer a Cozy Corner." *Sports Illustrated* 63 (23–30 December 1985), 45–48, 50, 55, 58, 61.

Edwards, Harry. "Sport within the Veil: The Triumphs, Tragedies, and Challenges of Afro-American Involvement." *Annals of the American Academy of Political and Social Science* 445 (1979), 116–127.

Eisenman, Patricia A., and C. Robert Barnett. "Physical Fitness in the 1950s and 1970s: Why Did One Fail and the Other Boom?" *Quest* 31, no. 1 (1979), 114–122.

Furst, Terry R. "Mass Media and the Transformation of Spectator Team Sports." *Canadian Journal of History of Sport and Physical Education* 3 (December 1972), 27–41.

Govan, Michael. "The Emergence of the Black Athlete in America." *The Black Scholar* 3 (November 1971), 16–28.

Graham, Peter J., and Horst Ueberhorst, eds. *The Modern Olympics.* Champaign, Ill.: Leisure Press, 1976.

Hanford, George H. *An Inquiry into the Need for and Feasibility of a National Study of Intercollegiate Athletics: A Report to the American Council on Education.* Washington: American Council on Education, 1974.

Henderson, Edwin B. *The Negro in Sports.* Rev. ed. Washington: Associated Publishers, 1949.

Johnson, Karen M., and Harry Fritz, eds. "The Phenomenon of the Olympic Games." 5 parts. *JOPERD* 55 (January 1984), 21–32; (February 1984), 19–30; (March 1984), 17–30; (April 1984), 15–29; (May 1984), 61–72.

Kennedy, Ray, and Nancy Williamson. "Money: The Monster Threatening Sports." 3-part series. *Sports Illustrated,* 17 July 1978, pp. 28+; 24 July 1978, pp. 34+; 31 July 1978, pp. 34+.

Lewis, Guy M. "Adoption of the Sports Program, 1903–39: The Role of Accommodation in the Transformation of Physical Education." *Quest* 12 (May 1969), 34–46.

Lipsky, Richard. *How We Play the Game: Why Sports Dominate American Life.* Boston: Beacon Press, 1981.

Miller, Geoffrey. *Behind the Olympic Rings.* Lynn, Mass.: H. O. Zimman, 1979.

Nixon, Howard L. "The Commercial and Organizational Development of Modern Sport." *International Review of Sport Sociology* 9, no. 2 (1974), 107–131.

Okafor, Udodiri Paul. *The Interaction of Sports and Politics as a Dilemma of the Modern Olympic Games.* Ph.D. dissertation, Ohio State University, 1979.

Petryszak, Nicholas. "Spectator Sports as an Aspect of Popular Culture—An Historical Review." *Journal of Sport Behavior* 1, no. 1 (1978), 14–27.

Powers, Ron. *Supertube: The Rise of Television Sports.* New York: Coward McCann, 1984.

Rader, Benjamin G. *In Its Own Image: How Television Has Transformed Sports.* New York: Free press, 1984.

Research Quarterly for Exercise and Sport Centennial Issue (1985): entire issue. A collection of historical studies on topics from the history of AAHPERD.

Riordan, James. "The Social Emancipation of Women Through Sport." *British Journal of Sports History* 2 (May 1985), 53–61.

Simri, Uriel. "The Development of Female Participation in the Modern Olympic Games." *Stadion* 6 (1980), 187–216.

Smith, Ronald A. "The Paul Robeson–Jackie Robinson Saga and a Political Collision." *Journal of Sport History* 6 (Summer 1979), 5–27.

———. "What's Wrong with AAHPERD Historically." *The Physical Educator* 38 (December 1981), 190–204. This article is followed by a counterargument by J. Thomas Jable. "AAHPERD: Professionals Proudly Promoting Physical Education." *The Physical Educator* 38 (December 1981), 205–211.

Sojka, Gregory S. "Evolution of the Student Athlete in America." *Journal of Popular Culture* 16 (Spring 1983), 54–67.

"Sport in America." *Quest* 27 (Winter 1977): entire issue.

Spring, Joel H. "Mass Culture and School Sports." *History of Education Quarterly* 14 (Winter 1974), 483–500.

Strenk, Andrew. "What Price Victory? The World of International Sports and Politics." *Annals of the American Academy of Political and Social Science* 445 (September 1979), 116–127.

Struna, Nancy L. "Beyond Mapping Experience: The Need for Understanding in the History of American Sporting Women." *Journal of Sport History* 11 (Spring 1984), 120–133.

Taafe, William. "TV to Sports: The Bucks Stop Here." *Sports Illustrated* 64 (24 February 1986), 20–22, 25–27.

Tait, Robin. *The Politicization of the Modern Olympic Games.* Ph.D. dissertation, University of Oregon, 1984. Microfiche.

Twin, Stephanie, ed. *Out of the Bleachers: Writings on Women and Sport.* Old Westbury, N.Y.: The Feminist Press, 1979.

Underwood, John. "A Game Plan for America." *Sports Illustrated,* 23 February 1981, pp. 64–65.

———. *Spoiled Sport: A Fan's Notes on the Troubles of Spectator Sports.* Boston: Little, Brown, 1984.

VanClief, Elizabeth W. *Influential Physical Education Books of the Twentieth Century.* P.E.D. dissertation, Indiana University, 1982. Microfiche.

HISTORICOPHILOSOPHICAL BIOGRAPHY SERIES: AAHPERD LEADERS

Bandy, Susan. "Clark Wilson Hetherington: A Pioneering Spirit in Physical Education." *JOPERD* 56 (January 1985), 20–22.

Bennett, Bruce L. "Dudley Allen Sargent: The Man and His Philosophy." *JOPERD* 55 (November-December 1984), 61–64.

Betts, Edith, and Hazel Peterson. "Dorothy Sears Ainsworth: Pioneer in International Relations." *JOPERD* 56 (May/June 1985), 63–65, 67.

Brunner, Ruth. "Old Doc Hitchcock: A Pioneer Physical Educator with a Humanistic Vision." *JOPERD* 53 (October 1982), 22–24.

Davenport, Joanna. "Thomas Denison Wood: Physical Educator and Father of Health Education." *JOPERD* 55 (October 1984), 63–65, 68.

English, Eleanor B. "The Enigma of Charles H. McCloy." *JOPERD* 54 (May 1983), 40–42.

Friedrich-Cofer, Lynette K. "The Legacy of Edward Hitchcock." *JOPERD* 56 (November-December 1985), 24–29.

Jable, J. Thomas. "Jay B. Nash." *JOPERD* 56 (September 1985), 55–57.

Kozar, Andrew. "R. Tait McKenzie: A Man of Noble Achievement." *JOPERD* 55 (September 1984), 27–31.

Kretchmar, R. Scott. "Thomas Denison Wood's Hope and Reality: A Philosophic Review." *JOPERD* 55 (October 1984), 66–68.

———, and Ellen W. Gerber. "Jesse Feiring Williams: A Philosophical and Historical Review." *JOPERD* 54 (January 1983), 16–17, 19–20.

Leigh, Mary. "Edward Hitchcock, Jr., Dean of the Profession." *JOPERD* 53 (October 1982), 19–21.

———, and Ginny Studer. "Eleanor Metheny." *JOPERD* 54 (September 1983), 74–77.

Mosher, Stephen D. "The Turning Point." *JOPERD* 54 (October 1983), 71–73. [Luther Halsey Gulick]

Pekara, Jean. "Luther Halsey Gulick: 'He Dreamed Dreams and Made His Dreams Come True.'" *JOPERD* 54 (October 1983), 69–70, 73.

Thomas, Duane L. "Clark W. Hetherington: Persuasive and Philosophic." *JOPERD* 56 (November/December 1985), 74–75.

See also the following books listed in the Resource Readings at the end of the book:

Baker; Baker and Carroll; Betts; Dulles; Espy; Gerber; Guttman, *The Games*; Howell; Kanin; Laforse and Drake; Lee; Lockhart and Spears; Lucas; Lucas and Smith; Mandell; Michener; Noverr and Ziewacz; Rader; Riess; Seagrave and Chu; Spears and Swanson; Underwood; Van Dalen and Bennett; Welch and Lerch; and Zeigler, *History*.

PART III

OUR FOUNDATIONS:
Physical Education And
Sport Knowledge

Courtesy Duke University Sports Information

INTRODUCTION: THE SPORT SCIENCE DISCIPLINES

We shall look briefly at each of the disciplines or subdisciplines generally accepted as part of the field of sport science or sport studies. Scholars accept either six or seven areas as separate: sport history (concerned with the when, where, and how of sport), sport philosophy (concerned with the what and why of sport), sport psychology (concerned with individual and group behavior), sport sociology (concerned with societal behavior and practices), sport physiology (concerned with the physical working of the body and with sports medicine), sport biomechanics (concerned with natural law), and (to some scholars) sport pedagogy (concerned with the process of motor learning and teaching).

The Philosophical Bases of Physical Education and Sport

chapter 7

Philosophy in Physical Education and Sport

The study of philosophy is important to physical educators, for in keeping with our whole-person concept of physical education, it helps us to develop personal philosophies that affect every area of our actions in our daily lives. To realize why we need to understand philosophy and the uses of philosophy, we need to look at three areas of interest: (1) the definition and application of philosophy in physical education and sport, (2) the major philosophical teachings, and (3) the newer area of sport philosophy.

The philosophy of sport is one of the newer areas of philosophic study. Some early writings on the philosophy of sport do exist, but this area of interest is primarily a development of the last two decades, particularly the 1970s. The Philosophic Society for the Study of Sport (PSSS) was founded late in 1972 at a regional meeting of the American Philosophical Association. The society, with its meetings and the publication of its *Journal of the Philosophy of Sport,* has led the way in promoting the philosophic study of sport and sport-related activities.

WHAT IS PHILOSOPHY?

Philosophy has long been a nebulous concept to students. It is difficult to define clearly, for historically the definitions may seem to be in conflict. Harold Barrow, who suggests that philosophy can be viewed several ways, presents three concepts of philosophy: (1) philosophy as "a study of the truth or the principles underlying all knowledge," (2) philosophy as "a study of the most general causes and principles of the universe," and (3) philosophy as "a system for guiding life."[1] As you can see, philosophy is not a small area of interest; it is so broad that it can be difficult either to define or to comprehend. Barrow views philosophy as both a process and its resulting product. The process is a method used to establish a system of values, while the product is the system of values that eventually is produced by the process.

Randolph Webster notes that the original meaning of philosophy was a "love of truth" or a "love of wisdom."[2] It was viewed as a search for both facts and values that are to be studied without any bias or prejudice. As he points out:

> Philosophy is concerned with questions of right and wrong, justice, freedom, and discretion. Though there is a distinction between philosophy and science, philosophy can be said to be a science since it organizes knowledge about man and the universe for the purpose of evaluation and comprehension.... Philosophy criticizes, evaluates the worth of things, and synthesizes facts; while science describes, discovers, and analyzes facts....[Scientists] know how [atomic energy] works and how to use it, but only philosophers deliberate about where and for what purpose it should be used. Both processes are essential.[3]

In ancient times, philosophy included the physical and social sciences, but as knowledge expanded and specialized disciplines developed, philosophy was eventually left with meaning, values, appreciation, interpretation, and evaluation as its subject matter.

Philosophy studies such ideas as the ultimate meaning of life. We might say that science studies what can be proved through physical experiments and evidence, while philosophy studies what cannot be proved by physical or tangible evidence. Philosophy is an attempt to extend meanings far beyond known facts to provide directions for each person's life. While Webster spoke of philosophy as a science, philosophy is not a science as we commonly conceive of science in the modern world. Philosophy tries to go far beyond science's cold, physical facts. We need to consider the relationship between philosophy and some other broad areas of life.

Some of the relationships between philosophy and science are discussed by David and Miller.[4] They note that science is a precise area that seeks to learn what can be proved with concrete facts, whereas philosophy goes beyond the facts and into areas of speculation that probably can never be proved. Actually, the scientific method of research is similar to the methods used in philosophy to gain knowledge. However, science requires observable data, while philosophy does not. Philosophy is concerned largely with meanings and values, while science is concerned with provable facts. The dividing line between philosophy and science is not always clear, and considerable overlapping between the two can be found. While science relies on "cold, hard facts," its directions, as much as those of any other area of study or life, are determined by human emotions and philosophies.

Religion is closely related to philosophy, for religion is philosophical by its nature. Religion is concerned with the idea of God and the relationship between God and people; it also is concerned with ethics and ethical practices. Religion is occupied with many areas of meaning in life for which there can be no scientific proof. Religion is often self-conscious about its lack of scientifically provable ideas, but that makes it no less valid an area of life or of concern than philosophy. Both religion and philosophy seek to go beyond the known and into the unknown, and each seeks to answer questions that science can never answer.

Art is also closely related to philosophy, for no scientific judgment or process can be involved in art. Art is an area of values in which people seek to express, fulfill, and understand themselves—a complex process that goes beyond the limitations of science. Art is, by its nature, subjective; it is concerned with an inner self that is beyond the bounds of science. Indeed, we might say that art and science are simply different approaches to reality.

History is also related to philosophy. Although historians try to follow scientific methods in studying history, their most vital concern is not the scien-

Ceremonial dances of primitive societies are manifestations of people's search for a supreme being. This photograph shows a public ceremonial dance about the creation, given at the circumcision ceremony of young boys in an aborigine tribe in Australia. (Courtesy Australian Information Service. Photograph by C. Mountford)

tific process they follow or their use of provable fact, but the subjective process by which they decide what is important—what facts they will use, what each fact means, how each fact fits together with other facts, and how to present and interpret the chosen collection of facts. Although the process of history is in many respects scientific and objective, the result is largely subjective, for each person's interpretation of a fact may be different. Each historian has a philosophy that is reflected in that historian's methods and conclusions, which helps to tie history closely to philosophy in many respects.

WHAT IS SPORT PHILOSOPHY?

The Rise of Sport Philosophy

William Harper suggests that physical education's interest in philosophic studies developed at the same time as its idea of a discipline in 1963. This was also the year in which the first issue of *Quest* was published, using the philosophic approach as a stated goal. Though research dating before this time can be found, Harper describes it as "a lengthy sort of prologue."[5] Elwood Craig Davis was an early leader in trying to explain the method, content, and application of philosophy to physical educators.

When *Quest* appeared in 1963, its stated purpose was to move physical educators to think about what they were doing and why they were doing it. It was a joint project of the National College Physical Education Association for Men (NCPEAM) and the National Association of Physical Education for College Women (NAPECW), now combined into the National Association for Physical Education in Higher Education (NAPEHE). At the same time, individuals such as Franklin Henry began suggesting that physical education should study the idea of a discipline more thoroughly by promoting the development of physical education's body of knowledge. Thus, both the philosophic and disciplinary approaches were evolving throughout the 1960s.

As the idea of a discipline of physical education developed, a major question was: What would be the focus of the discipline? A popular response (though not the only one) was "sport," now sometimes broadened to "playful activities." The early philosophic studies were general, concentrating on comparing and contrasting the basic schools of philosophy. There were only a few in-depth studies such as those done by Johan Huizinga (written in 1938, but translated into English only in 1955) and Roger Caillois (1958 and 1961). Though those studies of play and games provided much food for thought, American physical educators were not quick to follow the ideas presented there. As interest in the concept of a discipline grew, however, interest in the scholarly study of sport grew, too. This led to the necessity of defining sport and explaining the part it plays in our culture.

The attempt to define and explain sport began to absorb more scholars' attention during the late 1960s and early 1970s as they considered the meanings of such critical terms as *play, games, sport,* and *athletics.* The major early questions concerned definition and significance: How do we define sport, and what is its significance in our culture (or any other culture)? By the early 1970s, the level of scholarly studies had risen sharply. We have already defined sport in Chapter 1, so now we need to discuss some of the focal points of sport philosophy and their implications for the physical educator.

What Is the "Sport Experience"?

Harold VanderZwaag and Thomas Sheehan have given an introductory description of the sport experience as a prelude to the understanding of the philosophic study of sport. They suggest that the sport experience of any person has three basic characteristics and may have another five occasional characteristics.[6]

The basic characteristics of the sport experience are *emotional, personal,* and *situational.* Rather than just being a physical experience, sport also causes emotional involvement. This is true for both participant and spectator. Sport involves competition, though not necessarily at a high level, and the physical aggressiveness that may be included also affects a person's emotional involvement.

At the same time, the sport experience is intensely personal. Each individual participates in or observes sporting activities for personal reasons or as a matter of personal taste. Even though a sport may be a team sport, each participant takes part for personal, rather than group, reasons.

The actual sport experience depends on the situation; it is difficult for a person who has not been in the same situation or a similar situation to understand the appeal or meaning of another person's sport experience. Though any sport experience has many common elements, other elements are seen only in a given activity.

Other characteristics may or may not be present in the sport experience of a person. Though the sport experience is personal, it also may be *social.* Special feelings may come from being on a team or from joining in a task performed as a team, which add a social effect to the already personal meaning of a sport experience.

The experience may mean *winning,* though victory is a complex concept. Because sport is competitive, winning is significant. For some persons, it is the victory that makes the sport experience mean what it does to them.

At the same time, the sport experience may mean *losing,* for where there are winners there will also be losers. Because in life there are victories and defeats, losing is as much a part of the experience as winning.

The sport experience *cannot be prescribed* or structured. Because it is a personal experience, no two people will react to the same thing in the same way, nor will they necessarily draw the same lesson from it.

The sport experience also *is not sacred.* While it is meaningful, it is not more meaningful than the other parts of a person's life.

VanderZwaag and Sheehan also discuss the conditions of the sport experience: where or when a sport experience might take place. They suggest seven conditions or situations in which the sport experience might occur.[7] The first they call the *memorable sport experience,* though some philosophers have used other terms such as "perfect moment" or "peak experience" to describe the same experience. It is that highly memorable action, perhaps a movement or a play, or a larger experience such as a championship game. It may be related to a victory, but it may not be. It can be simply an aesthetic experience, the sense that everything one has trained for seems to come together in a perfect moment of skilled sporting expression.

Another situation is the *sporting classic,* a major competitive event that may be watched as a spectator or participated in as a contestant or coach. Examples of sporting classics are events like the Olympic Games or the World Series. One aspect of a sporting classic forms another of the conditions for the sport experience—the *atmosphere of a sport.* It cannot be defined clearly, but participants and spectators have "felt" the atmosphere that is present at many sporting activities. Another aspect of the high-level sport experience is the *elements of perfection* that can be found in some sports. Some sports have the potential of perfection, such as bowling with a 300 game or baseball's no-hitter or golf's hole in one. Some sports are subjectively scored and permit perfect scores, such as the 10.0 in gymnastics. Such elements of perfection give another potential sporting experience to participant and spectator.

The *team experience* is yet another situation in sport. It includes the aspects of making the team and that of being a member of a "special" team such as an undefeated or championship team. There is the aspect of *lifetime enjoyment through sport,* for the sport experience does not have to be a short-term matter. It can extend over a lifetime, since many sports can be followed throughout the span of an average life. Finally, the sport experience can come from *just playing,* the chance simply to participate when one usually is not able to do so.

What Does the Sport Philosopher Do?

Perhaps this is the most difficult aspect of sport philosophy for most people to understand, since the work of the philosopher is mental and is not easily observed. VanderZwaag and Sheehan summarize the essential task of the sport philosopher as having three elements, each a part of describing the sport experience.[8] First, the setting must be provided so that the circumstances under which the experience took place will be clear. Second, the critical elements of the experience must be cited. This means those elements that contributed to the experience must be given. Finally, the broader meaning of the experience must be probed. What are the implications of the experience? Ultimately, the philosopher is concerned with the significance of the experience. What is significant about the sport experience?

The sport philosopher attempts to define and clarify sport and the sporting experience in order to determine the place and meaning of sport in our lives. The philosophic study of sport, like any other specialized field, has its methodology. We shall discuss that methodology later in this chapter.

Why Study Sport Philosophy?

William Harper suggests three reasons for the philosophical study of sport, pointing out that these reasons do not exhaust the legitimate possibilities.[9] The first reason for the study of sport philosophy is *to discover what there is to know*. In essence, we want to learn what is known about sport, including play, games, exercise, and athletics.

Our culture has many beliefs about sport, but which beliefs are really proven? Many of the popular ideas about sport have rarely been studied closely, such as the relationship between sportsmanship or character development and sports participation.

The second reason for studying sport philosophy is *to guide practical actions*. Serious thinking about sport can provide answers that can be of use in planning what we will try to do in sport. Knowledge should be applicable to some purpose, if possible. This is an important function of some of the answers we may gain from sport philosophy, for they can provide guidance for the future of sport.

The third reason for studying sport philosophy is *to produce a deeper understanding*. Many of our sport studies must be described as mere wadings into the shallows of sport, rather than as dredgings of the depths of the subject. Our knowledge and understanding of sport are minimal in comparison to what we need to know. A deeper understanding of sport helps us in learning more about humanity—the essential condition of the peoples of the earth, their wants, and their needs.

WHAT IS THE METHOD OF PHILOSOPHIC STUDY IN SPORT?

The question of method in philosophic studies is often confusing to the beginner. Ultimately, any philosophic question is subjective; empirical research is not possible, for strictly speaking, the phenomena are not observable. Indeed, VanderZwaag and Sheehan state that "there is no common methodology for sport philosophers" primarily because of the highly individual nature of the process, though they do suggest that analysis and synthesis are the "two pillars of integrity" in philosophic research.[10]

The three basic approaches to philosophic study are speculative (suggesting possible answers to a question), normative (suggesting guidelines or norms), and analytical (evaluating the ideas of others). The areas or methods of philosophic study are the historical background study, the varied interpretation method, the value judgment, clarifying the main issues, and determining relationships to similar concepts.

The philosophic and scientific research methods in organizing research studies are similar. However, we need to look at several other research methods to provide a broader exposure to the many possible approaches to philosophy. Kathleen Pearson suggests two research approaches that can be used as part of a brief self-study program. The first is called the "goodness of fit approach," for it is similar in approach to the statistical study that compares how closely two statistical models agree. In this case, the researcher takes a suggested paradigm or model (such as those for the relationships of play, games, sport, and athletics presented earlier), and studies whether another example conforms to the suggested one. The second method is the "implications approach," in which the researcher studies what something would be like if it did conform to a given model, or studies the implications of such a condition.[11]

Robert Osterhoudt suggests that the basic method used in philosophic studies is a systematic "dialectic," or dialogue, of either of two types: speculative or critical. He suggests that both types are valuable, however, for "without the speculative, philosophy would be reduced to logic, without the critical, to poetry. Philosophy is wholly neither."[12]

Seymour Kleinman has argued the idea of developing a "correct" theory of sport. He suggests that theories put structure and limits on sport that close it to anything beyond its imposed bounds, whereas sport demands openness. Kleinman discusses three methods of theorizing: formal description, logical description, and phenomenological description. Formal description tells the properties or characteristics of a phenomenon, logical description studies how a term is used in the language, and phenomenological description studies the experience itself. The latter method is Kleinman's preference, for it concentrates on the phenomenon as it happens, without limits.[13] As Osterhoudt puts it, phenomenology's method is "pure subjective consciousness."[14] Osterhoudt also notes, however, that phenomenology does not examine many aspects of life that need to be examined, so in some respects it is not as free of "unreflective assumptions" as it supposes.[15]

While this is by no means an exhaustive examination of the methods of philosophic inquiry, it should provide some idea of the processes. We now want to turn our attention to the branches of philosophy.

THE BRANCHES OF PHILOSOPHY

Several branches of philosophy form the field (Figure 7.1). When we think of philosophy, we usually think of *metaphysics,* which is concerned with the nature of reality and being. Will Durant described metaphysics as a study of the "ultimate reality" of everything, for it tries to answer questions about what is real and what really exists.[16] It is concerned with questions of reality that cannot be answered scientifically.

A second branch of philosophy is *epistemology,* which is the study of the theory of knowledge. It is a study of how to obtain knowledge and what kinds of knowledge can be obtained, or what can be learned and how it can be determined. It considers the processes of perception (how we see things) and knowledge, including the process of learning, which we sometimes call the "scientific method."

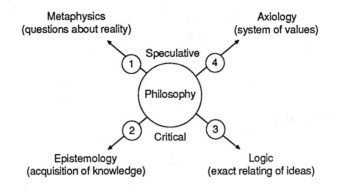

Metaphysics
(questions about reality)

Axiology
(system of values)

Speculative

Philosophy

Epistemology
(acquisition of knowledge)

Critical

Logic
(exact relating of ideas)

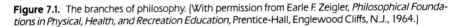

A Formula for Action
present values + scientific advances + conditioning of emotions = *what we do*

Figure 7.1. The branches of philosophy. (With permission from Earle F. Zeigler, *Philosophical Foundations in Physical, Health, and Recreation Education*, Prentice-Hall, Englewood Cliffs, N.J., 1964.)

A third branch of philosophy, *logic*, is concerned with the relationship of ideas to each other. It is interested in the ideal method used for thought and research, the steps that should be followed in relating one idea to another, or in proceeding from one idea to another more advanced one. For many people, logic is the most important area of philosophy.

A fourth branch of philosophy is *axiology*, which is the study of values in general terms; it considers the nature and kinds of values. Rather than studying axiology itself, we are more concerned with two of its subdivisions, ethics and aesthetics, which are more specific areas that study more specific questions.

Ethics is concerned with morals and conduct, with trying to decide on proper rules of conduct. It is a study of ideal conduct and the knowledge of good and evil. It seeks to determine what actions are right and wrong, or what people should and should not do.

Aesthetics, which deals with the nature of beauty, is subjective. Earle Zeigler has defined aesthetics as the "theory or philosophy of taste," for what does and does not constitute beauty is a matter of personal taste.[17]

We now need to look more precisely at the major questions philosophy tries to answer; we can then develop a clearer perception of the directions that philosophical studies can take.

THE QUESTIONS OF PHILOSOPHY

The major questions or concerns of philosophy are classified by James Baley and David Field as falling into nine areas, though their list is not necessarily exhaustive:[18]

1. *Nature of the universe.* In ancient times, philosophical discussion concerned the origin and nature of the earth and what basic materials had

been used in its development. Today this issue is of little concern to philosophers, for it has been largely taken over by the scientists.

2. *People's place in the universe.* Are human beings just other animals, or are they supreme creatures? Are they important or unimportant? Are they the masters of their own destiny, or is their fate controlled by higher forces?

3. *Determination of good and evil.* Are there any absolute measures for determining good and evil, right and wrong? Do such standards vary according to the situation involved? What constitutes "the good life"? These questions are still considered important today, and in many respects they are of great concern to physical educators in their teaching and in their practices.

4. *Nature of God.* Is there a God, or do gods exist? Is there some supreme being, and if so, what are its characteristics? Where do we find God, and what is God's relationship to people? These are some of the important questions involved in the philosophy of religion.

5. *Soul and immortality.* This area of concern may be related to the previous issue, depending on the philosophy and beliefs of the person involved. Do we possess a soul, that is, some inner part that is intangible and has no parts that can be seen or felt? When we die, does the soul die also, or does it continue to live on in some other place or some other form? This area of philosophy goes into the age-old religious questions regarding life after death: Is there life after death, and if so, what is it like?

6. *People's relationship to the state.* This area is a growing concern as the rapid expansion of the world's population brings on increased governmental regulation and monitoring of people's lives. What is the best form of government? Who should reign supreme—the people or the state? Is the answer to the question of supremacy an absolute, or can it change as circumstances change?

7. *Role of education.* What is the role of education in the social structure? What part does it play, and what should be its goals? These questions are crucial, for they determine how a civilization reproduces itself or fails to do so. What should be taught in education, and how should it be taught?

8. *Relationship between mind and matter.* How do people affect, and how are they affected by, their environment and surroundings? Which is superior—mind or matter—or is one superior to the other? How do they relate to each other?

9. *Implications of philosophy for physical education.* Though not a question of pure philosophy, this area of concern refers to physical education in the broad sense, including such related areas as health and recreation. How do the answers—those we have determined for ourselves as being the best—to the questions in the first eight areas affect our program of physical education?

As Baley and Field point out:

> Philosophy is man's effort to see the universe in a coherent, systematic, and meaningful way. It gives our actions direction. If our objectives, principles, and methods are to be consistent, we must possess a reasonably well thought-out

philosophic position. Otherwise, we are likely to be like the horseman who tried to run off in all directions at once.[19]

The questions that we seek to answer by our study of philosophy are used to help clarify our ideas and beliefs regarding life and how it should be lived. Philosophy can deal with both general and specific questions. Those questions help to make our purposes and goals clearer. By doing so, they play a major role in determining how we shall view physical education and sport and their function in society, what our thinking about physical education and sport will be, and what we shall try to do with them.

ISSUES IN SPORT PHILOSOPHY

To understand the kinds of problems studied by sport philosophers, we need to discuss some of the issues and areas of philosophic interest. We shall give a general idea of what the sport philosopher seeks to do in each area, rather than present a philosophic study of each area. Nine such areas of philosophic interest will be examined in this way.

The Nature of Sport

The first question or problem that the sport philosopher faces is that of defining the field of study: What is the nature of sport? What is and is not sport? We already have discussed this question in Chapter 1, for we have considered the elements of the sport experience and the definition of sport and its relationship to play, games, and athletics. Ellen Gerber and William Morgan begin their book with a discussion and supporting readings that are concerned with this question, for as they note, "fundamental to an examination of sport in its diversified and meaningful roles is an understanding of its nature as a phenomenon."[20] They briefly discuss four techniques that can be used to contribute to such an understanding: definition, characterization, classification, and comparison.[21]

Definition is the application of inductive reasoning to define sport in terms of those activities that are considered genuine sport. It provides a generalized idea of what sport is. *Characterization* uses deductive logic to determine the common elements or characteristics of sport. After the basic characteristics have been determined, the philosopher will try to discover the basic relationships. This is accomplished by *classification*, the grouping of subjects or activities according to similar elements. Finally, the philosopher will use the technique of *comparison* to see if the theorized elements do indeed hold true when compared with other activities.

The task of defining the nature of sport or of arriving at a theory of sport is such that not all philosophers agree that it is possible. Frank McBride is one philosopher who argues that the concept of sport is too vague and too complex to be defined in a single concept, if it can be defined accurately at all.[22] The differences often seem to be semantic; they consist of disagreements over the exact meanings of words. Part of the problem is that many terms are used interchangeably, especially in the United States, so that often different people use the same term as having conflicting meanings. A common example is use of the terms *sport* and *athletics*. They are used frequently in the United States to mean the same thing, though most philosophers agree that they overlap but are not the same. A scholar from another nation might have less trouble in defining these terms, for they probably have had different meanings from the beginning. This is only one example of the problems inherent in trying to devise a generally accepted concept or definition of the nature of sport.

Sport and Metaphysical Speculation

Metaphysics is essentially a study of reality, though in sport philosophy it is similar in some respects to the study of the nature of sport. Gerber and Morgan briefly discuss metaphysical speculation in sport, noting that three questions are asked of reality. The first question asks what reality is regarding the nature of the world (cosmology), though modern science has largely replaced that research topic. The second question asks what reality is regarding a divine entity or condition (theology), though theological studies have largely separated from philosophy in modern times. The third question asks the nature of reality from the standpoint of human existence (ontology), which is the primary modern focus of philosophic research. This is the most common type of study in metaphysics and sport, particularly the being status of sport from the standpoint of human existence.[23]

Metaphysical speculation in sport is concerned with such themes as the mind-body relation, finity and infinity, time, space, and freedom. It especially notes how sport is similar or dissimilar to other human movement phenomena, such as exercise, play, dance, and games. Gerber and Morgan suggest three approaches that may be used. The first approach develops the implications of major philosophic schools of thought (such as idealism) for issues that are central to sport. The second approach develops the implications of the philosophic systems of major philosophers (such as Plato) for issues of interest to sport. The third approach, which is the most difficult because it requires greater "philosophic acumen and originality," is to move into a direct philosophic examination of a major issue. Though metaphysical speculation may appear rather pointless, it does have important implications, for as Gerber and Morgan point out, the ways in which people view sport are reflected in their attitudes toward sport. Thus metaphysical speculation can be used by the sport philosopher to discover how people see, approach, and use sport.[24]

The Body and Being

The area of body and being essentially defines the relationship that exists among the mind, body, and soul, including the relative values of each "dimension."[25] The concept of a body–soul or mind-body relationship has been a matter of philosophical interest since the time of Plato. Plato viewed the body negatively and sport positively, and the resulting place of physical education and sport due to those opinions has caused much interpretive argument among philosophers of physical education and sport.

Phenomenologists (researchers of the nature of phenomena) do much work in the philosophic interest area of the body and being. They approach their study from the unusual (in terms of tradition) point of view of the body as the primary self rather than the mind or soul. Essentially, these philosophers examine the connection between sport and the body by studying the body experience in different sport or physical situations and by noting how it differs in nonphysical situations.

Sport as a Meaningful Experience

Sport as a meaningful experience is another complicated topic for, as Gerber and Morgan note, it deals with the "mysterious relationship between subject and object."[26] Experience lies in the realm of epistemology (the gaining of knowledge), as all questions of truth or confirmation of knowledge relate to experience. Farber cites these six universal characteristics of experience: (1) it is temporal in character, (2) it has elements of organic, physical, and cultural relatedness, (3) it involves the past, present, and future, (4) it has a space-time locus, (5) it involves some object or phenomenon in the experience, and (6) it is of various types, such as perceptual, imaginative, or conceptual.[27]

Each experience is different. It is peculiar to the person having the experience, for each person perceives things differently. This factor makes philosophic studies of meaningful experience even more difficult. Issues that are studied include those such as why people play, great moments in sport (such as when records are set), peak experiences, and the idea of the perfect moment. A peak experience or perfect moment does not demand championship skill levels, for it does not require records or other attributes of "great moments." The peak experience is "that moment when the person is totally involved, in control, and effortlessly touching that flow of personal perfection."[28] It is that time when a person fulfills or surpasses his or her potential in a movement experience, when everything comes together. It is a moment crystallized and held in time to be remembered, relived, and refelt and to be examined as a perfect moment in the future. It is perhaps the essence of the sport experience.

Sport Versus Physical Education: Philosophic Conflicts

The biggest problem in the conflict of sport versus physical education is the confusion over the difference between sport and athletics. The athletics-physical education relationship has been difficult in the United States since before 1900. Harper and others suggest that a clear understanding of the problem is complicated by the many myths that survive, five of which they mention.[29]

The first myth is the spurious continuum, the idea of a continuum running from play to games to sports (represented often by intramurals) to athletics.

The ancient Greeks tried not only to appreciate beauty but also to define it in their philosophies. Myron's famous *Discobolus* (discus thrower) is a classic example of the physical beauty the Greeks often portrayed in sculpture and other art forms. (Courtesy The Bettmann Archive)

In reality, athletes rarely come from intramural programs; in fact, intramurals are more often the final resting place of those who are unable to compete at the interschool level, rather than those preparing to do so or not wishing to do so. The second myth is that there is only one viable model for the sports program. There are several models, depending on the group setting the standards, which vary greatly. The third myth is that certain attitudes (such as sportsmanship and fair play) are inherent in the game. The fourth myth lies in the definitions used in athletics and physical education (such as those used for the terms *play, games, sport,* and *physical education*) because the definitions are imprecise. The fifth myth results from disregarding the historical origins of athletics, for the conflict in means and goals between athletics and physical education can be seen as far back as the ancient Greeks. Much work is needed in this controversial area, for the problems are real and immediate.

Sport and Aesthetics

Aesthetics is concerned with the question of what is beautiful. Some of the most complex of philosophical issues fall into this area of study: it includes questions of beauty, taste, and the nature of the aesthetic experience.[30] Some of the problems studied relate to what art is, what beauty is, and what constitutes aesthetic quality. Sport has long been seen as a good subject for works of art, and now sport itself is increasingly seen as an art form. Moreover, participation in sport can be an aesthetic experience. This leads to an even more difficult philosophical problem: the question of when a phenomenon has the quality to be considered art.

The area of aesthetics is beginning to receive more attention from sport philosophers, as in Peter J. Arnold's writing on "movement as a source of aesthetic experience."[31] The most extensive study at this time is Benjamin Lowe's *The Beauty of Sport: A Cross-Disciplinary Inquiry*.[32] The philosophic interest area of sport and aesthetics has been promoted more recently among professional physical educators with the founding of a Sport Art Academy within AAHPERD.

Sport and Values

The area of values represents perhaps the most critical aspect of sport concern for many people, since the moral or behavioral values expressed by sports participants are a concern to many observers. Are values taught in sport settings? Are they inherent in sport or in games? These questions lie at the crux of the education-sports-athletics dilemma, for one of the great all-time arguments for athletics was that it taught "sportsmanship" (though no evidence has ever backed up this admirable philosophy). Although we shall discuss some of these matters in more detail in the following chapter, we do want to mention two related concerns or problems that are also popular areas of study for the sport philosopher: the fair play-sportsmanship concern and the concept of the amateur.

The Concept of Fair Play and Sportsmanship

The place of values and moral education needs to be considered much more closely than it has been in the past, as Delbert Oberteuffer long ago suggested.[33] Harper and others have stressed the need for the development of ethical guidelines for amateur sport.[34] James W. Keating has given considerable attention to competition and the competitive experience, including questions of ethics, particularly in studies such as "Sportsmanship as a Moral Category."[35] Peter McIntosh has devoted an entire book to the historical and philosophical consideration of the concept of fair play and ethics in sport and education. He notes that while interest in the idea of moral education is increasing, too little attention has been paid to the roles of physical education, play, and sport in moral education.[36] Justice lies at the heart of the concept of fair play, yet the ideals of sportsmanship and fair play seem to be drifting farther and farther away from the common practice in modern sport. As such, this area is of critical interest to teachers and coaches.

The Concept of the Amateur

The concept of the amateur gains attention every four years with the return of the Olympic Games and the perennial argument over which athletes are really amateurs by the standards of the Olympics. The difficulty is that amateurism is defined by the motive of the athlete rather than by any concrete activity. Keating notes that many widely conflicting definitions are in use.[37] The French root of *amateur* means "lover," for the amateur is supposed to be one who performs an activity out of love for the activity rather than for any monetary reward or utilitarian reason. Amateur standards vary widely from sport to sport and from country to country. Athletics, however, tends toward professionalism because of its quest for excellence or results. Professionalism is the current direction even within the modern Olympic movement. Few world-class athletes are true amateurs, in the traditional sense of the word; perhaps none are.

Denney suggests that three standards of sports participation are found in the United States: The first is a business standard (the athletics model), the second is a social class standard (the "gentleman" amateur versus the nongentleman "professional"), while the third is that of the educational community and is torn between the other two models.[38] Weiss notes that "an amateur, strictly speaking, is one who plays a game for no other reason than to play it," rather than having some end other than the playing as the primary objective.[39] This concept does not rule out the desire to win—only the idea that victory is the major reason for playing.

Recent studies in the social science areas have begun to deal in depth with the concept of amateurism. Eugene Glader has done a detailed historical study of the concept of amateurism in athletics,[40] while Robert Stebbins has studied the concept from the sociological viewpoint.[41] There is still much room for further philosophic study of the difficult concept of amateurism in the modern world.

CONTEMPORARY PHILOSOPHIES OF EDUCATION AND PHYSICAL EDUCATION

Five major philosophies are examined most often in relationship to physical education today: naturalism, idealism, realism, pragmatism, and existentialism. As the study of philosophy in physical education and sport develops, less emphasis is placed on the traditional schools of philosophy as a subject of study. However, a brief study will give you a basis for understanding the development of educational philosophies. At the close of this section we shall also take a brief look at humanism and the eclectic approach to philosophy.

Naturalism

The term *naturalism* has as its root word *nature*. Naturalism is a belief that the laws of nature govern everything in life, and that because nature is unchanging, anything of value will always work. At the same time, naturalism emphasizes individualism by considering the person more important than society as a whole. Though naturalism puts societal goals below individual goals in importance, it still accepts the need for a social system to prevent chaos. This acceptance does not make the social system good; it is simply necessary.

In education, natural means is the desired method; that is, the process should be geared to the student rather than the student fitted into the process. The teacher is as much guide as teacher, for while the teacher primarily helps the student see how to learn, nature does the teaching. The student must make an active effort to learn, with punishments and rewards a part of the process as in nature. The rate of learning depends on the student, since the educational process requires a physical and mental balance rather than the promotion of one over the other.

In physical education, naturalism is concerned with the development of the whole person, rather than just the physical aspect. Physical activity can be a major source of the overall development of the student (especially with younger children, as in Rousseau's *Emile*). Play is an important part of the learning process, but it can be self-directed individual activity as well as group activity. Though competition is natural, it is not strongly emphasized, as the concentration is on the individual. The competition is against oneself. Teaching is at the rate of the student's needs, with reasonably democratic, informal teaching methods.

Zeigler suggests that naturalism has one strength and one weakness, and that they are the same: The philosophical practice of naturalism is extremely simple.[42] This simplicity can be an advantage, for most people find a simple education a relaxing change. On the other hand, it may be a disadvantage because the approach of naturalism may be too limited to prepare the student to cope with an increasingly complex world. A simple education may be a handicap rather than an asset in an advanced, scientifically oriented civilization. Naturalism was a popular philosophy during the 18th and 19th centuries, but it is no longer a major educational philosophy.

Idealism

The term *idealism* derives from the root word *idea*; idealism focuses on the mind. As everything is interpreted in terms of the mind, all reality comes from the mind. People's rational (reasoning) powers help them to find the truth, though they may use scientific methods to help in the discovery. According to idealism, people are more important than nature, for their mind interprets everything in nature for them. Ideas are true and never change, so moral values also never change. People have the free will to choose between right and wrong.

Since most of the educational process under idealism is concerned with the mind, much objective content is used. Because education develops the individual personality under idealism, the development of moral and spiritual values is important, too. The teacher creates a learning environment, but the student is responsible for motivation and learning. Many teaching methods may be used, but education takes place primarily through the active effort of the student to learn.

Though physical education can make a major contribution to the development of the intellect, idealists consider physical education less important than the more thought-oriented educational activities. Because physical education is based on known truths, principles, and ideas that do not change, the program can be rather fixed and formal, though not without variety in activities and teaching techniques. The teacher is an important example to the students, a role model in the use of ideals and values.

Idealism is a well-developed, broad philosophy for education and physical education. It gives the student a strong place in the universe by helping to develop a feeling of individual importance. It permits a broad physical and intellectual development, with play and recreation making important contributions. At the same time, some people object to the idealist notion of teaching values that have been established by past experience; less interest is shown today in the idea of dedication and sacrifice for older ideals. Moreover, some teachers' actions may contradict the values they seek to teach; as the saying goes, "Actions speak louder than words." The idealist educational program may give little attention to the body, for its primary concern is with the development of the mind. People's conflicting ideas of work and play can make the application of physical education under idealism difficult to explain, for people may have difficulty in accepting that play can have values as great as those of work.[43]

Realism

Realism falls between naturalism and idealism. It believes that the physical world of nature is real, so people should use their senses and experiences to understand it. Experimental means, such as the scientific method, help realists discover and interpret the truth. They believe that the physical things that happen result from the physical laws of nature. Realists also hold that the mind and body cannot be separated: one is not superior to the other. While naturalism does not permit religion (it puts nature over everything) and idealism does permit religion, realism permits its adherents to go either way in determining their beliefs.

The first concern of the realist educational process is to develop the student's reasoning power, because that power is considered essential to further learning. Scientific, objective standards are used for everything, with an orderly, scientifically oriented process and curriculum.

Physical education is valuable in the realist curriculum, for it results in greater health and productivity. Realists believe that a healthy person can lead a fuller life. The realist physical education program is based on scientific knowledge and uses many drills to instill knowledge according to scientific progression. Social behaviors and life adjustment are considered important benefits of recreational and sporting activities.

Zeigler points out that realism encourages people to accept the world as they find it, for the world of cause and effect cannot be changed. Physical education has a clear function in realism: It provides a healthy physical basis for life. At the same time, realism advocates a lower status for physical education, since it is primarily required to give a vigorous physical basis for life. However, realism does give a more clearly defined place for physical education in the educational process than many other philosophies. The authoritarianism suggested by the realist acceptance of standardization and drill learning is not consistent with the needs of democratic societies. In realism, little emphasis is placed on societal needs and trends.[44]

Pragmatism

Pragmatism was once called experimentalism, because it is based on learning from experiences or experiments.[45] The idea behind pragmatism is that since change is a characteristic common to everything in life, success is the only reliable judge of any theory or truth; anything that is true can be proved. Success in social relations is also stressed under pragmatism. The philosophy emphasizes societal living and the preparing of people to take their places in society so that they can live in harmony with one another.

The basic pragmatic educational tenet comes from John Dewey, who stressed "learning by doing" or gaining knowledge through experience. At the same time, the emphasis is on the student rather than the subject area; the idea is that each person is a bit different, so all students should not be forced into the same mold. Problem solving (experience) is the basic educational method, with the ultimate judgments made in terms of becoming a productive member of society. The emphasis is on developing the *total* person—mind, body and soul—using a broad process.

According to the pragmatic view of physical education, physical activities have social value, since they help to integrate students into society by teaching them how to act and react with other people. The curriculum is based on the needs and interests of the students and offers a variety of activities to provide a multitude of experiences. The problem-solving method is used even in physical education, since creativity and the ability to widen one's experiences can result. The teacher is concerned with motivating the individual student rather than with relying on a standardized program.

Zeigler notes that pragmatism is a practical approach to education that breaks down the distinctions between life in and out of school. It teaches people to cooperate by using a broad program based essentially on whatever works. Physical education is important in pragmatism, because it has broad social uses. However, pragmatism's experimental approach to education is difficult to apply to physical education because an unmanageable multitude of goals can result. The pragmatic philosophy of education has no fixed aims or values, and therefore it does not provide the stability and direction that many students need.[46]

Existentialism

Some people argue over whether existentialism is a philosophy, for its basic concern is the individual. Everything is judged in terms of the individual, with each person interpreting experiences individually and developing a personal system of values. Under existentialism, the person is more important than society, so the concern is not with whether an individual fits into society. Because an existentialist believes nothing can be done to change things, existentialism is often considered a negative, hopeless philosophy.

Butler maintains that no one has tried to apply existentialism formally to either education or physical education.[47] However, the implications of the philosophy on education can be surmised. Under existentialism, education would be viewed as a process of learning about oneself and of developing one's own beliefs. The school would be used only to provide a learning environment. The student would control the curriculum and methods, with the teacher acting as a stimulator. Responsibility toward oneself rather than toward others or society would be stressed. The students would be made aware that they have to bear full responsibility for the consequences of their decisions.

In physical education, existentialism would allow freedom of choice in the program, which might take any form and therefore could not be planned ahead by the teacher. Many activities would be used, with play resulting in the development of creativity. The teacher would act as a counselor by showing the students the various available activities, while the students would be ultimately responsible for selecting the activities in which to participate.

From these suppositions concerning an existentialist education, the philosophy would appear to have only one real strength: its emphasis on individuality, which makes each student important. Each person has a status not granted by any other philosophy, since the existentialist educational process revolves totally around each student's personal needs and wishes. This apparent strength of an existentialist education is also its greatest weakness, however, because the importance each student would be accorded in the school community could never be realized in the outside society. As a result, a student would not be prepared to work within the social system. The suggestion that society is unnecessary to each person is an approach better suited to anarchy. The overriding flaw of absolute individualism makes existentialism seem an unlikely choice as the sole basis of a successful program of mass education.

The Humanistic Approach to Education

Zeigler defines humanism as "a position in which concern for man's welfare is central; [it] stresses the importance of man in working out his own destiny."[48] Bucher gets closer to the heart of the current educational concept of humanism with his definition of it as "a revolt against depersonalization and...the emergence of the belief that every human being is an individual and should be treated as an individual rather than as part of a larger group."[49] Frost speaks of the "humanization of education" that is needed.[50] In contrast, the expansion of technology into education emphasizes the impersonal, nonhumanistic direction that may be the future of mass society.

The humanistic approach to education attempts to counter the effects of the depersonalization that is a natural outgrowth of crowded societies by trying to show concern for every person. It encourages the involvement of everyone in the educational process, not just some of the members of a class.

The humanistic approach in education is an attempt by educators to return to a basic concern for each person. It is not an attempt to make each person the center of everything in education; it is simply an effort to ensure that each person retains a personal identity in society. The approach tries to maximize students' potential contributions to society, while it tries at the same time to develop maximum student self-respect. Physical education can play a major role in the trend toward humanism, for its activities include close primary contact between individuals and groups.

The Eclectic Approach to Philosophy

We have now studied the major philosophies and approaches to philosophy that affect our practices in physical education and our concepts of it. Each student must develop a personal philosophy of life, of education, and of physical education. The last approach for the student to consider in developing a personal philosophy is the eclectic approach to philosophy. Zeigler defines eclecticism as "the practice of combining a variety of theories from different philosophical schools into a body of fairly compatible beliefs."[51]

We might view the eclectic approach as a supermarket, "pick-and-choose" development of a personal philosophy; each student takes whatever is agreeable from the different philosophies and gradually constructs a personal philosophy that may bear no resemblance to any single philosophy of physical education. Zeigler suggests that the eclectic approach is an immature stage in the development of a philosophy. However, this approach is common among educators and philosophers.

HOW DO WE APPLY PHILOSOPHY IN PHYSICAL EDUCATION?

Philosophy is a vital part of the process of developing physical education programs, for it is a major influence on the early stages of program planning. Figure 7.2 roughly illustrates the steps leading from what we already know (facts) through what we theorize and believe (our personal philosophy) through the various stages of development until we arrive at the actual policies and procedures that we shall use in administering a physical education program.

We begin at the lowest level with *facts,* or the base of information that has been proved conclusively. If no base of proven fact is at the root of a physical education program, the program will simply be an experimental vehicle of questionable value. In a time of increasing demand for accountability, the chances of success for such a program are slight.

We next apply our personal *philosophy* to the facts we have at our disposal. In essence, we take what we know and add to it what we believe. We use our

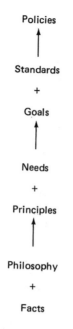

Figure 7.2. The developmental process of the total physical education program.

philosophy to try to determine fundamental *principles* on which we shall base our program. Webster has defined a *principle* as "a fundamental truth or cause...which serves as a guide for conduct and procedure...a guide which is used in the attainment of an aim or objective."[52] Principles are viewed as fundamental laws, though they are closer to universally accepted hypotheses or theories, for principles *can* change.

When the principles that apply to the program have been determined, the next step is to ascertain the *needs* of the program, that is, what the people need in the program being designed. Blending the needs of the program with the principles that are involved then produces the *goals* of the program.

The goals may include a number of closely related aims and objectives, which are simply more specific aspects of the overall goals of the program. The goals of the program may be expressed in terms of gaining or developing knowledge (cognitive goals); attitudes, appreciations, and a sense of values (affective goals); and skills (primarily psychomotor goals in physical education).

When the goals of the program have been determined, the *standards* that will be used in evaluating the goals must next be developed. The standards are evaluative criteria that set the level of the desired outcomes. For example, if a certain skill is to be developed, how thoroughly must it be developed to satisfy the goals of the program?

The program will be administered by the *policies and procedures* that result from the combination of desired goals and suggested standards for the program. The policies and procedures state how the actual program will be run in terms of administration, requirements, and application of the curriculum.

At the heart of the entire resulting physical education program is the philosophy of the program, for philosophy enters the planning process in developing a program at the earliest stages and thus determines the areas that will be emphasized within a particular program. Because of the crucial part philosophy plays in planning the program, the personal philosophy of each person involved should be thought out as clearly as possible, for philosophy's ultimate effect on the program is considerable.

So far we have attempted to explain the *why* of philosophy, rather than the *what*. Although we have discussed briefly what the study or process of philosophy is, we have primarily discussed its value to physical educators, or why we study philosophy. In an age increasingly concerned with science, we tend to forget the importance of things that cannot be tested against concrete facts.

As science has made rapid advances, many scientists have become concerned with how their discoveries will be applied and have thus moved from science into philosophy. Science developed theories that led to the first nuclear weapons, but many scientists then moved into the area of philosophy, because they were concerned with the *morality* of such weapons. Do human beings have a moral right to develop such weapons? To use them? Questions such as these are philosophical, for they cannot be answered with simple facts.

The rise of questions of this nature has shown us repeatedly that while we are moving toward the "two cultures" of C. P. Snow, both cultures are still tied to the realm of philosophy. Unanswerable or untestable questions exist in every discipline and field of learning, and if answers to such increasingly difficult questions are to be found, all fields of learning must be familiar with the nature and uses of philosophy. The concept of the ultimate value of all learning will come to us from our studies in philosophy, not solely from those in our separate fields.

We have discussed the meaning and use of philosophies as well as their basic teachings regarding education and physical education. You can now study the philosophies and decide what your own personal philosophy of education and physical education will be when you lead the life of a physical educator.

While this overview of philosophy in physical education and sport has been brief, we still need to study the ethical dilemmas that we face in physical education and sport. They will be the concern of the next chapter.

NOTES

1. Harold M. Barrow, *Man and His Movement: Principles of His Physical Education*, Lea & Febiger, Philadelphia, 1971, p. 18.
2. Randolph W. Webster, *Philosophy of Physical Education*, Wm. C. Brown, Dubuque, 1965, pp. 3–4.

3. Ibid.
4. Elwood Craig Davis and Donna Mae Miller, *The Philosophic Process in Physical Education,* 2d ed., Lea & Febiger, Philadelphia, 1967, pp. 23–29.
5. William A. Harper, "Philosophy of Physical Education and Sport (A Review of the Literature)," in *Exercise and Sport Sciences Review,* vol. 2, ed. Jack H. Wilmore, Academic Press, New York, 1974, pp. 239–263.
6. Harold J. VanderZwaag and Thomas J. Sheehan, *Introduction to Sport Studies: From the Classroom to the Ball Park,* Wm. C. Brown, Dubuque, 1978, pp. 113–128.
7. Ibid., pp. 120–125.
8. Ibid., pp. 125–127.
9. William A. Harper, "The Philosophical Perspective," in *Foundations of Physical Education: A Scientific Approach,* ed. Richard S. Rivenes, Houghton Mifflin, Boston, 1978, pp. 45–46.
10. VanderZwaag and Sheehan, p. 142.
11. Kathleen Pearson, "A Self-Study Guide: Two Approaches to Doing Philosophy of Sport and Physical Education," in *A Self-Study Guide for the Philosophy of Sport and Physical Education,* ed. R. Scott Kretchmar, Sport Philosophy Academy, Brockport, N.Y., 1978, pp. 10–18.
12. Robert G. Osterhoudt, *An Introduction to the Philosophy of Physical Education and Sport,* Stipes Publishing Company, Champaign, Ill., 1978, pp. 8–9.
13. Seymour Kleinman, "Toward a Non-Theory of Sport," *Quest* 10 (May 1968), 29–34.
14. Osterhoudt, pp. 96–97.
15. Ibid., p. 98.
16. Will Durant, *The Story of Philosophy,* Pocketbooks, New York, 1954, p. xxviii.
17. Earle F. Zeigler, *Philosophical Foundations for Physical, Health, and Recreation Education.* Prentice-Hall, Englewood Cliffs, N.J., 1964, p. 22.
18. James A. Baley and David A. Field, *Physical Education and the Physical Educator,* 2d ed., Allyn & Bacon, Boston, 1976, pp. 227–232.
19. Ibid., p. 231.
20. Ellen W. Gerber and William J. Morgan, *Sport and the Body: A Philosophical Symposium,* 2d ed., Lea & Febiger, Philadelphia, 1979, p. 1.
21. Ibid., pp. 2–3.
22. Frank McBride, "Toward a Non-Definition of Sport," in Gerber and Morgan, pp. 48–52.
23. Gerber and Morgan, pp. 69–72.
24. Ibid., p. 71.
25. Ibid., pp. 145–147.
26. Ibid., pp. 201–203.
27. Cited in Gerber and Morgan, p. 201.
28. Kenneth Ravizza, "Raising the Consciousness of the Human Movement Experience," in Kretchmar, *A Self-Study Guide,* p. 20.
29. William A. Harper et al., *The Philosophic Process in Physical Education,* 3d ed., pp. 250–259.
30. Gerber and Morgan, pp. 315–317.
31. Peter J. Arnold, *Meaning in Movement, Sport and Physical Education,* Heinemann, London, 1979, pp. 120–161.
32. Benjamin Lowe, *The Beauty of Sport: A Cross-Disciplinary Inquiry,* Prentice-Hall, Englewood Cliffs, N.J., 1977.

33. Delbert Oberteuffer, "On Learning Values Through Sport," *Quest* 1 (December 1963), 23–29.
34. Harper et al., pp. 231–238.
35. James W. Keating, *Competition and Playful Activities*, University Press of America, Washington, 1978, pp. 39–53.
36. Peter McIntosh, *Fair Play: Ethics in Sport and Education*, Heinemann, London, 1979.
37. Keating, pp. 25, 27.
38. Cited in Harper et al., pp. 252–253.
39. Paul Weiss, *Sport: A Philosophic Inquiry*, Southern Illinois University Press, Carbondale, p. 198.
40. Eugene A. Glader, *Amateurism and Athletics*, Leisure Press, Champaign, Ill., 1978.
41. Robert A. Stebbins, *Amateurs: On the Margin Between Work and Leisure*, Sage Publications, Beverly Hills, Calif., 1979.
42. Zeigler, pp. 65–66.
43. Ibid., pp. 241–244.
44. Ibid., pp. 162–164.
45. Ibid., p. 69.
46. Ibid., pp. 109–110.
47. J. Donald Butler, *Four Philosophies and Their Practice in Education and Religion*, 3d ed., Harper & Row, New York, 1968, p. 462.
48. Zeigler, p. 320.
49. Charles A. Bucher, *Foundations of Physical Education*, 8th ed., C. V. Mosby, St. Louis, 1979, p. 37.
50. Reuben B. Frost, *Physical Education: Foundations, Practices, Principles*, Addison-Wesley, Reading, Mass., 1975, p. 24.
51. Zeigler, p. 319.
52. Webster, p. 148.

SUGGESTED READINGS

Best, David. *Philosophy and Human Movement*. London: George Allen and Unwin, 1978.
Bressan, Elizabeth S., and Willy Pieter. "Philosophic Processes and the Study of Human Moving." *Quest* 37, no. 1 (1985), 1–15.
Brohm, Jean-Marie. *Sport: A Prison of Measured Time*, trans. Ian Fraser. London: Ink Links, 1978.
Case, Bob. "Eastern Thought and Movement Forms: Possible Implications for Western Sport." *The Physical Educator* 41 (December 1984), 170–175.
Fox, Richard M. "The So-Called Unreality of Sport." *Quest* 34, no. 1 (1982), 1–7.
Fraleigh, Warren. "The Philosophic Society for the Study of Sport: 1972–1983." *Journal of the Philosophy of Sport* 10 (1983), 3–7.
Guthrie, Steven P. *Is Sport Art?: Philosophical Analysis of a Problem of Definition, and Classification through Identifying Exemplars and Prototypical Attributes*. Ph.D. dissertation, University of Oregon, 1985. Microfiche.
Harper, William A. "Philosophy of Physical Education and Sport (A Review of the Literature)," *Exercise and Sport Sciences Review*, Vol. 2., ed. Jack Wilmore. New York: Academic Press, 1974.

Harris, Janet C. "Broadening Horizons: Interpretive Cultural Research, Hermeneutics, and Scholarly Inquiry in Physical Education." *Quest* 35, no. 2 (1983), 82–96.

———. "Hermeneutics, Interpretive Cultural Research, and the Study of Sports." *Quest* 33, no. 1 (1981), 72–86.

Hellison, Donald R. *Humanistic Physical Education*. Englewood Cliffs, N.J.: Prentice-Hall, 1973.

Kebric, Robert B. "The Mythology of 'Ideal' Sport." *The Physical Educator* 40 (December 1983), 194–199.

Kew, Francis C. "Values in Competitive Games," *Quest* 29 (Winter 1978), 103–112.

King, Linda. "Philosophy in Coaching." *The Physical Educator* 38 (December 1981), 180–182.

Kleinman, Seymour. *Mind and Body: East Meets West. Big Ten Body of Knowledge Symposium Series, Vol. 15*. Champaign, Ill.: Human Kinetics, 1986.

Kretchmar, R. Scott. *A Self-Study Guide for the Philosophy of Sport and Physical Education*. Brockport, N.Y.: Sport Philosophy Academy, 1978.

———. "Shared Honor." *Proceedings, National Association for Physical Education in Higher Education Annual Conference* 2 (1980), 108–124.

Lenk, Hans. "Philosophical Considerations in Human Performance." *The Academy Papers*, no. 18 (1984), 118–129.

———. *Social Philosophy of Athletics*. Champaign, Ill.: Stipes Publishing Company, 1979.

Meier, Klaus V. "An Affair of Flutes: An Appreciation of Play." *Journal of the Philosophy of Sport* 7 (Fall 1980), 24–45.

———. "A Meditation on Critical Mass in the Philosophy of Sport." *Journal of the Philosophy of Sport* 10 (1983), 8–20.

Metheny, Eleanor. *Movement and Meaning*. New York: McGraw-Hill, 1968.

Morgan, William J. "Social Philosophy of Sport: A Critical Interpretation." *Journal of the Philosophy of Sport* 10 (1983), 33–51.

Ravizza, Kenneth Henry. *A Study of the Peak-Experience in Sport*. Ph.D. dissertation, University of Southern California, 1973. Microfiche.

Shogan, Debra A. *The Nature of Man in Contemporary American Physical Education Philosophy*. M.A. thesis, University of Western Ontario, 1976. Microfiche.

Siedentop, Daryl. "The Humanistic Education Movement: Some Questions," *Issues in Physical Education and Sports*, ed. George H. McGlynn. Palo Alto, Calif.: National Press Books, 1974.

Snow, C. P. *The Two Cultures: and A Second Look*. Cambridge: Cambridge University Press, 1964.

Theberge, Nancy. "Toward a Feminist Alternative to Sport as a Male Preserve." *Quest* 37, no. 2 (1985), 193–202.

Thomas, Carolyn Elise. *The Perfect Moment: An Aesthetic Perspective of the Sport Experience*. Ph.D. dissertation, Ohio State University, 1972. Microfiche.

Watson, Scott B. "The Legitimization of Sport: Pindar and Weiss." *Quest* 35, no. 1 (1983), 37–45.

Zeigler, Earle F. "What Do I Believe? (A Self-Evaluation Check List for Professionals in Sport and Physical Education)." *The Physical Educator* 37 (December 1980), 197–201.

———. "Without Philosophy, Coaches and Physical Educators Are 'Unguided Missiles.'" *The Physical Educator* 37 (October 1980), 122–127.

See also the following books listed in the Resource Readings at the end of the book:

Arnold; Caillois; E. C. Davis; Ellis; Fraleigh; Gerber et al.; Gerber and Morgan; Harper; Horrow; Huizinga; Jerome; Keating; Leonard; Lowe; McIntosh, *Fair Play*; MacLeod; Mihalich; Murray; Novak; Orlick; Osterhoudt; Rigauer; Sanborn and Hartman; Siedentop; Slusher; Thomas; Ulrich and Nixon; VanderZwaag; Weiss; and Zeigler, *Sport Philosophy*.

chapter 8

Problems and Ethics in Sport and Physical Education

No field is without problems, but the problems we encounter in physical education and sport can be particularly difficult. In many cases we find ourselves caught in ethical dilemmas, unsure as to what is the best or most proper thing to do. We shall look first at some current problems in physical education and sport, and then we shall turn to a discussion of ethics in physical education and sport, though the emphasis will be on the sport setting.

PROBLEMS IN PHYSICAL EDUCATION AND SPORT TODAY

Problems in sport affect physical education, for the public views the two areas together, and the majority of American coaches are in that field. Sport has changed considerably in recent decades, with the development of television and other media coverage, coupled with the large sums of money that are involved. At the highest levels of competition, athletics can become almost a full-time job. Are such requirements by coaches or a school ethical, even with scholarships? Here is an overview of the problems and risks of one popular sport—football:

"I wanted to be the starting quarterback and a Phi Beta Kappa at the same time," [the athlete] says. Through hard work and long hours he became both. He has a double major in economics and psychology....

When he talks of his decision to quit football you hear tones of frustration about how college sports can practically consume the lives of the young athletes who play them.

"For me it was 12 months a year," [he] says. "You never really got to stop. When you come to college, it becomes such a regimented program. It can get monotonous. A lot of guys lose interest...."

The life of a football player, he'll tell you, is a lot less thrilling than the glory the rest of the world sees on Saturday afternoons.

"When you come to college," he says, "you notice it's no longer a game you're playing. It's a job."

As a football player [he] had to eat breakfast every morning by 8. If he missed breakfast, he had to go through the "[Team] Reminder," a disciplinary measure requiring grueling early morning runs. He had to finish all his classes by 1 P.M. in order to eat lunch at 1:15 at a players' "training table." Next came meetings with the coaches, film-watching sessions and scouting reports. At 3:30 his ankles were taped for practice, which lasted until 6:30. After that he had to lift weights and shower. Between 7:30 and 8:30 it was back to the training table for dinner.

"For those 12 hours you haven't been able to study," [he] says. "You're starting out at 9 o'clock at night, worn out from the day you've been through. You get back to your dorm room, and you've got that book on your desk right next to your bed. And right over there's the TV. That's where a lot of the fun is lost. A lot of players give in."

[He] frequently studied until 3 or 4 A.M. During one season he lost 15 pounds and had to have nutrients injected intravenously the day before games to have enough stamina to play.

"College football is one of the biggest industries in America," he says. "Big industries require a lot of people. Athletes bring in tons of revenue for the university but end up with a transcript not showing much. Too many guys are going out and saying, "What do I do now?" In essence, they're being exploited."

[Though he] started at quarterback for two years, [he] has left the team and will not play next fall. Instead, he has decided to follow his academic interests, which he hopes will lead him to graduate studies in business and maybe a Rhodes scholarship....

For [him], college always represented more than a chance to play football because, he says, there comes a time when you must understand your abilities and your limits.

"I think my potential in other areas is better than my potential in pro football," [he] says. "The bottom line is your potential in life, getting where you want to in life."[1]

This example of what it is like to play football at a high level can be seen in many other sports. Academic success and the enjoyment of college life are not the only things at risk. A note on "the football knee" points out that 70 percent of professional football players have knee surgery by age 26, 50 percent of all running backs require knee surgery, and 50,000 pieces of knee cartilage are removed annually by American surgeons.[2]

The physical risks also reach into the aftereffects of some of the more questionable training procedures in sports. These procedures include the use of steroids and human growth hormone, blood replacement techniques (blood doping), and other developing training methods. The risks reach into every modern sport; football is only a more prominent example.

We shall look briefly at four areas of problems in physical education and sport today. The first problem area is *the abuses of sport*. One writer has listed some of these abuses : direct or indirect payments to students for athletic purposes, encouragement of students to move from college to college for athletic purposes, lack of faculty control in games and grounds, coaches of questionable morals and influence, and bad moral effects of games when rules are broken or evaded.[3] These abuses, incidentally, were the subjects of a complaint made in 1903; thus, while the abuses of sport may be more intricate today, they are not new. Indeed, they were present at Olympia 2500 years ago. Many of the problems of abuses in sport need to be corrected, but while educators must show leadership in this area, there seems to be no sign of interest in a massive investigation such as the one conducted by the Carnegie Foundation in the 1920s. The mushrooming evidence of drug abuse on a large scale, ranging from narcotics to steroids to prescription medicines, shows the need for a major study of what we are and should be doing in sports.

Many Americans were shocked early in 1985 when they learned that Olympic cycling medalists from the United States admitted to blood doping before their competition. A magazine article stated that eight cyclists blood doped either before the U.S. Olympic trials or before the Games themselves. In addition, 86 American athletes in other sports failed drug tests given by the United States Olympic Committee in the nine months before the 1984 games.[4]

The same issue of the magazine gave an account of how the sudden death (from natural causes) of a Dutch runner at an American university led to the accidental discovery of widespread use of illegally obtained prescription drugs by college athletes, supplied by college coaches and others.[5] Several coaches were eventually fired, but the case probably represents the tip of the iceberg. Many athletes have too little faith in their ability to reach the top legally; the drugs they may take can be dangerous. Indeed, we still know little about the long-term effects of medium and high dosages of drugs such as anabolic steroids.[6]

The overemphasis on winning and success have led to a sports world that is far from clean. Young athletes, and their teachers and coaches, need a well-developed sense of ethics, of right and wrong, to decide which course to pursue as they develop.

A second problem area is the question of *overemphasis on sports in the schools*. If we consider sports to be a genuine contribution to the educational process, as most physical educators do, then we would expect them to be important. In many cases, though, sports seem to be overemphasized, that is, not pushed for lessons but promoted simply for the victories and fame that can be gained. As physical educators, we need to give serious consideration to this problem of competitive sports overemphasis, for it reflects on our physical education programs as well.

A prominent example is the Jan Kemp case at the University of Georgia in 1986. Jan Kemp was a remedial English instructor in a program called the Developmental Studies Program. The program was designed to assist students who had been admitted to the university but were not academically ready to do college-level work. Such students were expected to pass the remedial-level courses by a certain deadline, or they were removed from the university.

The university dismissed Kemp in 1983, but she filed a legal suit, claiming that she was fired for objecting too strongly to the favorable treatment given to the athletes. In early 1986, she won her suit against the university. The jury agreed that the athletes had been treated preferentially, that Kemp was fired because of her objections to athletes getting passing grades when they had failed, and that teachers were pressured to give good grades to the athletes.[7]

Shortly after the jury decision, the university president resigned, just after the state board of regents delayed renewing his contract. An audit report by the Board of Regents of the University System of Georgia showed that athletes had been given preferred treatment, under pressure from the athletic department, and with the knowledge of the university's president, according to a number of university officers. The report stated:

> Apparently because of the large number of academically deficient athletes who were admitted to the university, the athletic department chose to fund directly the establishment of a Developmental Studies laboratory that was subsequently used as a route for an athlete to bypass the established academic standards of the approved Developmental Studies Program.[8]

While the Georgia case was widely publicized, similar examples can probably be found at many other colleges and universities in the United States. What do practices such as this say for the ethical standards maintained by a school, its administration, and its coaches, if they develop and encourage a system for using academically unqualified athletes until their eligibility expires?

Why did a massive system of competitive sports in the schools develop in the United States, yet not in any other country? Does the American concept of mass education have anything to do with it? Other nations have mass public education; is their concept of education different from ours?

Did schools in the United States stop being seen by the public as a place of education, becoming instead a center for "youth activities"? Did the school become a place for young people to stay busy and play while waiting to grow up and move out into adult society?

Texas was the first state to try to change the direction of school sports with its "no pass, no play" policy in 1985. Though it resulted in many athletes losing their places on the teams, it has received strong support from parents and the courts.

Marian Kneer has suggested that physical education and athletics "need a divorce," that the problems that grew from trying to teach and coach at the same time cannot be solved except by separating the jobs. She argues that the teaching of physical education has been badly damaged, so the profession needs new answers.[9]

A third problem area is *whether competitive sports are overemphasized in the physical education program*. Although competitive sports may be overemphasized by less skillful teachers, a good teacher will prepare a well-balanced program that exposes students to all areas of physical activity. As physical educators, we need to evaluate our programs constantly to ensure that we are providing physical *education*, not simply promoting physical *competition*. This is an area of great professional concern.

The fourth problem area is still controversial: *What is the relationship of physical education and sport?* In the eyes of the public, the two areas are one. The need to share facilities, equipment, and even budgets causes conflict. Each area is affected by the public reputation of the other. Whether physical education and athletics wish to be a single area, they are often forced together by the public. The question of which area will carry the greater influence, if either one, has not yet been settled.

HOW DOES ETHICS RELATE TO SPORT AND PHYSICAL EDUCATION?

We discussed ethics briefly in Chapter 7 and defined it as concerned with morals and conduct, with trying to decide on proper rules of conduct. We said that it is a study of ideal conduct and the knowledge of good and evil, and that it seeks to determine what actions are right and wrong, what should and should not be done. The greatest problem that we face in discussing ethical problems is that no single perspective is absolute. Each person may have a different belief about what is right and wrong, and we have no objective standards by which we can judge some issues. For this reason, we need to understand that the ethical standards discussed in this chapter reflect the ethical views of the author.

Ethics is vital to the successful functioning of any society; that is, people must have standards of value by which they live. The development of ethical standards has long been considered a vital part of the educational process. The Greeks spoke of the development of character as one of the most, if not *the* most, vital concerns of education. Many educational goals were optional, but character was a goal that could never be dropped.

If we agree that we need to develop character, or ethical standards, what does that need have to do with sport and physical education? We often refer to sport and physical education as a laboratory of human experience, for there, more than in any other organized area of the educational process, students are likely to show their inner selves. Sport and physical education challenge the student both physically and intellectually, and in the heat of intense competition, a person's true values often show. One person may be more concerned with fair play, while another person may try to win in any possible way. This is the ultimate test of ethical standards, and no other area of educational endeavor is so likely to put the student to the test.

Sport poses a dilemma in modern life, no less than in ancient times. H. A. Harris discussed the problem in the conclusion to his book *Greek Athletes and Athletics*:

> Not only are games pleasant to play but many of them afford great enjoyment to spectators; all the problems of modern sport spring from this simple fact. In logical language the essence of sport is the enjoyment of the players; the pleasure of spectators is an accident....So long as sport is true to itself, the only purpose of the organization of it is the enjoyment of the players; as soon as the interests of the spectators are allowed to become predominant, corruption has set in and the essence of the game has been lost. In other words, sport can be an entertainment for spectators, but what is primarily entertainment for spectators can never be sport in the true sense of the term.[10]

Originally sport was for the competitors, but in modern times the influence of television has increased the problem of the entertainment dilemma. When sport is still purely for the athlete, however, it is an excellent test of ethical behavior. Because sport and physical education can provide such a fertile ground for learning and testing ethical behavior, we face our next problem: Should physical educators teach ethics and values?

SHOULD ETHICS AND VALUES BE TAUGHT IN SPORT AND PHYSICAL EDUCATION?

If sport and physical education really are a "laboratory of human experience" as we claim, what better place could be found to try to teach ethics and values to the future leaders of the world? Delbert Oberteuffer has suggested that this issue is a major area of concern in contemporary physical education.[11] Whenever lists of objectives for physical education have been prepared, we see the development of social and moral competences included as a major concern. The supporters of sports programs have argued frequently that the contribution that the programs make to developing character is a major reason for having them.

We might be more accurate if we suggested that sport provides the opportunity to *display* character rather than to develop it, but the ties between ethical character and sport and physical education are strong and of an ancient heritage. As physical educators and coaches, we have an obligation to try to teach ethics and values, for in the ultimate judgment, it may be the most important lesson we teach.

Although we have faced the question of ethics in physical education and sport for many years, only recently has much attention been placed on the question. The most complete discussion of the history of ethics in sport and physical education, as well as of some of the related issues, is Peter McIntosh's *Fair Play: Ethics in Sport and Education*.[12]

HOW DO WE TEACH ETHICS AND VALUES?

As physical educators and coaches, we teach ethics and values largely by example. Although we may talk about living by rules and treating others fairly, our students and athletes will be far more influenced by our practices than by what we say. People's true ethical beliefs are reflected in their daily actions. Telling a class to treat everyone fairly does a teacher no good if the teacher does not treat the students fairly. The old saying that "actions speak louder than words" is true when we speak of ethical behavior. We are unlikely to teach good character if we exhibit poor character. Teachers and coaches must be constantly aware of the effect of their actions on their students and athletes, for young people will imitate their coaches and teachers in the belief that their actions are examples of accepted and proper conduct and ethics.

Today the concern over ethical behavior is rising as society becomes more aware of the need for ethical character in its members. The increasing consciousness of the need for the development of the older concept of ethical character is reflected by the reappearance of discussions of ethics in newer textbooks. Our programs need to return to a stress on character, ethics, and sportsmanship.

This exaggerated drawing of an early Princeton-Yale football scrimmage indicates how college athletics may have earned the bad reputation they had before 1900. (Courtesy The Bettmann Archive)

THE "ETHIC" OF BIG-TIME SPORT: WHY SPORT HAS A POOR REPUTATION

Students and athletes learn many lessons from competitive sports, and not all of them are good lessons. Most people realize that competitive sports do not have a very good reputation today, particularly in the areas of ethics and values. When we think of sport today, we are often thinking of what has come to be called big-time sport, that is, top-level competition combined with large budgets. We may look at such competition in terms of professional athletics, or perhaps college or high school sports, but whatever the level of competition, many lessons are to be learned.

Sport has developed a poor reputation for many reasons. What philosophies and practices have given sport this questionable reputation? One reason for many problems is that coaches and athletes at lower levels of competition try to imitate the practices they see in the big-time sports programs. Practices that might seem acceptable in professional athletics (which is essentially entertainment, just as a circus is) are often inappropriate in amateur athletics. Unfortunately, however, we see many of the ideas of professional athletics at the lowest levels of competition. That they reach these levels of sport and remain there must be the responsibility of the teacher–coach, for unless the teacher–coach opposes the practices, they will continue to spread. The following ideas or thumbnail philosophies are examples of practices that should be discouraged if sport is to be educational and attempt to develop a consistent system of values.

The Supreme Importance of Victory

Two aspects of the overemphasis on victory might be called the "winning is the only thing" ethic and the "agony of defeat" syndrome. The "winning is the only thing" ethic comes from the saying, popular among coaches, that "winning isn't everything, it's the *only* thing." This idea, which is often attributed, probably incorrectly, to professional football coach Vince Lombardi, has been used by coaches on all levels to justify questionable practices ranging from mistreatment of their athletes to outright violations of the rules of sport. The basic idea expressed here is that the only point of athletics is victory, so anything that is done to win is acceptable. The end justifies the means. At best, this is a gross abuse of the idea of sport as a contributor to the educational process. If this is the philosophy of a school's coach or teacher, the school should have no sports program, for this motto has not the slightest pretense of moral or educational values or ethics.

The "agony of defeat" syndrome covers the total range of sports, which is apparently "the thrill of victory, the agony of defeat." One small question arises in response to this view: *Why* should we think that defeat must result in agony? We compete with the hope of winning, but if we have given our best and still lose, why should we feel agony? One dictionary definition of agony is "intense suffering." Should this realistically be our response every time we lose? Many coaches call sport a "training ground for life," but if agony is a person's response to every defeat in life, would that person be considered well adjusted? Defeat is a disappointment, sometimes an intense one, but the idea that it should be agony is another abuse of the place of sport in education and in life.

When we coach or compete in sports, we want to win. Winning, or trying to win, is a natural desire of the human race. It is true that we can liken life to a competition, but if we make victory with no holds barred the goal of life, we have removed most of the potential quality of that life. If victory is our ultimate lesson in school athletics, we have no lesson worth teaching, for the desire to win is inherent. The value of sport in the school curriculum lies in the other values that we teach or promote as we teach and train and compete. Victory is neither the only goal nor the highest goal in educational sport and physical education.

Poor Sportsmanship

Sportsmanship has been used for many years as an example of the best trait that athletics can develop. Unfortunately, no evidence shows that competitive sports participation does develop sportsmanship. We *do* have some evidence that sports competition can inhibit or lessen sportsmanship. Poor sportsmanship may be primarily a result of the examples given by coaches and teachers to their teams and to other students as they pursue victory and fame.

The proverb that "nice guys finish last" is a good example of what is wrong with educational sport, for too many coaches and athletes have tried to live up to this rule. The idea is that decency is a sign of weakness, that a person who shows signs of character probably does not have the force of will to become a champion. This belief may motivate coaches to abuse their athletes and to abandon any ethical standards in the pursuit of victory, because they do not think they can win if they play by the rules. If "nice guys finish last," sport will finish in that position in the list of educational priorities.

We might call the other aspect of poor sportsmanship the idea that "the Lord (or coach) loves a poor loser." We are increasingly treated to the spectacle of athletes who throw temper tantrums whenever they lose. This action is then cited by the coach or sports announcer as a sign of competitiveness or

© 1973 United Feature Syndicate, Inc.

spirit. If we want to be honest, it is a sign of childish immaturity, for most people are expected to have outgrown such behavior by the time they enter elementary school. Coaches and athletes do not like to be referred to as cases of "retarded emotional development," but the poor losers are just that. A person who cannot lose with dignity is not psychologically prepared to benefit from a competitive experience. Whether we can teach sportsmanship in the schools, we should at least demand that it be exhibited by any person who wishes to compete or to coach.

The Lack of Joy in Sport

We traditionally think of sports activities as activities that people enjoy or that are fun to do. One aspect of contemporary sport seems to be the idea that sport should not be fun, because winning or losing is too serious to permit sport to be enjoyed. One example of this idea is similar to the last point made under poor sportsmanship. "Show me a good loser, and I'll show you a loser," as some coaches put it, is another example of an immature approach to sport. When we express the idea that only winning has a value, we are ignoring an important point: Everyone loses at some time. Philosophies of this sort are self-defeating, for they turn everyone into losers. If everyone who participates in athletics will end up being called a loser, who will want to participate? Sport simply becomes futile under those conditions.

Another view of the no-joy-in-sport philosophy is expressed by the coach who says, "We're here to win, not to have a good time." If this is the coach's philosophy, the team has already lost, for the education this program will produce is entirely negative. We have all seen examples of the coach who believed that smiling was a sign of a poor competitive attitude. Whose attitude is really the poor one in this case? If there is no fun in sport, what will our competitive athletes be like in the future? Will they continue the idea that success equals misery?

The Place of Education in Sport (Dead Last)

We might refer more accurately to this as the place of the *educator* in sport, for we are concerned with the dedication of the coach to teaching. Most coaches in our schools will state that sport is an important part of the educational process. The question is whether their practices uphold their claim of believing the statement. We might cite as an example the "dedicated teacher" syndrome, or the coach whose educational approach is best reflected in his defensive statement, "I get paid to win, not to teach." The most obvious fact in the statement is that this coach is not a teacher and does not consider himself a teacher. Moreover, the statement makes the observer suspect that the coach has never been remotely interested in being a teacher. The statement itself is, in some cases, undoubtedly true, but it is not a particularly supportable defense for doing a poor job, or no job, of teaching. A coach with this philosophy teaches athletes far more than he or she realizes—primarily things schools would prefer not to have taught.

Sports as Money

We might view money as the greatest force affecting athletics today, for it lies at the heart of so many abuses of the educational goals of sport. The problem is a form of the Midas touch: Athletes hope that everything they touch will pay off in dollars and cents. It is reflected in the coach whose primary concerns are salary and fringe benefits. We see it increasingly in the high school athlete whose primary concern about a college is "What will you give me?" Many of today's high school athletes are about as interested in the ethics of scholarships and fringe benefits as is a professional athlete: *not at all*. Too often we see the picture of a functionally illiterate all-star high school athlete from a poor family who, after barely escaping high school, suddenly acquires a car, an improved wardrobe, perhaps a well-paid summer job, and the status of "amateur" college athlete. Too many coaches and athletes today believe that the cardinal rule of athletics is "money talks." What lessons are they teaching to their athletes and to the public?

The Nutcracker Reflex

A favorite saying of coaches is that "when the going gets tough, the tough get going." The sentiment is worthy, for it teaches the rewards of sticking with a task until it is completed. Unfortunately, it also may be the catchword signaling the abuse and dehumanization of a coach's athletes. As teachers and coaches, we should be sure that the goal for which a student athlete is working is worthy of the effort required. Abuse simply for the sake of proving toughness or desire is never justified in an educational context.

The Rodney Dangerfield Syndrome, or Why the Coach Gets No Respect

Perhaps the greatest failing of physical educators is reflected in the growth of the idea of the anti-intellectualism of athletics and coaches. Sport is not usually thought of in an educational or intellectual sense primarily because of the actions of coaches. In our society the coach has come to be viewed as dedicated but not at all intellectual. Coaches are widely viewed as relatively ignorant people who have little interest in educational matters and even less understanding of education. Unfortunately, because coaches and teachers of physical education often remain aloof from the rest of the school staff, many teachers hold this low opinion of their coaching colleagues. While much of the responsibility for this view lies with the poor job of public relations performed by physical educators, actual abuses are also at the heart of the matter.

Coaches who try to have an athlete's grade changed for the sake of the student's eligibility are showing fellow teachers they have no concern for education or the primary task of the institution. Teachers who automatically give athletes good grades perform the same negative task in the eyes of the other teachers. College coaches who enlist their all-star recruits as physical education majors regardless of the students' qualifications or interests show their own lack of respect for physical education's integrity as a field of study.

The use of the physical education major as a haven for the academically inept athlete has long been a popular concept among educators and citizens outside the field of physical education. One reason for the poor reputation of physical education as a subject area is the number of students majoring in the subject who are not in college for an education, but who have come to be college athletes for as long as they can stay eligible. Physical education has suffered from the perpetuation of this sort of ignorance on the part of its coaches for far too long.

A psychological study of successful coaches has revealed that one of their characteristics is conservatism, or a resistance to change that is greater than the average person's resistance to change.[13] Coaches tend to be inflexible in their practices, which is more than likely to bring them into conflict with other teachers who do not share their views. Such inflexibility, however, does not have to be a negative trait. If physical education teachers and coaches will work with their colleagues in other areas and let their colleagues see that their interests go beyond the gymnasium and playing fields and that they do want to maintain academic integrity, they can gradually overcome the often negative image of physical education teacher–coaches.

These brief examples are not all of the abuses that have contributed to giving athletics and physical education a poor reputation. We discussed others earlier in the chapter. We have taken decades to work ourselves into our current position, and changing that position will be neither easy nor quick. Now that we have considered some of the things that have hurt the reputation, we need to look at the positive side of the task: our challenge. If we agree that physical educators should try to teach ethics and values, what ethical and value problems should we be teaching?

WHAT ARE THE ETHICAL PROBLEMS WE FACE?

Values Taught to Athletes and Students

One of our first ethical problems is a dual one: What values *do* we teach to our athletes and students, and what values *should* we teach to them? To answer the first part of this question, we must return to our earlier discussion of the way we teach with our actions. Regardless of what we say, the people we influence are watching what we do to see whether our practices live up to our theories.

The late 1960s was a time of much complaining about teachers and coaches being hypocrites, people who pretend to believe in one thing, or teach it, while they are doing something else that contradicts what they teach. If teachers do not live up to the theories they teach, they will have a negative influence on their students. We must *live* what we teach.

To answer the second part of our dual ethical problem—What values should we teach our students and athletes?—we could suggest many different values or aspects of ethical character that should be taught as a part of the educational process. Instead, we shall discuss five basic areas of ethics or values: justice and equality, self-respect, respect for others, respect for rules and authority, and a sense of perspective or relative values. This list is not intended to cover everything in the domain of values and ethical practices. It is simply a sampling of some broad areas that the teacher–coach should keep in mind.

Justice and Equality

Probably the greatest wish of any student or athlete is a simple one: fair and equal treatment. Students want a genuine opportunity to learn, to be exposed to what the teacher is teaching, as well as a fair opportunity afterward to show what they have learned. Too often the average or poorly skilled student in physical education is neglected in favor of the gifted student. Educators should assist all students, regardless of their relative ability. Physical educators most often fail to help the students of lesser ability in physical activities, because they tend to neglect them. This practice is not just; it is unfair treatment of the student by the teacher.

Educators can fail to treat students equally because the students are different in any of several ways. We commonly think of the students who have not been given equal opportunity because they are of a different race than their teachers or other students. Teachers are equally unfair if they neglect a student whom they consider to be in a different social or economic group than the other students. A teacher also can fail students by neglecting them because they are not of the same sex as the teacher or other class members. Finally, teachers fail to treat some students fairly by giving them less attention because their level of physical ability, whether high or low, is different from that of the rest of the group.

The problem is complicated in athletics, for coaches have a tendency to give more attention to the more gifted athletes. This tendency is natural, because the ultimate success of the team will likely ride more heavily on the shoulders of the more able athletes than on those of the other team members. Even so, a difference in physical talents should not affect the way the coach treats the athletes. All athletes should be treated equally, regardless of their respective abilities. The coach should work with all the athletes as much as possible. Athletes will remember how the coach treated them long after they have forgotten everything else the coach taught.

Respect and Consideration for Oneself

A coach who downgrades the athletes on a team, or a teacher who does the same thing to the members of a class, will lessen their chances of success. A student or athlete needs self-respect and a positive self-image to be a success.

The teacher–coach who treats all students equally will have made a major step in this direction, for no student will believe that he is unimportant or undeserving in the eyes of the teacher.

The teacher–coach should try to stress several concepts that relate to building students' self-respect. First, all that anyone can ask of people is that they do their best. If the teacher or coach demands that the students give their best, they will likely give it. However, a class or team that gave its best and was still unsuccessful should not be abused. If a runner competes and runs faster than ever before, does anyone have a right to complain if she still lost the race? Teachers cannot expect more than students have to give, though they can raise the goals of the students to a higher level.

A second concept related to self-respect is the Golden Rule: Treat others as you wish to be treated. This rule holds true for teachers, coaches, students, and athletes. Self-respect is a delicate area, and students often feel insecure in the educational or athletic environment. The teacher can do much to remove the insecurity and help the student to develop a sense of self-respect that will lead to greater self-confidence and self-reliance.

Respect and Consideration for Others

Students and athletes need to learn to respect other people, whether their classroom or competitive counterparts, teachers, coaches, or any other person. The student needs to learn the value of treating other people with re-

W. H. Freeman

spect. The athlete who treats an opponent with respect is far more likely to receive the same treatment in return. In a competition where the athletes treat each other with respect, the competition will be much more enjoyable for everyone involved. We have grown too accustomed to the idea that opponents are supposed to be abused; coaches are failing in their ethical duties if they teach that type of conduct. Coaches should, instead, encourage students to extend respect to everyone, including parents and teachers.

When we speak of students and athletes learning respect, we need to remember that many athletes and students learn about respect from what they see their coaches do. A coach who screams at officials every time the team receives an adverse call is destroying any real opportunity to teach respect. Athletic competition may seem like war at times, but it is not. An opponent or official who makes a judgment call against a team does not become a target for abuse in a sports program that is concerned with any aspect of ethical character. Coaches must *show* respect to *teach* it.

An aspect of learning to respect others relates to how the coach treats the athletes, or how a teacher treats the students. A teacher and coach must always be concerned with the students' and athletes' rights and feelings. A student should not become a target of ridicule because of an error, nor should the athlete who has an undesirable characteristic be subject to the coach's abuse. When teachers or coaches abuse students or athletes, the climate of respect disintegrates; a position of authority never includes the right to ridicule or abuse another person.

Respect for Rules and Authority

Students and athletes need to learn to respect rules and authority, for without them a society will not function. The first requirement in teaching this respect is that the rules need to be worthy of respect. The teacher–coach who makes ridiculous rules simply to have rules to enforce only complicates matters. The teacher–coach should set no requirements except those that genuinely contribute to the task at hand.

One aspect of respect for rules is how we teach the rules. Rules are designed guidelines of conduct in sport; they tell what can and cannot be done. The teacher or coach can abuse the rules without explicitly violating them by pushing them to the allowable limits. We sometimes hear the distinction made between the letter of the law and the spirit of the law. The letter of the law refers to what the law says shall be done, but underlying the law is the spirit of the law, which is the intent of the law. What is the *purpose* of a rule? If a rule is designed to make basketball a noncontact game, what are coaches teaching if they hunt technicalities that may be used to help the team physically abuse an opponent? If we teach the rules and then teach how they can be broken without detection, what are we teaching? The object of all rules and laws is justice—to allow each person a fair opportunity.

We have to realize that living in a democracy requires respect for other people and respect for the rules. If we do not respect other people, we shall not be able to get along with them. The result is conflict—an end to peace. If we do not respect the rules of society, the result is anarchy, or disorder. A life of freedom and democracy is based on respect for our fellow citizens and our laws.

A Sense of Perspective or Relative Values

An important aspect of values concerns the viewpoints or perspectives we hold. We need to consider several questions related to the value of sport. We shall not seek ultimate or final answers, for these questions should not be answered and passed over quickly. They require much thought and study.

A first question, perhaps the most important one, is: *How important is sport?* Where do we place sport in the educational spectrum and in our lives? What part does sport play in life? For each of us, the answer or answers to the question of the importance of sport will give some indication of the part sport plays in our educational philosophies. Some of our answers may indicate that sport is more important than it should be, but as educators, we need to place sport in a proper perspective.

A second question is: *What is the proper relationship between sport and physical education?* We must determine the educational relationship between physical education and sport to be assured that sport receives the proper emphasis in an educational program but not an overemphasis.

A third question is: *How necessary is victory?* Do we believe in the idea of victory at any price? The value we place on athletic victory, which can be a choice between means and end in education, does much to show our ethical standards in sport. We have looked at some of the current problems in sport, such as steroid use, the use of other drugs, and blood doping. We must decide whether victory is more important to us than the educational values of competitive sports.

A fourth question concerns *academic integrity.* As educators we must decide what we stand for. Are we semieducators who will bend the academic rules to help ourselves gain a valuable athlete? Do we want our school to bend the rules to allow us to enroll a student who is unqualified to enroll or unprepared for the academic work expected of the typical student? Are we really educators if we encourage the academically inept to come to school because they are good athletes? We might consider the comments of Jacques Barzun in this area: "The analogy to athletics must be pressed until all recognize that in the exercise of Intellect those who lack the muscles, coordination, and will power can claim no place at the training table, let alone on the playing field."[14]

TOWARD AN ETHICAL FUTURE

In most of this chapter we have discussed various aspects of ethics and ethical problems and their relation to sport and physical education. People believe that ethical character and the learning of values are important aspects of education, but they are not sure how important they are, where they fit in, or exactly what we can do about them. Delbert Oberteuffer commented on our need to learn more in this area in this way:

> What we needed in physical education was full-blown research and clinical experience in the relation of movement to the teaching of ethics and morality, to the improvement of psychological states, and the cultivation of social gain between people and groups.... What kind of manpower does our society need for its preservation? This is the compelling question from the standpoint of national need and people in physical education had better have an answer or they will be lost in the oceans of sweat recommended by the muscle-building anti-intellectual.[15]

The future leaders of the nation in physical education and sport will determine the ethical practices and subsequent reputation of sport and physical education in the future. Whether physical educators are viewed as a group of not-too-bright, not-too-ethical jocks as they have sometimes been viewed in the past is up to future teachers and coaches. We need to see a major improvement. Let us hope that the next generation of teachers will be more committed to the ideals of education and therefore more concerned with their own and their students' and athletes' ethical practices.

As educators and coaches, we should stand for something positive. We should have positive standards that show our respect for ourselves and others, our interest in fairness and justice, and our commitment to a strong sense of ethics. When we teach and coach, we can do no better than to convince those we teach that the often-quoted lines by the sportwriter Grantland Rice are the best judge of our ethical behavior:

> For when the One Great Scorer comes
> To write against your name,
> He marks—not that you won or lost—
> But how you played the game.

NOTES

1. Matt Schudel, "Kevin Anthony, Former Athlete," Raleigh (N.C.) *News and Observer,* March 4, 1986, p. 6A. Used with permission.
2. Sports Features Syndicate, March 1986.
3. D. A. Sargent, "History of the Administration of Intercollegiate Athletics in the United States," in *Chronicle of American Physical Education,* ed. Aileene S. Lockhart and Betty Spears, Wm. C. Brown, Dubuque, p. 272.
4. Bjarne Rostaing and Robert Sullivan, "Triumphs Tainted with Blood," *Sports Illustrated* 62 (21 January 1985), 12–17.
5. Bill Brubaker, "A Pipeline Full of Drugs," *Sports Illustrated* 62 (21 January 1985), 18–21.
6. Terry Todd, "The Steroid Predicament," *Sports Illustrated* 59 (1 August 1983), 62–66, 68–71, 73–75, 77.
7. William Nack, "This Case Was One for the Books," *Sports Illustrated* 64 (24 February 1986), 34–36, 41–42.

8. "Ga. Report Says University Chief Knew Athletes Were Favored," *New York Times News Service*, 4 April 1986.
9. Marian E. Kneer, "Physical Education and Athletics Need a Divorce," *JOPERD* 57 (March 1986), 7.
10. H. A. Harris, *Greek Athletes and Athletics*, Indiana University Press, Bloomington, 1966, p. 189.
11. Delbert Oberteuffer, "On Learning Values Through Sport," *Quest* 1 (December 1963), 23–29.
12. Peter McIntosh, *Fair Play: Ethics in Sport and Education*, Heinemann, London, 1979.
13. Bruce Ogilvie and Thomas A. Tutko, *Problem Athletes and How to Handle Them*, Pelham Books, London, 1966, pp. 23–24.
14. Jacques Barzun, *The House of Intellect*, Harper & Row, New York, 1959, p. 95.
15. Oberteuffer, pp. 23–29.

SUGGESTED READINGS

American Council on Education: Commission on Collegiate Athletics. Text of recommendations on collegiate athletics. *Chronicle of Higher Education* 19 (9 October 1979), 4–5.

Arnold, Peter J. "Three Approaches Toward an Understanding of Sportsmanship." *Journal of the Philosophy of Sport* 10 (1983), 61–70.

Blucker, Judy A., and Sarah W. J. Pell. "Legal and Ethical Issues Essential for Professional Preparation Curricula." *JOPERD* 57 (January 1986), 19–22, 28.

Bredemeier, Brenda J. "Moral Reasoning and the Perceived Legitimacy of Intentionally Injurious Sports Acts." *Journal of Sport Psychology* 7 (June 1985), 110–124.

——, and David L. Shields. "Values and Violence in Sports Today: The Moral Reasoning Athletes Use in Their Games and in Their Lives." *Psychology Today* 19 (October 1985), 22–25, 28–29, 32.

Case, Robert W., and Robert L. Boucher. "Spectator Violence in Sport, A Selected Review." *Journal of Sport and Social Issues* 5 (Fall-Winter 1981), 1–14.

Chambers, Robin L. *Sportsmanship in a Sporting America: Tradition, Ideal, Reality*. Ed.D. dissertation, Temple University, 1984. Microfiche.

Collins, Robert M. "Richard M. Nixon: The Psychic, Political and Moral Uses of Sport." *Journal of Sport History* 10 (Summer 1983), 77–84.

Corbin, Charles B. *The Athletic Snowball*. Champaign, Ill.: Human Kinetics Press, 1978.

DeFord, Frank. "No Longer a Cozy Corner." *Sports Illustrated* 63 (23–30 December 1985), 45–48, 50, 55, 58, 61.

——. "Religion in Sport." 3-part series. *Sports Illustrated*, 19 April 1976, pp. 88+; 26 April 1976, pp. 64+; 3 May 1976, pp. 42+.

——. "The Toughest Coach There Ever Was." *Sports Illustrated* 60 (30 April 1984), 44–61.

Development of Human Values Through Sports. Reston, Va.: AAHPERD, 1974.

Fielding, Lawrence W. "From Skill to Innuendo: The Greening of American Gamesmanship." *Canadian Journal of History of Sport* 15 (December 1984), 30–44.

Feigley, David A. "Is Aggression Justifiable?" *JOPERD* 54 (November-December 1983), 63–64.

Figley, G. E. "Moral Education Through Physical Education." *Quest* 36, no. 1 (1984), 89–101.

Fraleigh, Warren P. *Right Actions in Sport*. Champaign, Ill.: Human Kinetics, 1984.

Freischlag, Jerry, and Charles Schmidtke. "Violence in Sports: Its Causes and Some Solutions." *The Physical Educator* 36 (December 1979), 182–185.

Gair, Chris, and William J. Baker. "The Manhood Game: American Football in Critical Perspective." *The South Atlantic Quarterly* 82 (Spring 1983), 145–153.

Gardner, Paul. *Nice Guys Finish Last: Sport and American Life.* London: Alan Lane-Penguin, 1975.

Geadelmann, Patricia L. "Physical Education: Stronghold of Sex Role Stereotyping." *Quest* 32, no. 2 (1980), 192–200.

Gilbert, Bil, and Lisa Twyman. "Violence: Out of Hand in the Stands." In *Sport in Contemporary Society,* ed. D. Stanley Eitzen. New York: St. Martin's, 1984, pp. 112–118.

Greenberg, Jerald, Melvin M. Mark, and Darrin R. Lehman. "Justice in Sports and Games." *Journal of Sport Behavior* 8 (March 1985), 18–33.

Greenspan, Emily. *Little Winners: Inside the World of the Child Sports Star.* Boston: Little, Brown, 1983.

Grundman, Adolph H. "The Image of Intercollegiate Sports and the Civil Rights Movement: An Historian's View." *ARENA Review* 3 (October 1979), 17–24.

Halberstam, David. *The Amateurs: The Story of Four Young Men and Their Quest for an Olympic Gold Medal.* New York: William Morrow, 1985.

Hanford, George H. *An Inquiry into the Need for and Feasibility of a National Study of Intercollegiate Athletics: A Report to the American Council on Education.* Washington: American Council on Education, 1974.

Harris, Janet C., et al. "Ethical Behavior and Victory in Sport: Value Systems at Play." *JOPERD* 53 (April 1982), 37, 98–99.

Horrocks, Robert. "Sportsmanship/Moral Reasoning." *The Physical Educator* 37 (December 1980), 208–213.

Hult, Joan S. "The Philosophical Conflicts in Men's and Women's Collegiate Athletics." *Quest* 32, no. 1 (1980), 77–94.

Johnson, William. "Steroids: A Problem of Huge Dimensions." *Sports Illustrated* 62 (13 May 1985), 38–42, 44, 49–50, 52, 54, 56, 61.

———. "You Ain't Seen Nothin' Yet." 2-part series. *Sports Illustrated* 55 (10 August 1981), 48ff; (17 August 1981), 26ff.

Kennedy, Ray, and Nancy Williamson. "Money: The Monster Threatening Sports?" 3-part series. *Sports Illustrated* 49 (17 July 1978), 28ff; (24 July 1978), 34ff; (31 July 1978), 34ff.

Kretchmar, R. Scott. "Ethics and Sport: An Overview." *Journal of the Philosophy of Sport* 10 (1983), 21–32.

Kutcher, Louis. "The American Sport Event as Carnival: An Emergent Norm Approach to Crowd Behavior." *Journal of Popular Culture* 16 (Spring 1983), 34–41.

Leach, B. E., and B. Conners. "Pygmalion on the Gridiron: The Black Student-Athlete in a White University." *New Directions for Student Services,* no. 28 (1984), 31–49.

Martens, Rainer. *Joy and Sadness in Children's Sports.* Champaign, Ill.: Human Kinetics, 1978.

Massengale, John D. "The Americanization of School Sports: Historical and Social Consequences." *The Physical Educator* 36 (May 1979), 56–69.

Meakin, Derek C. "Moral Values and Physical Education." *Physical Education Review* 5 (Spring 1982), 62–82.

Mechikoff, Robert A. "The Olympic Games: Sport as International Politics." *JOPERD* 55 (March 1984), 23–25, 30.

Miller, Donna Mae. "Ethics in Sport: Paradoxes, Perplexities and a Proposal." *Quest* 32, no. 1 (1980), 3–7.

Miller, Geoffrey. *Behind the Olympic Rings.* Lynn, Mass.: H. O. Zimman, 1979.

Mudra, Darrell. "A Humanist Looks at Coaching." *JOPERD* 51 (October 1980), 22–25.

Nikou, Nick, and Bob Dinardo. "Academics Versus Athletics: Are the Pressures Too Great?" *JOPERD* 56 (October 1985), 72–73.

Nixon, Howard L. "The Commercial and Organizational Development of Modern Sport." *International Review of Sport Sociology* 9, no. 2 (1974), 107–131.

Overman, Steven J. "Exercising for Dollars." *JOPERD* 54 (October 1983), 68, 74. On using physical activities as fund-raisers. Letters in response, *JOPERD* 55 (January 1984), 11.

"A Plan for Cleaning Up College Sports." *Sports Illustrated* 63 (30 September 1985), 36–37.

Powers, Ron. *Supertube: The Rise of Television Sports.* New York: Coward McCann, 1984.

Rader, Benjamin G. *In Its Own Image: How Television Has Transformed Sports.* New York: Free Press, 1984.

Randall, Lynda E. "A Code of Ethics for Physical Education: Do We Need It?" *Proceedings, National Association for Physical Education in Higher Education Annual Conference* 4 (1983), 77–83.

Sabock, Ralph J. *The Coach.* 3d ed. Champaign, Ill.: Human Kinetics, 1985.

Savage, Howard J. *American College Athletics,* Bulletin 23. New York: Carnegie Foundation for Advancement of Teaching, 1929. Microcard.

"Shame of College Sports, The." *Newsweek,* 22 September 1980, pp. 54ff.

Shea, Edward J. *Ethical Decisions in Physical Education and Sport.* Champaign, Ill.: Charles C Thomas, 1978.

Smith, N. J., R. E. Smith, and F. L. Smoll. *Kidsports: A Survival Guide for Parents.* Reading, Mass.: Addison-Wesley, 1983.

Sojka, Gregory S. "Evolution of the Student Athlete in America." *Journal of Popular Culture* 16 (Spring 1983), 54–67.

"Sports Gambling: Special Report." *Sports Illustrated* 64 (10 March 1986), 30ff.

"Sports: How Dirty a Game?" Forum in *Harper's* 271 (September 1985), 45–56.

"Sports Participation as a Builder of Character." 3 articles in *Sport in Contemporary Society,* ed. D. Stanley Eitzen. New York: St. Martin's, 1984, pp. 167–192.

Stein, Harry. *Ethics (and Other Liabilities): Trying to Live Right in an Amoral World.* New York: St. Martin's, 1982.

Stoll, Sharon K. "What Is Ethical and What Is Not: A Philosophical Stance for The Physical Educator of the 80s." *The Physical Educator* 39 (December 1982), 181–184.

Strenk, Andrew. "What Price Victory? The World of International Sports and Politics." *Annals of the American Academy of Political and Social Science* 445 (September 1979), 116–127.

Sweet, Judith M. "Intercollegiate Athletics: More Than a Game." *Proceedings, National Association for Physical Education in Higher Education Annual Conference* 2 (1980), 98–107.

Tait, Robin. *The Politicization of the Modern Olympic Games.* Ph.D. dissertation, University of Oregon, 1984. Microfiche.

Templin, Thomas J., and Maria T. Allison. "The Sportsmanship Dilemma." *The Physical Educator* 39 (December 1982), 204–207.

Thomas, Carolyn E. "Ethical Considerations." In *Sport in a Philosophic Context.* Philadelphia: Lea & Febiger, 1983, pp. 170–210.

———. "Thoughts on the Moral Relationship of Intent and Training in Sport." *Journal of the Philosophy of Sport* 10 (1983), 84–91.

Todd, Terry. "The Steroid Predicament." *Sports Illustrated* 59 (1 August 1983), 62–66, 68–71, 73–75, 77.

Tutko, Thomas, and William Bruns. *Winning is Everything, and Other American Myths.* New York: Macmillan, 1976.

Underwood, John. *The Death of an American Game: The Crisis in Football.* Boston: Little, Brown, 1979.

———. "A Game Plan for America." *Sports Illustrated* 54 (23 February 1981), 64ff.

———. "The Shame of American Education: The Student-Athlete Hoax." *Sports Illustrated* 54 (19 May 1981), 36ff.

———. *Spoiled Sport: A Fan's Notes on the Troubles of Spectator Sports.* Boston: Little, Brown, 1984.

VanDyke, Roger. "Aggression in Sport: Its Implications for Character Building." *Quest* 32, no. 2 (1980), 201–208.

Wandzilak, Thomas. "Values Development Through Physical Education and Athletics." *Quest* 37, no. 2 (1985), 176–185.

Wendt, Janice C., and John M. Carley. "Resistance to Title IX in Physical Education: Legal, Institutional, and Individual." *JOPERD* 54 (September 1983), 59–62.

Zeigler, Earle F. "Application of a Scientific Ethics Approach to Sport Decisions." *Quest* 32, no. 1 (1980), 8–21.

———. *Ethics and Morality in Sport and Physical Education: An Experiential Approach.* Champaign, Ill.: Stipes Publishing, 1984.

See also the following books listed in the Resource Readings at the end of the book:

Baker; Baker and Carroll; Cashman and McKernan; Coakley; Hargreaves; Horrow; Keating; Koppett; Laforse and Drake; Lipsky; Lipsyte; Lucas; Lucas and Smith; McIntosh; Mandell; Michener; Murray; Nixon; Novak; Rader; Underwood; and Weiss.

The Scientific Discipline Bases of Physical Education and Sport

chapter 9

The Social Sciences of Physical Education and Sport

STUDYING PHYSICAL EDUCATION AND SPORT IN THE SOCIAL SCIENCES

Physical education and sport studies have been traditionally associated with studies in the physical and biological sciences, but in recent years, increasing attention has been paid to the potential of sport or human performance research in the social sciences. We can simplify the distinction between the physical and biological sciences and the social sciences by looking at the former as concerned basically with physical phenomena, while the latter are concerned with social phenomena. The most commonly understood social sciences in sport studies are psychology, sociology, and history. As we have already discussed sport history in depth, now we shall look briefly at the study of sociology and psychology in sport and human performance to give a clearer idea of the focus and method of both in sport studies. We shall also look at motor learning, which has branched from psychology yet also includes aspects of the physical and biological sciences.

SPORT SOCIOLOGY

What Is the Focus of Interest?

Sport sociology is concerned with the social behavior of people in the sport setting, both individual and group behavior.

This broad area is sometimes described as studying the sociocultural processes and institutions as they relate to and are affected by sport and sporting behavior. Sport is a significant part of our social order. It is often described as a "microcosm of society," that is, a small-scale model of what the whole society is like. The sport sociologist studies how people interact with each other in a sport setting to determine how the process of sport affects their development and socialization, or how people fit into society.

How Did It Develop?

Sport sociology is largely a recent area of sport research, though a few of its scholarly works go back to the early years of this century. Examples are H. Steinitzer's *Sport and Culture* (1910), H. Risse's *Sociology of Sport* (1921), Johan Huizinga's *Homo Ludens* (1938), and Roger Caillois's *Man, Play, and Games* (1958). The International Council for Sport and Physical Education (ICSPE) formed an International Committee for the Sociology of Sport (ICSS) in 1964. John Loy traces early suggestions for sport sociology as a subdiscipline to E. Popplow (1951) and H. Plessner (1952) in Europe,[1] while in the United States recommendations were made by Gerald Kenyon and John Loy in 1965,[2] with more specific definitions of the subject area made by Loy in 1968.[3]

Indeed, sport sociology was one of the first of the sporting disciplines or subdisciplines to develop its own scholarly organizations and publications apart from the usual small groups of physical educators that operate within larger general conventions. The first international and regional meetings had begun by the late 1960s, with a variety of scholarly publications appearing during the 1970s. Even so, in 1980 Loy described the field as being short of what he calls "critical mass," not yet having enough specialists to investigate a wide range of concerns and integrate sport sociology strongly into either physical education or sport sociology as a critical part of the academic structure.[4]

What Are the Major Topics of Study?

Two aspects of society are studied by sport sociologists: social institutions, such as schools or other organizations, and social processes, such as the development of social status or prestige within a group or community. At the same time, the important part that sport plays in the schools and in the community as children grow up requires that we learn as much as we can about how sport affects the social aspects of the growing process. Only with such knowledge in hand can sport be used in the most beneficial way in helping children to grow into healthy, socially useful adults.

Areas of research in sport sociology include sport and social institutions (such as schools and politics), social stratification (how people fit into social classes or are classified socially by others), and socialization (how people or groups interact and are affected by each other). Among the many subtopics that are studied in relation to individuals and groups in sport are sexual differences and roles, racism, religion, values and ethics, economics, politics, leisure and work habits, ethnic groups, and social change.

Small-group concerns include such topics as interactions among people and subgroups, leadership, socialization, and such traits as delinquency and aggression, social mobility, the relationship of morale and self-concept to success, the development of character, and similar aspects of social development. At the same time, sport socialists are concerned with developing better theories defining and explaining sport and its effects in society, along with the improvement of research techniques used in the field.

As an example of areas of research interest, we can look at the seven topics suggested by Martha Wilkerson and Richard Dodder as functions of sport in society:[5]

1. An emotional release (in a socially acceptable way)
2. The affirmation of identity (develop a sense of personal identity)
3. Social control (develop conformity and predictability)
4. Socialization (establish common values and acceptable behaviors)
5. A change agent (social interactions, assimilation, upward mobility)
6. A collective conscience (to enforce patterns of proper behavior)
7. Success (a way to attain success through participation or spectating)

They pointed out that these functions can become negative as well as positive.

What Is the Method of Research?

Social aspects of life are difficult to research, for they provide little truly objective data. Group and individual behavior are studied by using sources such as interviews, official statistics (which often are based on subjective judgments), library and archival research, questionnaires, surveys, documents, direct observation, and controlled experimentation.[6] Such sources are rarely objective, however, since they require the opinion of an individual or group to determine a status or change. As a result, sociological research results often are considered controversial.

What Are the Research Outlets and Sources of Information?

The International Committee of Sport Sociology (ICSS) has regular international sport sociology seminars. Professional groups that have some sport sociology research presented at their conventions include the North American Society for the Sociology of Sport (NASSS), the Sport Sociology Academy in the National Association for Sport and Physical Education (NASPE) area of AAHPERD, the American Sociological Association, the American Anthropological Association, the Association for the Anthropological Study of Play, the North American Society for Sport History (NASSH), and the Popular Culture Association.

Publications that include sport sociology research include the *International Review of Sport Sociology*, the *Review of Sport and Leisure*, the *Journal of Sport and Social Issues*, the *Canadian Journal of Applied Sport Sciences*, *Leisure Sciences*, the *Journal of Sport Behavior*, and the *Journal of Leisure Research*. Some sport history meetings and periodicals publish studies that can be termed sport sociology, since areas of sociology may be studied in their historical context such as whether sports participation was widely used in blending early immigrant groups into the existing communities in the United States. Some sport sociology studies may also be found in meetings and publications relating to sport psychology, sport philosophy, and popular culture.

SPORT PSYCHOLOGY

What Is the Focus of Interest?

Sport psychology is concerned with studying human behavior in the sport setting. In the realm of sport studies, psychology is often studied in two aspects: motor skill learning and performance, which is common to both physical education and sport, and sport psychology. A broader term, motor behavior, may also be used. The study is concerned with the psychological factors affecting the learning and performance of physical skills and with how individuals are affected by both internal and external factors.

It includes studying how people learn physical skills (motor learning), and it also includes studying the effects of different stimuli on the performance of

Coaches use sport psychology in helping athletes to prepare for high-level competition and deal with the stress that they face on those occasions. (Courtesy *Raleigh News and Observer.* Photo by Thomas Green)

those skills (sport psychology). It studies the effect on performance of such factors as motivation, arousal, anxiety, personality, and social and other factors.

Sport psychology is a field that has received much attention in the 1980s. In the last few years, psychologists in the Western world have become increasingly active in working with athletes and teams, but in the Eastern European socialist countries sport psychology clearly has been present in the preparation of high-level athletes. This is the direction of the future. Coaches, teachers, and parents are becoming more concerned not only about preparing athletes for highly skilled performance but also about protecting the emotional and psychological health of athletes, for the psychological stress level of elite sport is high.

How Did It Develop?

Dean Ryan wrote an overview of the development of sport psychology,[7] noting that among the earliest works in sport psychology were two books by Coleman R. Griffith, *Psychology of Coaching* (1926) and *Psychology and Athletics* (1928). Clarence Ragsdale published an early work, *The Psychology of Motor Learning* (1930), and John Lawther published *The Psychology of Coaching* in 1951. Even so, sport psychology was relatively new territory when large-scale interest began to develop in the 1960s.

The International Society of Sports Psychology was organized at the First International Congress of Psychology of Sport in Rome in 1965, while the North American Society for the Psychology of Sport and Physical Activity (NASPSPA) was founded in 1966, with Arthur Slater-Hammel as its first president. When the idea of discipline-centered academies to promote scholarship appeared in the early 1970s, the Sport Psychology Academy was begun in 1975, with the related Motor Development Academy following in 1979. Both are branches of psychology, and both have specialists within AAHPERD, the professional arm of physical education.

What Are the Major Topics of Study?

Sport psychology studies such issues as the nature of motor skill, performance, and learning, and the psychological characteristics of the performer. The factors that are studied include those affecting physical performance such as motivation, the distribution of practice, and the principle of specificity. Other topics have already been mentioned in defining the field. The difference in those factors in the teaching situation and the coaching situation is primarily one of the level of skill and intensity of the performer, as the basic factors and principles are the same.

What Is the Method of Research?

Some sport psychologists are debating the direction to be taken in sport psychology research, particularly in methodology. Rainer Martens has called for more emphasis on "field" research, that is, research that studies performance where it takes place—on the track or playing field—rather than traditional laboratory research. In the past, most research was done with individuals or groups in a laboratory setting, a carefully monitored environment, but today surveys and field observations are being used more often. Standardized tests are used for many studies of personality. Martens notes the existence of the question of why sport psychologists spend so little time studying sport, or applied research. In response, he suggests that more theory-building work is necessary and that doing it will require more time studying sport where and as it takes place.[8] While Martens does not call for the abandonment of laboratory research, he is concerned about the lack of effect of sport psychology research on the world of sport.

> Have you not wondered why sport psychology, as we know it, has had little to no influence on the world of sport? It is not because the coaches and athletes are unreceptive to information from our field; indeed they are eager for such information. It is, unfortunately, because our insights have not been challenging, the issues studied have not been critical, and our data are not convincing to the *vital* issues in sport. Thus, experiential knowledge and common sense have been more appealing, and usually more beneficial, than knowledge from sport psychology research.[9]

Martens does note that field research can be just as erroneous as any other type of research, but says that laboratory research often is not useful in the field situation. The essential problem is the complexity of human behavior. So many factors can affect a single situation that it may be impossible to determine how to change the factors if we want to increase or decrease some element of performance.

Siedentop agrees with Martens's suggestions that the field would be the best place for research in psychology and with the idea that new theories would be more likely to develop from field research that is concerned with applied problems.[10] However, Siedentop does not agree with all of Martens's ideas. He notes that "sport psychology will become more accepted in the 'field' if it adopts a more client-centered approach."[11] Sport psychologists are beginning to react to this call for more applied research into the actual sporting practice instead of lab experiments that often bear little fruit in the field.

Much work remains to be done by sport psychologists in terms of field and laboratory research; actual work with coaches, athletes, and teams; the monitoring of programs such as youth sports; and interpreting and teaching what we have learned to the teachers and coaches of the future.

What Are the Research Outlets and Sources of Information?

While articles relating to sport psychology may be found frequently in the *Research Quarterly for Exercise and Sport* and occasionally in *Quest*, the primary scholarly publications are the *International Journal of Psychology of Sport*, the *Journal of Sport Psychology* (begun in 1979), *Medicine and Science in Sports*, the *Journal of Motor Behavior*, and *Perceptual and Motor Skills*.

MOTOR DEVELOPMENT AND MOTOR LEARNING

What Is the Focus of Interest?

Motor development and learning are concerned with the development of a person's physical skills and performance. It can be studied in two aspects. *Motor development* is concerned with physical ability and skill improvements that are primarily a result of maturation, while *motor learning* is concerned with improvements that can be attributed primarily to practice and experience.

How Did They Develop?

While motor development and motor learning branched from the field of psychology, they have developed into specialties of their own. As Siedentop notes, "much of the early [research] was dominated by practical investigations....[Since 1960], however, there has been much more theory-oriented research and gradual acceptance of an information-processing view of motor skill acquisition and performance."[12] Teachers were concerned with the most effective methods for teaching physical skills, so most of their earlier research tested specific methods or schemes of teaching. Gradually, researchers began to work more toward formulating and testing theories of motor development and motor learning.

The field of motor behavior, motor development, and motor learning is a broad one, with a long historical background in the field of psychology through its early interest in learning (not necessarily of physical skills). We are concerned primarily with physical skills, particularly those in the sporting situation.

What Are the Major Topics of Study?

George Colfer et al. gives examples of the topics that are included in the study of motor development and motor learning.[13] Under motor development, the following topics are included:

1. Heredity versus environmental influences in motor development—This is the physical skill version of the traditional "nature or nurture" question. What is the influence of heredity on motor development, and what is the effect of the environment surrounding the learner?
2. Relationships between age and sex and motor performance—How does the expected motor performance level differ from one age or sex to another?
3. Fundamental motor skill development—Through what stages do people pass when learning a given physical skill?
4. Perceptual-motor development—How does the coordination of a person develop, and what effect does coordination have on learning in other areas?
5. Intelligence and motor performance—Does the level of intelligence affect

the speed of learning physical skills? Can the learning of physical skills raise a person's intelligence level?

6. Cognitive processes and motor performance—How does a person process information when learning physical skills? How much information can be processed?

7. Physical fitness and children—How does the fitness level of children differ from that of adults? Do exercise programs help children?

8. Youth sports development—What are the effects of youth sports programs on children? At what age are specific organized sports appropriate for children?

Under motor learning, the following topics are studied:

1. The stages of learning—What are the steps and characteristics of the different stages of learning physical skills?

2. Memory and motor performance—What is the effect of memory on the learning of physical skills?

3. Motor control—How is the performance of physical skills controlled by the human body?

4. Knowledge of results—What is the most effective way to use knowledge of results in teaching physical skills?

5. Practice conditions—What are the most effective conditions for practicing physical skills?

What Is the Method of Research?

Research in motor learning is becoming increasingly complex. Antoinette Gentile, in an overview of significant research over the decade of the 1970s, noted that the experimental tradition in motor learning in 1970 was still that of experimental psychology. By 1980, however, as more sharply focused theories and research topics appeared, experiments were based more on the methods of behavioral neurophysiology.[14]

What Are the Research Outlets and Sources of Information?

Professional organizations that are concerned with motor development and motor learning include the Motor Development Academy of NASPE, a part of AAHPERD, and the North American Society for the Psychology of Sport and Physical Activity (NASPSPA). Publications that use research in the field include the *Research Quarterly for Exercise and Sport*, published by AAHPERD; the *Journal of Human Movement Studies*, published quarterly in England; the *Journal of Motor Behavior*; *Motor Skills: Theory Into Practice*; and *Perceptual and Motor Skills*. In addition, periodicals listed in sport psychology and, in some cases, pedagogy may produce some scholarly research in the field.

Now that we have taken a brief look at some of the social sciences of sport and human performance, we need to look at two disciplines in the biological and physical sciences: exercise physiology and biomechanics.

NOTES

1. John W. Loy, et al., "The Emergence and Development of the Sociology of Sport as an Academic Specialty," *Research Quarterly for Exercise and Sport* 51 (March 1980), 91–109.
2. Gerald S. Kenyon and John W. Loy, "Toward a Sociology of Sport," *JOHPER* 36 (1965), 24–25, 68–69.
3. John W. Loy, "The Nature of Sport: A Definitional Effort," *Quest* 10 (1968), 1–15.
4. Loy, et al., "The Emergence...of the Sociology of Sport," 98–101.
5. Martha Wilkerson and Richard A. Dodder, "What Does Sports Do for People?" *JOPER* 50 (February 1979), 50–51.
6. Harold J. VanderZwaag and Thomas J. Sheehan, *Introduction to Sport Studies*, Wm. C. Brown, Dubuque, Iowa, 1978, pp. 175–176.
7. E. Dean Ryan, "The Emergence of Psychological Research as Related to Performance in Physical Activity," in *Perspectives on the Academic Discipline of Physical Education*, ed. George A. Brooks, Human Kinetics, Champaign, Ill., 1981, pp. 327–341.
8. Rainer Martens, "About Smocks and Jocks," *Journal of Sport Psychology* 1 (1979), 94–99.
9. Ibid., 95.
10. Daryl Siedentop, "Two Cheers for Rainer," *Journal of Sport Psychology* 2 (1980), 24.
11. Ibid., 2.
12. Daryl Siedentop, *Physical Education: Introductory Analysis*, 3d ed., Wm. C. Brown, Dubuque, 1980, p. 112.
13. George R. Colfer et al., *Contemporary Physical Education*, Wm. C. Brown, Dubuque, Iowa, 1986, pp. 99, 102.
14. A. M. Gentile, "Most Significant Research of the Past Decade: Motor Learning and Control," *The Academy Papers*, no. 16 (1982), 29–39.

SUGGESTED READINGS

Bird, D. M., and D. Ross. "Current Methodological Problems and Future Directions for Theory Development in the Psychology of Sport and Motor Behavior." *Quest* 36, no. 1 (1984), 1–6.

Coakley, Jay J. *Sport in Society: Issues and Controversies*. 3d ed. St. Louis: C. V. Mosby, 1986.

Curry, Timothy J., and Robert M. Jiobu. *Sports: A Social Perspective*. Englewood Cliffs, N.J.: Prentice-Hall, 1984.

Edwards, Steven W., and Shelley A. Huston. "The Clinical Aspects of Sport Psychology." *The Physical Educator* 41 (October 1984), 142–148.

Eitzen, D. Stanley, and George H. Sage. *Sociology of North American Sport*. 3d ed. Dubuque, Iowa: Wm. C. Brown, 1986.

"The Games of Summer: Playing to Win in Politics and Sports." *Psychology Today* 18 (July 1984), 18–44. Five articles on sport psychology.

Gentile, A. M. "Most Significant Research of the Past Decade: Motor Learning and Control." *The Academy Papers*, no. 16 (1982), 29–39.

Greendorfer, Susan L. "A Challenge for Sociocultural Sport Studies." *JOPERD* 54 (March 1983), 18–20.

———. "Emergence of and Future Prospects for Sociology of Sport." In *Perspectives on the Academic Discipline of Physical Education*. Ed. George A. Brooks. Champaign, Ill.: Human Kinetics, 1981, pp. 379–398.

Gruber, Joseph J. "Most Significant Research of the Past Decade: Physical Activity and Emotional Health." *The Academy Papers*, no. 16 (1982), 49–58.

Harris, Janet C., and Roberta J. Park, eds. *Play, Games, and Sports in Cultural Context.* Champaign, Ill.: Human Kinetics, 1983.

Hatfield, B. D., and D. M. Landers. "Psychophysiology—A New Direction for Sport Physiology." *Journal of Sport Psychology* 5, no. 3 (1983), 243–259.

Heyman, S. R. "The Development of Models for Sport Psychology: Examining the USOC Model." *Journal of Sport Psychology* 6, no. 2 (1984), 125–132.

Hollands, R. G. "The Role of Cultural Studies and Social Criticism in the Sociological Study of Sport." *Quest* 36, no. 1 (1984), 66–79.

Kiester, Edwin, Jr. "The Playing Fields of the Mind." *Psychology Today* 18 (July 1984), 18–24.

Kleinman, Matthew. *The Acquisition of Motor Skill.* Princeton, N.J.: Princeton Book Co., 1983.

Leonard, Wilbert Marcellus, II. *A Sociological Perspective of Sport.* 2d ed. Minneapolis: Burgess, 1984.

Loy, John W., et al. "The Emergence and Development of the Sociology of Sport as an Academic Specialty." *Research Quarterly for Exercise and Sport* 51 (March 1980), 91–109.

Luschen, Gunther, and George Sage, eds. *Handbook of Social Science of Sport.* Champaign, Ill.: Stipes Publishing, 1981.

Mechikoff, Robert A., and Bill Kozar, eds. *Sport Psychology: The Coach's Perspective.* Springfield, Ill.: Charles C Thomas, 1983.

Morgan, William P. "Physical Activity and Mental Health." *The Academy Papers*, no. 17 (1983), 132–145.

———. "Selected Psychological Factors Limiting Performance." *The Academy Papers*, no. 18 (1984), 70–80.

Nixon, Howard L., II. *Sport and the American Dream.* Champaign, Ill.: Leisure Press, 1984.

Oglesby, Carole A., ed. *Women and Sport: From Myth to Reality.* Philadelphia: Lea & Febiger, 1978.

Oxendine, Joseph B. *Psychology of Motor Learning.* 2d ed. Englewood Cliffs, N.J.: Prentice-Hall, 1984.

Rarick, G. Lawrence. "Most Significant Research of the Past Decade: Motor Development." *The Academy Papers*, no. 16 (1982), 40–44.

Sage, George H. *Motor Learning and Control: A Neuropsychological Approach.* Dubuque, Iowa: Wm. C. Brown, 1984.

———. "Sociocultural Aspects of Physical Activity: Significant Research Traditions, 1972–1982." *The Academy Papers*, no. 16 (1982), 59–66.

Schmidt, Richard A. *Motor Control and Learning: A Behavioral Emphasis.* Champaign, Ill.: Human Kinetics, 1982.

———. "Past and Future Issues in Motor Programming." *Research Quarterly for Exercise and Sport* 51 (March 1980), 122–140.

Silva, John M., III, and Robert S. Weinberg, eds. *Psychological Foundations of Sport.* Champaign, Ill.: Human Kinetics, 1984.

Singer, Robert N. *The Learning of Motor Skills.* New York: Macmillan, 1982.

Stallings, Loretta M. *Motor Learning: From Theory to Practice.* St. Louis: C. V. Mosby, 1982.

Suinn, Richard M. "The 1984 Olympics and Sport Psychology." *Journal of Sport Psychology* 7 (December 1985), 321–329.

——. *Seven Steps to Peak Performance.* Toronto: Hans Huber, 1986.

Umphlett, Wiley Lee, ed. *American Sport Culture: The Humanistic Dimensions.* Lewisburg, Penn.: Bucknell University Press, 1985.

Widmeyer, W. Neil. *Physical Activity and the Social Sciences.* 5th ed. Ithaca, N.Y.: Mouvement Publications, 1983.

Williams, Harriet G. *Perceptual and Motor Development.* Englewood Cliffs, N.J.: Prentice-Hall, 1983.

See also the following books in the Resource Readings:

Ball and Loy; Caillois; Coakley; Eitzen and Sage; Huizinga; Loy and Kenyon; Loy, McPherson, and Kenyon; Luschen; Michener; Snyder and Spreitzer.

chapter 10

The Biological and Physical Sciences

EXERCISE PHYSIOLOGY

What Is the Focus of Interest?

Exercise physiology is concerned with how the body reacts to and functions during exercise. The effects of training are a critical facet of exercise physiology research, which makes it perhaps the most important of the sport studies, for it is concerned with all aspects of how the body adapts to exercise. This includes such concerns as the function and contraction of the muscles, the workings of the nervous system during physical activity, the functions of the respiratory system, and the working of the cardiovascular system.

At the same time, this area of study is often considered to include sports medicine, an equally important and growing area of study. Sports medicine is concerned with both treating and preventing athletic injuries. In turn, this broad interest in the health of the physically active body also can include adapted physical education, or developmental activities for the physically or mentally handicapped or disabled. The sports medicine specialist is concerned with preventive training, treatment, and equipment that assist the performer in staying healthy; nutrition; drugs and ergogenic aids; the treatment and rehabilitation of injuries; and ethical matters related to the training, exercise, and treatment of athletes.

How Did the Field Develop?

Exercise physiology is one of the oldest areas of research in physical education. A major early researcher was A. V. Hill, whose influential work included the book *Muscular Activity* (1925). While the first exercise physiology laboratory seems to have begun at Harvard University in 1892 under the direction of George Fitz, M.D., it lasted only a short while and was quickly forgotten by physical educators.[1] Much of the early research in the United States was done at the later Harvard Fatigue Laboratory, which was started in 1927, soon after Hill's book appeared, and continued its work for almost 20 years. Early American textbooks in the area included those by J. J. McCurdy (1928) and Peter V. Karpovich (1933).

The last two decades have seen a surge of interest in exercise physiology. It has been one of the fastest-growing areas of concentration for graduate studies in physical education, with perhaps the most advertised job opportunities of any area of the field during the mid-1980s. Opportunities for trained exercise physiologists expanded beyond the university to the private sector, with positions in corporations and fitness facilities that were concerned with occupational health. While the corporate interest grew in the 1970s with an emphasis on executive health and fitness, by the 1980s companies were expanding their interest to their employees at all levels. This surge of interest from companies was a result of a leap in the cost of health insurance, with the belated recognition from the companies that employees who are healthier are more productive and cost less in health benefits.

What Are the Major Topics of Study?

Sport physiologists are interested in topics such as muscular functions, the nervous system and its operation, respiratory function, cardiovascular function, muscular strength and endurance, cardiovascular endurance, the effects of exercise, defining and measuring physical fitness, the development of fitness, the physiology of performance, and the effects of ergogenic aids (drugs and hormones) on the body and its development and performance. John Faulkner and Timothy White listed nine topics (which can overlap) as current areas of research emphasis in 1981:[2]

1. Substrate utilization during exercise
2. Kinetics of oxygen uptake
3. Anaerobic threshold
4. Efficiency of physical exercise
5. Factors limiting performance
6. Environmental influences on performance
7. Mechanisms of muscular weakness and fatigue
8. Physiological adaptations to conditioning programs
9. Role of endurance conditioning in the prevention of and rehabilitation from disease

They also suggested that too few specialists have addressed their research to major topics of concern, theorizing that, at least in part, it is because many sport physiologists did not receive as strong a background in the sciences as did the researchers who were major students in anatomy, biology, chemistry, or physiology.

What Is the Method of Research?

The sport physiologist conducts research studies in a physiology laboratory, using such equipment as treadmills, exercise bicycles, oxygen-measuring equipment, and equipment that measures chemical characteristics of the body. Computerized monitoring and measuring equipment is developing rapidly, requiring some understanding of the developing technology in that area also. The sport physiologist works basically in areas related to chemistry. Most of the sport physiologist's work takes place in the laboratory, but an increasing amount of research is being done "in the field," testing athletes where and when they perform. The importance of the research of the physiologist is great, for such work cuts to the heart of the training system;

Exercise physiologists conduct research studies in laboratories, using treadmills, oxygen-measuring equipment, and computerized monitoring and measuring equipment. (Courtesy Erik Palmer/Miller High Life News Bureau)

unless an athlete is trained to a fine edge and to the highest level, good mechanics and well-planned psychological preparation will not be enough to result in high-level performances.

What Are the Research Outlets and Sources of Information?

Groups interested in the study of sport physiology include the Exercise Physiology Academy of AAHPERD, which encourages scholarly study among the professional membership; the American College of Sports Medicine (ACSM), which encourages and publishes research in that area; and the National Athletic Trainer's Association (NATA), which encourages study in that area. The American Medical Association has a Committee on the Medical Aspects of Sports that actively works with physicians and keeps them informed of matters relating to sports problems, injury, and treatment. The work of this committee has become especially important because of the great increase in participation in competitive sports and the related rise in sports injuries, many of which are treated by doctors who normally do not work with sports injuries.

Publications in the field include the *Research Quarterly for Exercise and Sport* published by AAHPERD; the *Journal of Applied Physiology,* the journal *Medicine and Science in Sports* published by the ACSM, *The Physician and Sportsmedicine, The Encyclopedia of Sport Sciences and Medicine* also published by the ACSM, *The Exercise and Sports Sciences Reviews,* and *Physiological Reviews.* Different groups interested in sports physiology hold many national and international conferences on the subject each year.

The future of sport physiology will probably include more coordinated studies with coaches that are designed to learn how to determine and properly monitor optimal training levels in exercise programs. These studies will use testing of the cardiorespiratory system and of blood chemistry. Much work in this area has already been done in East Germany and the Soviet Union.

Currently, sport physiologists are conducting much research in prevention of athletic injuries and in development of better programs to prepare people for exercise programs and help them recover swiftly from injuries. At the same time, work is also being done to prepare more athletic trainers and to educate more doctors in sports medicine so that prevention and treatment will be raised to a higher level in the United States.

In addition, sport physiologists are doing work in areas related to the needs of the physically handicapped. This work includes the development of rehabilitation methods and programs and the development of more "normal" programs of physical education and sport for the handicapped. The impetus that federal regulations provided (e.g., Public Law 94-142) that require the mainstreaming of handicapped individuals into nonhandicapped programs has resulted in far more attention and money for this area than at any time in the past.

Exercise physiologists, medical workers, and physical therapists now develop programs to use in helping people with heart problems. (Courtesy DUPAC, Duke University Preventive Approach to Cardiology)

BIOMECHANICS

What Is the Focus of Interest?

Biomechanics is concerned with the effects of natural law and forces on the body in sport. It has developed from the field of kinesiology, which is also a study of movement. Kinesiology has two basic areas: anatomical kinesiology, which is concerned with the construction and working mechanisms of the body, and mechanical kinesiology, which is biomechanics or the mechanics of the human body. Anne Atwater suggested that kinesiology is more properly an interdisciplinary area of study, covering facets of anatomy, biomechanics, and physiology.[3] In sum, sport biomechanics is the study of the human body and how the laws of physics apply to it. We still find some controversy over the exact distinction (if any) between kinesiology and biomechanics.

How Did the Field Develop?

Studies of kinesiology can be seen from the 1800s, when the first cameras were developed that could photograph a moving object ("freeze" it in time, essentially). While Aristotle is sometimes called the father of kinesiology, motion study really began in modern times. Eadweard Muybridge first photographed moving animals such as a running horse using a series of cameras with strings to trigger each camera as the horse passed. By this method, the first examination of the actual running pattern of a horse was made in 1872. After the motion picture camera was developed, such studies could be made more easily.

One of the first major books studying human movement was Jules Amar's *The Human Motor* (1924), while writings by Nicholai Bernstein on "biomechanics" were appearing in Russian by 1926. Archibald Hill, notable for his work in exercise physiology, was also influential in this area during the 1920s. The first textbook in the United States was Arthur Steindler's *Mechanics of Normal and Pathological Locomotion in Man* (1935).[4] Textbooks, mostly titled "kinesiology," appeared in increasing numbers until the 1970s, when the "biomechanics" titles began appearing. Specialists have become better prepared in the scientific side of the field, and increasingly sophisticated research equipment (high-speed cinematography, video techniques, computer-digitized graphics, and such) are being used. Increasingly, scholars are emphasizing both basic and applied research, working to wed our knowledge to our practices.

What Are the Major Topics of Study?

Peter Cavanaugh and Richard Hinrichs, while discussing the "state of the art" of biomechanics in 1981, presented a list of topics that covered the "core elements of the discipline."[5] They included the following:

1. The measurement of motion (how to make it more accurate)
2. Errors in data collection (because moving objects are hard to measure with much accuracy)
3. Kinematic analysis (studying an object's motion independent of the force causing the motion)
4. Body segment parameters (developing more accurate estimates or measures)
5. Kinetic analysis (of both internal and external forces affecting an object's motion)
6. Modeling and simulation (to predict actual behavior)
7. The analysis of sports equipment

At the same time, they note that sport biomechanics is still, relatively speaking, in its infancy. Thus, the areas of concern are still developing, as is the technology used in conducting biomechanical research. The work requires an understanding of its relationship to the learning in other areas of specialization.

What Is the Method of Research?

Research in biomechanics breaks down into two large categories: fundamental study of the process of simple movements, and analysis of motor skills, which are far more complex and pertinent to sport skills than are simple movements. J. Ann Carr discusses seven types of research found in biomechanics. They are cinematography, stroboscopy, force platform studies, electrogoniometry, electromyography, telemetry, and computer-based studies.[6]

Cinematography uses motion picture photography to study movement. High-speed individual pictures are taken of many parts of a single continuing motion. Stroboscopy employs a similar photographic technique, except that an entire skill is captured in a single picture. A stroboscopic light flashes at preselected intervals of time during the performance. Only the positions of the body photographed during the light flashes will show up on the picture, thus providing a representative view of the entire pattern of a motion.

A force platform measures the force pushing against it, such as the amount of push a jumper uses in leaving the ground. It is used in studying the size and direction of forces, as well as their duration, and helps give a clearer idea of the variables in performances of skills such as the sprint start (by the time and amount of force exerted against the starting blocks, and when each foot pushes and stops pushing).

Electrogoniometry records changes in joint angles with electrical instruments, giving a clearer idea of the sequence and ranges of motion followed in performing a skill. Electromyography uses electrical instruments to record the work of muscles during the performance of skills. It can tell what muscles are used in a skill, what muscles only assist with the skill, and what sequence of muscles is used in performing a complex skill. Telemetry uses electrical instruments to record electrical "events" in the body, which means any physical activity that can be converted into an electrical signal such as a heartbeat. Small radio transmitters are then used to send the signal to recording instruments so that the performer can be studied while taking part in a normal performance; such methods can be used to record the activity of the heart of someone competing in a one-mile race.

Computers are being increasingly used to help analyze complex skill performance. In fact, they can now be used to simulate skill activities. The mechanical characteristics of a performer, such as a discus thrower, can be fed into a computer and displayed on a screen, along with information on the thrower's performance. The computer then can simulate or predict how far the discus would have been thrown if certain improvements in the thrower's technique had been made. This gives the performer a clearer idea of how a skill can be improved and the potential gain that might come from this improvement.

The motion analyses of biomechanics look at two aspects of motion study: kinematics and kinetics. Kinematics seeks information on the motion of the body, regardless of what causes the motion. Kinetics studies what causes the body to move the way it does. There are many other subdivisions of areas within biomechanics, such as mechanics and dynamics, and even lower subdivisions, such as fluid mechanics, but these are better discussed in a biomechanics course. Kinetics and kinematics themselves are subdivisions of dynamics, which is simply the study of motion.

What Are the Research Outlets and Sources of Information?

Many groups are concerned with sport biomechanics, and numerous meetings are held at the national and international levels to discuss research in the field. The International Society of Biomechanics (ISB) was founded in 1973, and the Olympic Scientific Congresses held before recent Olympic Games have offered an outlet for research and communication. Members of the American College of Sports Medicine (ACSM) are involved in biomechanics research. The American Society of Biomechanics first met in 1977, while within AAHPERD the discipline-oriented Kinesiology Academy is devoted to encouraging scholarship in this area.

The International Society of Biomechanics, which has a congress every two years, publishes the *International Series on Biomechanics*, with many articles from each congress. The most recent collections are *Biomechanics VIII* (2 volumes, 1983) and *Biomechanics IX* (2 volumes, 1985). The *International Journal of Sport Biomechanics (IJSB)* was begun as a quarterly in 1985. The International Series on Sports Science (ISSS) includes volumes on biomechanical topics. *The Journal of Biomechanics* has been published since 1968. *The Physician and Sportsmedicine* includes articles on biomechanics, as does the *Research Quarterly for Exercise and Sport*, a publication of AAHPERD.

The future of biomechanics should include more joint research projects, either with motor-learning specialists interested in determining how skills are learned and what the most efficient teaching procedures are, or with coaches interested in improving the technical performances of athletes through use of the scientific expertise and research capabilities of modern programs. The use of biomechanics in sport and athletics is already a conspicuous part of Eastern European athletics, with East Germany and the Soviet Union leading the way in the application of research capabilities to athletic performance.

NOTES

1. Walter P. Kroll, *Perspectives in Physical Education*, Academic Press, New York, 1971, pp. 186–199.
2. John A. Faulkner and Timothy P. White, "Current and Future Topics in Exercise Physiology," in *Perspectives on the Academic Discipline of Physical Education*, ed. George A. Brooks, Human Kinetics, Champaign, Ill., 1981, pp. 76–89.
3. Anne E. Atwater, "Kinesiology/Biomechanics: Perspectives and Trends," *Research Quarterly for Exercise and Sport* 51 (March 1980), 194.
4. Ronald F. Zernicke, "The Emergence of Human Biomechanics," in *Perspectives on the Academic Discipline of Physical Education*, ed. George A. Brooks, Human Kinetics, Champaign, Ill., 1981, pp. 124–136.
5. Peter R. Cavanaugh and Richard N. Hinrichs, "Biomechanics of Sport: The State of the Art," in *Perspectives on the Academic Discipline of Physical Education*, ed. George A. Brooks, Human Kinetics, Champaign, Ill., 1981, pp. 137–157.
6. J. Ann Carr, "The Biomechanical Perspective," in *Foundations of Physical Education: A Scientific Approach*, ed. Richard S. Rivenes, Houghton Mifflin, Boston, 1978, pp. 103–110, 125–129.

SUGGESTED READINGS

Adrian, Marlene J. "Biomechanics: Theory into Practice." *Proceedings, National Association for Physical Education in Higher Education Annual Conference* 4 (1983), 38–50.

Borer, Katarina T., et. al. *Frontiers of Exercise Biology.* Champaign, Ill.: Human Kinetics, 1983.

Brancazio, Peter J. *SportScience.* New York: Simon & Schuster, 1984.

Buskirk, Elsworth R. "The Emergence of Exercise Physiology in Physical Education." In *Perspectives on the Academic Discipline of Physical Education*, ed. George A. Brooks. Champaign, Ill.: Human Kinetics, 1981, pp. 55–74.

Cavanaugh, Peter R., and Richard N. Hinrichs. "Biomechanics of Sport: The State of the Art." In *Perspectives on the Academic Discipline of Physical Education*, ed. George A. Brooks. Champaign, Ill.: Human Kinetics, 1981, pp. 137–157.

Edington, D. W. "Most Significant Research of the Past Decade: Physiology of Exercise." *The Academy Papers*, no. 16 (1982), 10–14.

"Exercise and Health." *The Academy Papers*, no. 17 (1983): entire issue.

Faulkner, John A., and Timothy P. White. "Current and Future Topics in Exercise Physiology." In *Perspectives on the Academic Discipline of Physical Education*, ed. George A. Brooks. Champaign, Ill.: Human Kinetics, 1981, pp. 75–96.

Fox, Edward L. *Sports Physiology.* 2d ed. Philadelphia: Saunders, 1984.

——, and Donald K. Mathews. *The Physiological Basis of Physical Education and Athletics.* 3d ed. Philadelphia: W. B. Saunders, 1984.

Groves, Richard, and David N. Camaione. *Concepts in Kinesiology.* 2d ed. Philadelphia: W. B. Saunders, 1983.

Hatfield, B. D., and D. M. Landers. "Psychophysiology — A New Direction for Sport Physiology." *Journal of Sport Psychology* 5, no. 3 (1983), 243–259.

Hay, James G. *The Biomechanics of Sports Techniques.* 3d ed. Englewood Cliffs, N.J.: Prentice-Hall, 1985.

——. "Most Significant Research of the Past Decade: Biomechanics." *The Academy Papers*, no. 16 (1982), 20–26.

Hinson, Marilyn M. "Applications [Biomechanics]." *The Academy Papers*, no. 16 (1982), 27–28.

Kneer, M. E., ed. *Basic Stuff Series: Kinesiology.* Reston, Va.: AAHPERD, 1981.

Kreighbaum, Ellen, and Katharine M. Barthels. *Biomechanics: A Qualitative Approach for Studying Human Movement.* 2d ed. Minneapolis: Burgess, 1985.

"Limits of Human Performance." *The Academy Papers*, no. 18 (1984): entire issue.

McArdle, William D., Frank I. Katch, and Victor L. Katch. *Exercise Physiology: Energy, Nutrition, and Human Performance.* Philadelphia: Lea & Febiger, 1986.

Moore, Kenny. "Watching Their Steps." *Sports Illustrated* 44 (3 May 1976), 80–84, 86, 89–90.

Pate, Russell R., Bruce McClenaghan, and Robert J. Rotella. *Scientific Principles of Coaching.* Philadelphia: W. B. Saunders, 1984.

Sharkey, Brian J. *Physiology of Fitness.* 2d ed. Champaign, Ill.: Human Kinetics, 1984.

Shephard, Roy J. *Biochemistry of Physical Activity.* Springfield, Ill.: Charles C Thomas, 1984.

Sinning, Wayne E. "Applications [Exercise Physiology]." *The Academy Papers*, no. 16 (1982), 15–19.

——. "Theory Into Practice: 'Update: Physiology of Exercise.'" *Proceedings, National Association for Physical Education in Higher Education Annual Conference* 4 (1983), 3–20.

Wells, Christine L. *Women, Sport and Performance*. Champaign, Ill.: Human Kinetics, 1985.

Zernicke, Ronald F. "The Emergence of Human Biomechanics." In *Perspectives on the Academic Discipline of Physical Education*, ed. George A. Brooks. Champaign, Ill.: Human Kinetics, 1981, pp. 124–136.

PART IV

WORKING IN TODAY'S WORLD

Courtesy Duke University Sports Information

chapter 11

Teaching in Physical Education and Sport: The Formal Profession

We discussed physical education both as a discipline and as a profession in Chapter 1. We now need to look more closely into some aspects of the profession of physical education so that you will understand more clearly what a profession is and what a professional does. We also shall study the different professional organizations in which physical educators are involved and the major publications that physical educators use. We shall conclude the chapter by discussing how the physical cceducation student works to develop professionally.

THE MEANING OF PROFESSIONAL

We shall use the term *professional* in its academic sense; that is, a professional is a member or practitioner of a recognized profession. In our case, the profession of physical education refers to teachers of physical education. To understand more clearly what this means, we shall review briefly our discussion of the profession from Chapter 1.

We used the six criteria or characteristics of a profession that were suggested by Abraham Flexner.[1] According to Flexner, these are the characteristics of a profession:

1. Intellectual activity (a "body of knowledge")
2. Practical use
3. Research resulting in new knowledge and ideas

4. Self-organization
5. Communication capacity (internal and external)
6. Altruism (dedication to helping others)

A profession needs to have an intellectual base. Though we may teach physical skills, an intellectual base of knowledge is required if we are to be fully effective teachers. This is a critical point, for the body of knowledge should be far broader and deeper than that possessed by a nonprofessional, such as an experienced athlete who has had no special training.

A practical use or application for knowledge must exist in a profession. It cannot be knowledge gained purely for purposes of possession; it must be knowledge that can be applied to some practical use, such as the development and improvement of people's health, skills, and fitness.

Research that results in new knowledge and ideas should be taking place in a profession. True professionals never stop trying to learn about their field, for this search for knowledge steadily increases their effectiveness.

Some formal self-organization or professional bodies should exist. These professional bodies assist in the fifth point—providing the capacity for communication—usually through professional publications and meetings.

Finally, an important characteristic of a profession is altruism. A profession exists to help others. Its members are concerned about the welfare of other people; they work to help protect or improve the lives of others.

Physical educators have argued for years whether physical education is a profession. Though time has passed since his description, we still accept Bucher's suggestion that it is still an *emerging* profession, one that is developing but has not fully arrived.[2]

An important distinction that we need to clarify is what a professional is *not*. A professional athlete does not meet the criteria for a member of a profession. Often students are confused about what a professional is because of their familiarity with the term "professional athlete." In that sense, "professional" means simply that the athlete performs for money. By that definition—lack of amateur status—every person who is employed is a "professional."

Remembering this distinction is important. A professional in the true sense is a member of a recognized profession, not simply any person willing to perform a task for money. A "roll out the ball" teacher is no more a true professional than the ordinary person on the street. A professional is trained to work *to high standards* in a field that meets the criteria presented earlier. Consequently, a true professional will have pride in his or her chosen profession.

MOVEMENT PEDAGOGY: THE DISCIPLINE SIDE OF TEACHING

Siedentop was one of the few who called for the inclusion of pedagogy in the disciplines.[3] Sport pedagogy is concerned with teaching, particularly the skills used in sporting situations. It includes teaching methods and many elements tied to the concern of the profession of physical education. The direction recommended by Siedentop is being pursued, and as he reported in 1982, "we have begun to develop a technology that someday could revolutionize the preparation of teachers and coaches in our field."[4] Ann Jewett, speaking on research progress in curricular studies, noted:

> Influence on performance has been limited to some extent by the overwhelming need for theory-building. A substantial effort has gone into the business of conceptualizing curriculum as a field of scholarly inquiry....Those who conceptualize the area [of curriculum and instruction] as pedagogy tend to include additional professional sub-areas so that pedagogy is viewed as including curriculum, instruction, supervision, and administration.[5]

Charles Corbin commented that both Siedentop and Jewett have correctly noted that the root of criticism of pedagogy as a discipline has been because of the lack of two factors—"sound research methodologies and basic theories." However, he cautions that the results of pedagogical research must be made usable by the practitioners if it is to be of true value.[6] Sport pedagogy is perhaps the least developed of our disciplines, but it has immense potential value to the field of sport studies and performance.

PROFESSIONAL ORGANIZATIONS IN PHYSICAL EDUCATION AND SPORT

Physical educators are involved in a multitude of professional organizations, the largest of which is AAHPERD. AAHPERD is a national organization dedicated to improving programs in all areas of physical education. With about 40,000 members nationally, AAHPERD represents the major voice of physical educators in the United States today. Six associations are included in the formal organization of AAHPERD; these represent the largest groups within the membership:

1. American Association for Leisure and Recreation (AALR) is concerned with promoting leisure services and recreation education at the school, community, and national levels.
2. Association for the Advancement of Health Education (AAHE) is concerned with programs of health education in the schools, communities, and colleges, as well as with health-oriented legislation.
3. Association for Research, Administration, Professional Councils and Societies (ARAPCS) might be viewed as a catch-all association of a number of smaller, more specialized interest groups, including administrators of different types of programs and persons interested in a number of areas of research in the field of physical education and sport.
4. National Association for Girls and Women in Sport (NAGWS) is concerned with women's athletics at all levels, and its work includes producing rule books and sports guides in many areas. The former inter-collegiate sports organization for women, the AIAW, grew from this association.

5. National Association for Sport and Physical Education (NASPE), the largest of the associations, is concerned with people whose primary working interest lies in the areas of physical education and sport, which are promoted at all levels.
6. National Dance Association (NDA) is concerned with the development of dance both inside and outside the educational systems of the nation.

AAHPERD works in many ways to advance the profession. It holds annual national conventions in the spring that are rotated among the six regional districts of AAHPERD. Each of the six districts also holds an annual convention, as does each state organization. These conventions provide an invaluable means of contact among physical educators of many different interests from across the country.

AAHPERD also produces many publications. In addition to regular magazines in the largest areas of interest, it produces many materials designed to assist the teacher, to clarify the work of physical educators, and to promote the areas within physical education.

All members of AAHPERD receive the newspaper *UPDATE* monthly during the school year (ten months). It gives current schedules of meetings and tentative programs of conventions, and provides a few articles of general interest to the whole profession.

The *Journal of Physical Education, Recreation and Dance (JOPERD)*, which is the most widely read physical education journal, also appears monthly during nine months of the school year. While JOPERD has less current news than *UPDATE*, it contains many timely articles on both teaching practices and theory, columns devoted to the many special interest groups within physical education, and information on new publications and products available to physical educators.

Health Education is the health educator's magazine, which appears six times yearly. It is concerned with all aspects of health education programs and practices.

Research Quarterly of Exercise and Sport is a journal devoted entirely to reports of completed research in the fields of physical education. Appearing four times annually, it is designed to stimulate and communicate research among physical educators. It has research articles in all areas of physical education, though it tends to lean heavily toward research in biomechanics, physiology, and motor skill learning.

Each member of AAHPERD receives at least two of the four publications cited. The publications serve to improve communication within the profession and also to help improve teaching practices within the field.

The American Academy of Physical Education ("the Academy") was started by a small group of prominent physical educators in 1926 to advance knowledge and raise standards in physical education and to honor physical educators who show superior accomplishments. Its members, now numbering more than 100, are elected by the other members. It is best known for its work in promoting excellence and in initiating the discussion of new ideas in physical education. It also publishes annually *The Academy Papers*, which contain papers presented by its members on matters of importance or topical interest to physical educators. It is the highest honorary group in health, physical education, and recreation.

The National Association for Physical Education in Higher Education (NAPEHE) was formed by the merger of the National College Physical Education Association for Men (NCPEAM), founded in 1897, and the National Association of Physical Education for College Women (NAPECW), which was founded in 1924 though its origins can be traced to 1909. The new association's first convention was held in Milwaukee in 1979. NAPEHE, as its name states, is concerned with physical education in the colleges.It publishes the semiannual monograph *Quest*, which is oriented toward the philosophical and social science areas of the field. It also publishes an annual *Proceedings* and a quarterly newsletter.

The American School Health Association (ASHA) was formed in 1926 by a group of physicians who were concerned about health services and instruction in the schools. Its members are people such as school nurses, who are involved in school health. It publishes the *Journal of School Health*, which appears ten times yearly.

The National Recreation and Park Association (NRPA) grew from the Playground Association of America, which was started in 1906. The association is concerned with all areas of recreation, parks, and park services.

The National Intramural Association (NIA) was founded in 1950. It is interested in promoting and expanding intramural activities and in promoting professional contacts among intramural directors. It has close ties to both AAHPERD and the NRPA, and it publishes the *Proceedings of the Annual Intramural Conference*.

The Phi Epsilon Kappa Fraternity was started in 1912. It is a national professional organization interested in promoting research and an international exchange of information in the areas of health education, physical education, recreation education, and safety education. It publishes the magazine *The Physical Educator*, which appears quarterly.

Delta Psi Kappa is a national honorary organization begun in 1916 for women professional students in health, physical education, and recreation, though it now allows male members. It works to raise professional standards and to encourage women to conduct distinguished research. It publishes *The Foil* twice each year.

The National Education Association (NEA), founded in 1857, is the nation's largest professional organization of teachers, with more than one million members. Its primary concern is promoting education in the United States while, at the same time, working for the best interests of the teachers. AAHPERD has been affiliated with the NEA. The NEA's most widely circulated publication is *Today's Education*.

There are many professional fraternities for all educators, just as there are fraternities for physical educators exclusively. A prominent example of the former is the Phi Delta Kappa educational fraternity, which works to advance educational standards and research and includes among its publications the monthly *Phi Delta Kappan.*

Many other national, regional, and local associations of teachers and coaches throughout the country are also of interest to physical educators, and just as there are many professional journals of education and physical education, there are also coaching journals and publications. Some of the publications are devoted to single sports, while others include all sports. Two of the most widely used coaching magazines are *Athletic Journal,* which has an emphasis slightly closer to the college level than *Scholastic Coach,* which is directed more toward the high school level. Because both periodicals cover all major sports and contain articles that relate to sport performance problems and practices, they are useful to coaches and physical education teachers. As a beginning teacher, you should try to become familiar with the publications available in the fields of education and physical education, and if you plan to coach, you should become well acquainted with the more specialized publications available in your coaching area of sport.

BECOMING AN INVOLVED PROFESSIONAL: DEVELOPMENT AND RESPONSIBILITIES

Becoming an involved, committed member of a profession is an ongoing process. As a student preparing for a career in the field of physical education, you are working to meet the minimal standards for admission to the profession. When you join the profession after graduation, you need to work to upgrade yourself as a professional. Beverly Seidel and Matthew Resick have written about the various aspects of becoming a professional, and we shall study briefly the categories or areas of professional commitment or involvement at both the student and practicing professional levels.[7]

School Selection

The future physical educator is first concerned with choosing a college or university for undergraduate or graduate preparation. In many cases, students give too little thought to an institution and what it has to offer. An undergraduate institution should have a strong major program in your area of interest, whether it be physical education, health education, recreation, safety education, or dance, for you are not likely to specialize beyond this point at the undergraduate level. In fact, you can receive good undergraduate training in the many combined health and physical education major programs that are found primarily in the smaller schools, though you should make sure that a broad, well-balanced preparation is available at the school.

You should study the requirements of a school for admission to its major program: What type of nonmajor courses are required by the department or the school? Who teaches the undergraduate students—the professors or teaching assistants? What kind of reputation does the school have in the state and in the region? Are its graduates respected? Are its graduates successful?

AAHPERD regularly revises a directory of all schools in the United States with major programs that may help in the selection of an undergraduate or graduate school.

The concerns just discussed change in emphasis when you prepare to go into graduate school. Matters such as the regional and national reputation of the school and department should be considered. What do the faculties of other schools think of the school and its graduates? Where do its graduates find employment? What are the admission and retention standards of the school? Are its professors respected specialists with advanced training in their areas of specialization? Where were the professors trained? Finally, you should remember that many benefits are gained by studying at several schools, rather than by earning all of the degrees at a single institution. Many reputable graduate institutions now are refusing to allow their students to earn all of their degrees through the doctorate at the same institution because of the risk of inbreeding and of developing a narrow, provincial viewpoint.

Library Development and Use

This category might be called "developing the tools of the trade," for at the undergraduate level it is concerned with building a strong personal library of professional publications and, at the same time, with learning to use the public or school library and its resources. Library skills are critical to success in professional work; you must be at home in the library, and your personal library should be broad. As you begin to work in specialized areas, however, a more narrow outlook of interests may be detected in the titles added to your personal library.

A common complaint is that too many physical educators seem to be non-readers and that their reading habits reflect a seeming lack of general education and only a narrow professional education. As professionals, we should read widely, including current newspapers and general periodicals as well as the professional publications, for such reading helps us to establish common lines of communications with persons who are not physical educators.

Professional Preparation

A good program of professional preparation is also essential. The physical educator needs a strong, broad undergraduate education, but the process of education does not end with a bachelor's degree. Not only do most states require further academic work before any type of permanent certification is awarded but also more specialized work such as is available in graduate programs will assist you in developing expertise in some area or areas. The process of professional preparation can consume many years, but it can be a challenging, stimulating experience rather than a discouraging one.

Professional Membership

Membership in professional organizations is one sign of true professional commitment. As an undergraduate, you will find such organizations as student major clubs and such professional fraternities as Phi Epsilon Kappa on campus. You also will find that reduced membership fees are available in most state organizations and in AAHPERD. These student memberships include most professional privileges, as well as subscriptions to the professional publications.

When you graduate and become a member of the profession, you should definitely become a member of AAHPERD and of the state-level version of AAHPERD. Membership in many other professional organizations, such as those mentioned earlier in this chapter, can also benefit an active professional. As a physical educator with a genuine commitment to the profession, you will want to be involved actively in some of these professional groups, since they are all dedicated to advancing the profession.

Professional Meetings

Professional membership shows some interest in the condition of the profession, but a real commitment involves attendance at professional meetings. Many types of professional meetings take place regularly around the world. The meetings are the most exciting means of communication among members of professional groups, for at these meetings the physical educator can meet many people from different backgrounds and share common problems and discoveries. In many respects, the greatest impetus to change may be said to result from the stimulus and challenge of professional meetings.

At the undergraduate level, you will find such activities as state student major conventions, which students completely plan and run. Attendance at these will help you to experience a feeling of involvement and to gain experiences and contacts that are similar to those gained at professional meetings. You also may wish to attend the specialized clinics that are held for such areas of interest as sports coaching or officiating particular sports, or the physical fitness and sport clinics of the President's Council on Physical Fitness and Sports. These meetings are useful because they can help to broaden your outlook and your experiences as a student physical education major.

As a practicing physical educator, you may still wish to attend the clinics, but you will probably become more aware of the regular professional conventions. Physical educators usually attend such meetings as the annual AAHPERD conventions held at the state, district, and national levels. As an involved physical educator, you should try to attend one or more of these conventions annually if possible, for the experience is invaluable. Most other professional groups have an annual convention, and the members are depended on to plan the meetings and the programs.

Mere attendance at the professional meetings is not enough, however. For a profession to grow and improve, its members must be directly involved in its activities. Many professionals have become involved in high-level organization work simply because no one else was willing to help. The opportunities for direct involvement at all levels of professional activity are great, and as undergraduate and graduate students, you should try to get involved.

Most larger conventions have special sections and meetings for students so you should not think that your involvement will not be wanted before graduation. There is room for any person willing to help.

Research and Writing

All too few physical educators are involved directly in research and in writing. A profession and discipline need continual research to grow. Only through research can we extend the boundaries of our knowledge and improve our practices. While the areas in which research can be useful are almost unlimited, physical educators as a group have been occasionally ridiculed for both the lack of research and for the low quality of some research projects. The only real solution for such shortcomings is to make the members of the field recognize that *every* member is capable of conducting research at some level. In many cases, members have not conducted research because they were not encouraged to and because they doubted their ability to do so successfully. While the lack of time is often used as an argument for research not being conducted, the real reasons are most likely to be lack of self-confidence and lack of encouragement. Physical educators should feel obligated to conduct research on some small scale regularly, whether it is major or significant research.

The same reasons cited for failing to do research are also cited for the failure of physical educators to write about their activities or the state of the profession. How many times have people read professional articles and reacted with "I could have written that"? So why was it not done? We need to write to share our ideas, our concerns, and our theories. Articles can show others how we solved the problems that they are facing.

A profession and a discipline run and grow on the professional meeting and the written word. Write about your ideas, and encourage others to write about theirs. Do not be afraid to write because you fear ridicule or lack confidence in your opinions. As physical educators, we must be willing to accept valid criticism if we are to grow as professionals; we also must encourage writing and research on a massive scale, not to inundate the field with poor-quality work but to increase the odds that we shall produce more and better scholars and writers to help us improve the field.

While the national meetings may be flooded with people willing to write and speak, this is not often the case at the district level, and only rarely is it the case at the state level. Get involved, and see where it leads you. The field of physical education will be the better for it.

Teaching

The public thinks of most physical educators as being teachers (as well as coaches), no matter whether this is the case. The physical educator should be dedicated to quality teaching, just as to quality research and writing, for our greatest contact with the public is as teachers. The future of physical education rests largely on the opinions of the future citizens whom we teach in the

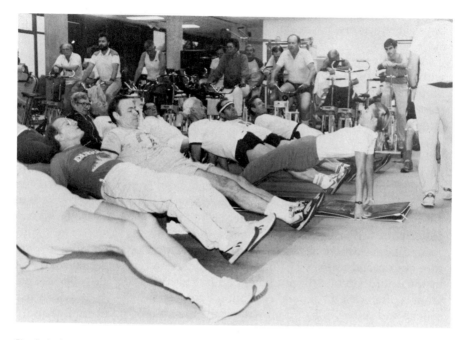

Physical educators work not only in the school systems but also at public and private recreational and fitness centers. (Courtesy DUPAC, Duke University Preventive Approach to Cardiology)

schools. Coaching is another form of teaching, when it is done well. We should attempt quality coaching, but it should never interfere with the quality of our teaching, for our teaching programs are also the base unit of our public relations programs.

Commitment

If any word is to be chosen to describe the most desirable characteristic in the professional physical educator, or in any member of any profession, it is *commitment*. True professionals must be committed to their fields. Only by being committed and totally involved physical educators can we hope to achieve genuine membership in our profession. Furthermore, our commitment will be most valuable if it is a *commitment to excellence*.

WHAT ARE THE COMPONENTS OF PROFESSIONAL PREPARATION?

The college training of the physical educator has traditionally been referred to as "professional preparation," according to the belief that teaching is indeed a profession. Such a formal training regimen is a relatively recent development in educational history, particularly in the broad areas that constitute physical education, for organized collegiate programs designed to train physical educators, particularly for teaching, are little more than a century old.

Although the physical educator may perform many different functions with little involvement in the educational systems, the traditional patterns of preparation have been teacher oriented. More programs now permit specialization that does not involve the teacher-training approach, but the primary orientation of the field is still toward teaching of some nature. The term *physical education* shows why this is true.

Our current patterns of professional preparation are largely a result of the development of the major in the normal schools, which were simply teachers' colleges. The teacher emphasis of those schools has had a major impact on how physical educators are trained. Physical educators have made attempts to ally themselves more closely with the sciences, but the traditional patterns are not easily changed.

Traditionally there have been four areas of professional preparation for future physical educators. The first area includes the *academic courses* required by the institution that the student attends. This portion of the collegiate program is often called "general education," for it is designed to provide every college and university student with academic training of a broad nature. It provides some concept of the breadth of human knowledge. This part of the preparation is commonly done during the first two years of college.

The second area of professional preparation is the *foundation sciences*, or those areas of science that must be a part of the physical educator's base knowledge if a good grasp of the major field is to be expected. The basic emphasis has been toward the biological sciences, especially anatomy and physiology. Increasing emphasis, however, is being directed toward an understanding of chemistry, which underlies biology (particularly in the area of exercise physiology), and toward more exposure to physics, which is necessary in studying aspects of movement, such as the mechanics of human movement and the outside forces that affect it.

The third area of professional preparation is often referred to as *professional education*. It comprises the major courses in education itself, which are entirely oriented toward teaching. It includes the student-teaching experience, which is generally considered the most valuable portion of the area. Student teaching is usually required for teacher certification if you wish to teach below the college level, and in some cases at the junior college level.

The fourth area of professional preparation is the area of physical education—the *major program*. In many colleges it is a combined major in health education and physical education, though it might be a major concentration in a single area of the broad field of physical education such as physical education itself, health education, recreation, dance, safety education, or any of the newer areas of specialization that are appearing as schools consolidate and more specialists are sought.

WHAT ARE SOME OF THE ISSUES OF TEACHER EDUCATION?

One of the oldest issues in the education of teachers is the question of time: How long should the training program last if it is to be effective? The generally accepted minimum is four years, though most educators insist that five years is a more reasonable period: four years to become well trained in the field of specialization, followed by a year devoted to the professional training in education. In many cases, however, the fifth year blends into work toward the master's degree.

A parallel issue to the time problem is the length of time required to complete the teacher preparation process. Some experts have argued that well-skilled teachers of physical education can be produced in two years, as they were in the early years of teacher training. Their argument is that the long time required to prepare teachers is largely wasted, because it simply keeps younger professionals out of an overcrowded marketplace as long as possible while providing more jobs to college teachers. Though the issue is more complex than this, at its heart lies a growing conviction that the preparation process has expanded to include too much busy-work, timeserving that serves

The future teacher and coach needs to develop personal performance skills to enhance demonstrations and to understand the learning process better. (Copyright Durham Herald Co., Inc. Photo by Jim Thornton)

no practical purpose and does not pay off in increased teaching skill or success.

Another issue causing considerable controversy is the amount of work devoted to the subject matter versus professional education training. The root of the issue is that more preparation is needed in the subject matter so that future teachers will know *what* to teach. Another argument is that the professional education training is more important, for it does not matter if someone has mastered the field, if he does not know *how* to teach it. This controversy may be the reason for the push toward the fifth year of preparation, for it permits more work in both areas.

A third persistent problem is the approach to the subject matter. Should it be taught with the emphasis on the subject matter itself, or should it be taught with the emphasis on how the students will teach it after they have graduated? In other words, should the instruction in teaching methods be integrated into the subject matter instruction, or should it remain segregated and taught in "methods" courses outside the subject courses?

A fourth problem is the question of whether there should be more philosophical or more scientific emphasis. The question arose early in the 20th century as educators sought to develop a "science" of teaching. They never succeeded, and the issue has not yet been settled. In a way, this controversy is an extension of the arguments about liberal arts versus sciences or the "practical" versus "theoretical," arguments still prevalent in education.

A fifth issue relates to laboratory experiences, or the time spent observing teaching activities and practicing teaching as students. The many points of view in this area range from involving the students regularly from the first year of college in small teaching-observation experiences, through the more traditional approach of concentrating the experiences during one or more terms of the last year of college, to the idea of requiring a full year or more of successful teaching before awarding certification.

A final persistent issue is the general education of the student. How much time should be spent in areas outside the major field and the other areas of study directly related to the teaching field? How broad should the general education be? Professional educators have frequently argued against additional work in general education, because they believe it further limits the amount of work that can be devoted to the areas in which the student hopes to teach. This issue involves us most with people outside the field, for at the heart of the issue is the far-from-simple question: What is education? What is its ultimate goal? What education is most worth having? The question has not been resolved for centuries, nor is it likely to be settled in the near future, but physical educators should not be too dogmatic or closed-minded to the views of the liberal arts supporters. By ignoring their areas of study, we may be isolating ourselves from the other areas of the educational experience more than we realize.

As we look at the broad area of physical education, the dichotomy between the arts and the sciences is still visible. Physical education is still torn over which way to go. As a result we are neither art nor science, though the tendency is toward the sciences. In health education, two directions may also be seen. The traditional approach has been to combine health with physical education, with between one fourth and one third of the time spent in health. Increasingly, specialization in health education begins at the undergraduate level rather than in the graduate schools as in the past. Recreation education also is developing rapidly as an undergraduate area of specialization. It may be the most rapidly developing specialization, particularly in a time of greatly increasing leisure time for people in many areas of the world.

TRENDS IN PROFESSIONAL PREPARATION

The professional preparation programs through which physical educators travel are gradually changing. Although the process is usually slow, it is also relatively constant. Because the needs of people change, the skills that physical educators need also change. These changing skills needs are reflected in changing patterns of professional preparation as schools try to find better ways to prepare their students to meet these needs. Several of the more noticeable trends in professional preparation programs should be understood clearly.

Increased Specialization

Perhaps the most noticeable trend in professional training is the increase in specialization; many more people are concentrating on smaller areas of the physical education fields. For example, more students are developing concentrations at either the undergraduate or graduate level in areas such as health education, recreation education, safety education, dance, athletic training, coaching, and adapted and therapeutic work. In the past the physical educator majored only in a broad degree that could be called health and physical education. The combined degree is gradually dropping from use as the specialist replaces the generalist. One reason for this is the increase in the size of schools as districts and schools consolidate, while another reason is the large increase in the number of teachers available. At the same time, a specific major field should develop a better teacher of health or of physical education rather than a marginally knowledgeable teacher of both. The gradual result of this increase in specialization is an expansion of the programs available to students in the many fields of physical education, which is a great improvement in the schools' services.

Certification of Coaches and Trainers

A number of states have begun to require certified coaches and trainers. By requiring some background training in these areas, such as the equivalent of a minor program in college, they can provide a safer, more knowledgeable level of coaching in the schools.

The concern over the safety of school athletes has increased rapidly in recent years, for as sports competition has expanded, so has the number of injuries. Too many schools have no trainers to work with problems of athletic injuries. Some states are working to establish groups of high school trainers who have been certified by the state so that injured high school athletes will receive better care as quickly as possible.

The move toward required certification of coaches and provision of trainers is extremely important with the greater use of part-time coaches in the schools. The last decade was a time of rapid expansion in sports for girls, but too few trained coaches were available. Part-time, nonschool coaches, sometimes with minimal training, were pressed into service to meet the immediate need. Unfortunately, the last decade was also a time of mushrooming numbers of legal liability suits against schools and individuals. Coaches need to be educated to know the risks that they create for their athletes and the legal risks that they themselves are taking on when they coach.

Elementary School Specialists

As the trend toward specialization continues, one of the rapidly growing specialties is the teacher of elementary school physical education. The elementary ages might be considered the most important ages for the application of good physical education programs, yet in many states, elementary school children are taught physical education by classroom teachers. The result frequently has been poor programs of physical education at a critical age for the development of coordination skills. Specialists are now being trained, however, who will either teach physical education at that level or act as consultants and supervisors of the physical education program at several elementary schools.

Adapted and Therapeutic Specialists

The areas of adapted physical education and therapeutic or physical rehabilitation are rapidly developing. This area is concerned with persons who cannot take part in the normal physical education programs. In the adapted area, special programs may be planned for persons with temporary injuries, for persons with below-average physical skills and abilities, and for persons who are mentally retarded or physically handicapped. An example of one of the programs that has developed from this type of work is the Special Olympics for the mentally retarded, which is growing rapidly across the nation. In the area of physical therapy or physical rehabilitation, the object is to work with people who are trying to make a comeback from a serious injury, disease, or handicap. Examples of responsibilities in this area include working with persons who have lost limbs and are learning to use artificial arms and legs, or working with persons crippled from the effects of diseases such as polio or muscular dystrophy to improve their ability to walk or master other common physical skills.

Courtesy DUPAC, Duke University Preventive Approach to Cardiology

Paraprofessional Training

The training of paraprofessionals or teacher's aides is still a small area of physical education training, but it is expected to grow rapidly in the future. The paraprofessional is a person who has had technical training, such as a one- or two-year program in a junior or community college, and who assists the teacher by fulfilling many of the duties that require less training. Examples of such duties are taking roll, issuing and receiving equipment, preparing facilities, and giving and grading tests. Essentially the paraprofessional is used to lighten the work load of the teacher by doing many of the time-consuming, nonteaching duties that cut into the teacher's actual teaching time.

After Graduation

The preparation of a physical educator does not end after graduation from college. Most teachers are faced with preservice and inservice training, or programs designed to keep them in touch with the latest developments in educational theory and practices. Many states require further college work at regular intervals, regardless of how long the teacher has been teaching. This trend is in keeping with the belief that the process of education never ends. Many other people pursue scholarly studies with no intention of teaching or coaching.

Whole-School Involvement in Teacher Education

This trend, which involves all the departments of the college in planning the teacher-training process, is a reaction to the problem of isolation of specialists in education and physical education. The tendency to try to do everything, including the academic preparation, wholly through the department of education can give teachers a rather limited idea of the views and knowledge of the areas in which they may be teaching in later years. The idea of involving all the departments on campus in planning the teacher-preparation programs and their content is a move to insure that the concern for methodology will not overlook or replace an equal concern that the teachers actually *know* something to teach.

Open Admissions Versus Higher Teacher Standards

This problem may have no solution. At the same time that educators are trying to raise the quality of teaching by requiring higher grades or levels of knowledge from prospective teachers, many schools have become open-admissions colleges. These colleges have few or no admissions standards: Any student may be admitted, regardless of ability or seeming lack of ability. There are many reasons for the rise in the number of open-admissions schools, but a major reason is the need to balance the earlier problems of discrimination in admissions. In an open-admissions school, every person has a chance to demonstrate the ability to do college work. This does not make higher standards impossible, or even necessarily more difficult to develop. The school can require that the bulk of the general education and foundational sciences course work, along with some introductory areas of physical education theory courses, be completed with set grade restrictions before the student is admitted to the profession preparation program. Although this work should be the equivalent of two years of college work, the student is not limited to two years to meet the requirements. Time can be permitted for academic deficiencies to be made up in addition to taking the required programs.

New Directions in Professional Preparation

During the mid-1980s, several professional groups studied educational patterns, then recommended major changes in the education of future teachers in the United States. The individual schools and states have set standards in the past, with a major emphasis on taking education and other teacher preparation courses during the four years of undergraduate study. The National Council for Accreditation of Teacher Education [NCATE] has worked to develop and enforce national standards for the teacher programs, though many schools are not members of NCATE.

A group of education-school deans from 28 universities formed a body known as the Holmes Group Consortium, dedicated to raising the quality of teacher education programs at their own institutions, regardless of whether other schools follow their lead.[8] The Holmes Group report was quickly followed by the report of the Carnegie Forum Task Force on Teaching as a Profession.[9]

Both the Holmes Group and the Carnegie Forum recommended major changes in the current patterns of teacher training. Among the suggestions were higher entry standards before students are permitted into the field, an undergraduate concentration on the subject field (rather than diluting those years with a heavy schedule of education courses), taking the teacher preparation courses during the fifth year of college, serving teaching internships as apprentice teachers, more thorough testing of prospective teachers, and developing national standards of preparation and certification rather than the current patchwork quilt of standards across the nation.

Whether their recommendations will be implemented, the dissatisfaction with the level of preparation of our teachers will result in at least some changes in our teacher preparation patterns. It may be years before we see whether those changes will be major ones, or simply minor modifications made to limit the criticism of teacher education programs

TOWARD THE FUTURE IN CURRICULAR PLANNING

Physical education, like all areas of education and life, is changing, and so must our patterns of teacher education change. One of our greatest problems, however, and the one that most hurts the reputation of educators, is our tendency to snatch an idea from the air and put it into effect in our programs with no greater justification than how nicely the theory rolls off the tongue at professional conferences. One reason for the disrespect with which educators are treated today is that, while claiming to know how to teach better than any "noneducators," we have shown no objective proof to establish that we know what we are talking about. This is a compelling reason to conduct research in pedagogy.

Before we make changes in our patterns of professional preparation, we should show (1) the value of the changes and (2) that the changes can work. If we cannot establish these two points, not only shall we receive no respect from the academic and nonacademic communities but also we shall *deserve* no respect. We should establish these values and outcomes before making the changes rather than after the fact, for changing before proving is ideology rather than education. This does not mean that we should not experiment, but we should not push for large-scale changes based on unproved ideas, as in the competency-based-teacher-education (CBTE) movement of the 1970s. It is difficult to plan education for the future, because we often have little idea of what the future holds either in educational practices and conditions or in job opportunities and needs. If we did have the answers to everything, much of the challenge of teaching would be gone.

One solid need of physical educators is for more work in the liberal arts and interdisciplinary studies areas. There are several reasons for suggesting this shift in direction. One is supplied by James B. Conant, whom many persons consider to be an opponent of physical education. No matter whether he is an opponent, he expresses some compelling arguments for such a broadening of the educational background of physical educators:

> Because the physical education teacher is likely to be a coach and because of the high visibility of the coaching staff, the road to administrative positions is open and attractive....The future is likely to be like the past in this respect. Unless there is a change in the direction of this trend, I conclude that *the physical educa-tion teacher should have an even wider general academic education than any other teacher* [italics added]....More likely than not, the [student] preparing to be a physical education teacher is, perhaps unconsciously, preparing to be an educational ad-ministrator. He [or she] needs to start early on a course of wide reading in the humanities and the social sciences.[10]

Large numbers of coaches eventually become administrators in the public schools, and Conant's suggestions are meant to direct their training toward the broader liberal arts studies that will make them more aware of the ideas and viewpoints of the other disciplinary areas of the educational spectrum. Although he touches on the edges of the reason for these wide studies, he misses one basic reason for them that should occur to most physical educators—lack of communication.

A great communications gap exists between physical educators and other educators, academic and otherwise, simply because we cannot speak their language. We sometimes seem out of touch with the liberal arts and with their required development of communications skills so that even if physical education has become more academically respectable, we seem to be unable to prove it or communicate it to the academic community outside our own field. There is little value in our telling ourselves that our field is a respectable area of the educational process; we must sell it convincingly to those who have no ties to the field. We must broaden our horizons so that we shall be able to open new lines of communication to the many academic fields with which we have no present communication. Only when they begin to under-stand us and we begin to understand them will physical education begin to attain the respect that we physical educators believe it deserves.

NOTES

1. Abraham Flexner, cited in Walter P. Kroll, *Perspectives in Physical Education,* Academic Press, New York, 1971, pp. 119–121.
2. Charles A. Bucher, *Foundations of Physical Education,* 6th ed., C. V. Mosby, St. Louis, 1972, pp. 9–18.
3. Daryl Siedentop, *Developing Teaching Skills in Physical Education,* Houghton Mifflin, Boston, 1976, pp. 12–14.
4. Ibid., "Recent Advances in Pedagogical Research in Physical Education," *The Academy Papers,* no. 16 (1982), 94.
5. Ann E. Jewett, "Most Significant Curriculum Research in the Past Decade," *The Academy Papers,* no. 16 (1982), 71.
6. Charles B. Corbin, "Applications," *The Academy Papers,* no. 16 (1982), 95–96.

7. Beverly L. Seidel and Matthew C. Resick, *Physical Education: An Overview*, 2d ed., Addison-Wesley, Reading, Mass., 1978, pp. 202–208.
8. Holmes Group Consortium, *Tomorrow's Teachers: A Report of the Holmes Group*, Holmes Group, Inc., East Lansing, Mich., 1986. Excerpted in *The Chronicle of Higher Education* 32 (9 April 1986), 27–37.
9. Carnegie Forum Task Force on Teaching as a Profession. *A Nation Prepared: Teachers for the 21st Century*, Carnegie Forum on Education and the Economy, Hyattsville, Md., 1986. Excerpted in *The Chronicle of Higher Education* 32 (21 May 1986), 43–54.
10. James B. Conant, *The Education of American Teachers*, McGraw-Hill, New York, 1963, pp. 185–186.

SUGGESTED READINGS

Alley, Louis E. "Two Paths to Excellence." *Quest* 34, no. 2 (1982), 99–108.

Betts, Edith. "Keepers of the Crown Jewels." *Quest* 35, no. 2 (1983), 75–81.

Broekhoff, Jan. "Physical Education as a Profession." *Quest* 31, no. 2 (1979), 244–254.

Burchner, Craig A. "Erroneous Assumptions in Graduate Physical Education." *Quest* 35, no. 1 (1983), 46–53.

Carnegie Forum Task Force on Teaching as a Profession. *A Nation Prepared: Teachers for the 21st Century*. Hyattsville, Md.: Carnegie Forum on Education and the Economy, 1986. Excerpted in *The Chronicle of Higher Education* 32 (21 May 1986), 43–54.

Cheffers, John T. F. "Concepts for Teacher Education in the 80s and 90s." *Proceedings, National Association for Physical Education in Higher Education Annual Conference* 2 (1980), 316–322.

"Competency Testing, State Certification, and Accreditation." Symposium in *Journal of Teacher Education* 35 (March-April 1984), 2–18.

Corbin, Charles B. "Applications [Pedagogy]." *The Academy Papers*, no. 16 (1982), 95–98.

"Current Challenge: Revitalization or Obsolescence?" *Proceedings, National Association for Physical Education in Higher Education Annual Conference* 5 (1984), entire issue.

Dodds, Patt. "Competency-Based Teacher Education: The Withered Rose." *Proceedings, National Association for Physical Education in Higher Education Annual Conference* 2 (1980), 301–310.

Feistritzer, C. Emily. *The Making of a Teacher: A Report on Teacher Education and Certification*. Washington: National Center for Educational Information, 1984.

Finn, Chester E., Jr., Mary Hartwood Futrell, and Myron Lieberman. Three articles debating teachers' unions and quality education. *Phi Delta Kappan* 66 (January 1985), 331–343.

Goldberger, Michael, and Steve Moyer. "A Schema for Classifying Educational Objectives in the Psychomotor Domain." *Quest* 34, no. 2 (1982), 134–142.

Graduate Education in Health Education, Physical Education, Recreation Education, Safety Education, and Dance. Reston, Va.: AAHPERD, 1974.

Holmes Group Consortium. *Tomorrow's Teachers: A Report of the Holmes Group*. East Lansing, Mich.: Holmes Group, Inc., 1986. Excerpted in *The Chronicle of Higher Education* 32 (9 April 1986), 27–37.

Jewett, Ann E. "Most Significant Curriculum Research in the Past Decade." *The Academy Papers*, no. 16 (1982), 78–81.

———, and Linda L. Bain. *The Curriculum Process in Physical Education*. Dubuque, Iowa: Wm. C. Brown, 1985.

Kaestle, Carl. "Education Reforms and the Swinging Pendulum." *Phi Delta Kappan* 66 (February 1985), 422–423.

Knoppers, A. "Professionalization of Attitudes: A Review and Critique." *Quest* 37, no. 1 (1985), 92–102.

Kroll, Walter P. *Graduate Study and Research in Physical Education.* Champaign, Ill.: Human Kinetics, 1982.

Lawson, Hal A. "Problem-Setting for Physical Education and Sport." *Quest* 36, no. 1 (1984), 48–60.

——, ed. *Undergraduate Physical Education Programs: Issues and Approaches.* Reston, Va.: AAHPERD, 1981.

Locke, Lawrence F., Kim C. Graber, and Patt Dodds. "Research on Teaching Teachers: Where are We Now?" *Journal of Teaching in Physical Education*, Monograph 2 (Summer 1984), entire issue.

Lopiano, Donna A. "The Certified Coach: A Central Figure." *JOPERD* 57 (March 1986), 34–38.

McBride, Ron E. "Some Future Considerations in Professional Preparation." *The Physical Educator* 41 (May 1984), 95–99.

Marsh, Jeannette J. "Measuring Affective Objectives in Physical Education." *The Physical Educator* 41 (May 1984), 77–81.

Marshall, James. *The Devil in the Classroom: Hostility in American Education.* New York: Schocken Books, 1985.

Morgan, S. R. "'A Nation at Risk!' Performance-Based Teacher Education Did Not Work." *College Student Journal* 18 (Fall 1984), 198–203.

National Association for Physical Education in Higher Education. *Annual Conference Proceedings: Theory Into Knowledge.* Vol. 4. Champaign, Ill.: Human Kinetics, 1983.

National Commission for Excellence in Teacher Education. "A Call for Change in Teacher Education." *The Chronicle of Higher Education* 30 (6 March 1985), 13–21.

Olson, H. C. "Changing Teacher Accreditation and Certification Standards: Selected Annotated Bibliography." *Action in Teacher Education* 6 (Winter 1984–1985), 69–77.

Olson, Janice K. "Research on Teaching in Physical Education." *Proceedings, National Association for Physical Education in Higher Education Annual Conference* 4 (1983), 52–66.

Powell, Kenneth E., Gregory M. Christenson, and Marshall W. Kreuter. "Objectives for the Nation: Assessing the Role Physical Education Must Play." *JOPERD* 55 (August 1984), 18–20.

Professional Preparation in Health Education, Physical Education, Recreation Education. Reston, Va.: AAHPERD, 1962.

"Profiles of Struggle." *JOPERD* 57 (April 1986), 32–63. A series of articles describing the difficulties of different teaching jobs of real teachers.

Rahni, Muhamad Ali A. *The Opinions of Curriculum Experts in the United States and Canada Regarding What Courses Should Be Included in the Undergraduate Professional Preparation of Physical Education Teachers.* M. S. thesis, Washington State University, 1983. Microfiche.

Schuman, Barbara J. *A Profile of Women Leaders in Physical Education, Sport, Athletics and Dance Organizations and a Study of Role Models and Mentors of the Leaders.* Ph.D. dissertation, University of Iowa, 1984. Microfiche.

Siedentop, Daryl. "Recent Advances in Pedagogical Research in Physical Education." *The Academy Papers*, no. 16 (1982), 82–94.

Sisley, Becky. "Coaching Specialization: The Oregon Program." *The Physical Educator* 41 (October 1984), 149–152.

Spears, Betty. "Building for Today and Tomorrow." *Quest* 34, no. 2 (1982), 89–98.

"Standards for Graduate Programs in Physical Education." *JOPERD* 55 (February 1984), 54–62.

Willgoose, Carl E. *The Curriculum in Physical Education.* 4th ed. Englewood Cliffs, N.J.: Prentice-Hall, 1984.

Woodring, Paul. *The Persistent Problems of Education.* Bloomington, Ind.: Phi Delta Kappa, 1983.

chapter 12

New Careers in Physical Education and Sport: Professions, Disciplines, and Crafts

WHAT IS THE JOB SITUATION IN PHYSICAL EDUCATION?

Today's student in physical education is increasingly concerned with the future job opportunities in the fields of physical education. The coming of the 1980s continued an economic decline that affected the hiring and retention practices of the schools and resulted in an unstable employment situation in the formerly stable area of teaching. Although there are many nonteaching options in physical education, we traditionally think of teaching when we ask of the employment situation in physical education.

The job market in education is tight, especially in physical education, for it is a popular teaching field. As a college major, it has been popular with athletes, many of whom are interested primarily in coaching in the schools. Although there was a shortage of teachers in the early 1960s, by the mid-1970s the education situation had reversed itself. The number of students in the public schools (through the high school level) was decreasing, while the number of teachers had increased far beyond the needs of the schools. A considerable oversupply of teachers had appeared in most subject and grade areas, and the number of teachers being produced each year exceeded the number of teaching vacancies by a significant margin.

During the 1950s and 1960s, the school population made rapid, vast increases. As the children reached school age who were born during the series of "baby booms" that began during World War II and continued through the

Korean War, the schools had to be enlarged rapidly; American education seemed to turn into an exercise in building construction. This expansion also was felt in the colleges and universities during the middle to late 1960s, for a larger proportion of the high school graduates were continuing their education past the high school level.

Two other developments of the 1960s furthered the growth of the post–high school student population: the rise of the community college and technical school across the United States and the trend of many schools toward an open-admissions policy. Although a few states, notably California, had strong systems of community colleges before 1960, the period of the 1960s saw almost every state begin to push the founding and development of local two-year community colleges that were oriented toward the work of the first two years of liberal arts and sciences college study and of technical schools that were oriented toward one- and two-year degree programs in many different trades. As a result, the post–high school population in education multiplied at a startling rate.

During the 1970s, evidence of a surprising reversal of the school population trend appeared. Adults were becoming more concerned with birth control, women were preferring to have fewer children, and the size of the typical

Courtesy DUPAC, Duke University Preventive Approach to Cardiology

family began to drop. Although the "zero population growth" goal of many birth-control advocates was hardly being realized, the number of students hit a high-water mark and then began a gradual decline. This decline is expected to continue for at least another decade.

The effect of the declining birth rate on the school population and teacher needs was compounded by another trend: the consolidation of schools, particularly the middle schools or junior high schools and high schools. Smaller schools were being combined into larger schools for several reasons. Two of the major reasons were (1) to permit the schools to offer a broader educational program while eliminating the unnecessary duplication of teachers within the school district, and (2) to allow the cities to try to end the age-old problem of racially segregated schools.

All the changes in education during the mid-1970s were further complicated by a long-lasting period of recession that affected the ability of the people to support the system of education as they had in the past. Though the oversupply of teachers seems to be ending and may even disappear in the 1990s, it is a cycle that may recur in the future.

What was the result of these several trends? The unexpected decline in the demand for teachers came at a bad time—just as the children of the "baby boom" began entering the market as newly qualified teachers. Because of the financial problems of the schools, many teachers lost their jobs.

What does the oversupply of teachers mean in practical terms? At the elementary through high school levels, two possibilities are obvious, but they have not materialized, partly because of the financial situation. First, the schools have an unprecedented opportunity to hire only the most qualified applicants as teachers and also to remove teachers who are poorly qualified or incompetent. Unfortunately, teachers are usually retained on the basis of seniority, and the quality of their work does not always figure in determining who will be released from employment. For the most part, the first possible result has failed to happen.

The second possible effect of the oversupply of teachers would result from the school's using them to make radical cuts in the size of the classes. A commonly held, though unproven, view of educators is that more and better learning is possible in a small class than in a large one. This lowering of pupil/teacher ratios also has failed to happen. In fact, the financial crunch has in many cases resulted in the release of so many teachers that the typical class size has increased despite the teacher surplus.

The situation is somewhat different at the college level. The increased number of two-year community colleges and technical schools, combined with the growing trend to continue school after high school, will probably result in continued increases in the college population. Although there is currently a teacher surplus at the college level, the opportunities for college teachers will probably improve again in a few years.

So what is the demand for physical education teachers? The demand for male teachers is small. In fact, there are far more qualified male teachers of physical education than there are jobs. Although there are more qualified females than jobs, the demand for women physical educators has been increasing. The controversial Title IX federal funding programs that were aimed at eliminating sexual discrimination in the schools resulted in a huge growth of women's sports in the schools and colleges, and the demand for women coaches is almost impossible to meet. While the job situation in physical education is better for women than for men, there are numerous exceptions for people with specialties, as we shall discuss later in the chapter.

TEACHING AS A CAREER: PROS AND CONS

Many people who consider physical education as a major field think in terms of teaching and coaching, yet they often give little thought to the good and bad points of teaching as a career. Before we can discuss the opportunities in the teaching areas of physical education, we need to understand the positive and negative factors that affect one's enjoyment of teaching.

Positive Aspects of Teaching

Teaching is generally considered to have many benefits as an occupation. The teacher has traditionally held a position of respect in the community. The reason for this respect can be traced to another aspect of the teacher's work, for the teacher makes a definite contribution to society. Teaching is vital to the survival of the community, and a good teacher is a positive influence on many young people.

Teaching is considered an occupation with good job security, though the recent financial crisis has affected this security to some degree. Generally speaking, teachers are well paid for their services. Although salaries might be higher, which can be said of almost any occupation, the last two decades have seen tremendous changes in the level of teachers' salaries. Also, teachers generally receive automatic pay raises each year, which is true of few other occupations. Teachers also enjoy the benefit of long vacation periods; they work an average of nine to ten months of the year. While the extra time may be devoted to an additional job, it is available for travel, study, and many other opportunities. The long vacation periods have made teaching attractive to persons who wish to have more free time to pursue their other interests.

Perhaps the greatest positive aspect of teaching as a career, however, is the personal satisfaction it provides. A person who really wants to teach will find many aspects of the work satisfying, for teaching carries a degree of personal involvement in the success of others that is found in few other occupations. Many teachers continue to teach for this reason alone.

Negative Aspects of Teaching

Too few prospective teachers stop to look at the negative aspects of teaching as a career, for teaching can have as many bad points as it has good ones. Perhaps the best-known negative aspect of teaching as a career is that teaching is an overcrowded field, though this is not a negative aspect of teaching as a practice. The competition for teaching jobs is difficult, and it becomes more difficult each year. More candidates are appearing annually, and often they are better qualified candidates for the available jobs in terms of educational training, degrees, and teaching experience.

While teaching has traditionally been a respected occupation in the abstract sense, many people increasingly view teachers as a body with a lack of respect. The schools and teachers have begun to suffer from a lack of support from a public that is becoming dissatisfied with the schools and their work. This problem carries over into the area of teachers' salaries. While teachers' salaries are not low, and while they have risen rapidly, they are low in comparison to the education and expense required to qualify for them. Schools much prefer to hire teachers with master's degrees, yet the salary increase gained by earning this degree represents only a fraction of the cost of the degree. Moreover, if the degree is earned in a full-time study program, the loss of a full year's teaching salary must be added to the cost of the degree. The educational requirements for the jobs are not consistent with the salaries offered when the requirements are met.

Finally, today's teachers are finding that they have increasingly heavy work loads, which makes doing a good job more difficult. A large surplus of qualified teachers is available, but fewer teachers are being employed because of the schools' financial problems. The result is larger student loads per teacher, combined with less time for recovering from and preparing for teaching the classes. The large quantities of paperwork that are a traditional part of the educational bureaucracy make the work load heavier, for too few school systems provide enough clerical workers or teaching aides to keep teachers from being bogged down in nonteaching duties.

To Teach or Not to Teach

As you can see, teaching has both its good side and its bad side. As a prospective teacher, you must look at both sides carefully, for you must decide which aspects of teaching carry the most weight for you. For many persons the overall satisfaction of a career devoted to helping people outweighs all of the negative considerations, while for other persons the work load or pay situation is enough to drive them away from teaching. You must decide which of these positive and negative aspects is most important to you as you consider teaching as a career.

BASIC QUALITIES OF THE SUCCESSFUL TEACHER

What makes a successful teacher? We have talked about the good and bad points of a teaching career, and later we shall discuss how the physical educator is trained for a career. What are the basic, general qualities needed if a person hopes to become a successful teacher? While each person can produce a list of suggested necessary qualities, we shall look at a brief list of important qualities for the successful teacher.

Teaching Personality and Interests

Successful teaching requires a good combination of personal qualities and interests. A good personality is necessary; the teacher should enjoy people, work well with them, and have a good sense of humor. The teacher must be interested in the educational process and in the students. A concern for the needs and interests of the students is an important part of successful teaching. Even if a prospective teacher possesses the other qualities already mentioned, a poor personality can severely hamper the chances of teaching success. A teacher must *want* to teach and must *enjoy* teaching.

Strong Educational Background

In addition to having intellectual ability, the successful teacher needs a good, broad educational background, which means more than having a good preparation in the major field. Teaching calls for a broadly based high school and college program of study in the liberal arts and sciences. The teacher needs to have some exposure to and understanding of the breadth of human experience and knowledge. The teacher's educational background and intellect are closely allied to the next quality.

Communication Skills

Teachers need to be skilled in both oral and written communication. They must be able to express themselves clearly—to be able to explain their thoughts and ideas to other people. Teaching also involves many written reports. In fact, much of what teachers learn comes from information that other teachers write. Without communication skills, successful teaching is almost impossible. Unfortunately, communication is one of the areas where today's prospective teachers are the weakest.

Health and Physical Skills

The successful teacher needs to be healthy, simply because the unhealthy person is physically less able to do a thorough job of teaching. This is particularly true in an area involving physical skills such as physical education. In physical education, the teacher must have good motor ability—a good combination of coordination, flexibility, strength, and speed.

The teacher needs to be skilled in performing the activities that are going to be taught for two reasons: (1) the teacher will have to demonstrate the skills in many cases, and (2) the teacher will have a far better understanding of the components of the skills and the problems that may be encountered by the student in learning the skills.

Intellectual Ability

If one single quality of the teacher is to be considered the most important, perhaps intellectual ability would be that quality. While a person does not have to be a genius to teach successfully, a person of poor or even average intellectual ability is at a distinct disadvantage. Good teachers must be able to understand what they are teaching at higher levels than those at which they may present the material to the students. Also, the teacher should be able to serve as an example to the students, which is difficult if the students consider the teacher an intellectual inferior. All education has an intellectual base, and a prospective teacher needs the intellectual ability and intelligence to work at a reasonable level of accomplishment. The teacher needs to be intelligent and have a strong interest in learning. A person with little respect for learning can hardly be expected to be a dedicated teacher.

TYPES OF TEACHING JOBS

When people think of employment opportunities in physical education, they first think of teaching opportunities. The field of physical education is so closely tied to teaching and coaching that we rarely stop to realize the many nonteaching opportunities. We should look at some of the many types of teaching jobs in the different areas of physical education, for it is a broader field than many people realize.

Physical Education

While we have consistently referred to physical education in the broad sense by including all the areas of the field such as health and recreation, we shall now refer to jobs in physical education under the narrow definition. Most physical educators who teach do so in the area that most people refer to as physical education. Although we usually think physical education teachers work with basic activity classes at the high school level, the field has many levels of teaching opportunities.

The lowest level of employment, in terms of age, is working with preschool and elementary school children. This age group is sometimes broken into two groups, with the younger group referred to as K–3, or kindergarten through grade three. Specialists rather than traditional classroom teachers are increasingly doing the teaching at this level. They most often work with movement education and perceptual motor activities instead of teaching games and sports skills, for children at this age benefit more from activities aimed at developing the most basic of movement skills.

The upper elementary grades are sometimes combined with the grades of the middle or junior high school to cover a range of grades from four through nine. For this age group, the teacher moves more into games and sports skills, though they are not of a strenuous nature, for the bodies of students in this age range are developing rapidly. Teachers working with this age group find that the wide range in body size, strength, endurance, and skills of their students requires careful adjustments in the physical education program. Many teachers who wish to teach at the high school level begin their teaching careers at the middle school level, in grades seven through nine.

The next level is the high school level—sometimes referred to as senior high school—which includes grades 10 through 12. At this level, the teachers ideally teach more advanced skills, more strenuous activities, and some lifetime sports, and they will work with coeducational activities. In most cases, the teachers at this level (and many teachers at the middle school level) are also involved in coaching some sports activities. At this level, the prospective teacher is likely to encounter job openings in private schools or academies as well as in the public schools. These private schools may have been started for a number of reasons, some of them academic, some religious, some essentially political.

Beyond the high school level are two basic types of educational institutions. One type is aimed at terminal degree programs of a practical nature. These are most often technical schools or community colleges whose programs usually last one or two years. Whether physical education is offered in such schools depends on the educational philosophy and goals of the state, county, or community sponsoring the school.

The other type of institution is the traditional college, such as the junior college (with two-year programs that are usually oriented to liberal arts) and the senior college or university (with four-year programs and, in many cases, graduate programs). The goals of these institutions may seem impractical, for they are usually not aimed at learning to perform a single, money-earning skill. Most of these institutions have physical education programs, and many of the colleges and universities also have programs for physical education majors.

At the college level, the teacher is more likely to be a specialist. Some college teachers primarily teach activity classes, and they may do most of their teaching in the narrow range of four to six specific activities rather than teach a little bit from every type of physical activity. Some college teachers work primarily in the teacher preparation program such as in the coaching theory area, the professional skills areas, the scientific foundations areas, or other theory areas like administration or measurement and evaluation. Some college teachers work primarily in intramural activities or in research areas, while others work primarily as administrators of programs in physical education. As the academic level at which the teacher works gets higher, the variety of teaching jobs increases considerably.

Many job possibilities in the teaching areas have been discussed by Sheldon Fordham, Carol Leaf, and others.[1] We have indicated the basic type of job that the physical education teacher performs through the college level, but there are other teaching possibilities in addition to those in the regular public and private schools. A teacher may work for the government and teach in schools on armed forces bases, both in the United States and in foreign nations. These teachers enjoy many of the benefits of governmental employment. A teacher may teach for the United States government or for a foreign government under government-sponsored programs such as the Peace Corps.

Health Education

Health education has become a field that is often separated from physical education. Health educators are concerned with improving the health knowledge and practices of all people, though we commonly think of this work being done with school-age people. More schools below the college level are now hiring specialists in health education instead of having the health education classes taught by the physical education teacher, who often has little training in health education. Many of the jobs in the field of health education and school health services are nonteaching jobs, which we shall discuss later in the chapter.

Recreation

Recreation specialists make up another rapidly growing group of workers, particularly at the community level. The number of recreation teachers is not great, though it is increasing. Recreation is taught primarily at the college and university level to persons majoring in the field of physical education or to persons planning to specialize in recreation and recreational services. As many nations become more affluent and leisure time increases, the recreation specialist will gain increasing importance both inside and outside the educational system.

Coaching

The coaching of athletic teams has traditionally been an important part of the teaching duties of physical educators in American schools. Many persons will argue over whether coaching is, in fact, a form of teaching, but when it is done well and with a regard to more than the immediate aim of victory, coaching can be an important type of teaching. Its effects seem to stay with students longer than other types of teaching.

Coaches are hired as teacher–coaches at the junior high or middle school level, at the high school level, and at the college and university level. While state regulations usually require a middle school or high school coach to be a teacher, this is not true at the college level. The larger the college is, the less likely the coach is to be a teacher as well. Coaching may be the most popular aspect of physical education activities to professionals. It is largely responsible for creating much of the interest of future physical educators in the field. The interest and importance of coaching can be exaggerated, but we should not overreact by trying to cast out coaches as unworthy physical educators, for they have much to contribute to the field.

Safety Education

Safety education is a broad area that includes all areas of safety practices, including driver education. Many states have begun to require all younger drivers to complete an approved course of driver education before they can receive a license to drive. Many insurance companies offer lower rates to young people who have completed driver education courses. Safety in the use of bicycles and recreational vehicles has been a more recent addition to many programs of safety education. The field is concerned with the development of consciousness of safety procedures and an awareness of the dangers that exist in many activities.

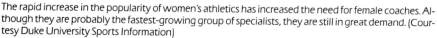
The rapid increase in the popularity of women's athletics has increased the need for female coaches. Although they are probably the fastest-growing group of specialists, they are still in great demand. (Courtesy Duke University Sports Information)

Dance

Teaching dance is also growing in interest in physical education. Many of the students who major or minor in dance activities become teachers either in the schools or by offering private lessons to students. While most teachers of dance are women, the number of men in dance is increasing. At the college level, students have become interested in learning folk dances of many nations as a recreational activity. At earlier ages, more students are specializing in activity areas, including dance, which is especially popular for young women. It offers many benefits in the development of coordination and grace.

The Need for Specialists

More specialists are needed in the schools in a number of areas. While physical education teachers and coaches are in oversupply as a group, many areas of teaching and coaching still are far from crowded. Special education has a shortage of teachers who can work with the exceptional child. Teaching special education classes or using "adapted activities," refers to teaching any person who is unable to benefit from the ordinary program of physical education activities. It can include working with gifted children, whose needs for more intellectual content or better approaches to physical activities are rarely met, with children who have mental disabilities (e.g., children who are retarded), or with children who have any type of physical disability (e.g., temporary injury, blindness, deafness, and diseases such as muscular dystrophy or polio). The need for people who are skilled in the special education area is great.

Specialists are needed in such areas as aquatics and gymnastics, for some specialized coaching areas are still far from crowded. The oversupply of coaches is primarily in the so-called major sports such as football and basketball. The number of different sports offered in the schools has expanded rapidly over the last decade, but the expansion is handicapped by a lack of trained coaches. Because some sports that were primarily regional are beginning to spread across the nation, specialists are now needed in parts of the country where these sports have been rare.

Specialists are also needed in the areas of lifetime sports and coeducational activities, which are expanding rapidly. Many schools have changed the orientation of their programs from fitness activities to lifetime sports, which requires some changes in the training of the teachers. At the same time, governmental regulations and popular demand are calling for a greater emphasis on programs of coeducational activities rather than those in which all classes are grouped by sex. This change in the composition of the classes can affect the teaching content and methods and require new training and teachers with different areas of specialization.

Women coaches are perhaps the fastest-growing group of specialists in the field today. The late 1960s and early 1970s brought a massive increase in the number of women's athletics teams at the high school and college levels. The need for trained women to coach these teams has far outstripped the supply, almost regardless of the sport. This need, combined with the somewhat limited number of women physical educators, has combined to open a strong job market for women physical educators who are specialists in one or more sports.

Elementary school specialists are another growing group. They have been in short supply, though many colleges have begun to graduate more such specialists to fill that void. More elementary schools are hiring specialists to teach physical education in the elementary school or to act as advisors or supervisors of the classroom teachers who may do the actual teaching in the lower grades. The demand at this level is increasing, and teachers of both sexes are needed. The traditional elementary specialist has been female, which has created a greater market for male specialists.

Challenge-oriented specialists are in increasing demand. Examples of people in this area of work are teachers or instructors in programs such as Outward Bound. These programs, which are designed to provide a tough challenge to the participants, began outside the school, but they are gradually being added to college and high school physical education programs.

They provide an extended test of the individual that is difficult to reproduce in the usual school situation.

New areas of scholarship are also appearing at the college level, though they may not be teacher-oriented activities. Increasing numbers of physical educators are beginning to specialize in research areas such as we have described in our discussion of disciplines. Areas of research related to the fields of physical education that have been opened in the last two decades include research in motor learning, the sport psychology and sociology fields, the history and philosophy areas of physical education and sport studies, and new dimensions of physiological research oriented toward sport. New opportunities are developing in these areas as they are opened by growing numbers of physical educators interested in concentrating in the scholarly studies areas of the field.

This survey is just a sampling of some of the types of teaching jobs available in physical education and its allied fields. While the field has an overall surplus of teachers, many areas within the field do not have enough teachers to supply their needs. As a prospective teacher, you can improve your employment potential by developing a specialty in some area in which the need for teachers is great. The teaching possibilities in physical education are by no means limited, unless your interests are limited to the most common, traditional teaching areas.

THE FUTURE OF TEACHING JOBS

As we have noted, the need for general teachers of physical education is low because of an oversupply of teachers. However, that oversupply is expected to disappear during the next decade, so the job market in teaching should improve steadily into the 1990s. Also, the demand will always be greater for the better-than-average graduate—the A or B students—than for the C students, who are in considerable oversupply. The prospective teachers who have the greatest chance of finding a job are those with good grades and at least one well-developed area of specialization, such as we have discussed in this chapter.

Too few students realize that many job opportunities exist outside the teaching field for majors in physical education and sports. The greatest demands are connected with the many recreational activities and services, which in turn create a market for sporting equipment and supplies. The student of physical education can, by studying the job market carefully and at an early stage in the training process, find many good potential forms of employment. However, the student who maintains only ordinary grades and does not develop any area of specialization will have a difficult time locating a job after graduation.

TYPES OF NONTEACHING JOBS

Not every student of physical education is interested in teaching as a career. While the basic orientation of the field is toward teaching, many other areas of work are available to the trained physical educator. Most of these are essentially areas of physical education, but some of the areas may require specialized degrees in other areas such as recreation or physical therapy. In some areas, a business minor or even a major may be helpful, especially in administrative positions that involve long-term planning or handling large sums of money.

Fordham and Leaf have discussed alternative career possibilities extensively, and Charlotte Lambert produced a list of 50 job possibilities that a physical educator might pursue.[2] Now we need to discuss some of the many nonteaching job possibilities.

Administration

Administrative work may be the end result of teaching in physical education, for the teacher may become the administrator of a large program or department of physical education. Administrators are needed in teaching areas, but they also are needed in areas not connected with teaching, such as sports programs. Sports administration can include work as an athletic director or as a business manager for school or professional sports teams. An administrator needs some academic training in administrative needs and procedures, in addition to practical experience, for a successful teacher–coach will not necessarily be a successful administrator.

The field of sport management has attracted much interest in the last decade. The large increase in people participating in recreational activities that require more formal settings, such as racquetball and squash, has created a market for administrators of such facilities and programs. Their qualifications include an understanding of the facilities and equipment needed for the activities, plus the business skills necessary to handle budgeting, staffing, and other administrative tasks.

A number of schools offer programs with a concentration in sport management, which usually involves a combination of physical education and business administration courses. With the growth of private sports and health clubs, the opportunities in this area are growing rapidly. The need for trained fitness instructors has boomed during the 1980s, though there are few widely accepted procedures for certifying people as trained for that job. Some physical educators are concerned about the lack of training of many people who work or advertise themselves as fitness specialists in health and fitness clubs.

Health Education and Services

While we think of the health education area as a teaching area, it is closely allied to many activities that do not involve teaching. This area of work includes school nurses and doctors, health specialists in the schools who either provide services or supervise health programs, occupational health workers on the job site, and workers in the many areas of public health services. Health educators may work for local, state, or national governments to provide services, give information, and develop health or health education programs to be used in schools or communities. Many trained administrators are needed for areas of health education work and services.

The field of health education and services has grown rapidly over the last decade. The expansion of local health services has created a need for more specialists trained to work in this area. More schools are offering specialized programs in health education and services. Administrators are needed to handle these expanding programs.

The increase has been large in the number of company groups that combine health care and instruction with recreational and fitness activities. This is a growing area for exercise physiology specialists, recreation majors, fitness instructors, and health care and health education specialists. Companies have found that when such broadly based programs are provided, their overall health care costs actually decrease. The combined effect is "preventive maintenance" for their employees. The growth of health maintenance organizations (HMOs—prepaid health care and maintenance programs) has been rapid in the 1980s. It opens another area of potential jobs, as groups follow unified programs to prevent illness, injury, and poor health instead of waiting until hospitalization is required.

Therapy and Specialized Training

While we usually think of therapy as physical therapy, which involves working with people who have temporary or permanent physical disabilities, the areas of therapy are much broader. The four basic types of therapy are physical therapy, corrective therapy, occupational therapy, and dance therapy. We shall briefly discuss each as a possible occupation.

Physical therapy is primarily physical activity that a physician plans to help people make a physical recovery from severe disease or disability. It is planned to correct problems that are primarily physical in nature, so it might be considered a more narrow area of corrective therapy. Although a physical education degree is helpful, a person needs specialized training before qualifying as a physical therapist.

Broader in scope than physical therapy, corrective therapy is concerned with the mental aspects of rehabilitation as well as the physical aspects. It is a team approach to rehabilitating people with physical and mental illness. Rather than treat only the physical symptoms, it aims at the mental and social problems that result from the disability. This area of specialization has developed largely since World War II. Educational programs in this field are approved by the American Corrective Therapy Association (ACTA).

Occupational therapy involves working with people who are emotionally disturbed or suffer from perceptual motor problems. Physical education activities are used as one of several approaches to the problems of the patients. As with other types of therapy, the occupational therapist needs special training beyond a bachelor's degree.

Dance therapy is a relatively new area of therapy. The dance therapist works with people of all ages in programs that use the expressive movement

Fitness and rehabilitation programs need specialists trained in physical exercise activities. (Courtesy DUPAC, Duke University Preventive Approach to Cardiology)

aspect of dance as a means of guidance and to improve communication among people with problems. The dance therapist needs training in dance, movement activities, and psychology to develop the broad background needed to work in this area.

Recreational Services

The recreation area is growing rapidly, for many small communities are developing programs of community recreation and recreational facilities, just as the large cities did years ago. People are needed to develop and administer recreational programs on a number of levels. Although community recreation is the area we think of most commonly, the government uses specialists connected with the National Parks system and civilians on military bases, many business and industrial concerns hire people to run company programs of intramurals and competitive sports, and many larger churches are hiring trained specialists to run church recreation programs.

As nations become more affluent, citizens gain much more free time. One of the major problems of the future may be the question of how we shall use our leisure time. The area of leisure services has become a major national business, with many millions of dollars spent annually on recreation and recreational supplies in the United States alone. Businesses are sponsoring recreational activities not only for the enjoyment of their employees but also because such activities tend to develop healthier employees. Churches are adding recreation programs to provide more acceptable activities for their members. The activities also help the churches in holding the interest of the young people. Church recreation is a rapidly developing area in the recreational services field.

The growth of the recreational services area in the public and private sectors has created a large market for recreational specialists. More college degree programs are being offered under titles that convey the broad scope of the ultimate field, such as recreation and leisure, park management, and leisure services. People are needed to plan, build, and operate parks—large and small, public and private. Leisure services, whether organized community recreational programs, privately financed business or religious programs, or unorganized activities that require maintained facilities, are going to be a strong area of need in the future, for the modern trend is toward shorter working hours and more leisure time. The broad field of recreation is one of the largest current growth markets for people interested in physical education.

Full-Time Coaching and Athletics

Many coaches at the college level devote their full time to coaching duties, while some coaches also run coaching clinics, schools, and camps, especially during the summer months. This type of activity has become popular in the United States during the last decade or so, and as the number of professional sports teams increases, more professional coaching positions are becoming available. In fact, this is another area in which training in sport administration would be useful.

Many high school and college athletes hope to make a career of professional athletics. The one thing to keep in mind in this area is that the competition is extremely keen. The odds against a high school athlete playing and doing well in college and then continuing on into professional sports successfully are in the million-to-one range. The most unfortunate aspect of the interest in playing professional sports and in coaching at a high level is that too many athletes neglect to prepare themselves to do anything else if they fail to meet their goal. A student interested in professional sports should be educated for a second career as a basic precaution.

Sports and Health as Business

Many "health clubs" have been opened to develop and maintain the health of anyone who will pay the bill regularly, while many existing sports clubs are devoted to particular sports, such as golfing, swimming, tennis, skiing, ice-skating, and bowling. Most of the sports clubs hire specialists as "club pros" who teach or coach the members in the activities of the sport. Although the primary prerequisite of a job of this nature is a highly developed level of skill in the chosen sport, a physical education background can be helpful in the teaching aspects of the duties. Health clubs can use people with training in physical education, though the dominant hiring interests of some of them seem to relate to an attractive appearance and the ability to sell memberships, rather than any evident ability to improve the health of a paying customer.

Some of the private sports concerns that run their own schools in a sport require trained teachers, while some organizations have set up resorts dedicated to a single sporting activity that requires highly skilled teachers. Some more general organizations, such as country clubs, also hire sports coaches to train private sports teams composed of the children of the club members.

Training in sport management also can be a useful asset in sports and health businesses. In many cases, the people beginning sports or health clubs are more knowledgeable in sport than in business practices, and as a result, someone with administrative training could help to stabilize the daily operations. Training in recreation or leisure services also might enable someone working in sports and health businesses to see needs that are not being met. By meeting those needs, the chances of success for the operation are increased greatly. Just as some people want a sports facility where they can exercise, others want organized activities, such as club intramurals, tournaments, or other competitive as well as social activities. Many areas of training and expertise can be useful in such a situation.

Sports Medicine and Athletic Training

A great need in sports is for more specialists in sports medicine (doctors) and for specialists in athletic training (paraprofessionals in athletic medicine).

The title "athletic trainer" can be confusing, for in amateur athletics the trainer does not really train the athletes or plan their program of training. The trainer is concerned with the care and prevention of athletic injuries. Prevention may include activities such as providing liquids for athletes to drink during workouts in hot weather or taping ankles or other body parts for safety or support before practice sessions or contests. Treatment includes first aid and emergency treatment of injuries and may include planning the program of rehabilitation for an athlete after an injury. The trainer may be considered an intermediate step between the coach and the physician who specializes in sports medicine. Well-trained, ethics-conscious athletic trainers are necessary to prevent the abuse of training and drug-handling practices that can occur in the treatment of athletic injuries. Ethically, the trainer cannot dispense drugs or give shots unless supervised by a physician, but in practice, this may not be the case. This is an area of major concern in modern athletics, for too few people are accustomed to dealing with athletic injuries.

Although specialized training is necessary, the need for people in the area of athletic injuries and their treatment is growing rapidly. Many states are moving to put trainers in the high schools, which would create a huge demand for certified trainers, both male and female. Not all colleges have athletic trainers at this time, but a move toward requiring trainers as a safety factor in athletics could make this area one with excellent job opportunities in the future. The National Athletic Trainers Association (NATA) has information on training programs and colleges with certified training programs. The number of doctors trained in handling sports injuries is also limited in most communities, though the addition of certified trainers in the community could improve this situation because the injuries would be fewer. The interested student should check with NATA to learn the certification requirements and to see which schools offer certified programs.

Sports Supplies and Equipment

As participation in sports and recreational activities increases, sales and business opportunities in sporting goods increase rapidly. Private companies need persons with an understanding of physical activities, both competitive and recreational sports. People are needed who are familiar with the equipment needs and changing demands. Many companies are specializing in the design and construction of athletic facilities, indoor and outdoor, and they need people with knowledge of the requirements of sporting events.

The area of sporting goods is another growth industry for the same reasons cited for recreational fields. People are needed to design improved equipment, to develop new markets, and to test and sell sporting equipment. The specialist in many activities may be able to determine unmet needs that could result in large business increases. To be successful in this area, considerable knowledge of sporting activities is needed, combined with business acumen and training. An understanding of the working of the human body also is needed when designing sports equipment, since the body determines the manner in which sports equipment must be used.

Publishers

Publishers of books on sports and textbooks in the area of physical education and its allied fields need people who are knowledgeable about physical education in several areas. Editors are needed who are familiar with the wants and demands for publications in areas related to physical education and sport. This type of job requires a knowledge of physical education and of writing and editorial skills. Other people are needed in the sales areas, including direct sales, which often involves traveling to sell books. These jobs require a knowledge of physical education and the comparative values of the available books, combined with sales ability and an understanding of the available markets for publications in the area of physical education and sports.

Another area of publishing that offers job opportunities for people who are knowledgeable about physical education is that of sporting magazines. Specialty sporting magazines aimed at people interested in depth in a single sporting activity experienced a time of growth in the 1970s. Magazines such as *Runner's World* showed that a sizable market was available to the publisher who knew an area well and was able to predict how great an interest in that area was held by the public. That growth has continued into the 1980s, as magazines and books devoted to newer activities, such as triathlon competitions, have appeared. Though many sporting magazines die almost as rapidly as they are born, a market still exists for knowledgeable people to act as writers, editors, and administrators.

Though this is only a brief overview of nonteaching jobs, you can see that the job market has much more to offer than simply teaching and coaching in the public schools. In a time of rapid societal change, you may have the opportunity to create an entirely new type of job in one of the growth areas of the 1990s.

NOTES

1. Sheldon L. Fordham and Carol Ann Leaf, *Physical Education and Sports: An Introduction to Alternative Careers*. New York: John Wiley, 1978.
2. Charlotte Lambert, "Career Directions, "*JOPERD* 55 (May-June 1984), 40–43, 53.

SUGGESTED READINGS

Andrews, Jerry W., C. Robert Blackmon, and James A. Mackey. "Preservice Performance and the National Teacher Exams." *Phi Delta Kappan* 61 (January 1980), 358–359.

Bianco, Albert, And Paul C. Paese. "So You Want to Be a Teacher/Coach." *JOPERD* 55 (January 1984), 55.

Clayton, Robert D., and Joyce A. Clayton. "Careers and Professional Preparation Programs." *JOPERD* 55 (May-June 1984), 44–45.

Considine, William J., ed. *Alternative Professional Preparation in Physical Education*. Reston, Va.: AAHPERD, 1979.

Cruikshank, Donald R. "What We Know About Teacher's Problems." *Educational Leadership* 38 (1981), 402–405.

Dunn, Diana R. "Economics and Equity: Critical Choices." *JOPERD* 55 (May-June 1984), 23–26.

Fain, Gerald, ed. "Employee Recreation," *Leisure Today*, in *JOPERD* 54 (October 1983), 31–62.

Fordham, Sheldon L., and Carol Ann Leaf. *Physical Education and Sports: An Introduction to Alternative Careers*. New York: John Wiley, 1978.

Frith, Greg H. *The Role of the Special Education Paraprofessional: An Introductory Text*. Springfield, Ill.: Charles C Thomas, 1982.

Heitzmann, William Ray, *Opportunities in Sports Medicine*. Lincolnwood, Ill.: National Textbook Co., 1984.

Kauth, Bill. "The Athletic Training Major." *JOPERD* 55 (October 1984), 11–13, 80–83.

Lambert, Charlotte. "Career Directions." *JOPERD* 55 (May-June 1984), 40–43, 53.

Monahan, Terry. "HMOs: Directing the Future of Sports Medicine?" *The Physician and Sportsmedicine* 14 (March 1986), 254–257, 261.

Nash, Heyward L. "How to Set Up a Sports Medicine Clinic." *The Physician and Sportsmedicine* 13 (June 1985), 168–174, 176.

———. "Instructor Certification: Making Fitness Programs Safer?" *The Physician and Sportsmedicine* 13 (October 1985), 142–144, 146, 151–152. 154–155.

Nelson, Katherine H. "Is Corporate Fitness Really the Career of the Future?" *The Physical Educator* 41 (May 1984), 100–103.

Parkhouse, Bonnie, ed. "Sport Management." *JOPERD* 55 (September 1984), 12–22.

Quain, Richard J., and Janet P. Parks. "Sport Management Survey: Employment Perspectives." *JOPERD* 57 (April 1986), 18–21.

Randall, Lynda E. "Employment Statistics: A National Survey in Public School Physical Education." *JOPERD* 57 (January 1986), 23–28.

Ravizza, Kenneth. "Enhancing Well-Being: An Old/New Role for Physical Education." *JOPERD* 54 (March 1983), 30–32.

Rog, James A. "Teaching and Coaching: The Ultimate Challenge." *JOPERD* 55 (August 1984), 48–49.

Roos, Robert. "Are Physician Credentials in Sports Medicine Needed Now?" *The Physician and Sportsmedicine* 14 (March 1986), 262–266, 268, 270.

Schell, B., et al. "An Investigation of Future Market Opportunities for Sport Psychologists." *Journal of Sport Psychology* 6, no. 3 (1984), 335–350.

Shields, Sharon L., ed. "The Physical Education Profession in the Corporate Sector: Its Role and Influence." *JOPERD* 55 (March 1984), 32–44.

"Sports Medicine Groups 1985." *The Physician and Sportsmedicine* 13 (November 1985), 143–145.

Templin, Thomas J., ed. "Profiles of Excellence: Fourteen Outstanding Secondary School Physical Educators." *JOPERD* 54 (September 1983), 15–36.

VanderZwaag, Harold J. "Coming Out of the Maze: Sport Management, Dance Management and Exercise Science—Programs with a Future." *Quest* 35, no. 1 (1983), 66–73.

Yessis, Michael. "Role of the Sports Interpreter/Translator in Promoting Sport." *The Physical Educator* 38 (December 1981), 187–189.

Zehring, John William. "How to Get Another Teaching Job and What to Do If You Can't." *Learning* (February 1978), 44–51.

chapter 13

The Technological Workplace Appears

We are now very much in a computer age, yet many people are not comfortable with even the idea of computers. Some people see computers as difficult to use and threatening to human peace of mind, a view that may be in part a result of our fictional literature about computers.

Since the 1920s our fiction has presented us with computers and robots that create dangers for us. From Karel Capek's early play *R.U.R.*, from which we get the term *robot* to HAL 9000 in the movie *2001*, from Tik Tok to the "cybernetic samurai," our fictional computers and the robots they often inhabit appear as threatening faces of the future. Though we also have been given other, nonthreatening (and even humorous) forms, as in the movie *Star Wars*, the talking appliances and depressed robot of Douglas Adams, and the helpful and sometimes protohuman characters of Robert Heinlein, many people still seem to view the technological future as a dark, threatening one.[1]

In reality, it is a promising future, though it is a challenging one. We need to be educated well to take full advantage of technology, yet it is not difficult in the sense we fear. Each new advance in computer hardware and software makes computers easier for anyone to use. You do not have to be able to write computer programs to be able to use computers well. Indeed, software programs are being made as nontechnical and user-friendly ("foolproof") as possible. Even so, they will be far simpler in a few more years.

To take full advantage of the computerized, technological society blossoming before us does not require technical training. In most cases, what you re-

BLOOM COUNTY   **by Berke Breathed**

ally need is to learn what practical uses you can make of new machines now and to develop some idea of what the future may hold. With this in mind, we shall first look at the computer in today's world, and then we shall make a projection into the workplace of the near future. For some of you, this future is already here.

THE COMPUTER REACHES THE MARKETPLACE·

Our world is changing rapidly, moving into a technological age that we scarcely dreamed of two decades ago. We read of failing industries and unemployed or unemployable workers, yet the total number of jobs available continues to increase. A sense of the type of change was carried in a statement made in 1983 by Ronald Reagan, speaking of the types of jobs that are now available and the education that they require.

"I'll read you the entire ad," said Reagan. "'Systems programmer—large-scale IBM, VTAM, TSO/SPF, ACF, CICS, OS/MFS.' The point is that we're in a new age. No longer do the ads simply offer jobs with good hours and no heavy lifting. You have to be a specialist to know what the ad is even about."

We are now in the computer age, and the face of the marketplace has changed radically in less than a decade. The impact reaches into the schools, affecting students and teachers even more than businesses. A businessman is concerned primarily with now, this year and next year. The teacher and student are more concerned with the effect of today's education on the student's life 10 and 20 years from now. Who knows what skills or knowledge we shall need then? The microcomputer is a symbol of the changes that have taken place.

A few years ago the distinction among a computer, a minicomputer, and a microcomputer was clear. It was a difference of size, price, and particularly memory capacity. A *computer* was a mainframe machine, as large as a standing file cabinet, and usually much larger. A *minicomputer* was less bulky and had less memory, but it was still expensive. A *microcomputer* could fit on a desk or under an arm, was relatively inexpensive, and had a very limited memory. It was useful only for smaller tasks, or as an alternate-location connector to a mainframe computer.

The distinction between the minicomputer and microcomputer essentially has disappeared, as much smaller storage media have multiplied the memory capacity of the smallest microcomputer by many times. Today when people refer to a computer, most often they mean a microcomputer, because micros have become so common and are so widely used. Far fewer people work directly with large mainframes, such as the larger IBMs and DECs, and fewer still work with the world's rare supercomputers, such as the CRAY-1 or CYBER 205.

WHAT IS A COMPUTER?

A computer is a machine that understands only two commands, which we think of as "yes" and "no." At the lowest level, its memory consists of single *bits*, each of which is a piece of material that can be electrically charged to be either off or on, states that programmers note as a zero or a one. Early microcomputers arranged those bits into eight-bit patterns called *bytes*.

A program builds a pattern of those zeroes and ones until it leads the computer to complete some function, which originally was the working of complex mathematical problems. The instructions to the computer are commonly called languages, because they are used to "talk" to the computer, to communicate with it. The combinations of zeroes and ones represent machine language. Above the level of machine language is a level called assembly language, which allows more complicated directions or commands. We usually think of programming in terms of the higher-level languages, such as COBOL, FORTRAN, BASIC, Pascal, C, Ada, and many others.

For a beginner to the world of computers, the best approach is to look at them as "black boxes." It does not really matter to you *how* a computer does something; what is important is knowing what it can do for you and what procedures you have to follow to make the computer do what you want. What happens inside the box is not important to you, so long as what comes out of the box is what you need. Using a computer is similar to watching television: We do not care how or why it works; we simply want to see a given program. As long as the television does what it is supposed to do for us, we do not really care how or why it does it. That degree of understanding is not necessary to meet our needs.

A general example of a computer arrangement is shown in Figure 13.1. The part labeled "computer" is the central processing unit (CPU), where the programs run and the calculations are made. This is where the main memory of the computer is located, with programs that are always present and cannot be changed (ROM—read-only memory) and the memory that holds temporary programs and does the calculations (RAM—random-access memory). The text or data entries and the results are usually viewed on a television-type (but more sharply focused) screen called a video display terminal (VDT). (An older term is CRT—cathode ray tube.)

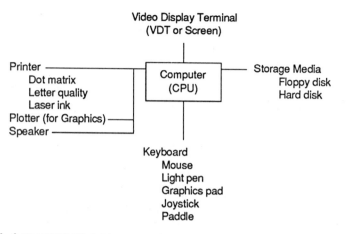

Figure 13.1. A computer hardware arrangement.

The programs that the computer runs (the software) are usually put into the computer from attached storage media sources, such as disk drives of either floppy disks (with small capacities) or hard disks (with large capacities). Programs and data can also be entered from the keyboard, which looks much like the keyboard of a typewriter. Signal entry is also possible (depending on the hardware and software combinations) with a "mouse" or rolling-ball unit (used to issue commands to the computer by the "point-and-click" method), light pens, graphics pads, joysticks, paddles, and even the touch of a finger to the screen.

While the results of the program can be seen on the VDT, they can also be saved on the storage disks and printed (to make hard copy) on a printer. The most common types of printers today are the dot-matrix printer (which quickly forms characters with a series of dots), the letter-quality or daisy-wheel printer (which is much slower but uses formed letters to strike a ribbon, just as a typewriter does, giving the highest quality print), and the laser-jet ink printer (quick, clear, and expensive). Plotters are used to print graphics, often in color. Sound programs can be output through the small speaker in most computers, though music synthesizers (like the MOOG) have more advanced systems.

Computer needs are given in terms of hardware and software. The hardware is all of the equipment that is used, and the software includes the programs that are used with the hardware. The recommended selection method is to choose software that meets your needs, then buy the computer and equipment that will run that software. (Different types of computers often cannot share each other's software; the problem of compatibility is always important.) Many books and magazines are produced to explain computers and computer programs and to help people decide what equipment they need. The computer field changes rapidly. Companies can appear and disappear rapidly, which is also a factor in computer decisions. At this time, the leading hardware includes Apple computers in the educational and small business fields and IBM and the IBM-compatibles (such as COMPAQ) in the larger business and scientific world. However, other major, high-quality computers are available.

THE EVOLUTION OF MICROCOMPUTER SOFTWARE PROGRAMS

A computer is of no use without software (computer programs) that allows us to communicate with the machine. Microcomputer software programs already enable one person to do tasks that required a small team of clerical workers ten years ago. This is largely the result of the lightning progress of the first decade in the life of the microcomputer. It began as a machine with a tiny memory, so that early programs had to be small and simple. Statistical processes were the original purpose for both large and small computers, but games soon appeared.

Today, we speak of the computer's memory in terms of "k," as in "64k." One k is a kilobyte, or a thousand (actually 1024) bytes or units of memory in their binary form. As the machine's memory increased from 16k to 48k and then to 64k, word-processing programs appeared, making the process of writing far simpler. The first spreadsheet programs then appeared for keeping columns of financial records that could be statistically manipulated. They allowed businesspeople to make "what if" decisions by changing parts of the data file, such as the number of units sold, to see what the result might be. They could then decide on the most cost-effective or profitable way to run their businesses.

Machine memory continued to increase, rising to 128k, then to 256k. The "integrated" software programs, which combine several types of programs into a single integrated or combined package, began to appear. They required much more memory, but their power and usability were also much greater. After a decade of microcomputer and software evolution, a high-level integrated program may include five elements: word processing, a financial spreadsheet, a database, a graphics program, and telecommunications capabilities (Figure 13.2). The word processor may include a spelling checker, with vocabularies now passing 100,000 words and allowing the user to add any professional terms that are not already included. It may even include a grammar checker to ensure that the sentence structure is correct. The user can take work from one part of the program, such as statistical tables and graphs, blend it into another part of the program, such as the word processor, develop a final report, then "mail" it somewhere else by telephone.

The memory storage capacity of microcomputers has risen and the size of storage media has decreased, from the early audio cassette tape storage through floppy disks to hard disks, which may be run either on board (inside the computer) or by peripheral disk drives (connected to the computer by cable). On-board memory capabilities of microcomputers have already risen above three megabytes (three million bytes), with attached hard-disk mem-

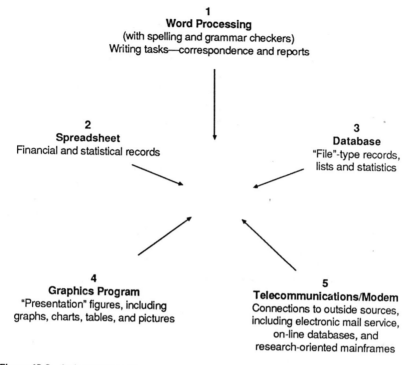

Figure 13.2. An integrated software program.

ory storage of 75 or more megabytes available. ROM (read-only memory) compact laser disks of 540 megabytes are expected during 1986. Microcomputers today may be 100 or more times as powerful as many mainframe computers were 15 years ago. Computers continue to decrease in size, and their capabilities to increase, with the currently estimated lifetime of a new state-of-the-art microcomputer system at not over 18 months before new developments make it a has-been. We are charging into the age of a marvelous technology.

Major changes in manufacturing techniques have accompanied the rapid growth of robotics; industrial robots now perform many heavy-duty and high-precision tasks that human workers previously did. At the same time, the use of three-dimensional computer graphics in CAD/CAM packages (computer-aided design and computer-aided manufacturing) has greatly changed the efficiency of designing goods and testing them before production models are constructed and has improved efficiency during the manufacturing process itself.

THE NEXT STEP IN COMPUTER USE: EXPERT SYSTEMS

We are now at the stage where *expert systems* are beginning to appear as microcomputer software. An outgrowth of artificial intelligence research, expert systems are programs designed to provide expert guidance, taking the place of an expert by making specialized knowledge easily available to the user.

Artificial intelligence is a field that studies learning and tries to recreate the learning pattern in computer programs. While intelligent machines have been developed, the definition of when a machine truly becomes intelligent has been revised many times. Expert systems form one branch of the field of artificial intelligence, but it is perhaps the most potentially meaningful one to educators.

As Donald Hillman notes, expert systems can be more accurately called "knowledge-based systems," as they are programs that use someone's expertise or knowledge in a given field.[2] The early expert systems were programs to assist doctors in diagnosing illnesses. As microcomputer capabilities have increased, expert systems have been produced for smaller machines. They are used most often in medical and business applications as aids in decision making or in the diagnosis of problems,[3] but they have great potential in sport applications also.

An expert system has three parts: a *database*, which has facts about the subject matter; a *rule base*, which is the list of rules an expert follows in solving problems; and a *rule interpreter*, which interprets the rules based on the facts in the database.

In essence, when an expert system is developed, a programming specialist called a knowledge engineer works with one or more experts in the subject area to determine the problem-solving process that an expert in that subject follows. As an example, if an expert system were being developed for football coaching, the programmer would want to know what logical process the expert coach follows in deciding what he will do. It is a process of learning that *if* this is the situation, *then* we shall follow procedure A, or *else* we shall follow procedure B (which may be yet another if-then-else structure).

To complicate the programming logic, people do not think like computers. A computer has only two possibilities, "yes" or "no," programmed one or zero. A series of steps in a computer operation is simply a long series of yes-no decisions. For people, the procedure is more complicated. We think with what has been called "fuzzy logic."

Fuzzy logic is the use of approximations and rough rules of thumb. We say that *if* this is true *and* that is true, *then* we shall follow procedure A, *maybe*. We do not say that if the other team is leading by exactly 11 points, we shall use procedure B. Instead, we say that if we are behind by "about" ten points *and* the competitive conditions are X *and* other factors are or are not present, *then* we shall try procedure B. An expert has many working rules of thumb about what to do in certain conditions. Those rules of thumb based on knowledge gained through experience are sometimes called *heuristics*. Heuristics includes expert knowledge, sometimes called intuition or insight. An expert may have a "feel" for a solution, based on a number of vague factors and on knowledge and experience gained over the years. Thus, a heuristic approach may solve a problem that an ordinary computer program would be unable to solve.

Expert systems written for nonprogrammers are now appearing for micro-computers.[4] Examples are programs such as Expert-Ease, M-1, and EXPERT-2. With these programs, nonspecialists can begin to develop their own expert systems programs. Programs such as these are sometimes referred to as "knowledge engineering environments" (or "tool kits"), as they come with a "shell" that is "the linguistic and reasoning mechanisms that interpret and draw conclusions from the knowledge."[5] In a few years we may have programs that can provide a coach with all of the knowledge of the most expert coach in the world, all available in response to "natural language" questions (using no computer codes) from the owner.

However, experts do not agree on the potential of expert systems. Hubert and Stuart Dreyfus have worked in artificial intelligence, yet they have written that expert systems may be of only limited value.[6] They argue that humans are not rule bound in making their decisions the way computers are, so that expert systems can never be better than advanced novices in their ability to deal with complicated problems. They liken the human mind to a hologram, arguing that the mind is more concerned with images than with words. While this is an area of controversy, much progress is being made toward producing useful expert systems for certain "real-world" applications.

We are seeing computers used heavily in many new areas. The technology we see used in medicine today will eventually appear in sport settings, at least as research and diagnostic tools.[7] The computer technology used in sport biomechanics has gained much media attention in the mid-1980s,[8] as has its use in assisting with the preparation of world-class and Olympic athletes.[9] Computers are appearing in health and fitness clubs, and inexpensive software is being sold for home fitness analysis, instruction, and record keeping.[10]

To ignore the computer in today's world is to ignore the present, and perhaps to write off many of our greatest possibilities for the future. Priscilla Norton has suggested that we need to be careful in how we use the new technology in education.[11] She points out that these new technologies affect how we think and learn, yet we still know little of their full effect on us and how they can be used most effectively in teaching and learning. In suggesting her imperatives for technology in education, she strongly urges educators to study technology and its role in change. She argues that we shall have to develop new definitions of learning, as well as new strategies for achieving it. We still have little idea of what direction education will take in our technological future.

A DAY IN THE LIFE: THE COMING TECHNOLOGY

Now we shall take a "real-life" look at the new and coming technology. What will life be like for the physical educator in our technological future? We shall look at a day in the life of several people with typical jobs in our field. A typical job often includes a combination of teaching, coaching, and administrative duties, so we shall look at specialists in each of those functions, with research added. The single difference is that we shall concentrate on what they will be doing with technology and on what technology may be doing with them.

While these views are speculative, essentially everything mentioned here is already in use in limited situations or will likely be possible within a few years. We think of future changes as fuzzy objects in a dim, distant future. As Steven Levy has pointed out, a microcomputer that is state-of-the-art today will remain as the leading model for only about 18 *months*.[12] That assumes that the rate of technological improvement does not increase, whereas it has been increasing geometrically for decades. Now, let's look at tomorrow.

The Researcher

We are accustomed to the idea of college professors doing research and to the idea that their research may involve new technologies. Our common image in this area is of the laboratory work that specialists in sport biomechanics and physiology do. Even so, other researchers such as sport sociologists and sport psychologists use advanced technology as well. For example, such researchers might use videotaping to permit more careful analysis of group dynamics and behavior in the teaching-learning situation, just as others will use on-line access to national or international databases for informational (written) research.

Many research projects begin with the writing of a research proposal, particularly if the researcher is applying for a grant to cover the costs of the research. Let us consider a researcher of the future who has undertaken a study of the endurance of college freshmen. Our researcher is working with two other professors on their research project, gathering data at three different universities across the country, while following a common research design. With a modem connecting their microcomputers to long-distance telephone lines, they hold a conference "call" by computer, jointly writing and polishing their research proposal. When it is completed, it is stored on the university's large mainframe computer and then downloaded to the microcomputers, where it is printed, giving each teacher a hard copy.

They will then use a project-manager software package to outline the steps they will follow as they conduct the research. It will help them to set their deadlines for the subparts of the research, monitoring their progress and providing time guidelines throughout the study.

As part of their research project, the teachers need to review the literature and research already done on their chosen subject. The hardest part of this task, locating all of the possible sources, is conducted with a computer search through several of the large national and international on-line databases. A person or institution pays a monthly fee for access to the database, with additional charges based on the amount of time using the database. The relevant titles will be listed (on the screen) to their computer, so they can store them on disk and print a hard copy at the same time. The researchers may even be able to have complete copies of the needed papers sent to them by computer.

To save money, their computer is programmed to make its calls to the databases during the night hours, when access rates are cheapest. It will then store the information, making it available for the researchers when they arrive in the morning. Throughout the project they will keep in touch with each other by electronic mail, leaving messages for their computers to mail to each other during the night.

As the project continues, the researchers will collect their data, using the computer as a monitor and measuring tool, storing and printing out the results as they happen. The computer will measure physical performance variables during treadmill runs. It will develop digitized pictures of the biomechanical movement patterns of athletes from filmed performances.

When the experimental part of the study is completed, the data will be analyzed by statistical packages used by the computer, and it will prepare tables illustrating the results of the study. If any graphics would be useful as illustrations, it will be able to prepare them automatically, in color and with a three-dimensional effect, if it would be appropriate.

The research paper will be written with word-processing software by merging the different sources into one larger whole, using the "cut-and-paste" method. An outliner will be used to develop the plan for writing the paper. Then the review of the literature articles will be downloaded from the mainframes and edited down to the necessary quotations or points of reference, with the proper citations attached. The references and keywords will be located automatically. If the project develops into a full book, the index can be prepared automatically, and the type can be set from the disk. The statistical tables will be shifted from the storage program to the growing final paper. The word processor will compile the paper, automatically checking for correct spelling and grammar. The final paper will be printed and collated in multiple copies in a high-speed, letter-quality printer, such as a laser-jet ink printer.

The paper may be sent to a professional journal by electronic mail. If it is published, it will be added to a number of electronic databases available to all paying subscribers. If it is not published, or if it is presented at a conference or convention, it may be added to some other database, such as the ERIC database used in education. During the entire process, from the original idea onward, no piece of paper has to be touched by any of the researchers until they have the final paper in hand (if then). It will not be necessary.

The Teacher

Our teacher is concerned first with planning the overall physical education program and the lessons to be taught each day. The teacher will use a simple graphics program to develop by computer overhead projections and slides to illustrate the points to be made in the lessons. Photographs that illustrate good technique or skill performance can be loaded into the computer with an optical scanner, then reproduced as transparencies or slides. The graphics that the teacher develops can be combined into a videotaped presentation (stored on cassette), with dubbed-in music added to accompany the parts of the presentation that have no dialogue.

All teachers have to keep detailed records, and our teacher is no exception. The teacher will store on computer disks all records of student attendance, grades, performance on physical tests, checklists of skills, lists of lockers and combinations, team or group assignments, and any other relevant information. The school has a central computer for most record keeping and to hold all of the major software programs that the administrators and teachers need. The teacher has a microcomputer in the gym office, but it is connected to the larger computer, so the teacher has all needed access and storage capacity.

The teacher may be involved in developing computer-aided instruction (CAI) or computer-aided learning (CAL). This might involve developing interactive teaching software, with which the student and computer can communicate with each other, so that the computer responds to whatever the student is doing. The teacher will use software to help develop a program for the students to use. This software will be able to do such things as:

1. Ask questions and then record and grade student responses
2. Give students their choice of directions or levels of study
3. Use game ("arcade") graphics to test some motor skills and reaction times of students
4. Tell students what their performance strengths and weaknesses are, then show how their weaknesses can be corrected
5. Play tunes to accompany "decision-time" thinking

As an example, a weight-training machine will provide color graphics showing the progression and effectiveness of a training session performed while using a computer software package interfaced with the lifting machinery. It will detect and explain weaknesses in each individual lift of a series, as well as problems from one lift to the next in a progression.

Perhaps holographic images will be improved enough for the image of a world-class athlete to be projected onto the gymnasium floor, demonstrating a sport skill. The students can walk around the image, watching the performance from different angles and having it projected at different speeds. They will see a performing, three-dimensional, solid-looking "ghost" figure as a demonstrating student instructor.

The Coach and Athletic Director

The coach will take advantage of an expert system to plan his training. He has a software program on how to coach basketball, and it was developed with the most famous (and successful) college coach in the country. When he has a question, he goes to his office, puts the computer on voice mode, then asks his questions just as if the other coach were physically present. The expert system program will speak in response to his questions, using whatever type of voice the coach prefers. Most of his questions will be answered in this manner, so that he is not at a great competitive disadvantage even though he is not yet an experienced coach. He has 30 years of expertise and experience available to answer almost any question that occurs to him.

The computer will keep detailed records of his team's training sessions. He can type them in or give them orally, letting the computer make the proper entries. His records of individual training are also saved, and they can be printed out as a daily record or in summary form, in either tables or graphs.

He has stored his game films on videotapes, though he may have some interactive instructional programs on videodisc also. He can ask the computer to run any tape or videodisc, moving quickly to the part he wants to see. He can also use the computer to make technique analyses of his athletes' individual performances, based on expert systems that take advantage of a team of coaches and biomechanical experts on sports techniques and movement.

On the weekend he will attend a national coaching clinic, but he will do it in his own office. The school's "earth station" (satellite dish) will receive the beamed telecommunications signal sent from a central source via satellite. The expert coaches giving the clinic will not leave their schools. A telephone hookup will allow all of the participants to ask questions personally of any of the experts. The expert coaches can televise live or taped demonstrations using their own athletes in their own gym. The financial affairs of the clinic will be handled completely by electronic exchanges between bank accounts, with no checks having to be written or bills to be mailed.

Like those experts, much of his athletic correspondence will be conducted by electronic mail, sent from the school office at night by the computer. If he is a college coach, it may be a major recruiting source for him. He will subscribe to databases that have information and contact sources for potential recruits across the United States and Canada, and possibly including Europe, Central and South America, Australia, and New Zealand. It will give a printout that the student provides, with pictures of ratings from coaches or personnel in the scouting service. The athletic department's computerized mailings will be sent to all prospects as often as the coach wishes, with each letter personalized in comments that apply only to that athlete and in the coach's apparently hand-signed autograph on each letter, all without the coach being involved.

Indeed, the coach will keep close to his rabid fans with his call-in hotline with messages that change daily, or even hourly. His school may cooperate by helping him to produce clinics and booster or alumni club visitations via satellite and television hookups (live), while producing videotape or videodisc presentations for other situations.

The Administrator

One headache for our administrator is scheduling, which includes scheduling the school's facilities, arranging the class schedules, and planning special events, including athletic contests. In scheduling the facilities, the administrator must look for the most effective use of (1) space, (2) time, and (3) cost (more heating or cooling or lighting is needed at different times of the day and night, as well as different times of the year). The computer maintains a detailed schedule of the physical education and athletic facilities, including the dates and times when each area is in use. It keeps records of the relative cost of a given facility at different times and dates.

In scheduling classes for the students, the administrator must decide (1) when to offer each class, (2) who will teach each class, and (3) where each class should be held. The computer handles the scheduling from two directions. It plans the teaching facilities for each class on the schedule, taking into account need and relative convenience of time choices. It plans the schedules for each student based on individual requirements balanced against the school's requirements.

The computer is used in scheduling special events. It may be used to analyze and determine the best time or date for an event. It will be used to arrange the athletic schedules, including the correspondence, contracts, and logistical arrangements that are needed. It may be used to record ticket sales, perhaps even to mail invitations and bills, while keeping the account books balanced.

Budgeting is an important task. The administrator will need to develop and carry out budget plans, which will be done with the spreadsheet software in the computer. The administrator can look at this year's expenditures, which have been recorded. From that, he or she can project how the rate of spending compares with the budget, helping to project the end-of-year result. When the next year's budget is being developed, he or she can use "what if" projections based on different student enrollments, school incomes, and other variables, giving a better idea of the effect of the different options on the final budget.

He or she will use project-managing software to make the task of planning complicated projects much simpler. The software will provide regular target dates against which the progress toward the final goal can be judged. This will assist in the planning and scheduling of any of the long-range projects of the department.

As with the researcher and the coach, electronic mail is used for much of the correspondence. This large school system finds it simpler than the old system of a traveling courier taking piles of loose memos to each school each day. Now the system runs an electronic bulletin board with the general messages, in addition to the computer calls with memos and other messages sent to each school during the night. Most school system paperwork, including budgets, travels by this method now.

Finally, administrators have meetings with their peers, meeting via a teleconference. Many meetings can be held this way, allowing the open communication among the members of a group, while saving much travel time and money.

The Olympic Coach

Developing world-class athletes is a task done at a far higher level than most people realize. It has become technological in many other nations, and is now moving in that direction in the United States. We shall see radical changes in the methods used to develop the most advanced athletes in the near future.[13] The work described here is more theoretical than the work described in the other areas, because ethical and philosophical questions are at issue. These actions may be possible, but we have many questions about whether they are proper and should be legal.

Many world-class athletes in different sports will be tested physiologically and psychologically, until we develop a clear pattern of the physical and mental traits of the champion in each sport. Children will then be tested while still in elementary school. Their athletic profiles will be compared with those of champions in each sport. Then the children will be directed toward the sport in which their inherent traits are most similar to the champion athletes. A 10-year-old may be directed toward speed skating or water polo rather than football or basketball.

As youths are trained for sports, those of greater potential will be tested more thoroughly. The common measures of heart, lungs, strength, and blood chemistry will be measured. Muscle biopsies will give a clearer insight into the qualities of the youth's muscular tissue characteristics. The joints will be tested for flexibility and resilience. Tests of balance and coordination will be made. Psychological profiles will be developed, and brain-wave scans will be made during rest, practice, and competition. The pattern of electrical impulses through the muscles will be tested.

The athletes may have their growth stimulated with steroids and human growth hormones, or they may have their maturation retarded with other hormones in sports where smaller bodies are an advantage, such as women's gymnastics. The electrical muscle patterns of champion athletes will be recorded and used to stimulate the motor patterns of the developing young athletes. Electrical stimulation will enhance their muscular strength while they rest and as they train.

During training, specialists constantly will monitor the blood chemistry and psychological states, along with biomechanical efficiency and precision. Experienced physiotherapists and sports physicians will treat injuries immediately. Massage will be provided as a regular part of training, along with relaxation biofeedback and motivational psychological training. The body will be monitored throughout each training session, with heart, respiration, and blood chemistry readouts at the training site as the athlete exercises. Sport physiologists will prescribe any needed changes in the training immediately, as the need arises.

In preparing for competition, a rigorous pattern of mental conditioning and psychological support will be used, along with biofeedback to enhance relaxation and help to prevent the athlete from becoming nervous or distracted about the competitions. Mental practice of the skills will be used, along with electrical stimulation of the motor patterns, visual cues through films and holographs of expert performances, and psychological support services.

During skilled performances and competitions, the athletes will be filmed at speeds of 10,000 frames per second, with the performances immediately digitized and replayed in three-dimensional computer graphics. The graphics will be used to demonstrate how the skill was performed, followed by a replay with the mechanical imperfections corrected, providing a readout of what the resulting performance would have been. The athletes will be given computerized biofeedback during the competition, sometimes with computer tones or auditory patterns, sometimes with actual spoken instructions from the coach or trainer.

Sports careers at the highest level may last much longer, because of the thorough, careful scientific and medical care provided to the athletes. On the other hand, bodies trained throughout the year at the most intensive level may not be able to perform at the highest level for more than one to three years. Whether athletes trained in this manner will be able to live "normal" lives afterward, or will have their permanent health or length of life affected, is another unanswered question. A brave new world may be at hand in athletics, a technological wonderland, but many questions remain about its ultimate meaning to *homo ludens* — man, the player.

Today and Tomorrow

Looking at microcomputers today, one author wrote that "The New Human Interface Comes of Age."[14] We are already in an age when we can control our microcomputers with the keyboard, light pens, a mouse, our voice, and the touch of our finger on the screen. Technology is advancing so quickly that often we are unaware of what we can do today, much less what our future possibilities may be. Most of the things mentioned in this chapter are "old" already (except for the holographic techniques). We need to become more aware of the technology available to us, so we can learn how it can be used to help others. In the area of technology, the future is now; indeed, it is almost the past.

NOTES

1. Arthur C. Clarke, *2001*, New American Library, New York, 1968; John Sladek, *Tik Tok*, Victor Gollancz, London, 1983; Victor Milan, *The Cybernetic Samurai*, Arbor House, New York, 1985; Douglas Adams, *The Hitchhiker's Guide to the Galaxy*, Arthur Barker, London, 1979; Morton Klass, "The Artificial Alien: Transformations of the Robot in Science Fiction," *Annals of the American Academy of Political and Social Science* 470 (November 1983), 171–179.
2. Donald J. Hillman, "Artificial Intelligence," *Human Factors* 27 (February 1985), 22.
3. Henry Fersko-Weiss, "Expert Systems Decision-Making Power," *Personal Computing* 9 (November 1985), 97–101, 103–105.
4. Joseph M. Ferrara, James D. Parry, and Margaret M. Lubke, "Expert Systems Au-

thoring Tools for the Microcomputer: Two Examples," *Educational Technology* 25 (April 1985), 39–41.

5. Paul Kinnucan, "Software Tools Speed Expert System Development," *High Technology* 5 (March 1985), 16.

6. Hubert and Stuart Dreyfus, "Why Computers May Never Think Like People," *Technology Review* 89 (January 1986), 42–61.

7. H. Garrett DeYoung, "State of the Heart," *High Technology* 4 (May 1984), 33–41.

8. Dwight B. Davis, "Sports Biomechanics: Olympians' Competitive Edge," *High Technology* 4 (July 1984), 34–41.

9. Karen Freifeld, "Personal Computers at the Olympics," *Personal Computing* 8 (July 1985), 116, 119, 122, 123, 127–128; Ken Sheldon, "Olympic Coaching by Computer," *inCider* 2 (April 1984), 36–39; and "Man Behind the U.S. Olympic Sports Medicine Committee," *Scholastic Coach* 52 (January 1983), 31–32, 78–80; (February 1983), 26–28, 58–60.

10. Karen Freifeld, "Body Management," *Personal Computing* 7 (August 1983), 60–65, 67, 69, 71, 156; and Sue Mott, "Computers Get a Health Club Workout," *Personal Computing* 9 (September 1985), 15.

11. Priscilla Norton, "An Agenda for Technology and Education: Eight Imperatives," *Educational Technology* 25 (January 1985), 15–20.

12. Steven Levy, *Hackers: Heroes of the Computer Revolution*, Doubleday, New York, 1984.

13. Mark Teich and Patricia Weintraub, "Ultra Sports," *Omni* 9 (August 1985), 39–40, 42, 44, 96–97, 100–101.

14. Jim Bartimo, "The New Human Interface Comes of Age," *Popular Computing* 10 (January 1986), 58–61, 63, 65.

REFERENCES

Adams, Dennis M., and Deborah A. Bott. "Tapping into the World: Telecommunications Networks and Schools." *Computers in the Schools* 1 (Fall 1984), 3–17.

Adams, Dennis M., and Mary Fuchs. "New Digitized Literacies: Mixing Visual Media, the Humanities, Print, and Computer-Based Technology." *Educational Technology* 25 (May 1984), 16–18.

Antonoff, Michael. "The Push for Telecommuting." *Personal Computing* 9 (July 1985), 82–85, 87, 89, 91–92.

Bartino, Jim. "The New Human Interface Comes of Age." *Personal Computing* 10 (January 1986), 58–61, 63, 65.

Bork, Alfred M. *Personal Computers for Education*. New York: Harper & Row, 1985.

Brod, Craig. *Technostress: The Human Cost of the Computer Revolution*. Reading, Mass.: Addison-Wesley, 1984.

Brand, Stewart, ed. *Whole Earth Software Catalog for 1986*. Garden City, N.Y.: Quantum Press/Doubleday, 1985.

Bright, George W., and John G. Harvey. "Computer Games as Instructional Tools." *Computers in the Schools* 1 (Fall 1984), 73–79.

Brodeur, Doris R. "Interactive Video: Fifty-One Places to Start—An Annotated Bibliography." *Educational Technology* 25 (May 1985), 42–47.

Brodie, David A., and David A. Thornhill. *Microcomputing in Sport and Physical Education*. Wakefield, England: Lepus Books, 1983.

Cicciarella, Charles F., ed. *Directory of Computer Software with Application to Sport Sci-*

ence, Health, and Dance. Urbana, Ill.: AAHPERD Research Consortium Computer Network Committee, n.d.

"Computers in Education: Where Do We Go From Here?" Symposium in *Educational Technology* 25 (January 1985), 7–55.

Davis, Dwight B. "Sports Biomechanics: Olympians' Competitive Edge." *High Technology* 4 (July 1984), 34–41.

Deaken, Joseph. *The Electronic Cottage.* New York: William Morrow, 1982.

DeYoung, H. Garrett. "State of the Heart." *High Technology* 4 (May 1984), 33–41.

Feigenbaum, Edward A., and Pamela McCorduck. *The Fifth Generation: Artificial Intelligence and Japan's Computer Challenge to the World.* Revised. New York: New American Library, 1984.

Fersko-Weiss, Henry. "Electronic Mail: The Emerging Connection." *Personal Computing* 9 (January 1985), 71–74, 76, 79.

———. "Expert Systems Decision-Making Power." *Personal Computing* 9 (November 1985), 97–101, 103–105.

Florman, Samuel C. *Blaming Technology.* New York: St. Martin's, 1981.

Forester, Tom, ed. *The Information Technology Revolution.* Cambridge, Mass.: MIT Press, 1985.

Freifeld, Karen. "Personal Computers at the Olympics." *Personal Computing* 8 (July 1985), 116, 119, 122, 123, 127–128.

Gindele, John F., and Joseph F. Gindele. "Interactive Videodisc Technology and Its Implications for Education." *T.H.E. Journal* 12 (August 1984), 93–97.

Gold, Jordan. "Do-It-Yourself Expert Systems." *Computer Decisions* 18 (14 January 1986), 76–81.

Heinich, Robert. "Instructional Technology and the Structure of Education." *ECTJ: Educational Communication and Technology* 33 (Spring 1985), 9–15.

Hoth, Evelyn K. "Debunking Myths about Computer Literacy for Teachers." *Educational Technology* 25 (January 1985), 37–39.

Hunter, C. B., Jr., and A. L. Wold. "Basic Guide to the Complete Educational Computer." *Media and Methods* 21 (November 1984), 13–23.

"The Impact of Technology on Teaching." Symposium in *VocEd* 59 (April 1984), 19–37.

Johnson, W. L. "Using a Systems Approach in Education." *Education* 105 (Winter 1984), 135–138.

Jonassen, David H. "Learning Strategies: A New Educational Technology." *PLET: Programmed Learning and Educational Technology* 22 (February 1985), 26–34.

Kearsley, Greg P. *Training for Tomorrow: Digitized Learning through Computer and Communication Technology.* Reading, Mass.: Addison-Wesley, 1985.

Kinnucan, Paul. "Software Tools Speed Expert System Development." *High Technology* 5 (March 1985), 16–20.

Kleiman, Glenn M. *Brave New Schools: How Computers Can Change Education.* Reston, Va.: Reston Publishing, 1984.

Logsdon, Tom. *Computers Today and Tomorrow: The Microcomputer Explosion.* Rockville, Md.: Computer Science Press, 1985.

Lu, Cary. "Making Computers Easier to Use." *High Technology* 4 (July 1984), 29–31.

McAleese, Ray, and Elizabeth B. Duncan. "Information Technology and an Educational Broadcasting Database." *PLET: Programmed Learning and Educational Technology* 22 (February 1985), 39–45.

McCorduck, Pamela. *Machines Who Think.* San Francisco: W. H. Freeman, 1979.

Masterton, P. "A Futurist Looks at Educational Technology, or Wheel Re-Inventing Reconsidered." *T.H.E. Journal* 11 (January 1984), 143–146.

Nathan, Joe. *MICRO-MYTHS: Exploring the Limits of Learning with Micros*. Minneapolis: Winston Press, 1985.

Norton, Priscilla. "An Agenda for Technology and Education: Eight Imperatives." *Educational Technology* 25 (January 1985), 15–20.

Papert, Seymour. *Mind Storms: Children, Computers, and Powerful Ideas*. New York: Basic Books, 1980.

Peterson, Dale, ed. *Intelligent Schoolhouse: Readings on Computers and Learning*. Reston, Va.: Reston Publishing, 1984.

"Planning the School of the Future: Proceedings of a National Study Conference." *Peabody Journal of Education* 62 (Winter 1985), entire issue.

Podemski, Richard S. "Implications of Electronic Learning Technology: the Future Is Now!" In *Educational Microcomputing Annual*. Vol. 1 (1985). John H. Tashner, ed. Phoenix: Oryx Press, 1985, pp. 27–29.

Roberts, Franklin C. "An Overview of Intelligent CAI Systems." *Peabody Journal of Education* 62 (Fall 1984), 40–51.

Robinson, Brent. "Media in Educational Research: Are the New Electronic Media a Threat to Literacy or a Challenge for the Literate?" *British Journal of Educational Technology* 16 (January 1985), 42–59.

Scandura, J. M. "Theory-Driven Expert Systems: The Next Step in Computer Software." *Educational Technology* 24 (November 1984), 47–48.

Simons, Geoff. *Silicon Shock: The Menace of the Computer Invasion*. Oxford: Basil Blackwell, 1985.

Smith, Peter, and Samuel Dunn. "Tomorrow's University: Serving the Information Society — Getting Ready for the Year 2000." *Educational Technology* 25 (July 1985), 5–11.

Stubbs, Malcolm, and Peter Piddock. "Artificial Intelligence in Teaching and Learning: An Introduction." *PLET: Programmed Learning and Educational Technology* 22 (May 1985), 150–157.

Tashner, John H., ed. "Journals and National Associations in Educational Microcomputing." *Educational Microcomputing Annual*. Vol. 1 (1985). Phoenix: Oryx Press, 1985, pp. 171–175.

Teich, Mark, and Pamela Weintraub. "Ultra Sports." *Omni* 9 (August 1985), 39–40, 42, 44, 96–97, 100–101.

Torrey, Lee. *Stretching the Limit: Breakthroughs in Sports Science That Create Super Athletes*. New York: Dodd, Mead, 1985.

Turkle, Sherry. *The Second Self: Computers and the Human Spirit*. New York: Simon & Schuster, 1984.

Unwin, Derick. "the Cyclical Nature of Educational Technology." *PLET: Programmed Learning and Educational Technology* 22 (February 1985), 65–67.

Van Horn, Mike. *Understanding Expert Systems*. New York: Bantam Books, 1986.

Wessner, Cecilia. "The Compleat Electronic Researcher." *Personal Computing* 8 (December 1984), 125–128, 131, 135–136, 140.

Williams, Dennis A. "How One School Does It Right." *Personal Computing* 9 (September 1985), 80–81, 83–85, 87.

Yazdani, Masoud. *New Horizons in Educational Computing*. New York: John Wiley, 1984.

PART V

PHYSICAL EDUCATION
AND SPORT TODAY
AND TOMORROW

Courtesy *Raleigh News and Observer.* Photo by Thomas Green

chapter 14

Current Issues in American Physical Education and Sport

While considering the status of American physical education and sport in the late 1980s, we shall look at three broad areas: issues in American education as a whole, issues in American physical education, and issues in American sport. We shall also discuss some new directions in which American physical education and sport are moving. A combined study of these four areas will present a fair idea of what is happening in American physical education and sport today. Although there is a gap in time between the writing and the reading of this chapter, the majority of the issues mentioned here will not have disappeared, despite the possibility that the current emphasis may have changed.

ISSUES IN AMERICAN EDUCATION

Many issues are argued in American education, but two led the way from the 1970s and well into the 1980s: the back-to-the-basics movement and the cost of education. The back-to-basics movement grew as a grass-roots revolt against the school curriculum; parents believed that the schools were spending too much time on the "frills" of education (the less academically needed areas) and that the students were not being taught such basics as reading, writing, and math. Supporters of the back-to-basics movement have cited the decline in scores on college-entrance examinations, such as the SAT, over the last two decades as evidence of lowered levels of student learning in the schools. While legitimate arguments for this statistical decline have been suggested, various research studies support the idea that the decline in the level of education of typical American students is genuine, rather than simply the result of testing flaws or statistical weaknesses as some critics have suggested.

Parents have suggested several causes for this apparent decline in student learning. Television viewing, which detracts from the amount of time that students spend on homework, is perhaps the most popular excuse for less achievement. Some parents say the decline in learning is due to the fact that teachers today assign little homework to be done. Others suggest that a major cause of lower levels of learning is the decline of discipline in the schools, as seen in several aspects ranging from physical discipline to the strength of passing standards. Much of the criticism of the schools reflected in the back-to-basics movement might be viewed as a belief that the schools have lost the idea of the work ethic, that they no longer teach the value of hard work to achieve success.

Some of this suspicion dates from the late 1960s and early 1970s when the idea of ungraded classes and more loosely structured requirements gained considerable popularity in the colleges. Graduates of teacher-training colleges carried this idea into the schools as young teachers. Some school districts began to revise programs on the basis of the idea that education would be more successful if the students decided what they should learn and if emphasis were placed on making courses more "relevant" to the students' daily lives. In conjunction with this idea, the concept of failure was removed from some programs. The theory behind this move to an ungraded system was that students would become more inner directed in a noncompetitive atmosphere. The students would learn more because they would see the value of what they were trying to learn, and, at the same time, they would try more difficult areas because they would have no fear of failure.

More experienced teachers could have predicted the problems with this type of educational system. "Relevant" was most often interpreted to mean "fun" and "easy"; the ungraded approach meant that few people cared whether a student worked or achieved. The system was a failure for the majority of students because it did not require the levels of achievement necessary for successful life after school.[1] The disastrous effects of this system became obvious when state legislatures, reacting to parental complaints, began to set levels of achievement to be met by testing before a high school degree could be awarded; though the levels required were modest, failure rates were startlingly high. This was the birth of the high school "competency" tests.

George V. Higgins writes of some of the problems that have developed from an educational system that claims every student is capable of doing everything equally well. In "Clumsy Oafs, Unlettered Louts," Higgins' character, the professor, makes these observations about such an educational system:

If you lie to a kid and tell him that he can do something when he knows very well that he cannot do it, he will try it. And of course he will fail. When you tell him that he has succeeded [as in schools without failure], he knows you are lying. He will never trust you again. He will be right. [After this happens in several grades] he will get the impression that people lie to him in order to get rid of him. This may be good training for the adult world, but it is poor training for performance in that world.[2]

Higgins points out that students begin to expect people to make allowances for them, which generally will not happen outside the schools. The result is students unqualified for college who demand simpler college courses. And without the multitude of weaker students, teachers would lose jobs. Higgins paints a discouraging picture of American education today, but it is largely an accurate picture.

While there have always been disagreements over what should be the major concerns of the schools, today there is an increasing realization that the schools are not doing their best in basic education. Students cannot read well; students cannot perform simple mathematical functions well. This observation does not refer simply to the weaker students. Today, many of the highest-scoring high school students who have been accepted into America's best universities must take remedial courses in reading and writing.

We live in an increasingly technological society. We cannot plan an up-to-date, relevant education because the technology of the modern world is expanding so rapidly that much of what we teach may be outdated by the time a textbook can be written and published. The basic skills of reading, writing, speaking, mathematics, logic, and mental and social flexibility or adaptability are perhaps the most important skills or attributes necessary for success in the modern world. Yet the typical American student is weak in these basic skills. As a result, the technological future can result in terrible failures in the simple ability to function efficiently in the everyday world.

We face the always complex question that lies at the heart of the development of any educational system: What education is most worth having? Regardless of the educational or technological level, certain skills are basic to achievement. The school years are a time of teaching and testing to prepare students for the more advanced levels of training needed for the jobs of the future. Yet, as technology advances, we increasingly see a developing class of people who are unable to cope with modern society—hard-core unemployables who have not developed sufficient skills to win any other than the most simple physical jobs. An educational system that set clear standards and requirements and enforced them could have prevented this problem rather than having social promotions in keeping with the "up or out" rule of education.

The demands of the back-to-the-basics movement are admirable and understandable in terms of the educational problems that its proponents are trying to correct. However, the unfortunate aspect of these demands is that they have come during a time of spiraling educational costs that are resulting in severe budget cuts in most school systems. These budget cuts, coupled with the demands of the back-to-the-basics movement, have resulted in the loss of supplementary programs, because they are thought of as frills, not as necessary parts of the educational program. This is unfortunate, for the need to tighten up educational requirements and strengthen learning in basic areas does not lessen the value of many supplementary areas of education that have been added to the comprehensive schools popular in the United States. While "reading, writing, and 'rithmetic" comprise the cornerstone of education, exposure to the arts, business courses, the sciences, technical programs, physical education, sports, and nonphysical extracurricular school activities can be equally important in developing the well-rounded citizen.

Teacher competence is another area of concern. Lowered educational requirements in the last two decades have resulted in many teachers who were trained in programs that had few requirements in terms of actual knowledge of the subject area. As a result of this situation, more states are developing an interest in requiring teacher candidates for state certification to take standardized tests to prove their competence in the subjects that they are to teach. The results of these tests have shown that many college graduates do not have the knowledge recommended for teachers in their subjects. Many arguments have been used for and against standardized testing as a part of teacher certification. While it is true that standardized tests cannot accurately show which candidates will be skillful teachers, such tests *do* indicate which candidates have the knowledge necessary to teach.

At the same time that teacher competence was beginning to be evaluated more carefully, teacher shortages appeared in a number of subjects. Current needs exist for math and science teachers. Specialists in bilingual education and in working with the handicapped are in short supply, too. Also, teachers are needed to fill positions in inner-city schools and in the more isolated rural schools.

A growing concern of teachers, students, and parents is school violence. Incidents of violence against students and especially against teachers have increased in recent years, lending an air of fear to some schools. While this problem has generally been viewed as an exclusive worry of inner-city schools, it is now becoming a more general school concern, since violence has become common in many schools throughout the country, regardless of their location or size.

One of the most difficult problems in American education is the question of moral dilemmas in the schools, including moral questions and concerns in the school curriculum. The idea of moral education has long been considered important in American schools, though religious education itself has traditionally taken place outside the schools in keeping with the Constitution and its requirement of the separation of church and state. However, this requirement does not affect areas that are considered moral education, such as ethical behavior or subjects that include moral questions or issues like sex education. The major dilemma is whether such subjects are the proper concern of the schools or should be left to the parents of the individual students. If such subjects are included in the curriculum, other dilemmas arise regarding the content and emphasis to be used in teaching the courses. Should certain moral or ethical standards be suggested or recommended? Should the students simply be directed to develop their own standards as they see fit?

These dilemmas in the area of moral education are made more difficult by the many conflicting views of citizens regarding the proper answers. While there is little disagreement with the idea that students need to learn to be concerned with moral issues and need to develop standards of conduct, the great disagreement lies in what standards they should develop, how these standards should be developed, and who has the responsibility to see that they are developed.

Another area of considerable concern and controversy is elitism, or education for the superior student as opposed to education for the "average" or typical student. The dispute over elitism affects such areas as subject matter and level, grading standards, educational emphases, and such related areas as sexism in education and education of the handicapped. For the most part, the American educational program has been directed toward the average student and planned at the level of this student. While this program may work well for that student, it sorely neglects the intellectually gifted student, the potential leader and discoverer of the future. The move toward education only at the average level of ability has been expressed partly as an education of the majority, but it has also carried clear elements of anti-intellectualism. That intellectual needs are neglected at many educational levels is an idea that was expressed in a letter of concern that two physical educators wrote who were responding to an article on standards for graduate study in physical education. They noted that even though the suggestions were for the graduate level of education, "it is appalling that enhancement of scholarship and research was absent from the list of recommendations."[3]

This problem of intellectual neglect stems partly from the popular idea that *elitism* is a dirty word, because it implies that some people are better than others. The schools should not accept the idea that one person is better than another, but they cannot afford to ignore the fact that one person may be more talented than another, for to ignore it is to deny and suppress that talent. The idea of education is to stimulate and expand each person within the limits of their ability. Elitist programs should be required; the law requires programs for the average and for those who are far below the average, yet the most talented people are often ignored unless they are athletes.

Elitist views have been condemned on the basis that they are not concerned with equality and with treating all students the same. However, people are not intellectually or physically equal and to deny that is foolish. Equality demands that each person be given the opportunity to reach his or her full potential, without that opportunity depending on another person's greater or lesser potential.

Many problems or issues are tied into the controversy over elitism. Competition as a part of the educational process is one issue. Some experts believe that competition is harmful to education, even while others believe that it is necessary, beneficial, and normal.[4] There is no denying that people have to compete when they are out of school, which some consider a justification for competition in the classroom, since it is supposed to be a preparation for real life.

A parallel concern with elitism is nonsexism, the idea of equality of education and opportunity regardless of sex as guaranteed in the 1970s by Title IX. During the 1970s, perhaps the greatest impact of Title IX was felt in school sports as women's teams expanded at a prodigious rate. The repercussions of Title IX were felt in academic areas also, for in the past, many courses had been viewed almost as the work for a single sex. Boys took shop courses, while girls took home economics. The fact that as adults both sexes need information in both these areas was disregarded. In a more subtle vein, women were sometimes discouraged from more scientific and technical areas of study because such areas were considered as not in keeping with women's talents. Also, women often were discouraged from undertaking graduate studies, as they were expected to get married and leave the job market at an

The population concentration of the United States is shifting toward more adults and elderly citizens, which creates new challenges in society, education, and physical education. (Courtesy DUPAC, Duke University Preventive Approach to Cardiology)

early age. Sexism was only another leaf on the tree of discrimination, as minority groups also were discouraged from some fields as less in keeping with their assumed talents. Discrimination suits became a factor of education in the 1960s and 1970s, under the 14th Amendment to the Constitution in both racial and sexual suits and under Title IX in sexual suits.

Education of the handicapped is another area of concern in education today. Under Public Law 94-142, the public schools have been required to give greater attention to the education of the handicapped, as the law guarantees free and appropriate education to all handicapped students. The law also encourages mainstreaming, putting students with learning disabilities into classes that normally have had no disabled students. The effect of PL 94-142 has been to create a number of controversial issues in education.

There is no denying that the handicapped have been shortchanged in education, and fortunately that situation is being rapidly amended as new programs for the handicapped are implemented. Several arguments against aspects of these new programs have appeared, however. These arguments are not over the rights of the handicapped to an education or to increased opportunities but over other concerns. One major concern is cost. Can the schools afford the massive costs of the new programs for the handicapped at a time when "normal" school activities are already being dropped from the curriculum because of money problems? At the same time, many people are concerned that mainstreaming may, rather than help to put the handicapped into the mainstream of society, simply drop the level of education offered to the nonhandicapped as they are forced to slow their classes to a level acceptable to those with learning disabilities. Opponents of mainstreaming see this as a denial of the rights of the majority who are not disabled.

Many educators are also concerned that some of the programs for the handicapped were developed only to take advantage of federal grants. These educators suggest that those really interested in helping the handicapped will help without grants and that many programs will disappear when grant monies disappear. In addition, there is concern over whether the handicapped are being used, or displayed for sympathy and money-raising purposes. This is a dehumanizing process, as Wilfred Sheed pointed out in his essay, "On Being Handicapped."[5]

The concept of adult education as a lifelong process, as a never-ceasing continuum from the time of birth throughout adult life and into old age, grew during the 1970s. Much of the credit for popularizing this concept must go to the local and community colleges that developed programs that cover areas of interest to all ages and groups within a community. Courses that are offered in these programs range from exercise to wine tasting to business to the arts. A brief study of the courses offered at any large community college will give a good idea of the breadth of experience and expansion of the concept of education in the modern American community.

Gerontology, the study of aging, is a growing area of interest to educators. As the youth boom passes into middle age, the average age of the population is rising. Improvements in health treatment and in disease control have continued to prolong life. Consequently, the proportion of elderly citizens is on the rise. Concern is growing to develop educational and physical programs of interest to these older citizens so that the quality of life may be improved for this group, which has been largely neglected in the past.

Bilingual education is another issue in contemporary education. The idea of bilingual education is that a student who does not speak English should be able to receive instruction in his or her native tongue (most often Spanish) until he or she is able to learn equally well in English. The basic concept is sensible, but difficulties have appeared as a result of expansion of this concept. The first difficulty arises from a growing tendency to use the foreign language program not as a temporary measure while English is being mastered, but as a continuing practice in place of mastering English. This situation has resulted in a massive need for bilingual teachers, few of whom are available.

At the same time, bilingual education has created a second difficulty: What can be done about a growing population that cannot mix with the majority of Americans because its members have made little effort to learn the language of their adopted country? The expansion of the idea of bilingual education has caused the weakening of the old concept of the United States as a melting pot of nations where foreign peoples are all blended together as Americans who speak a common language. People who retain another preferred language without learning the native language leave themselves outside the mainstream of the society in which they live, weakening their chances of success even as they weaken the cohesiveness of that society. The controversy over what bilingual education should be in the schools is still a great question to be solved in the future.

Another issue in contemporary American education concerns alternative educational institutions. Many different forms of education are available today—some formal, some less formal, and others extremely experimental. Traditional American education is conducted in a formal school setting, with concrete courses that meet at regular intervals for a set period of time and that are followed with examinations. A record of achievement is kept in terms of course units, hours, or some other unit of quantitative measure. A diploma or degree requires a set quantity of these units or hours.

Religious groups started most of the early American schools, particularly as a way of educating ministers. During the 1700s and 1800s the idea of public education began to grow, eventually resulting in the public school system and in state colleges and universities. Over the last several decades, private institutions have begun to appear in greater numbers as alternative institutions. These institutions take many different forms. Some are religious or political schools started as alternatives to public education. These schools have been designed to meet needs that parents did not believe the public schools were meeting or to avoid problems that the parents saw in the public schools. Some of these have taken the form of public or private elite institutions—schools for the intellectually gifted—though these are not large in number. Other alternative schools were started to emphasize special areas of student talents, such as training schools in the arts or sciences. Other institutions, such as open schools, were started in response to the desire to implement experimental educational programs.

At the college level in the 1960s and 1970s, a greater variety in educational offerings appeared because of expansion of the community colleges, which offer credit and noncredit courses in a vast range of interests. Moreover, the idea of permitting students to develop some of their own courses in more specialized or unusual areas became popular in many colleges. Life-experience schools also appeared. These nstitutions give college credit and degrees based on a person's personal experiences rather than formal training. External degree programs expanded, too, as more colleges began offering courses by mail or by television. These programs have made college credit and diplomas available to people who are unable to attend college in the traditional manner.

The most controversial of these new college programs is that offered by the life-experience schools. Too often these schools award degrees, including doctorates, based primarily on payment of a large tuition. They may have no campus, library, or faculty. An example of the alternative graduate school is Nova University in Florida, which offers external doctorates in public and educational administration. This university has a minimal campus staff, relying instead on faculty members from other institutions who are paid to work with the individual students.[6] There is little formal course work; instead, the emphasis is on a small number of limited seminar-type courses and a work project of a dissertation nature. The idea of the external degree will probably remain a controversial topic in the educational mainstream for some time, since many educators view most of the external degree programs simply as "mail-order degrees." Whether this criticism is true or whether the life-experience schools are the "wave of the future," as they describe themselves, remains to be seen.

A continuing issue in American education is the place of sport and sporting competition in the educational process. The first facet of the issue is simply whether the school is a legitimate place for sporting competition, even though longstanding tradition and public interest appear to accept it as a legitimate site. The second facet of the problem relates to the intensity with which the program should be conducted, that is, whether the success factor should be the major emphasis of the program or whether more attention should be paid to the personal development of the students and to the lessons that can be learned through competition in sports activities.

Another facet of the question, a most controversial one, relates to the ages of the participants: At what age should students be exposed to competitive athletics? A related problem centers on the concerns of how strongly a competitive emphasis should be placed on the program and how seriously young athletes should train or be made to train. This problem becomes more critical as we view the developments in international competitive sport, particularly the advances made in the competitive levels of Eastern European athletes. The native countries of these athletes put children with athletic potential (some younger than 10 years old) into intensive training schools that are often located in major cities far from their homes, and then monitor all aspects of the children's education, growth, and development. In fact, accusations have been made that drugs such as steroids are administered to these children to develop desired body characteristics.

Currently, most American competitive school sports appear at the junior high or middle school level (grades seven through nine), though intramural competitions may appear at the elementary school level. Some children begin competitive athletics, either through the schools or through community programs, at or before the age of 10. Such programs can be beneficial if their administrators are concerned individuals who realize that the body of young children is vulnerable to abuse, overload, and contact injury. Administrators of these programs also must consider psychological development of the young athlete. The place of competitive sports and youth sports is still an area of great controversy in American education.

While this list of issues in American education can hardly be called definitive, it does give an idea of the many areas of question and controversy in contemporary education. Education is not a placid, never-changing stream. An educator must be aware of the questions that concern fellow educators, parents, and students, and at the same time, an educator must be flexible enough to adapt to the changing educational scene.

ISSUES IN AMERICAN PHYSICAL EDUCATION

Perhaps the most critical issue in American physical education today is the question of the value of the physical education program. As money becomes less available, school programs come under close scrutiny, and the question of what programs are most valuable is raised. Physical educators are placed in the position of defending the worth of their subject in the larger program of education.

Because sports have been popular in schools and communities, many physical educators assume that physical education's place in the curriculum is safe—a risky assumption. Under newly popular methods of program assessment, a program must prove the need for its very existence rather than simply defend a request for a larger budget or for an expanded program. A quality physical education program must show that it has clear, useful, attainable goals, that it has a well-rounded program to attain those goals, that it regularly tests to determine that progress is being made, and that it succeeds in meeting its goals.

Physical educators are agreed that their subject is a vital part of a well-rounded educational program, that it makes vital contributions to meeting the needs of growing students, and that it affects intellectual growth just as it affects the development of physical health and coordination. However, too little is done to show the public the value of a good physical education program. Instead, the public often sees physical education as the tail end of the athletic program. This weak public relations effort must be corrected.

A second issue in American physical education relates to the emphasis of the individual physical education program, for the phrase "physical education program" does not refer to a single model used across the country. Each school system—and sometimes each individual school—has its own practices regarding the emphasis of its physical education program. The major emphases that are seen fall roughly into the areas of sports, fitness, and lifetime sports.

Some programs emphasize competitive sports, particularly those sports that are used at the individual school. The classes are devoted to the development of playing and tactical skills in a series of competitive sports such as football, basketball, and baseball. While efforts may be made to relate the work in these sports to overall physical development, the emphasis can too easily turn toward the production of strong competitive teams and the locating and training of young athletes for those sports from the physical education classes. Thus the physical education program becomes a "farm system" for the athletic department, run by and for the coaches, with more regard for how physical education can meet the needs of the athletic program than for how it can meet the needs of the students.

A second emphasis found in programs is that of fitness, with the primary goal of such programs being the development of a high level of physical fitness in the students. This orientation is especially strong during times of war. Fitness-centered programs tend to ignore basic motor skill development and the more social and intellectual aspects of physical education that are found in good programs.

Fitness is a worthy goal that is found too rarely in current programs, and a well-planned program can develop a high level of fitness without emphasizing the calisthenics and conditioning approach to class instruction. However, fitness can become a narrow focus for a program aimed at the growing student; consequently, a broader goal is needed.

A third emphasis seen in physical education programs is lifetime sports. A program emphasizing lifetime sports uses sporting activities that people of any age can follow, and therefore teaches skills that the students can continue to enjoy through middle age and into their later years. For example, few 50-year-olds can play football, but volleyball and badminton are excellent sporting activities at any age.

A program of lifetime sports does not mean that fitness cannot be developed. The fitness effect of any activity is largely dependent on the intensity used in participating rather than on some set fitness value that is the same regardless of how hard a person plays. For example, a younger person will find that badminton can be an extremely taxing activity from the fitness standpoint, yet an older person can play just as enjoyable and competitive a game at a lower level of intensity more suited to his fitness level. The same reason accounts for the popularity of games such as volleyball and slow-pitch softball—these games can be enjoyed almost regardless of the skill or fitness level of the players involved.

A second advantage of lifetime sports is that they are more easily used in coeducational and mixed-age classes than competitive sports and fitness activities, which require greater homogeneity of skill or fitness levels. As many classes are now mixed, this point has gained increasing importance. Games such as volleyball and slow-pitch softball work as well in coeducational classes as in single-sex classes, for neither the less skilled or less fit individuals nor the shorter or lighter individuals are put at any great disadvantage.

The emphasis of a physical education program tends to change gradually over a long period of time. This is not as bad a characteristic as it might appear to be, for it shows that the program can be responsive to the needs and interests of the society it seeks to serve. The early emphasis of many programs was on health, leading to fitness; a sport orientation eventually replaced this emphasis except during times of war. Most recently, lifetime sports became prominent, but changes are likely to continue. Programs are now beginning to respond to the New Games concept, the idea of cooperative rather than competitive group physical activities. Programs will continue to respond to new leisure patterns in the future as they have in the past.

A third issue has already been mentioned, for it is not specific to the physical education program alone—money. The issue is simple: When the budget crunch hits, does physical education have a place in the school program? More must be done to prove the place of physical education in any program of general education. In some cases, the question is seen as a choice between physical education and competitive sport, with one sacrificed to save the other. However, physical education seeks to help every student, while competitive sport is oriented toward the most skilled. While the most skilled deserve the chance to develop their talents to the fullest, that right does not overcome the right of the majority of the students to have their needs met. One complaint against physical education in the past has been that physical educators, as coaches, have preferred the elitist approach, neglecting the average students in favor of developing the skills of the talented few who can be successful in competitive sports. This is never a proper direction for a teacher to take.

A fourth issue, which is really a realm of issues, is the concern of problems in physical education, all of which overlap issues already cited. We shall look briefly at five problems: teacher competence, program emphasis, group instruction divisions, public relations, and athletics.

Teacher competence is a concern in all subject areas, but physical educators cannot afford to ignore this critical concern of the public. Too often, physical educators are viewed as poorly trained or inadequately educated individuals interested primarily in coaching athletes. While many physical educators coach, coaching is only a small part of the task that physical educators face.

Any competent teacher needs a strong academic education, for the acquisition of concrete and theoretical knowledge is essential before one is able to teach. In the past, as in the present, conflict existed between those physical educators who want greater emphasis placed on the discipline side of physical education—the acquisition and spreading of a scholarly base for physical education—and those who advocate the pedagogical or teaching side of physical education. This conflict has been described at times as the teachers versus the scholars, but this description is an unfortunate oversimplification, for the pedagogically oriented people should be no less scholars than are the discipline-emphasis people.

The question has been raised whether people trained only in the discipline have the knowledge of teaching theory and the physical skills necessary to teach and coach. Meanwhile the counterargument suggests that those who concentrate on the teacher-education side do not have the content—the scientific knowledge—necessary for correct and useful teaching and coaching. Physical educators must solve this nagging problem and create cohesive programs of professional preparation that can produce legitimate teacher–scholars.

At the same time, physical educators must carefully consider the most beneficial choice of program emphasis. It would be helpful if research were conducted to determine the most useful program in national terms, so that physical educators could recommend a reasonably concrete national program of physical education for students by age, with the evidence to support the value of the chosen emphasis, activities, goals, and so forth. Such a program could then be promoted in a unified manner across the country, while local modification would be possible to adapt the national program to meet any unusual local needs.

The matter of group instructional divisions has caused increasing problems because of federal intervention in local programs. Far more classes are taught on a coeducational basis than in the past; mixing of different age, sex, and ability levels is increased. The introduction of handicapped individuals through mainstreaming further complicates the picture, as does the introduction of multilingual requirements in areas having several non-English-speaking language groups in the schools. Physical educators must decide how best to meet these rapidly changing complications of the instructional program so that the effectiveness of the program will not be lessened.

Physical educators must be more conscious of public relations. This is the weak point in a budget crunch, for the group that has not considered public relations in the past is more likely to find its programs damaged, if not removed, when the supply of money diminishes. The physical education program must make a strong effort to *prove* its value, if it hopes to be protected by the public when money shortages come.

Finally, athletics is a persistent problem to physical educators. The issue often becomes teacher versus coach—a question of which person or emphasis controls the overall physical program of the school. Is the physical education program run to benefit the athletic program, or is athletics simply another facet of the program? If a physical educator primarily emphasizes the sports program, a budget cut may limit the physical education program severely, and this would affect the needs of far more students than those affected by the sports program. The intent of this comment is not to suggest that school sports are not a valuable adjunct to the school program; it is simply to point out that sports are more a dessert or side dish in relation to physical education, which is the main course.

ISSUES IN AMERICAN SPORT

Although we could cite many issues in sport today, we shall look primarily at the problems that we see reflected in school sports. We discussed aspects of these problems in Chapter 8 when we looked at ethical problems. We might say that the major issue is the growth of Big-Time Sport, with most issues appearing related to that umbrella concept.

The appearance and growth of Big-Time Sport in the public schools can be viewed as a larger version of the popular comparison of baseball as played by the cartoon character Charlie Brown and his friends to baseball as played by a highly organized Little League program. Many writers have also described it as the "professionalization of amateur sport."

An example of this approach is the turning of a sports program's emphasis away from the participants (and the benefits they gain from taking part) and toward the spectators. Booster clubs put increasing amounts of money into the sports, facilities become elaborate (especially for the spectators), the number of coaches and the rewards for coaching increase considerably, and often the actual number of sports and participants decreases (because the school does not want to "dilute its efforts" and perhaps field weaker teams in the "money sports." The ultimate emphasis is on the success of a few teams as well as on the revenue that they produce. Teams become not a growth experience for the athletes but a public relations and financial venture for the school.

The biggest issue, mentioned several times, is the relationship of sport to education. The question is not what part sport does play in education, but what part it *should* play. What is its proper place in the education of the young people? Is it so important that the intellectual education of the students is less important than their striving for athletic excellence?

Texas has been the first state to take a hard look at the future of its students and to see that the first task of the school is to educate, to pass intellectual learning on to the next generation. A state law was passed that required a student to pass every course being taken or be dropped from the athletic program until the grades were improved.

Among the unique arguments against the law was the idea that a major function of high school was to qualify youths for athletic scholarships to college, even if their grades indicated that they either were not prepared or were not mentally talented enough for college academic work. A more understandable fear was that students would avoid the more challenging academic courses for fear of losing their chance to play at sports. However, this fear (a legitimate one) was weakened by the high proportion of students who failed at least one course, regardless of how easy their academic schedule should have been. This failure rate said much about their seriousness.

In fact, the United States has developed the reputation of having the least academically strenuous educational program in the world. Arthur Powell and his co-authors, in fact, referred to the "shopping mall high school" after an extensive study of American education.[7] As one student said, "It's a big job to make up a curriculum that everybody can do." The writers compared American schools in the 1980s to a shopping mall, trying to have something for every level of ability, and as a result having no standard education that all students receive.

Sport in the schools is symptomatic of the problem, for too often students (and many coaches) seem to think that the purpose of the school is to provide a support system for athletic teams, rather than that the teams are just a part (and not the most important part) of the educational process.

We see the problem of elite athletics as the ethic of Big-Time Sport reaches to the high schools and even lower. Sports should give the athletically gifted a chance to achieve higher things, but if sport is such an educational experience, the less talented students should have a place. The less intelligent students are offered classes at their level of ability, not barred from school.

We also face ethical dilemmas, as we have already seen. Do we learn to respect others, to play fairly and by the rules when we take part in school sports? Do we learn good sportsmanship, or do we gradually become a nation of immature sports whiners, as has been too often the image in professional sports such as tennis? What lessons about life and adulthood do we first learn and then teach through our participation in sports?

What is the effect of violence in sports? Is it a reflection of a more violent world? The world has never been peaceful in the past, but has violence become more acceptable in sport? And if it has, does it carry over into real life, making violent acts more acceptable off the playing field? The famed soccer riots of 1985 that killed dozens of people and caused the barring of British professional teams from playing in Europe are not a new type of problem. However, it seemingly is becoming more common. Is sport the cause, or is it just an innocent bystander, used by violent people as an excuse for their acts?

Drug use is a growing problem in sport today. Is the use of any type of drug to enhance performance or training in any way *ever* acceptable from an ethical or sporting point of view? Whether it is the use of anabolic steroids or human growth hormone by a high-level athlete, the use of stimulants or depressants, or the use of narcotics by any athlete or coach, the problem is of critical importance.

At the same time, this reflects another aspect of the Big-Time Sport syndrome, the growing professionalism of sport at all levels. As we noted when discussing the rise of modern sport, professionalism is one of the characteristics of modern sport. Should an Olympic-level athlete be paid to train or perform? Should a college athlete receive payments? Should high school or lower-level athletes be paid to perform? If they are paid, how can we say that sport belongs in the schools? No one has ever expected payment for simply learning; it is an obligation and a necessity for survival.

Sport is a controversial topic in education and society. We need to look at the issues that appear and consider them carefully, not just from the view of the athlete or coach, but from the view of the fan, the spectator, and the opponent, for all of these people have valid reasons both to support and to oppose sport.

NEW DIRECTIONS IN PHYSICAL EDUCATION AND SPORT

Now that we have considered a limited number of the issues and problems in physical education and sport today, we need to consider even more contemporary concerns of American physical education: What are the new directions toward which physical education seems to be moving?

Physical educators are trying to determine the most useful and effective programs for the future, and this effort has led to many suggestions for the ideal school program. Paul Darst suggests that one reason programs have been unable to prove their effectiveness is that they seek to meet too many goals, such as accomplishments in physical fitness, motor skills, mental abilities, and personal social-emotional adjustment. He suggests that a more reasonable goal is to try to convince students to incorporate physical activities into their life-styles.[8] This suggestion is in keeping with the trend toward lifetime sports—programs that concentrate on activities that are appropriate for every age group.

The lifetime-sports approach has already been mentioned. The program goes beyond simply learning the skills to the level of stressing the pleasure of participation in the activities. If a student does not enjoy an activity, that activity rarely will be used in later life. Leisure activities of adults are, by definition, activities of choice; they are pastimes that adults find pleasurable. If this aesthetic appreciation of physical activity is not a part of the program, few students will be inclined to continue with the activities in later life.

At the same time, the 1980s have seen two conflicting trends in physical education: the rising popularity of high-risk activities and program-threatening rises in the costs of liability insurance. The growth of outdoor activities that involve physical risk (rock-climbing, hang gliding, white-water kayaking, and others) has been rapid. Triathlon competitions (swimming, bicycling, and running long distances) have boomed during the 1980s, just as road races did in the 1970s. Unfortunately, many participants are poorly trained, poorly conditioned, and careless in their approach to these activities, which have a much higher potential for life-threatening accidents.

At the same time, insurance companies have been hit hard by large awards from injury and negligence suits. The results have been prohibitively high insurance rates, dropping many activities, and the risk of severe limits being placed on sporting and recreational activities. Equipment manufacturers can be put out of business with one large award, in some cases ending the supply of safety equipment for a sport. Public parks have sometimes been closed, and community recreation programs have been shut down. No good answers have been found to these conflicting trends.

The New Games approach is another growing area in physical education. It is especially useful in the elementary school, for it introduces young students to organized physical activities in which cooperation is emphasized more than competition. Young children may find some aspects of competition frightening, particularly if they are overemphasized, as can happen in competitive sports. The New Games approach places more emphasis on mass participation and cooperation to meet a group goal rather than on competition against a person or team to achieve a personal advantage. The New Games activities might be viewed as an ideal learning experience for children growing up in a mass society, since cooperation is far more critical to survival than competition in a crowded world.

Coeducational activities have become increasingly important in the physical education program. While some mixing of the sexes did occur in classes in the past, it usually was limited to such activities as dancing. Federal regulations have rapidly increased the mixing of the sexes in those activities that are not considered physical contact (rough) activities. While this direction has disadvantages, including some instructional problems created by the more diverse interest, skill, and performance potential levels, mixed instruction is still appropriate in as many areas as possible without interfering with normal student progress.

A fourth direction in physical education is the trend toward fitting special populations into the regular physical education program. One example of this trend is mainstreaming, or the inclusion of those with physical or mental handicaps in regular classes. More concern also is being shown for physical activity programs for the aged. Indeed, even competitive activities are growing rapidly in the areas for special populations. The Special Olympics provides competitive opportunities for people with mental handicaps, while a handicapped Olympics and many competitive sports have been organized for people with physical handicaps. Over the last decade, the trend toward "master's competitions" in many different sports has been growing. Participants compete according to ten-year age brackets, which begin with age 40. For example, there might be a race for ages 40 to 49 and another for ages 50 to 59. In some cases, the age groups might be lowered to cover ages 35 to 39, or even 30 to 39. The result is to include more middle-aged and older adults who are interested in competing and training with people of their own age and ability levels. Many people who did not participate in sports in their school years are learning the pleasures of competition in later life.

American education is always in a state of change. The rethinking and revision in education is ceaseless because of changing ideas of what the duty of the school is toward the community, changing community needs, changing societal conditions, and changing theories of education. This is as it should be, for no system can afford to assume that it cannot be improved. This is what provides the eternal challenge of education.

NOTES

1. Robert L. Ebel, "The Failure of Schools Without Failure," *Phi Delta Kappan* 61 (February 1980), 386–388.
2. George V. Higgins, "Clumsy Oafs, Unlettered Louts," *Harpers*, (May 1980), 60–63.
3. Steven N. Blair and Russell R. Pate, Letter to *JOPERD* 51 (September 1980), 12.
4. Joseph Wax, "Competition: Educational Incongruity," and Michael Grenis, "Individualization, Grouping, Competition and Excellence," *Phi Delta Kappan* 57 (November 1975), 197–200.
5. Wilfred Sheed, "On Being Handicapped," *Newsweek*, (25 August 1980), p. 13.
6. Beverly T. Watkins, "Nova U. Keeps Up the War with Its Critics," *Chronicle of Higher Education* (3 November 1980), 13–14.
7. Arthur G. Powell, Eleanor Farrar, and David K. Cohen, *The Shopping Mall High School*, Houghton Mifflin, Boston, 1985.
8. Paul W. Darst, "Learning Environments To Create Lifelong Enjoyment of Physical Activity," *JOPERD* 49 (January 1978), 44.

SUGGESTED READINGS

Adler, Mortimer J. *The Paideia Proposal.* New York: Macmillan, 1982.

Annarino, Anthony A. "Changing Times: Keeping Abreast Professionally—A Dilemma?" *JOPERD* 55 (May-June 1984), 32–34, 52–53.

Austin, Dean A. "Economic Impact on Physical Education." *JOPERD* 55 (May-June 1984), 35–37.

———, ed. "What's GOOD About Physical Education? *JOPERD* 54 (September 1983), 45–56.

Baker, Keith, et al. Three articles on the problems of discipline, order and violence in the schools. *Phi Delta Kappan* 66 (February 1985), 482–496.

Boyer, Ernest L. *High School: A Report on Secondary Education in America.* New York: Harper & Row, 1983.

Brod, Craig. *Technostress: The Human Cost of the Computer Revolution.* Reading, Mass.: Addison-Wesley, 1984.

Broderick, Robert. "Noncertified Coaches." *JOPERD* 55 (May-June 1984), 38–39, 53.

Bunting, Camille. "Wilderness Learning and Higher Education." *The Physical Educator* 37 (December 1980), 172–175.

Case, Bob. "Hosting the Olympic Games: An Economic Dilemma." *The Physical Educator* 39 (December 1982), 208–211.

Clark, Burton R. "The High School and the University: What Went Wrong in America." *Phi Delta Kappan* 66; Part 1, February 1985, 391–397; Part 2, March 1985, 472–475.

Considine, William J., et al. "Basic Instruction Programs: At the Crossroads." *JOPERD* 56 (September 1985), 31–54.

Corbin, Charles B. "Is the Fitness Bandwagon Passing Us By?" *JOPERD* 55 (November-December 1984), 17.

Cusick, Philip A. *The Egalitarian Ideal and the American High School: Studies of Three Schools.* New York: Longman, 1983.

Daniel, Charles, ed. "Moving into the Third Age." *JOPERD* 57 (January 1986), 30–63. Articles on work in gerontology.

"Drug Testing in Sports." Symposium in *The Physician and Sportsmedicine* 13 (December 1985), 69–75, 78, 80–82.

Ebel, Robert L. "The Failure of Schools Without Failure." *Phi Delta Kappan* 61 (February 1980), 386–388.

Edwards, Harry. "The Black 'Dumb Jock': An American Sports Tragedy." *The College Board Review* no. 131 (Spring 1984), 8–13.

——. "The Free Enterprise Olympics." *Journal of Sport and Social Issues* 8 (Summer-Fall 1984), i–iv.

Finn, Chester E., Jr., Mary Hartwood Futrell, and Myron Lieberman. Three articles debating teachers' unions and quality education. *Phi Delta Kappan* 66 (January 1985), 331–343.

Fraleigh, Warren P. "Unresolved Tensions in College Physical Education—Constructive and Destructive." *Quest* 37, no. 2 (1985), 134–144.

French, Ron, and Hester Henderson. "Teacher Attitudes Towards Mainstreaming." *JOPERD* 55 (October 1984), 69–71.

Gaskins, Samuel E., and William F. deShazo III. "Attitudes Toward Drug Abuse and Screening for an Intercollegiate Athletic Program." *The Physician and Sportsmedicine* 13 (September 1985), 93–97, 100.

Gaudiano, Michael G. "High Risk Activities: In Physical Education?" *The Physical Educator* 37 (October 1980), 128–130.

Goodland, John I. "The Great American Schooling Experiment." *Phi Delta Kappan* 67 (December 1985), 266–271.

Gray, David, and Hilmi Ibrahim, eds. "Leisure Today—Recreation Experience." *JOPERD* 56 (October 1985), 27–58. Articles including information on activities involving risk or adventure.

Griffin, Pat. "Coed Physical Education: Problems and Promise." *JOPERD* 55 (August 1984), 36–37.

Hage, Philip. "Sports Medicine Clinics: Are Guidelines Necessary?" *The Physician and Sportsmedicine* 10 (October 1982), 165–166, 169–172, 177.

Hall, M. Ann. "The Player, the Woman, and the Necessity of Feminist Scholarship." *Proceedings, National Association for Physical Education in Higher Education Annual Conference* 3 (1982), 48–55.

Hawley, Willis D. "False Premises, False Promises: The Mythical Character of Public Discourse about Education." *Phi Delta Kappan* 67 (November 1985), 183–187.

Hayden, Sandy, Daphne Hall, and Pat Steuck. *Women in Motion.* Boston: Beacon Press, 1983.

Holyoak, Owen J., et al. "Critical Issues in Sport and Physical Education." *JOPERD* 56 (August 1985), 13–57.

Horton, Lowell. "What Do We Know About Teacher Burnout?" *JOPERD* 55 (March 1984), 69–71.

Howell, Jill. "Wellness for the Practitioners." *JOPERD* 54 (October 1983), 37, 55.

Jensen, Marilyn A., ed. "Computer Applications." *Leisure Today*, in *JOPERD* 55 (April 1984), 31–62.

Johnson, Martin W. "Physical Education—Fitness or Fraud? A Call for Curricular Reform." *JOPERD* 56 (January 1985), 33–35.

Kaestle, Carl. "Education Reforms and the Swinging Pendulum." *Phi Delta Kappan* 66 (February 1985), 422–423.

Kelley, E. James, and Shelby Brightwell. "Should Interscholastic Coaches Be Certified?" *JOPERD* 55 (March 1984), 49–50.

Lawson, Hal A., ed. *Undergraduate Physical Education Programs: Issues and Practices.* Reston, Va.: AAHPERD, 1981.

Locke, Larry, Pat Griffin, and Thomas Templin. "Profiles of Struggle." *JOPERD* 57 (April 1986), 32–63. Articles on different teachers' problems.

Lohman, T. G., and B. H. Massey, eds. "A Fit America in the Coming Decade—1985–1995." *JOPERD* 55 (November-December 1984), 24–60.

McGinnis, J. M., et al. "Summary of Findings from The National Children and Youth Fitness Study." *JOPERD* 56 (January 1985), 43–90. Four reactions, 92–93.

Maggard, Nadine J. "Upgrading Our Image." *JOPERD* 55 (January 1984), 17, 82.

Marshall, James. *The Devil in the Classroom: Hostility in American Education.* New York: Schocken Books, 1985.

Massengale, John D. "AAHPERD's Role in the Perceived Quality of Physical Education Graduate Faculty." *JOPERD* 54 (September 1983), 57–58, 64.

Miller Lite Report on American Attitudes Towards Sports, 1983. Milwaukee: Miller Brewing Company, 1983.

National Commission for Excellence in Teacher Education. "A Call for Change in Teacher Education." *The Chronicle of Higher Education* 30 (6 March 1985), 13–14, 16–21.

National Commission on Excellence in Education. *A Nation at Risk: The Imperative for Education Reform.* Washington, D.C.: Government Printing Office, 1983.

Orlick, Terry. *Winning Through Cooperation: Competitive Insanity–Cooperative Alternatives.* Washington, D.C.: Acropolis Books, 1978.

Perry, Jean L., ed. "The Role of Women in Sport." *JOPERD* 57 (March 1986), 33–64. A series of articles on different subtopics.

Powell, Arthur G., Eleanor Farrar, and David K. Cohen. *The Shopping Mall High School: Winners and Losers in the Educational Marketplace.* Boston: Houghton Mifflin, 1985.

Powell, Kenneth E., Gregory M. Christenson, and Marshall W. Kreuter. "Objectives for the Nation: Assessing the Role Physical Education Must Play." *JOPERD* 55 (August 1984), 18–20.

Roos, Robert. "Are Physician Credentials in Sports Medicine Needed Now?" *The Physician and Sports Medicine* 14 (March 1986), 262–266, 268, 270.

Rosenholtz, Susan J. "Political Myths about Education Reform: Lessons from Research in Teaching." *Phi Delta Kappan* 66 (January 1985), 349–355.

Sanborn, Marion Alice, and Betty G. Hartman. *Issues in Physical Education.* 3d ed. Philadelphia: Lea & Febiger, 1982.

Sedlak, Michael, et al. *Classroom Perspectives on High School Reform: Bargains, Student Disengagement, and Academic Learning.* New York: Teachers College Press, 1985.

Shanker, Albert. "The Revolution That's Overdue." *Phi Delta Kappan* 66 (January 1985), 311–315.

Shea, Edward J. "Research Synthesis: A Coherent View of Physical Education." *JOPERD* 56 (November-December 1985), 45–47.

Sizer, Theodore R. *Horace's Compromise: The Dilemma of the American High School.* Boston: Houghton Mifflin, 1984.

"Sorry, Your Policy Is Canceled." *Time* 127 (24 March 1986), 16–20, 23–26. A look at the problems caused by soaring insurance rates.

"Standards for Graduate Programs in Physical Education." *JOPERD* 55 (February 1984), 54–62.

Teague, Michael L., and Kenneth E. Mobily. "Rustproofing People: Corporate Recreation Programs in Perspective." *JOPERD* 54 (October 1983), 42–44.

Thomas, Jerry R. "Physical Education and Paranoia—Synonyms." *JOPERD* 56 (November-December 1985), 20–22. Reply by Shirl J. Hoffman, 23.

Van Handel, Peter J., et al. "Sports Physiology At the USOC Training Center." *JOPERD* 55 (April 1984), 17–22.

Woodring, Paul. *The Persistent Problems of Education.* Bloomington, Ind.: Phi Delta Kappa, 1983.

See also in Resource Readings:

Kroll; Siedentop.

chapter 15

International Physical Education and Sport Today

The advances in technology during the 20th century have resulted in a shrinking world. We find ourselves increasingly caught up in events around the world because communications have become almost instantaneous, with travel not far behind. Nations are forced into contact with each other, often with awkward results because neither nation really understands the other. The study of comparative physical education is an attempt of physical educators around the world to learn about each other and to share an understanding of their national programs.

WHY STUDY COMPARATIVE PHYSICAL EDUCATION?

This chapter is concerned with what physical educators are doing in other nations around the world today. Such a study is sometimes called a cross-cultural study of education, or comparative education.[1] Lynn Vendien and John Nixon give five reasons for making comparative studies of the physical education programs in other nations. First, the studies help educators to learn about the different programs around the world. Second, the studies can assist in developing talent in constructive leadership by studying other systems in a way that will enable educators to make comparisons. This requires educators to decide whether one system might be better than another one, or whether their own systems are necessarily best for their respective societies. This process is essential to the continual improvement of any educational system. Third, the educator is able to learn about the goals, ideas, and experiences of other cultures or societies. This knowledge is helpful in determining whether the system that has evolved is fulfilling the needs of the society. If it is not doing so, such knowledge can assist in determining how the program has moved away from the needs of a society. Fourth, comparative studies can help educators to assess and improve their own educational systems by allowing them to see how other nations with similar and dissimilar systems have tried to meet their educational needs. Fifth, such studies can help to promote international professional collaboration, particularly within the areas of educational research. Comparative studies of international education can thus be one more facet of international understanding that leads to better and more peaceful relations among the many nations of the earth.

Our comparative study has been based on several assumptions. First, we assume that any educational system is patterned at least partially after the traditional values and practices of its culture. Any nation's educational system is expected to be largely a reflection of that nation's interpretations of its history, its traditions, and the cultural practices it has followed throughout its history. The educational system will be an attempt to maintain the traditions of a nation and pass them on to the nation's youth.

Second, if the country was at one time the colony of another nation, we assume that the former colonial power influenced its educational system strongly, and perhaps permanently, and therefore it will be less strongly developed according to its own cultural traditions. A colony usually inherits an educational system similar to the native educational system of the ruling country, for the ruling power believes its own system is the best one. However, because the ruling power developed the system, with little or no regard for the culture or tradition of the colony, it may be almost useless for mass education of the "natives," as it takes little account of their cultural needs and patterns. This pattern is most easily seen in the former colonies of the British Empire where very "English" schools were started. Usually these schools preserved British social class distinctions that did not even exist in the colony where the schools were located; the schools were based on the cultural traditions and social patterns of the English, though they could serve almost no genuine cultural function for the natives of the colony.

The third assumption in our comparative study is that if the country is what we refer to as a newly emerging nation, it often faces two dangers, either of which is risky to the nation's educational future. The first danger is that the new country will perpetuate the inherited educational system that the colonial ruler developed and thus continue a system that has little true relationship to the culture of the new nation. The problems are essentially those noted in the previous paragraph. The other side of the coin constitutes the second problem: The new nation will drop the old colonial system of education that it has inherited, but will at the same time simply adopt a copy of some other Western nation's educational pattern, with little regard for whether that new educational system will fully meet its needs. Each nation's educational system, however, should meet the cultural patterns and traditions of that nation if it is to be a truly effective system of education.

Fourth, the newly emerging nations face the risk of assuming that the quality of their new programs is acceptable, thus leaving their new educational system in its original state. Any educational system should be in a constant state of change, even though that change is gradual, for societies and cultures themselves are constantly in a state of change. The educational system must be gradually evolving to meet society's changing needs and to prevent education's gradual obsolescence. The new nations need to be continually assessing and revising their programs in an attempt to bring them closer to the needs of their own culture, just as the older nations must do if they are to continue to improve. No educational system can remain static unless the nation wishes to stop progressing, for cultural life depends on change and growth. By failing to grow, an educational system begins to die.

Most educational programs that are now developing in the non-Western nations are under the influence of Western ideas and educational patterns. Unfortunately, these educational patterns are based on Western culture, which may not be consistent with the cultural patterns and needs of a non-Western nation.[2] When the barbarians invaded the Roman Empire, they often wanted to adopt the Roman system, which they considered good. The end result was the destruction of the Roman system, for it was not culturally suited to the barbarian nations. The strength of the Romans' system came from their adopting a bit of the native culture of each conquest, while leaving the basic traditional cultural patterns of the conquered people largely unchanged. The Romans were able to strike a happy medium between preserving their own culture and preserving the native culture, which permitted the conquered people to be ruled with a much greater stability than might otherwise have been the case. Neither the Romans nor those they conquered were expected to adopt a system radically different from the one they had traditionally followed.

Several problems may be created by wholesale adoption of Western educational patterns by non-Western nations. One problem may stem from whether the native country has a people who are basically either competitive or noncompetitive. Many nations are not competitively oriented, and if this is the case, adopting Western educational patterns may cause many inconsistencies. The Western patterns are usually strongly oriented toward competition, both inside and outside the classroom.

Another problem concerns the program for women in the schools. In some cases the program might simply be a copy of the men's program, while in other cases it might be a separately developed program. The difference can be quite important, for much depends on the place of women in a particular country. In some nations women do not hold the same rank or relative equality with the men, as they do (increasingly so) in the Western societies.

The schools should reflect the cultural patterns of the native country, for otherwise the result may be rather unpleasant to a nation that discovers its national educational system produces a massive change in its cultural patterns, as was the case in Iran in the late 1970s.

A third problem concerns the differences in the need for physical activity in different nations. Most of the Western nations whose educational patterns might be copied are composed of relatively affluent people who greatly need programs involving considerable physical activity. Most newly emerging nations and many non-Western nations are less affluent, however, and their people, who are more involved in physical labor in their daily lives, need less physical activity in their physical education programs. The educational pattern thus needs to reflect the needs of the local people, rather than the needs of an unseen nation far away.

A fourth area that can result in problems is dance. It is used far more in non-Western societies than in the West, and any program of physical education should reflect this cultural difference. Since dance is an important part of the cultures of many nations, it should play a much greater part in the educational process of those nations than in others where it is not. Again, the educational patterns of any country should reflect that country's own culture and needs.

A study of the practices of other nations around the world can be a major contribution to international understanding. The idea of improving international relations has been a concern for centuries. Baron Pierre de Coubertin, of France, was concerned with this lack of understanding between nations when he began working to revive the Olympic Games. When the games were revived in 1896, a major concern was to develop fellowship and understanding among the athletes of many different nations. During the time of the ancient Greeks the Olympic Games had been a time of peace and harmony, when people from all nations could meet and mingle in peace. Coubertin stressed this aspect of free movement by the athletes—their getting to know their opponents from around the world. As a result of his emphasis on the cultural aspects of the Olympic Games, the modern games also were tied into displays of art and other cultural activities.

This contribution to international understanding was an important part in the formation of the United Nations in 1945. Previous attempts to provide a place for the world's nations to meet and exchange their views, such as in the League of Nations, all eventually failed. The United Nations was formed after World War II as an attempt to provide a forum where the nations could discuss their common problems and explain their views to each other.

Many of the conflicts in the modern world have been a result of misunderstandings or failures of nations to communicate clearly with each other. As the world advances technologically, such misunderstandings become increasingly risky, for acts that might be interpreted as aggressive moves by a nation can be spotted almost immediately, and retaliation can be instantaneous. The risks of accidental war in a world filled with guided nuclear missiles set to go into action almost automatically are great indeed. The nations of the world need a forum where they can learn what their counterparts around the world have, want, and are doing. Some channels of communication *must* be established between nations, if only as an attempt to prevent accidental wars.

Each of the many international groups in the world today has some particular area of special interest. Our primary concern is with the international organizations that function in the areas of education, physical education, and sport. As there are multitudes of organizations in these areas, we shall concern ourselves primarily with the larger and more important of the international organizations.

We can advance no claim that international understanding and good will are the only goals of international relations, especially in the area of sport. Sport is an international language, and as such it can serve many other national interests. The commonly expressed reason for international sports competition is as a medium of cultural exchange. However, sport also can serve as a vehicle of international prestige, for individual and team championships at the international level can improve the prestige a nation feels on the international front. Competition also can serve as political propaganda. While winning is related to international prestige, tours by national teams can be used not only to impress other nations with one's prowess in sport but also to show one nation's regard for the esteem of another nation or the desire for good relations with that nation. For example, the first improvement in relations between Communist China and the United States was the so-called Ping-Pong diplomacy. When the Americans were invited to send their best table-tennis players to meet the Chinese in a series of matches, the invitation served notice that China was ready to improve relations with the United States in other areas as well.

International sports competition also can be used to bolster national pride. The success of a nation's athletes in international competition can develop a strong feeling of pride among the nation's citizens, especially the smaller nations and the newly emerging nations. This national pride in the success of their athletes can be seen in the reactions to the success of the athletes of the newly emerging African nations in the 1968 Olympic Games in Mexico City and the successes of the Kenyan and Finnish athletes in the 1972 games in Munich.

INTERNATIONAL ORGANIZATIONS

A major international organization in the area of education is the World Confederation of Organizations of the Teaching Profession (WCOTP), founded in 1952. It works to organize teachers around the world to promote education for the purposes of international understanding; it also looks after the interests of teachers and tries to improve the training of teachers and the programs they teach. With headquarters in Washington, D.C., WCOTP works with the United Nations in some areas of international educational concerns and holds regular conferences around the world. One of its members is the International Council on Health, Physical Education, and Recreation (ICHPER), a physical education group.

ICHPER was founded in 1959 at a meeting of the WCOTP. With headquarters in Reston, Va., ICHPER assists the WCOTP in fulfilling its goal by working with organizations concerned with the broader aspects of physical education, including health and recreation, internationally. It works in the areas of studying the preparation of teachers, exchanging information on national programs, promoting exchange programs in physical education, and conducting special international studies and holding international conferences concerned with international problems in physical education. It holds a world conference every year.

The International Federation of Physical Education (FIEP) was begun in 1923 and has its headquarters in Lisbon, Portugal. Its object is to promote physical education for all people, regardless of sex or age. It promotes research and the communication of ideas between nations by sponsoring exchanges of teachers and scholars between interested nations. It holds regular international meetings.

The International Council of Sport and Physical Education (ICSPE) was established in 1960 and has its headquarters in Munich, West Germany. Its primary goals are to improve cooperation between all groups interested in physical education and sport and to interpret the cultural values of physical education and sport. It has regular international meetings every two years.

The International Olympic Academy was established in 1961 to promote and maintain the ideals of the original Olympic Games. Its headquarters are in Athens, Greece, and it is connected to both the Hellenic Olympic Committee and the International Olympic Committee. The International Olympic Academy conducts annual summer sessions at the site of ancient Olympia as one way of achieving its objectives.

The International Association of Physical Education and Sport for Girls and Women (IAPESGW) was begun in 1953 to bring together women around the world who were working in physical education and sport. It also cooperates with other organizations that promote sport activities. The IAPESGW tries to improve school programs through international exchanges of people and ideas. It has a world meeting every four years.

Some organizations are concerned purely with sports, unlike the groups that are concerned with education or physical education and include sports primarily as an added area. The major sport organization is the International Olympic Committee (IOC), established in 1894 to revive the ancient Olympic Games. It has conducted the Olympic Games every fourth year since the first modern games in 1896, and it tries to encourage sports competitions that are in keeping with the ideals of the ancient Olympic Games. It deals strictly with the Olympic Committees of the member nations, such as the United States Olympic Committee (USOC), rather than with the national governments, for it seeks to keep all political considerations out of the Olympic Games. Some of its intended patriotic moves have gradually led the modern Olympics closer toward being an international political contest (e.g., the use of national anthems and flags at awards sessions and recognizing the athletes' home nations as much as their individual skills).

The International Amateur Athletic Federation (IAAF) was begun in 1912 to promote friendly sports competition between nations without any type of discrimination on any grounds. Its emphasis on fair competition has resulted in its being the body that makes and revises the rules and regulations governing international and Olympic track-and-field athletics (simply called *athletics* in most nations outside the United States). It also is the agency that approves world records. The rules are revised at its international meetings, held every two years. Membership of a nation depends on that nation's chosen representatives being accepted into what amounts to a "gentleman's club" composed primarily of rich, elderly men, much in the tradition of 19th century British athletics where it was considered unseemly for the common people to be permitted to compete in sports. This attitude can be seen in

National boundaries momentarily forgotten, Rafer Johnson, of the United States, and C. K. Yang, of Taiwan, collapse against each other after finishing first and second in the Olympic decathlon in Rome in 1960. It was this kind of international fellowship that Coubertin wanted to promote when he worked for the revival of the Olympic Games in the late 19th century. (John G. Zimmerman/Sports Illustrated)

many of the organization's regulations relating to amateurism that make it difficult for anyone but the relatively wealthy to be "pure" amateurs. Consequently, most nations interpret the rules in this area with considerable latitude, while the IAAF and IOC studiously attempt to look the other way.

The International University Sports Federation (FISU), with headquarters in Louvain, Belgium, was founded in 1948. It tries to promote international physical education among students by sponsoring international sports conferences and contests for university students (the World Student Games or Universiades, every two years). It has regular international meetings every other year.

The International Military Sports Council (CISM), also begun in 1948, tries to promote equality within the various armies of the world, while it encourages friendly relations and sports ties among the world's armies. With headquarters in Brussels, Belgium, it promotes international championships in many sports and also holds an annual meeting.

In addition to these organizations that are oriented primarily toward sports are many international organizations whose goals are related to physical education or sport but whose primary goals are more specialized. One such group is the International Federation of Sport Medicine (IFSP), established in 1928 and headquartered in Brussels. Its goals are to develop physical and moral health through physical education and sports activities. It also makes scientific studies in this area; these are concerned with the effects of sport on healthy people and with the problems of injuries and disabilities in sport. It has regular conventions every four years.

The International Recreation Association was begun in 1956 and has its headquarters in New York City. Its goals are to promote recreation and to provide international recreational services. It is a consultant to the United Nations, and conducts exchange programs to study recreational programs around the world.

The International Union for Health Education was begun in 1951 and has its headquarters in Paris. Its objectives are to promote better health through educational means and to promote the exchange of current information in health education. It has a regular convention every third year.

The International Youth Hostel Federation, which stems from an organization begun in 1932, is located in Copenhagen, Denmark. It tries to promote cooperation among national organizations while promoting international understanding among young people. Its primary mode of improving international understanding is to make inexpensive travel possible by providing places around the world where traveling youth can stay at minimal expense. This organization is most active in Europe.

The People-to-People Sports Committee was started privately in 1956 to promote international understanding and sports competition. It does so by sponsoring touring teams in many sports and by working in other ways to promote international sports.

UNESCO, the United Nations Educational, Scientific and Cultural Organization, was established in 1945 and has its headquarters in Paris. Its goals are to contribute to peace and security in the world by promoting cooperation among the nations in improving education, science, and culture, while stressing a basic respect for justice and individual human rights. It has an international meeting every two years.

The World Alliance of Young Men's Christian Associations, with headquarters in Geneva, Switzerland, was first begun in 1844. Its goal is to help YMCAs around the world. Its sister organization is the World Young Women's Christian Association, located in the same city, which was begun in 1848. Its more broadly based work includes the goals of international understanding, basic human rights, and improved social and economic conditions for all people. It has a large world meeting every four years.

The World Health Organization (WHO), with headquarters in Geneva, Switzerland, was organized in 1948 as an agency of the United Nations. Its ultimate goal is to help all people attain a high level of health, which it has defined as "a state of complete physical, mental, and social well-being and not merely the absence of disease or infirmity." It meets annually and provides assistance to any world government that requests it.

In addition to these specialized international bodies, which represent only a small number of the many international organizations, are many international sports organizations. Almost every sport that has participants in many countries has at least one international organization that keeps its rules updated, verifies world records (if the sport has such records), and provides for international competition and world championships. These organizations are too numerous to list in a short chapter, but some examples are the International Amateur Basketball Federation, headquartered in Munich, Germany; the International Gymnastics Federation (FIG), located in Geneva, Switzerland; and the International Amateur Swimming Federation, located in Jenkintown, Pennsylvania.

INTERNATIONAL COMPETITIONS

There are many international sports competitions, but the most important are the Olympic Games. Although the ancient Greek games were dissolved in A.D. 394, they often attracted scholars' attention over the next 15 centuries. The most prominent among the number of people who worked to revive the ancient Greek competition was Baron Pierre de Coubertin (1822–1908), of France.

The International Olympic Committee was formed in the 1500th anniversary year of the abolition of the Greek Olympic Games, with the revival of the games as its goal. Two years later, in 1896 in Athens, the first modern Olympic competition was held. The games are now held in every fourth year, or Olympiad, as were the ancient games, though world wars caused their cancellation in 1916, 1940, and 1944. A decision was made to add winter sporting events in 1908, but the now-separate winter Olympic Games were not held until 1924. More nations now take part in the Olympic Games than in any other internationally organized program except the United Nations.

The competition is open to both men and women in a large number of Olympic sports, but the number of activities has become so large and unwieldy that suggestions have begun appearing for the summer games to be separated into several parts by different sports and placed at different sites around the world. The primary reasons for this suggestion are: (1) the games represent a tremendous expense for any city to assume, (2) the large number of competitors and visitors puts an almost impossible strain on the facilities, housing, traffic, and police work of all except a few of the world's largest cities, and (3) the extreme visibility of such a concentrated sports event has made it seem an ideal place for political demonstrations and possible terrorism, such as the political demonstrations in Mexico City in 1968 and the murder of Israeli athletes by terrorists in Munich in 1972. The modern Olympic Games are currently facing perhaps the most difficult period of their survival; the danger is that their very popularity will destroy them.

A second major world championship event is the Universiade or the World Student Games of the FISU. The first competition was held in 1947, and the event is now held every odd-numbered year. Multitudes of university students from around the world take part in these games, which include a number of sports.

A third world meet, though one of more limited entry standards, is the World Maccabiah Games, which is patterned after the Olympic Games but

The Olympic Games are not always above political interference, as shown in this cartoon about the 1976 Olympics. Political interference was as great in the 1980 and 1984 games, and it will be just as much an aspect of the 1988 games as it has been in the past. (Courtesy Doug Marlette and the *Charlotte Observer*)

limited to Jewish athletes. First held in 1931, this competition in many sports is held every fourth year in Israel.

Many area championships that are held regularly involve only a portion of the world's nations. These contests are frequently patterned after the Olympic Games, though they may not include as many different sports within their competitive structures. The oldest example is the Asian Games, first held in 1913. Although the competition has changed its frequency and the nations involved in the competition a number of times since then, it is now essentially a sport competition for nations in continental Asia, ranging from Turkey to China, but not including the Soviet Union (much of which is in Asia). These games now meet every four years.

Another major competition is the Commonwealth Games, sometimes called the British Empire and Commonwealth Games. Begun in 1950, it also meets every fourth year, midway between Olympic Games. It is limited to the past and present members of the British Empire and the countries in the British Commonwealth.

The Pan-American Games represent a multisport championship for nations of the Western Hemisphere (North, Central, and South America). First begun in 1951, the Pan-American Games are held every four years, during the year before the Olympic Games.

Various European championships, usually involving single sports, also are held at varying intervals. The European nations, as well as the Soviet Union, are the participants. Most commonly a European championship is held every fourth year, usually between the Olympics like the Commonwealth Games. In track-and-field athletics an annual meet called the European Cup, which has qualifying meets to cut down the number of contestants, was added in the 1970s, as was the World Cup, followed by a World Championships in 1983.

Other competitions represent many smaller regions, while some represent individual sports. An example in team sports is the World Cup, the championship competition in soccer (football). The final playoffs involving a small number of national teams are held every four years, between the Olympic years, but the national teams qualify for the World Cup Final through a series of playoffs spread over the two years prior to the final.

World championships are held at some regular interval for most separate sports, though not all world championships are designated as such. The rules of the IAAF state that the Olympic Games also will serve as the world championship event for track-and-field athletics, though it is rarely referred to in that way. There are, however, dozens of world championships held during the period of every Olympiad, some of which are connected to the Olympic Games and some of which have no connection to the Olympics at all.

ORIENTATIONS OF PHYSICAL EDUCATION PROGRAMS

Physical education programs can vary greatly from nation to nation, for each nation has its own goals and orientation for a program. One of the traditional orientations for several thousand years has been toward military fitness. This major objective of physical education programs in the past can still be seen to some degree today. As we have seen in our historical review, it becomes important during times of war when national goals are to produce healthy young people who will be physically ready for military service. Military fitness is perhaps the most limited goal of a physical education program.

A second program orientation is toward competitive sports training. While the objective of these programs is partially to develop the skills and fitness of all the students by providing basic training in the techniques of competitive sports, they also can be used as "talent hunts," that is, to locate students with the potential to become outstanding athletes. In the past, programs of this nature that have been seen in the United States were community programs used to locate athletic talent for school teams. Today when such programs appear, they are more often on a national scale and are used to locate students who have the potential to become national or world-class athletes; the athletes are then given training on a higher level in the hope that they will ultimately bring athletic prestige to the nation.

The third orientation, that of the lifetime sports program, is seen primarily in the more affluent nations. In a program of this nature, the objective is to teach skills in sports that can be enjoyed throughout life, almost regardless of age. The hope is that the students will take part in physical activities and maintain at least minimal fitness throughout their lifetime. This approach is seen most frequently in nations where the people have more money and leisure time, for a citizen in a poverty-stricken nation generally does not have the time (or the facilities or inclination) for such activities.

A fourth orientation might be called cultural fitness, for it places emphasis on activities that are rooted in the culture of the nation. For example, a country might stress only its traditional activities, such as national dances and sports, and put little emphasis on activities used in other nations, regardless of their world popularity. This type of program is more likely to be seen in smaller nations or in nations that have been ruled by other countries and are striving to develop a national consciousness or self-image.

A fifth orientation, total fitness for life, is sometimes tied into the program as part of the total educational process. We refer to this approach when we speak of education both of and through the physical. The emphasis is not on any single area of fitness or training; instead, the concern is for the final outcomes of the educational process, whether physical, social, mental, or moral.

SOME NATIONAL PHYSICAL EDUCATION PROGRAMS

We shall discuss some of the practices of physical education around the world by looking at the educational systems in several countries, each of which can represent a number of other countries of a regional or ideological type. These five systems will be examined: (1) the English educational system, which has been copied around the world as a result of England's former position as the world's foremost colonial power, (2) West Germany's system, which is representative of the European programs of physical education, (3) the Soviet Union's system, which provides an example of a system in a totalitarian state, (4) Japan's system, which is to some degree representative of a modern Asian system (though it has limitations that we shall discuss later), and (5) Kenya's system, which serves as an example of programs in the newly emerging Third World nations.

England

The English educational system has been copied around the world in many respects, for at one time the British Empire encircled the globe. When educational systems were developed in the British colonies, they were for the most part copies of the traditional English system of education.

The system in England was once composed largely of privately run, elitist institutions that catered primarily to the upper classes. During the 20th century, the emphasis has shifted more toward mass education. The total fitness concept is the basic emphasis of the English physical education program, which is used as one more phase of an educational process aimed toward the ideals of social democracy.

England has long been a citadel of games and sports, but these activities are used in an extremely independent way. There is little reliance on coaches or formal organizations. The activities are self-organized and the participants control them, much like American sport in its developmental stages in the 19th century before the schools took control away from the students. In England, the tradition is sport, as opposed to the American emphasis on competition, which is not entirely the same. The primary emphasis of English sport is the fun of the competition.

While the English educational pattern in the past was largely upper-class education in private schools (referred to as "public schools"), that tradition has largely passed from common practice. Most English children are now educated in free, genuinely public schools. All children are required to attend school from the ages of 5 to 15. Considerable variety is available in English education, for the English try to adapt their educational practices to the many differences in ability and aptitudes that can be found among the students.

As the English free schools have improved in quality, the proportion of students in the public schools has dropped to about 10 percent of the student population. In the public-school pattern, students attend kindergarten from about the ages of 5 to 8, then a preparatory school from the ages of 8 to 13, and finally a private secondary school from the ages of 13 to anywhere between 16 and 18.

Attendance at these schools is followed by education at the university level. Some, but not many, preparatory schools are boarding schools, while most secondary private schools are of this type. Most schools have required games or sports activities on at least four afternoons weekly. Frequently physical education specialists are available, though their functions are often less authoritarian than in the American schools.

In the free schools, the classroom teachers usually teach physical education to the students at the lower levels. In the first several years of school, the emphasis is on movement education activities, with two short lessons daily between the ages of 5 and 7; later the daily lessons include some sports activities. As the students get older, more sports activities are added. At the secondary level, trained specialists do much of the instruction. The girls have activities such as "educational gymnastics," dance, and games and sports, while for boys the emphasis is on strength and mobility activities in the games and sports. At the secondary level, physical activity is commonly scheduled for four class periods per week, two of which are for games and sports. During the last year or so of secondary school, the number of class periods may be decreased as the student prepares for university entrance examinations.

For the secondary students, choosing which of the four types of secondary schools to attend depends on their career plans or occupational directions. Students are given standardized intelligence and achievement tests before entrance to the secondary schools as an aid in determining what type of school they should attend, but controversy regarding this testing practice is still considerable.

The most common type of secondary school today is the modern school, which is designed to meet the needs of most of the students. The second type is the grammar school, which emphasizes the academic areas of the humanities and sciences and which parents prefer as the best route to a university. The third type of school is the technical school, which emphasizes training in trades or industrial work, similar to technical schools in the United States. Another type of school, which is commonly called the comprehensive school and which is similar to American high schools, combines all three of the basic types of English secondary schools into a single school.

At the university level, physical education activities usually are not required; they are most commonly voluntary activities oriented toward recreational games and sports. Although most universities have physical education personnel, this staff assists students, but does not plan their programs. The students, who may occasionally hire a professional coach, usually organize, finance, and often coach sports organizations.

A governmental educational authority must certify and approve the teacher of physical education as a qualified teacher. Certification can be achieved by taking a three- or four-year teacher-training course at a teacher-training college or university. Some colleges specialize in preparing teachers of physical education, though they are of recent origin. A university graduate in another field can take a one-year course of specialization in physical education to become a certified physical education teacher.

Professional coaching has not been a prestigious career in England, and the coaches in the past were athletes who had no educational training. Most sports competition is through clubs, which may or may not hire coaches. A number of sports organizations have developed systems of coaching examinations that are used to certify coaches in a single sport on a local, regional, or national level. Because the overwhelming emphasis of sports competition in England has been the fun of sport rather than the success of competition, the coach has not been lifted to the exalted status sometimes seen in the United States.

West Germany

An example of European programs of physical education is the program of the Federal Republic of Germany (West Germany). The basic emphasis of the West German program lies somewhere between the total fitness concept and that of developing competitive sports. The physical education program is firmly tied to national sports bodies, which have strong national organizations to push sports competition among the youth of the nation. The government sponsors many competitive events for the students.

The educational program is now a decentralized one, with each of West Germany's 11 states directing the physical education program in its area. (This arrangement is similar to the state-oriented organization in the United States.) Although the centralized structure of education was broken up after the fall of the Nazi government, the federal government of West Germany still issues guidelines with suggestions for school requirements.

Daily play and instruction are recommended during the first two years at the elementary or primary level. Thereafter, the recommendations call for three hours weekly of gymnastics and play activities, with an additional two hours weekly of games and sports, either in the form of competition or of sports clinics. The two types of secondary schools are the professional school, which basically provides an academic preparation for university training, and the vocational school. Although the same suggestions are made for physical education in both types of secondary schools, a vocational school allots little time to physical education, and the actual number of class hours of activity in a professional school is sometimes less than the recommendations because of the time needed for academic studies.

The greatest emphasis in the curriculum is on gymnastics, which is largely an outgrowth of Friedrich Jahn's work in the early 1800s. Much work is also done with games and play activities during the early years of school, while in the later years the program moves into a heavily sports-oriented emphasis. Physical education is not a major part of the curriculum at the university level; it is geared primarily toward voluntary recreational activities, as in the English system.

Teachers at the intermediate or secondary level must be certified as teachers in two subjects, one of which is physical education. The process is usually satisfied by a three-year teacher-training program in the universities. One- and two-year teacher-training programs are also available, partially in response to the shortage of physical education teachers in the schools. During the last two decades, development of many sports training centers has accompanied the great national emphasis on developing facilities for play, recreation, and sport.

Soviet Union

An example of physical education in a totalitarian system is the program of the Union of Soviet Socialist Republics (the Soviet Union, or Russia). No single emphasis exists in the Russian program unless the improvement of the physical health and condition of the state might be described as one, but concurrently several emphases are evident. First is the concept of total fitness, which is used to develop a social-minded, healthy citizen. Mixed in are both a military-fitness emphasis, stressed through a concern for defense (Russia has long national borders and lost many millions of its strongest youths during World War II), and a sports-training orientation, which is stressed for the attendant national prestige achieved through sports successes.

The educational system has been slightly decentralized, but the programs throughout the nation follow governmental guidelines. Daily activity requirements in the schools include 10 minutes of in-place exercises at the start of every school day, in addition to the required physical education classes. The required class activities are split between (1) exercises and sport-type activities and (2) special technique work in a single sport. This second part is organized a bit like the lifetime sports idea in the United States, for it is designed in part to develop a level of skill and appreciation that will encourage the student to continue participation in the activity long after leaving school.

Other governmental programs strongly supplemented the school physical education program. Summer camps, which are made available for most age groups, stress physical activities, though many nonphysical activities also are included. The Sport Badge awards are used to reflect achievement levels in activities and lead up to the highest level, the Master of Sport. These awards are prestigious, for they require increasing levels of physical fitness in addition to successful completion of the advanced sports tests. The *Spartakiadas* are regular national sports competitions that are used both to promote physical education and to locate athletes who may be developed to the highest levels of achievement. These events are promoted through a huge system of local sports clubs.

The high status of physical education in the Soviet Union has resulted in many candidates for admission to the teacher-training programs, which in turn has resulted in higher admissions standards. The entrance examinations that a prospect must pass include tests of intellectual ability, physical fitness, degree of social adjustment, and leadership abilities. Limited class space has created keen competition among quality students.

There are three levels of teacher training in the Soviet Union. The lowest level requires a five-year course that follows eight years of primary school. Its graduates are assistant instructors who usually continue their studies in night classes. The second level is more academic and usually operates through a department of physical education at a teacher-training institute. Its graduates teach in primary or secondary schools, depending on the level of their academic training. A trend toward upgrading the lowest-level program to the middle level has developed in recent years.

The highest level of training occurs in the physical education institutes, which offer both undergraduate and graduate instruction. These institutes usually include departments to train sport coaches, for official coaches must be graduates of a physical education institute. A great deal of scientific research in sport is conducted in the Soviet Union, so a prospective coach needs special training to be able to interpret and apply the results of the research. The graduates of the institutes teach and administer programs at the highest levels.

The basic education of a prospective teacher in the Soviet Union may be summarized as a rough balance among three areas: (1) the physical fitness of the prospective teacher, (2) a high level of theoretical knowledge, and (3) the knowledge and skills of teaching theory and techniques.

Japan

Japan's educational system is representative of the Asian countries to some degree, even though many aspects of its school programs have been built on the model of the United States' school system. This American influence is a result of United States military control and intervention in Japan after World War II. The basic emphasis of the Japanese program of physical education is total fitness—the education of the whole person—including physical development, citizenship, and healthful leisure activities. Physical education is required in the schools from the elementary level through the university level.

Students are required to attend school for nine years (six years of elementary school and three years of junior high school), which may be followed by three years of senior high school and four years of university training. A multitude of activities are used in the school physical education program to meet its broad emphasis.

During the elementary school years, students have 45 minutes of activity three times each week under the direction of their classroom teachers. At the junior and senior high school levels, two or three classes of 50 minutes each are allotted per week to teaching more advanced skills. Traditional Japanese sports and activities are also added at these levels. Some theoretical studies are provided to show the benefits of exercise and its place in an individual's life.

At the university level, four credits are required in physical education, though two of them may be lecture-type courses in areas such as health education. The course offerings are diverse, in the tradition of the American system. While sports are first offered at the junior high school level, an attempt has been made to organize national programs of competitive sports under educational auspices to avoid the effects of competition that might be considered harmful or might not contribute to educational ends.

Teachers must be certified, which requires completion of either a two-year or four-year program of professional preparation; the four-year graduates teach at the higher school levels. The teacher-training programs are modeled largely on the American system of teacher preparation. At this time, only a few graduate programs in physical education are available in Japan, so many students undertake graduate studies in universities in other countries, such as in the United States.

Kenya

Kenya represents the newly emerging, underdeveloped nations of the world that are sometimes referred to as the Third World. Kenya was once a colony in the British Empire and is now a member of the British Commonwealth. Consequently, many aspects of its physical education program have developed from programs that the British began. The program was formerly one of physical training (primarily calisthenics), but the primary emphasis

Abebe Bikila, of Ethiopia, shown here winning his second Olympic marathon in Tokyo in 1964, was one of the first prominent African athletes to receive world attention. Since his time, many other and newer African nations have increased their international prestige by their successes in sport. (Courtesy AP/ Wide World Photos, Inc.)

today is on developing individual character. The broad program also stresses total fitness and the development of the whole person.

Kenya is still in the process of imprinting its own national identity on its program of physical education and its requirements. Kenyan physical educators are faced with the problem of limited facilities for physical education activities, and this hampers many of the efforts for a broadly based program. At the secondary school level, each student must take two periods per week of physical education, though other games and swimming also are provided. Activities are generally in three areas: (1) games (including team sports), (2) dance, and (3) swimming and athletics (track and field).

As is the case with many of the newly emerging nations that are seeking to establish national and international identities, Kenya is striving to develop a competitive international sports program. Much effort is made to attract students and adults to sports, both to provide recreational activities and to serve as an athletic talent hunt. Kenya suffers from a shortage of facilities and a lack of national and especially international competition. The nation is seeking to develop its full potential in sport, for much national pride has resulted from its successes in Olympic competition.

All teacher-training programs in the universities require some work in physical education, and all teachers are considered qualified to teach physical education, since they have at least a minimal background. Teacher-training programs are still being developed, and Kenya is appreciative of the benefits it can receive from international exchanges of teachers and from opportunities for its students to be trained in the universities of other countries. Kenya still has many problems in its developing educational system, but, as the nation develops, its educational system will continually progress too.

By studying the physical education programs and patterns of teacher preparation in other nations, we can broaden our understanding of those nations and of physical education, for we begin to see physical education through many other eyes. International studies can be one more link toward world understanding.

NOTES

1. C. Lynn Vendien and John E. Nixon, *The World Today in Health, Physical Education, and Recreation,* Prentice-Hall, Englewood Cliffs, N.J., 1968, pp. 5–6.
2. Ibid., pp. 8–9.

SUGGESTED READINGS

Ahrabi-Fard, Iradge. *Implications of the Original Teachings of Islam for Physical Education and Sport.* Ph.D. dissertation, University of Minnesota, 1975.

Arlott, John, ed. *The Oxford Companion to World Sports and Games.* London: Oxford University Press, 1975.

Bennett, Bruce L., Maxwell L. Howell, and Uriel Simri. *Comparative Physical Education and Sport.* 2d ed. Philadelphia: Lea & Febiger, 1983.

Cantelon, Hart, and Richard Gruneau, eds. *Sport, Culture, and the Modern State*. Toronto: University of Toronto Press, 1982.

Espy, Richard. *The Politics of the Olympic Games: With an Epilogue, 1976–1980*. Berkeley: University of California Press, 1981.

Graham, Peter J., and Horst Ueberhorst, eds. *The Modern Olympics*. Champaign, Ill.: Leisure Press, 1976.

Guttmann, Allen. *The Games Must Go On: Avery Brundage and the Olympic Movement*. New York: Columbia University Press, 1984.

Hardman, Ken. "The Development, Structure and Promotion of Sport in the Federal Republic of Germany." *Physical Education Review* 5 (Spring 1982), 45–61.

Herndon, Myrtis E. *Theses and Dissertations Related to Comparative/International Education, Physical Education, Sport, and Dance*. Published by the author, Hiram, Ohio, 1973.

Jeffries, Stephen C. "Sport and Education: Theory and Practice in the USSR." *Quest* 36, no. 2 (1984), 164–176.

Johnson, William, ed. *Physical Education Around the World*. Champaign, Ill.: Stipes Publishing, 1980.

Kanin, David B. *A Political History of the Olympic Games*. Boulder, Colo.: Westview Press, 1981.

Levin, Cathryn L. *Nationalism in Sport*. M.A. thesis, California State University, Long Beach, 1975.

Lowe, Benjamin, David B. Kanin, and Andrew Strenk. *Sport and International Relations*. Champaign, Ill.: Stipes Publishing, 1978.

Lucas, John A. *The Modern Olympic Games*. San Diego: A. S. Barnes, 1980.

McIntyre, Thomas D. "Sport in the German Democratic Republic and The People's Republic of China: A Sociopolitical Analysis." *JOPERD* 56 (January 1985), 108–111.

Ndulue, John Chika. *Selected Aspects of Physical Education in Advanced Countries Around the World With Implications for the Developing Areas, Especially Africa*. M.S. thesis, University of Illinois, 1974. Microcard.

Okafor, Udodiri Paul. *The Interaction of Sports and Politics as a Dilemma of the Modern Olympic Games*. Ph.D. dissertation, Ohio State University, 1979.

Riordan, James, ed. *Sport Under Communism: The USSR, Czechoslovakia, the G.D.R., China, Cuba*. Montreal: McGill-Queen's University Press, 1977.

Rust, Val D., and Terry Schofield. "The West German Sports Club System: A Model for Lifelong Learning." *Phi Delta Kappan* 59 (April 1978), 543–546.

Schneidman, N. Norman. *The Soviet Road to Olympus: Theory and Practice of Soviet Physical Culture and Sport*. Champaign, Ill.: Human Kinetics, 1978.

Seagrave, Jeffrey, and Donald Chu. *Olympism: A Cross-Disciplinary Analysis of the Olympic Movement*. Champaign, Ill.: Human Kinetics, 1981.

Simahara, Nobuo K. "Japanese Education and Its Implications for U.S. Education." *Phi Delta Kappan* 66 (February 1985), 418–421.

Strenk, Andrew. "Diplomats in Track Suits: The Role of Sports in the Foreign Policy of the German Democratic Republic." *Journal of Sport and Social Issues* 4 (Spring-Summer 1980), 34–45.

Van Dalen, Deobold B., and Bruce L. Bennett. *A World History of Physical Education*. 2d ed. Englewood Cliffs, N.J.: Prentice-Hall, 1971.

Zilberman, Victor. "Physical Education in USSR Schools." *JOPERD* 55 (August 1984), 64–68.

chapter 16

Toward the Twenty-First Century: New Directions and Future Concerns in Physical Education and Sport

After studying where physical education has come from, what it is, and how we are prepared as physical educators, we still face a major concern: What does the future hold for physical education? What are the developing trends in our lives, and what effect will they have on our field 10, 20, or 30 years from now? We need to consider not only trends and directions that seem to be apparent in education and society today but also some of the problems that we are facing in education and society.

TOWARD THE FUTURE

The future has always fascinated people. As we study the history of literature, we find many examples of people's predictions of the future. Writers have expressed their views of the future, sometimes as a warning and at other times as a suggestion of what the ideal society should be. The suggestion of an ideal lies behind Plato's *Republic* in ancient Greece, and Thomas More's *Utopia* written in the 16th century. Examples of other views of the future and its possible problems are found in Aldous Huxley's *Brave New World*, George Orwell's *1984*, and Alvin Toffler's *Future Shock*. While we want to know what the future holds, the thought of the changes it may bring leaves many of us apprehensive. We know with certainty that changes will take place, but we do not know whether the results will be better or worse for the human race.

The last several decades have seen the rise of an area of study called futurism or futuristics, which is an attempt to examine the future scientifically. Whereas previous study of the future consisted of attempts to predict or to plan a "perfect" society, such as the ideas of the Utopians who took their name from the title of More's 16th-century work, modern study is inclined more toward predicting the future than toward designing it. Madge Phillips has cited Henry Winthrop's contention that sociologists prefer futurism because of their belief in a value-free discipline.[1] However, even predictions of the future are based on perceived or inherent value systems. World trends, particularly those relating to population-growth problems and to energy and food shortages have resulted in widespread interest in predicting what the future holds.

The Problems of Predictions

While educational theorists are usually full of ideas about how to improve education and society, a "mood of caution" has overtaken many educators, according to *U.S. News and World Report*.[2] During the last two decades, educators have been given unprecedented opportunities to put their theories into action, but the results have rarely been impressive. Theorists are becoming more cautious in their predictions of successful, meaningful change, for too many of their earlier predictions have failed to come true.

At one time the population was expected to rise indefinitely; the school population, and therefore the need for teachers, also would rise forever into the future. Many schools began expansion programs with this prediction in mind, just as masses of teachers began to be turned out. We discovered, often too late, that this prediction was incorrect. A change in family habits has taken place: a trend toward smaller families. The result has been a leveling off of the school-age population, so that around 1982 the number of students at each grade level was expected to stabilize.[3] The college population is expected to continue to increase, though this prediction is not related to a population increase but to a change in societal views of the college experience. The population of the United States is expected to keep slowing its growth until it reaches approximately 250 to 300 million people, at which point it *may* stabilize, though this stabilization is difficult to predict. Because many other parts of the world have done nothing to decrease the growth rate, however, the world population will continue to rise at a phenomenal rate.

World Trends

Several world trends are easily visible. The most visible of these is the population explosion we have already discussed. The number of people in the world is increasing rapidly, with the greatest rates of increase most often found in the nations that are least able to support their present populations. Such growth creates a great conflict both within and among nations, as the wants and needs of the people clash with the concrete problem of availability of resources.

Another problem is the growth of the industrialized world into a heavily technological world. The knowledge explosion has tended to move people toward more specialization as it becomes less possible for a person to have a broad store of the world's knowledge. The world is increasingly computerized and miniaturized, so that many of the older distinctions between regions and people no longer hold true. Many of the old regional differences among areas of the United States are all but impossible to discover today, for the influences of national television, instant world news, and increasing wealth at most levels of society have done more in a generation to make the United States a single people of a single nation than all the changes of the past two centuries.

The technological world is a complex one; today more than ever the person who hopes to survive and be a successful, contributing member of society needs many skills. Our educational process must change to meet these technological needs so that schools can help prepare tomorrow's citizens to fulfill their roles in society. The old-fashioned education was designed to prepare a person for a civilization that was also old-fashioned. We must prepare people to live in the future rather than in the past or even in the present.

The knowledge explosion is another trend that has created educational conflicts. We cannot expect students to gain more than a portion of the world's knowledge, but we face the dilemma of deciding what portion of that knowledge will be most valuable. The period of the 1970s seems to have ushered in a new aspect of education in the United States that has not existed before: a massive disagreement over what the people want from education and the schools. The result of this discord is confusion; different schools are trying different approaches to education. The results tend to be confusing rather than enlightening. The question is asked and repeated: What knowledge is most worth having? Educators do not agree on the answer.

Another trend is the emergence of the Third World, which we discussed in Chapter 15. These nations were previously the world's "have-not" nations, but they are now becoming factors in world politics because of the size of their populations or because of other factors such as the petroleum reserves of the Arab nations. In fact, some authorities have suggested the emergence of a Fourth World, a nearly permanent, overcrowded, underprivileged group of nations, since a number of the Third World nations became wealthy as a result of their oil or mineral reserves and were thus more able to cope with the problems of emerging into a modern, highly technological world.

The Third World nations have acquired an important status in world politics because their population growth affects the future of the planet's life-support resources and because the money that some of them have come to control is sufficient to exert a strong force on the world economy. As these nations work toward political maturity, the other nations of the world must work to help them understand the long-term effects of their actions on the world, but the emphasis must be on international understanding and tolerance.

Another trend might be termed the growth of ethical dilemmas. The problems causing the dilemmas are those, as we have mentioned in our discussion of ethics, involving questions for which there may be no clear right or wrong answers. An example of an ethical dilemma is how to deal with the effects of the world population boom, for the growth in the world population is a serious threat to the ability of the world to support its citizens. The natural need is for a world policy of birth control, but many newly emerging nations see such a suggestion as a threat to their power; they believe that the suggestion is made in an effort to keep their nations small and weak. Such nations face the dilemma of having small populations that they can feed or large populations that will face starvation.

The same ethical choice appears in the problems of environmental concerns that we might refer to as economy versus ecology. Industrialization may hurt the ecology of a nation, yet the effect of strict measures to safeguard the ecology may be a weaker economy. The issue in some cases has been simplified to jobs or the ecology, and many people believe that any possible compromise will hurt both to some degree. In a problem of this sort, there may not be a right answer, but if this generation cannot solve the problem, the next generation will have much greater problems to solve.

Another ethical problem of sorts is the question of education of the masses. Each nation has its own ideas regarding who should be educated and to what extent they should be educated. The United States has traditionally attempted to educate a larger proportion of its people than any other nation on earth. Is this idea the best one in modern times? Should every person be educated? If so, what should be the process, what should be the content, and to what degree should they be educated? Again, there is no correct answer to problems of this nature. Each nation must make its own educational decisions for the future, but as the world changes, these decisions affect the other nations more than ever before.

When we look at these and all the other current trends, we realize we are facing different aspects of a single problem: The earth is continually changing. Nothing remains the same, including us. We must prepare ourselves for the future, and we must prepare physical education for the future. Our first big question is what the future holds for physical education.

TRENDS AND DIRECTIONS IN EDUCATION AND SOCIETY

In considering the trends and directions of apparent changes today, we want to look at three areas of trends: those of society, of the schools or education in general, and of physical education in particular. Societal trends give us a broad picture of what the future may hold, while school trends give us a more specific idea of the directions that physical education might take. A study of the trends and directions in physical education will give us our clearest idea of the implications of the future for physical educators.

Societal Trends and Directions

The population change is perhaps the most noticeable societal trend, and it has a great effect on the directions of most changes we anticipate. While only a few decades ago the population of the United States was expected to continue to increase in a geometric progression, we have already begun to see the death of that trend. The birth rate in the United States has begun to decline, though in the foreseeable future it is not expected to reach the "zero growth" rate (where the birth rate is equal to the death rate) that many advocates of population control are suggesting and that would result in a stable population level.

The gradual stabilizing of the United States population will require much rethinking of national educational priorities. The unexpected decrease in students means less need for teachers. This reason for the oversupply of teachers is further complicated by the fact that the number of trained college graduates who expect to go into teaching will continue to grow for years. The oversupply of teachers can be both a curse and a boon, for while it means more unemployed teachers, it also means an increased chance to enlarge the number of highly qualified teachers and to remove the poorly qualified.

The growth in world wealth has resulted in an increased availability of leisure activities for the general population, particularly in the United States. This trend creates a need for people who can teach and direct programs of recreational activities; it also creates a greater need for the teaching of recreational skills and attitudes toward exercise in the schools. Growth also will be seen in programs relating to relaxation skills and tension relief, especially as society becomes more technological and complex.

Concern for the environment also has increased in recent years, as people have become more conscious of nature and civilization's impact on it. As people become more concerned about the environment, they also become more involved in the developing programs of outdoor education and recreation. Environmental concerns will tie in with the increase in leisure time to lead to an explosive growth in the recreational area of physical education.

The problems seen in these societal trends are essentially aspects of two factors, one physical and the other philosophical. The physical factor is the mushrooming population, for it impacts on all other areas of life, both in terms of the ultimate resources available to the earth's inhabitants and in the resulting potential quality of life for those inhabitants. Many of the earth's resources, such as food supplies, can be replenished, but others, such as fossil fuels, are nonrenewable. When the planet's petroleum reserves are gone, as they are expected to be in no more than half a century, alternative energy sources will be necessary.

Greater populations mean greater drains on limited resources, such as energy supplies, and limit the ability of the planet to provide optimum shelter and nourishment. The result is an increasing dichotomy between the "haves" and "have-nots," with the subsequent social unrest that such division creates. Many wars result from the simple need of an overcrowded society to provide more room for too many people or to find more sources of food. The ultimate impact of the population increase, which on a world scale shows little sign of slowing, is vast. Mass starvation can certainly be an expected result of too many people in areas that cannot support large populations. If major weather changes occur, such as the drought that created the Dust Bowl of the Middle West during the 1930s, whole nations can starve.

The other factor, which is philosophical in nature, is the popular Western idea of progress.[4] This concept, which is the belief that whatever happens can be improved on, affects our attempts to improve learning, to improve standards of living, and indeed, even our concept of modern sport, for the idea of the "record" is tied to the idea of progress. However, Western society is now facing a dilemma, for this philosophy is becoming suspect in the face of rising populations and diminishing world resources.

School Trends and Directions

Many changes are appearing on the school scene today. The first really noticeable trend is the gradual decrease in and stabilization of the student population, which we have already discussed. Although the student population will stabilize through the high school level, it will continue to increase at the college level for some time. In this case the growth results not from any population change, but from a change in the American attitude toward post-high school education, combined with the radical growth of two-year schools in the United States during the 1960s and 1970s. More technical schools, community colleges, and junior colleges are providing a much greater variety of programs to high school graduates than ever before. Thus, the trend toward continuing one's education after completion of high school has been great.

The concept of education is also changing, as is the question of the proper emphasis of the educational process. A battle has developed between the cognitive and affective domains of educational objectives. The "taxonomy of educational objectives," a method of classifying more exactly the many objectives of education into types and their meanings, was developed by Benjamin S. Bloom and others.[5] According to this method, the objectives of education fall into three broad categories, or "domains":

1. *Cognitive*—This area might be thought of as factual, for it includes the gaining of knowledge and its use by the person. It is the area of intellectual abilities and skills.
2. *Affective*—This area involves our attitudes and values, or how we feel about things; the quality of our character; and our appreciations and interests. While most education has traditionally been in the cognitive domain, the affective domain is increasingly being emphasized in the educa-

tional process. The greatest difficulty with teaching in the affective domain is determining what is to be taught and then devising an objective
test to determine the degree of success or failure of the learning, for attitudes and appreciations are difficult to test objectively. The idea of putting a feeling into words *precisely* is a contradiction in terms.

3. *Psychomotor*—Bloom also refers to this area as the "manipulative or motor-
skill area,"[6] which gives a clear indication of the meaning of the term, for it
is concerned within the development of the motor skills of the student.

While we are not concerned with studying the nature of the taxonomy and
its educational application (for this area of study is in another part of the program of professional preparation), the conflict its appearance has generated
will last for years to come. It has brought forth once more an opposite aspect
to be considered within current educational disagreement: the back-to-basics
movement.

Today's student appears to have poorer language and math skills than the
typical student of 20 or even 50 years ago. Among the often-given reasons for
this decline in basic skills, or the three Rs, are the rise of permissive education, a move away from discipline and direction in the schools, and a move
toward emphasizing the affective domain—attitudes and appreciations—
rather than knowledge and concrete skills. One result of the dissatisfaction of
many parents with today's public education is rising attendance at alternative
institutions.

The number of "alternative schools," both public and private, has been increasing over the past several years. The first schools known as alternative
schools were originally started to provide a more humanistic or free-form
educational environment, but the term is now being used for almost any
school that differs from the typical public school in method or emphasis.
Some alternative schools are designed to provide students with more discipline and direction; others are planned to reemphasize basic education; and
still others (primarily private schools) wish to provide a more religious or patriotic environment. This movement also may be partially a result of the modern "homogenized" school, an attempt to remove anything that might be
considered the least bit controversial from the educational program. The rise
of multitudes of special-interest pressure groups who attack anything in the
schools that they do not consider agreeable with their own personal values
has sometimes created an atmosphere similar to that during the "red scares"
of the 1920s, 1930s, and early 1950s.

The rise of interest in the affective domain results from the feeling that
people need a greater concept of values, and that a vital part of the educational process is the development of attitudes and appreciations consistent
with those of the society in general. This interest in what might be called
moral education is an attempt to recreate what is seen as a lost "culture of responsibility" in the midst of what Christopher Lasch has called a "culture of

narcissism."[7] It is a desire to produce a society that understands that citizens in a crowded society have certain strong responsibilities to each other rather than an unimpeded right to do as they wish, regardless of its effect on others.

One reason for disagreements with the idea of affective education is that its supporters often forget that it can be developed only on a cognitive base, for facts must come before theories and values if the theories and values are to survive. Proponents of affective learning sometimes overreact by rejecting the cognitive domain, without realizing that the affective cannot survive without the cognitive base. For an education to be well rounded, however, *both* areas need to be developed. There is no reason for a battle between the cognitive and affective domains.

One outcome of this conflict over what the schools should teach has been an increasing community involvement in the schools. More citizens are interested in what is happening in the schools and are working to make the school programs more responsive to community and citizen needs. An attitude is developing that education is a lifetime experience rather than something that happens inside a schoolhouse within a certain age span of each person. Education is seen as less a function of age and more a continuing experience as the knowledge and interests of each person change throughout life.

This involvement and change in attitudes is reflected by an increasing move toward relevance in education. People are beginning to demand that education be functional, that it be relevant to their needs when they are outside the school. These concerns are part of the demand for accountability of the schools and of the teachers, who are expected to show that they are indeed accomplishing something in the schools, and to show that it is *worth* accomplishing. There is massive resistance to the old idea of the school as an ivory tower where reality and the outside world never enter. Today the outside world is moving into the school and the educational process.

A greater consciousness of a future of work is being developed in students as career training develops. It shows students the place of work in society, teaches them about work, and introduces them to many career options at an earlier age. It is intended to counteract the problem of students who graduate from school with absolutely no idea of what they want to do in the future, and in many cases, with no idea that they *need* to do anything.

Another trend is toward humanizing the curriculum. One complaint about education has been that it dehumanizes students, or puts them into a lowly position of little respect or human value. The humanization of education and the curriculum is one aspect of affective concerns. Increased emphasis is put on the idea of caring for the students. The curriculum also is becoming more flexible as more and more options are being designed to vary the curriculum to fit the needs of the individual student rather than bend the student to fit the curriculum. Use of block or modular scheduling, along with a growth in independent study and advanced placement testing, also is increasing.

The school curriculum has become broader, with more areas of study and interest permitted than in previous decades. The narrow bounds of traditional educational subjects and interests are gradually disappearing, as more interdisciplinary studies appear and cross the boundaries of subject matter. In physical education, the program is becoming much broader, with a move toward lifetime sports and lesser-known sports and fitness activities in the place of the small number of traditional sports and calisthenics-oriented fitness activities. More electives are being permitted in the schools, though the idea of a totally elective program has shown little sign of public acceptance, or of success if it were allowed.

The broader curricular pattern has led to Richard Gross's suggestion of seven new Cardinal Principles of Education to replace the 1918 list.[8] His revision is an attempt to put the principles into a modern world-society. To show how they contrast to the original list, we shall place them side by side:

Seven Cardinal Principles (1918)	Gross's Cardinal Principles (1978)
1. Health	1. Personal competence and development
2. Command of fundamental processes	2. Family cohesiveness
3. Worthy home membership	3. Skilled decision making
4. Vocation	4. Moral responsibility and ethical action
5. Civic education	5. Civic interest and participation
6. Worthy use of leisure	6. Respect for the environment
7. Ethical character	7. Global human concern

As we can see, the old and new cardinal principles are equally broad, yet the new principles are a bit more in touch with what we see as necessary functions of education in a modern world.

The decade of the 1970s was a time of great changes in education, and Ben Brodinsky has summarized some of the most meaningful events.[9] The events give some indication of directions for the future. Brodinsky selected ten events, but we shall mention only four: handicapped rights, women's rights, accountability, and affirmative action.

The first event is represented by bills such as Public Law 94-142 that, combined with court rulings, have required schools to provide conditions under which handicapped people can share equitably in the activities of nonhandicapped people. The effects of this legislation have ranged from the correction of facilities to provide easy access for physically handicapped persons to the implementation of "mainstreaming" or the inclusion of physically or mentally handicapped students in classes with students who do not share those characteristics.

Another event of the 1970s, the emergence of women's rights in education, was affected by laws such as Title IX. Title IX outlawed discrimination against women in educational areas, and the courts ruled that interschool athletics was among those areas. The result was an unbelievable boom in women's athletics. The trends created by Title IX presently show little sign of slowing down.

The 1970s also saw the development of the accountability movement, which is tied in with the back-to-basics movement. Together, these movements have been responsible for placing heavier requirements on students and teachers. Students are being asked to prove their learning by passing basic tests of competence. Meanwhile, teachers are being required to show precisely what changes they expect to produce in students and how they will test the production of those changes. Teachers also are being asked to prove that they are sufficiently skilled or knowledgeable to produce changes in their students.

Affirmative action began to affect hiring practices in teaching in the 1970s. Greatly increased opportunities in the educational job market for racial minorities and women have resulted from this event.

Teaching methodology is undergoing many innovative changes today. Specialists are being used more, as are such teaching techniques as team teaching (several teachers instructing a single class) and differentiated staffing (staff members teaching primarily in their areas of specialization rather than in all areas of their subject). A much greater use of teaching machines and audiovisual media is also evident. The laboratories that have been developed use taped sound cassettes, video cassettes, records, slide shows, or films as a part of the teaching process. More teachers than ever before are trying experimental teaching and learning methods and tools. The growth of innovative teaching techniques has been rapid, and it is not likely to slow down much.

Physical Education Trends and Directions

Physical education is beginning to emerge as a discipline, as we discussed earlier. The development of a discipline is helping to put the field of physical education on a more academic footing and is also raising the standards of education that the field requires.

The increased specialization of teachers will show up clearly in physical education, for it is a broad field with many potential areas of specialization. More people will develop teaching or research specialties, which will result in better-qualified teachers and which can permit the *hiring* of better-qualified teachers. However, the tradition has been to retain older teachers on the basis of seniority rather than on teaching quality or qualifications, and this practice could hamper the development of a better, more academically qualified body of physical educators and other teachers.

More specialized degrees may appear, and some schools likely will begin to concentrate their undergraduate or graduate programs in one or two specialized areas of physical education rather than try to prepare generalists in a world that specialists are increasingly taking over. Not only will more specialized fields develop but also students majoring in physical education will probably be required to work more in skill-development activity areas in the future.

Among the growing specialties for workers are the areas of adapted and handicapped activities, that is, working with people who are physically or mentally unable to participate in the regular physical education program or with those who need some type of rehabilitation program. Government studies indicate that about 11 percent of the students in the United States have some type of handicap such as speech impairment, learning disability, mental retardation, emotional disturbance, or other problems that remove them from the regular school programs.[10] More services will be provided to students who are disadvantaged, whether for physical, mental, or emotional reasons, or, as in the case of members of minority groups, for primarily social or economic reasons.

A greater variety of activities and areas of interest will be developing in the next decade or two. Women's sports activities grew rapidly in the 1970s, but the growth rate has leveled off. The rise in nonvarsity club sports in the colleges might be considered a return of the athletic programs to the students for their enjoyment and a move away from athletic departments and coaches as a way of life and as a business. A parallel trend toward physical education as a purely elective subject is also growing.

Finally, there is an increasing emphasis on the social and aesthetic areas of physical education and sport, both as studies and as simple areas of personal interest. Physical educators are following their interests into areas of dance, the liberal arts, humanities, psychology, and sociology. These are just a few examples of broad aspects of study that physical educators are using more and more. The emphasis on aesthetics, the joy and beauty of movement, is growing.

PROBLEMS AND CHALLENGES IN PHYSICAL EDUCATION

Although many problems and challenges face educators in general and physical educators in particular, we shall look at only half a dozen problems and challenges as examples of what the future holds for us. We could cite many more examples, but these few are enough to give a general idea of the scope and nature of the existing problems and challenges.

The Place and Function of Physical Education in Education

This issue is the source of a number of long-standing questions: What is the place of physical education in the educational process? What function does it fulfill? Can we justify it as a part of the curriculum? Can we justify requiring it of all students? These questions are being asked, loudly and often, across the country, and as physical educators we must have answers that will satisfy our critics. In a time of accountability, we must show that physical education has a definite, positive value in the educational process, and we need to show why physical education is a vital part of the curriculum.

At the same time, the place of athletics in education and its relationship to physical education are becoming grave concerns. In periods of much tighter budgets, schools must be far more careful about where they direct their expenditures. Questionable practices are attracting more attention to mismanaged sports programs.[11] Also, many benefits that school athletics promise are now coming under fire as unproven or unprovable. Sports programs will be studied much more closely rather than blindly supported. Even where programs continue, problems in providing skilled coaches will rise, for many schools have moved to accept part-time coaches to meet the increased number of school teams under Title IX. While this has resulted in more opportunities for competition, it has not increased the number of available jobs, and it may have resulted in the schools using less skilled coaches. Indeed, Lasch has argued that "games quickly lose their charm when forced into the service of education, character development, or social improvement."[12]

Other Curriculum-Oriented Problems

Many curricular problems exist in education and physical education. In addition to the need to make the curriculum more relevant, which we have already discussed, we need to establish educational priorities for our society if we are to settle some of the long-standing issues. We need to end the separation of reality and education, but we cannot go so far into the idea of "relevance" that we succumb entirely to the idea of having the student at any age plan the curriculum for us. As one educator said, "The trouble with gearing a curriculum to the interests of children is precisely that: they *are* children. But education is for life."[13]

We do not want to plan an inflexible curriculum, however. We must be open to change and innovation. Students need to have options that will permit them the optimum realization of their latent talents. For this reason the students need to be included in program planning and evaluation, for the programs are supposed to be designed to benefit the students, not the teachers.

We also have discussed the cognitive–affective struggle—the quarrel between advocates of learning the three Rs and the proponents of learning values or of unstructured education— earlier in this chapter. Theodore W. Hipple makes an interesting observation in this area by remarking that "the chief weakness in contemporary education may not lie within the institution itself, but within the expectations held for it by the larger society."[14] We might say that people have used it as a means to an end (employment, societal law and order, discipline) but have not considered it valuable for itself alone. Perhaps we use it simply to make up for our own personal mistakes, shortcomings, and failures.

We also face the challenge of developing more and better leaders, for physical education is not a field noted for its nationally recognized leaders or au-

W. H. Freeman

thorities. At the same time, we need to develop greater creativity, an ability to think and act innovatively, in our practitioners. Reuben Frost has suggested the term *copeability* as a great need—the development of the ability to cope with problems and to solve them.[15]

A need also remains for the academic physical educator with strong skills in all the communications arts. Physical educators have not been very successful in communicating to the public either the values of physical education or the need for physical education. One reason for this lack of success has been the narrowly defined education that we discussed in the chapter on professional preparation. The new physical educator needs to be skill oriented— capable of demonstrating as well as teaching the skills used in any class. At the same time, she must be broadly educated in the liberal arts and sciences to be able to converse meaningfully with people in all academic fields. For too long the physical educator has been cut off in the gym, with a reputation of having few interests beyond the sports pages. That type of physical educator cannot survive in the modern world, much less the future, because that type has become an educational dinosaur.

We particularly need to work to make athletics more genuinely educational. One of the greatest failures of physical educators is that we seem to lose sight of the purposes of physical education and education where school athletics is concerned. We have had no real action to correct the gross ills of sport since the 1929 Carnegie Report (and even that had little noticeable effect on college practices). Many people outside the field are questioning the value of athletics in the schools, and if we do not move to show and practice the positive values, we may find sports starting to disappear from the trimmed budgets of the future.

Oversupply of Teachers

We also have discussed the oversupply problem at some length. We need to raise the standards of admission to the field of physical education to reduce the glut of potential physical education teachers joining an already-overcrowded field. Raising admissions standards may be the best way to make a major improvement in the quality of physical education teachers and programs.

A parallel problem has been grade inflation, the awarding of higher grades than students deserve for their achievements. This problem, which hampers the ability of employers to evaluate candidates for jobs, may lead to more use of standardized testing to determine which candidates really possess the knowledge and skills needed to perform successfully.

The Gap Between Research and Practice

We need to work to close the gap between our current teaching methods and facts and what we have discovered about teaching and skill acquisition in research. We have allowed a gap to appear between the physical educators who are researchers and those who are practitioners. We need to work to see that we improve the practice of physical education as a result of the research we are doing in physical education.

Financial Problems

In the early 1970s, school budgets across the nation began facing severe budget problems. These problems have continued to grow. They were partially a result of a temporarily down economy, but they also include a warning for the future: Money is going to be less available. If physical education expects to continue to receive a fair share, we must prove the value of our programs to the schools. Otherwise, we may see our programs dropped or at least cut back severely. The same difficult lesson is doubly true for athletics in the schools. We must show the value, or our programs will be included among the frills that disappear when money is less available for the schools. We must be more conscious of budgets and more careful of our spending habits.

Alienation of Students

The "turned-off" student may be the greatest problem in education today: Can the student who is not interested in school be reached? The problems of drug and alcohol abuse that we see in students and the larger society are symptomatic of a sense of loss of personal worth, a feeling of making no contribution to anything. In part, such feelings of alienation are probably a result of overcrowded population conditions, but we must try to cope with the problem of alienated students, for the consequences of a large number of alienated people are grave. This worry is one of the major reasons for the interest in humanism in education.

Again, Toward the Future

Looking toward the future, we might consider two points raised by Warren Fraleigh in discussing the curricular implications for physical education.[16] The first is the increased movement toward a leisure society, which has major implications for our field. Fraleigh points out that while this movement can provide greater opportunities for human fulfillment, it also can result in meaningless discretionary time that is simply wasted. We have rarely considered this side of the coin. Furthermore, Daryl Siedentop raises a larger question, for he argues that leisure time is not increasing except in comparison to the last century.[17] He claims that we have far less leisure time than those living in the past centuries when there were far more holidays. Siedentop further suggests that physical education will be stronger when leisure time is redefined to lose its connection to work as "non-work" that permits an individual to return to work refreshed and ready to do a better job. Instead, he suggests that leisure should be defined in terms of its part in contributing to the "good life"; he believes that leisure's potential to enhance the quality of life should be stressed.

Fraleigh's second point is that a major continuing trend is the increasing attention to the needs and expressions of the human body. While this trend has many positive benefits that can be used to provide a focus for better programs of physical education, it also can simply become "a simplistic, indulgent hedonism," a not uncommon sight in the present. Indeed, some of the more faddish physical activities of the late 1970s and early 1980s show much of this characteristic. The jogging and running and road-racing crazes have attracted millions of people, yet multitudes seem to be more concerned with wearing the most expensive, stylish equipment and being seen in large races that they are physically unprepared to attempt. Road races have thus frequently turned into stylish mass "be-ins" rather than competitive sports. Triathlons are now becoming the replacement for road races. The faddish aspect of fitness can be seen distinctly in the many popular health clubs that emphasize attractive facilities for socializing and hire only marginally prepared teachers.

Zeigler has written of four important facets of the present and future: communication, diversity, cooperation, and readiness for change.[18] We have already mentioned the need for communication abilities and skills. Technological progress has made the world an infinitely small place in many respects, and the future physical educator must be prepared to be an active, skilled part of it. This calls for broader education and training, but it also calls for more active work to develop the skills of reading, writing, and speaking at all levels of ability.

Diversity is a mark of any large civilization. The strength of American society has been in large part a result of the diversity of abilities and experiences brought into its culture by the many immigrants absorbed into its society over a period of centuries. Being different should not be discouraged, for from it often come new breakthroughs. A society that discourages diversity, preferring strict conformity instead, generally is less able to cope with change and has to improvise to meet the rapidly changing needs of a highly technological society.

The growing world population makes cooperation an increasingly important need. In an overcrowded world, cooperation is essential to survival. One reason for the interest in the New Games concept is that it might be considered the "athletics for the overcrowded society," with its emphasis on cooperation rather than competition. Competition is natural and will not disappear; however, survival in a mass society requires that people also learn the skills and value of cooperation.

Readiness for change is a necessary ability or outlook in modern society. Change is inevitable; while some people will resist change, those who are more adept at survival will be prepared to accept change and learn to adapt. Education faces the difficult task of trying to develop this readiness for change, or adaptability, for it must prepare people not only for what is but also for what will be, even though what is to come is unknown. Thus, teachers must prepare their students from a "blind" position—an ignorance of the future. What is important, however, is that students learn to adapt to and accept change; they must learn to work with new situations. This adaptability is critical to any individual's ability to cope with the modern world.

Throughout this text we have looked at physical education as a broad field in the context of its historical past, its patterns of development, its function in today's society, and the trends it will most likely follow into the future. You now should have some idea of what physical education is about. We have tried to show physical education as an important part of the total educational process, without making exaggerated claims for it.

Courtesy Duke University Sports Information

Physical education is a worthy field, for in its activities and experiences we can find elements of value to people of all ages and conditions. The greatest question that faces physical educators today is not anything we have looked at directly in this text, but it is another question concerning the future of physical education: When you have become a physical educator, what will you do with it? What directions will physical education take under your guidance and leadership? That is the most important question about the future of physical education.

NOTES

1. Madge Phillips, "The Challenge of Change for Physical Education in the 1980s: Sociological View," *The Academy Papers*, no. 13 (1979), 51.
2. "Crisis in the Schools," *U.S. News and World Report*, 79 (1 September 1975), 42–59.
3. National Center for Educational Statistics, *The Condition of Education*, U.S. Government Printing Office, Washington, D.C., 1975, p. 132.
4. Robert Nisbet, *The History of the Idea of Progress*, Harper & Row, New York, 1980.
5. Benjamin S. Bloom, ed., *Taxonomy of Educational Objectives: Handbook I: Cognitive Domain*, David McKay Company, New York, 1956; and David R. Krathwohl, Benjamin S. Bloom, and Bertram B. Masia, *Taxonomy of Educational Objectives: Handbook II: Affective Domain*, David McKay Company, New York, 1964.
6. Bloom, p. 7.
7. Christopher Lasch, *The Culture of Narcissism*, W.W. Norton, New York, 1978.
8. Richard E. Gross, "Seven New Cardinal Principles," *Phi Delta Kappan* 60 (December 1978), 291–293.
9. Ben Brodinsky, "Something Happened: Education in the Seventies," *Phi Delta Kappan* 61 (December 1979), 238–241.
10. National Center for Educational Statistics, p. 164.
11. John Underwood, "The Writing on the Wall," *Sports Illustrated*, 52 (19 May 1980) 36+; Barry D. McPherson, "Sport in the Educational Milieu," *Phi Delta Kappan* 61 (May 1980), 605–606.
12. Lasch, p. 100.
13. Max Rafferty, *The Future of Education: 1975–2000*, ed. Theodore W. Hipple, Goodyear Publishing, Pacific Palisades, Calif., 1974, p. 167.
14. Theodore W. Hipple, ed., *The Future of Education: 1975–2000*, Goodyear Publishing, Pacific Palisades, Calif., 1974, p. 135.
15. Reuben B. Frost, *Physical Education: Foundations, Practices, Principles*, Addison-Wesley, Reading, Mass., 1975, p. 92.
16. Warren P. Fraleigh, "A Philosophic Basis for Curriculum Content in Physical Education for the 1980s," *The Academy Papers*, no. 13 (1979), 20–26.
17. Daryl Siedentop, *Physical Education: Introductory Analysis*, 3d ed., Wm. C. Brown, Dubuque, Iowa, 1980, pp. 229–231.
18. Earle F. Zeigler, *Issues in North American Physical Education and Sport*, AAHPERD, Reston, Va., 1979, pp. 278–279.

SUGGESTED READINGS

Academy of Leisure Sciences. *Values and Leisure and Trends in Leisure Services*. State College, Penn.: Venture, 1983.

Adler, Mortimer J. *The Paideia Proposal*. New York: Macmillan, 1982.

Bain, Linda L., et al. "Becoming Future Oriented in Professional Preparation Curricula." *Proceedings, National Association for Physical Education in Higher Education Annual Conference* 3 (1982), 93–114.

Bork, A.M. "Computers in Education Today—and Some Possible Futures." *Phi Delta Kappan* 66 (December 1984), 239–243.

Brod, Craig. *Technostress: The Human Cost of the Computer Revolution*. Reading, Mass.: Addison-Wesley, 1984.

Brodinsky, Ben. "Something Happened: Education in the Seventies." *Phi Delta Kappan* 61 (December 1979), 238–243.

"Browning of America, The." *Newsweek*, 23 February 1981, 26+.

Cetron, Marvin, Barbara Soriano, and Margaret Gayle. *Schools of the Future: How American Business and Education Can Cooperate to Save Our Schools*. New York: McGraw-Hill, 1985.

———, and Thomas O'Toole. *Encounters with the Future: A Forecast of Life into the 21st Century*. New York: McGraw-Hill, 1982.

Cheffers, John T.F. "Concepts for Teacher Education in the 80s and 90s." *Proceedings, National Association for Physical Education in Higher Education Annual Conference* 2 (1980), 316–322.

"Energy." *National Geographic* 159 (February 1981): entire issue.

Goodland, John I. *A Place Called School: Prospects for the Future*. New York: McGraw-Hill, 1983.

McBride, Ron E. "Some Future Considerations in Professional Preparation." *The Physical Educator* 41 (May 1984), 95–99.

Naisbitt, J. *Megatrends: Ten New Directions Transforming Our Lives*. New York: Warner, 1982.

Pearson, Kathleen. "Applied Futurism: How to Avoid Professional Obsolescence." *The Physical Educator* 39 (December 1982), 170–175.

Phillips, Madge. "The Unfinished Agenda." *Quest* 33, no. 1 (1981), 3–13.

Projections of Education Statistics to 1990–91. Washington, D.C.: National Center for Educational Statistics, 1983. Suggests that increasing public and private school enrollments (elementary and secondary education) could result in teacher shortage by the late 1980s.

Razor, Jack E. "Meeting the Challenge: Physical Education in the Late 1980s." *Proceedings, National Association for Physical Education in Higher Education Annual Conference* 4 (1983), 68–76.

Siedentop, Daryl. *Physical Education: Introductory Analysis*. 3d ed. Dubuque, Iowa: Wm. C. Brown, 1980. Chapters 14 and 17.

Spears, Betty. "Building for Today and Tomorrow." *Quest* 34, no. 2 (1982), 89–98.

Watts, G.E. "America's Changing Workplace: The Challenge Ahead." *New Directions for Higher Education*, no. 44 (1983), 83–91.

Welsh, Raymond. "Sharpening Our Professional Focus." *JOPERD* 54 (November/December 1983), 13–15.

Zeigler, Earle F. *Issues in North American Physical Education and Sport*. Reston, Va.: AAHPERD, 1979. Section 7, "Looking to the Future," pp. 237–288.

———. "Sculpting the Future." *JOPERD* 54 (January 1983), 15.

Resource Reading Materials

This list of books and magazines is a departure point for students and teachers interested in a deeper study of aspects of physical education and sport. It is by no means all inclusive.

RESOURCE BOOKS

AAHPERD. *Directory of Graduate Physical Education Programs*. Reston, Va.: AAHPERD, 1982.

Arlott, John, ed. *The Oxford Companion to World Sports and Games*. London: Oxford University Press, 1975.

Arnold, Peter J. *Meaning in Movement, Sport, and Physical Education*. London: Heinemann, 1979.

Baker, William J. *Sports in the Western World*. Totowa, N.J.: Rowman and Littlefield, 1982.

———, and John M. Carroll, eds. *Sports in Modern America*. St. Louis: River City, 1981.

———, and James A. Rog, eds. *Sports and the Humanities: A Symposium*. Orono: University of Maine at Orono Press, 1983.

Ball, Donald W., and John W. Loy, eds. *Sport and Social Order: Contributions to the Sociology of Sport*. Reading, Mass.: Addison-Wesley, 1975.

Bennett, Bruce L., Maxwell L. Howell, and Uriel Simri. *Comparative Physical Education and Sport*. 2d ed. Philadelphia: Lea & Febiger, 1983.

Betts, John Rickards. *America's Sporting Heritage: 1850–1950.*. Reading, Mass.: Addison-Wesley, 1974.

Boutilier, Mary A., and Lucinda SanGiovanni. *The Sporting Woman*. Champaign, Ill.: Human Kinetics, 1983.

Brodie, David A., and John J. Thornhill. *Microcomputing in Sport and Physical Education*. New York: Sterling, 1984.

Brooks, George A., ed. *Perspective on the Academic Discipline of Physical Education: A Tribute to G. Lawrence Rarick*. Champaign, Ill.: Human Kinetics, 1981.

Caillois, Roger. *Man, Play, and Games*, trans. Meyer Barash. New York: Free Press, 1961.

Cantelon, Hart, and Richard Gruneau, eds. *Sport, Culture, and the Modern State*. Toronto: University of Toronto Press, 1982.

Cashman, Richard, and Michael McKernan, eds. *Sport: Money, Morality and the Media*. Kensington, NSW: New South Wales University Press, 1981.

Cavallo, Dominick. *Muscles and Morals: Organized Playgrounds and Urban Reform, 1880–1920*. Philadelphia: University of Pennsylvania Press, 1981.

Chu, Donald. *Dimensions of Sport Studies*. New York: John Wiley, 1982.

Coakley, Jay J. *Sport in Society: Issues and Controversies*. 3d ed. St. Louis: C. V. Mosby Co., 1986.

Curry, Timothy J., and Robert M. Jiobu. *Sports: A Social Perspective*. Englewood Cliffs, N.J.: Prentice-Hall, 1984.

Davis, Elwood Craig, ed. *Philosophies Fashion Physical Education*. Dubuque, Iowa: Wm. C. Brown, 1963.

Davis, Lenwood G., and Belinda S. Davis. *Black Athletes in the United States: A Bibliography of Books, Articles, Autobiographies and Biographies on Black Professional Athletes in the United States, 1800–1981*. Westport, Conn.: Greenwood Press, 1981.

Dulles, Foster Rhea. *A History of Recreation: America Learns to Play*. 2d ed. Englewood Cliffs, N.J.: Prentice-Hall, 1965.

Eitzen, D. Stanley. *Sport in Contemporary Society: An Anthology*. 2d ed. New York: St. Martin's, 1984.

——, and George H. Sage. *Sociology of American Sport*. 3d ed. Dubuque, Iowa: Wm. C. Brown, 1986.

Ellis, Michael J. *Why People Play*. Englewood Cliffs, N.J.: Prentice-Hall, 1973.

Espy, Richard. *The Politics of the Olympic Games: With an Epilogue, 1976–1980*. Berkeley: University of California Press, 1981.

Figler, Stephen K. *Sport and Play in American Life: A Textbook in the Sociology of Sport*. Philadelphia: W. B. Saunders, 1981.

Fraleigh, Warren P. *Right Actions in Sport: Ethics for Contestants*. Champaign, Ill.: Human Kinetics, 1984.

Frey, James, ed. *The Governance of Intercollegiate Athletics*. West Point, N.Y.: Leisure Press, 1982.

Gerber, Ellen W. *Innovators and Institutions in Physical Education*. Philadelphia: Lea & Febiger, 1971.

——, et al. *The American Woman in Sport*. Reading, Mass.: Addison-Wesley, 1974.

——, and William J. Morgan, eds. *Sport and the Body: A Philosophical Symposium*. 2d ed. Philadelphia: Lea & Febiger, 1979.

Gratch, Bonnie, et al. *Sports and Physical Education: A Guide to Reference Resources*. Westport, Conn.: Greenwood, 1983.

Gruneau, Richard S. *Class, Sports and Social Development*. Amherst: University of Massachusetts Press, 1983.

Guttmann, Allen. *From Ritual to Record: The Nature of Modern Sports*. New York: Columbia University Press, 1978.

——. *The Games Must Go On: Avery Brundage and the Olympic Movement.* New York: Columbia University Press, 1984.

Hargreaves, Jennifer, ed. *Sport, Culture, and Ideology.* Boston: Routledge & Kegan Paul, 1982.

Harkness, Don, ed. *Sports in American Culture, 1980: Proceedings of the 1980 Congress.* Tampa: American Studies Press, 1980.

Harper, William A., et al. *The Philosophic Process in Physical Education.* 3d ed. Philadelphia: Lea & Febiger, 1977.

Harris, Janet C., and Roberta J. Parks, eds. *Play, Games and Sports in Cultural Contexts.* Champaign, Ill.: Human Kinetics, 1983.

Hart, M. Marie, and Susan Birrell. *Sport in the Sociocultural Process.* 3d ed. Dubuque, Iowa: Wm. C. Brown, 1981.

Higgs, Robert J. *Laurel and Thorn: The Athlete in American Literature.* Lexington: University Press of Kentucky, 1981.

——. *Sports: A Reference Guide.* Westport, Conn.: Greenwood, 1982.

Horrow, Richard B. *Sports Violence.* Arlington, Va.: Carrollton Press, 1981.

Howell, Reet. *Her Story in Sports: An Historical Anthology of Women's Sports.* West Point, N.Y.: Leisure Press, 1982.

HPER Omnibus. Reston, Va.: AAHPERD, 1976. Includes contributions from sixteen winners of the Gulick Award, AAHPERD's highest honor.

Huizinga, Johan. *Homo Ludens: A Study of the Play-Element in Culture.* Boston: Beacon Press, 1950.

Jerome, John. *The Sweet Spot in Time.* New York: Summit Books, 1980.

Johnson, William, ed. *Sports and Physical Education Around the World.* Champaign, Ill.: Stipes Publishing, 1980.

Johnson, William O. *All That Glitters Is Not Gold: The Olympic Games.* New York: Putnam, 1972.

——. *Super Spectator and the Electric Liliputians.* Boston: Little, Brown, 1981.

Kanin, David B. *A Political History of the Olympic Games.* Boulder, Colo.: Westview Press, 1981.

Keating, James W. *Competition and Playful Activities.* Washington, D.C.: University Press of America, 1978.

Koppett, Leonard. *Sports Illusion, Sports Reality: A Reporter's View of Sports, Journalism, and Society.* Boxton: Houghton Mifflin, 1981.

Kroll, Walter P. *Graduate Study and Research in Physical Education.* Champaign, Ill.: Human Kinetics, 1982.

Laforse, Martin W., and James A. Drake. *Popular Culture and American Life: Selected Topics in the Study of American Popular Culture.* Chicago: Nelson-Hall, 1981.

Lee, Mabel. *A History of Physical Education and Sports in the U.S.A.* 5th ed. New York: John Wiley, 1983.

Leonard, George B. *The Ultimate Athlete.* New York: Viking Press, 1975.

Lipsky, Richard. *How We Play the Game: Why Sports Dominate American Life.* Boston: Beacon Press, 1981.

Lipsyte, Robert. *Sports and Society.* New York: Arno, 1980.

——. *SportsWorld: An American Dreamland.* New York: Quadrangle, 1975.

Lockhart, Aileene S., and Howard S. Slusher, eds. *Contemporary Readings in Physical Education.* 3d ed. Dubuque, Iowa: Wm C. Brown, 1975.

——, and Betty Spears, eds. *Chronicle of American Physical Education, 1855–1930.* Dubuque, Iowa: Wm. C. Brown, 1972.

Lowe, Benjamin. *The Beauty of Sport: A Cross-Disciplinary Inquiry.* Englewood Cliffs,

Lowe, Benjamin. *The Beauty of Sport: A Cross-Disciplinary Inquiry.* Englewood Cliffs, N.J.: Prentice-Hall, 1977.

Loy, John W., Barry D. McPherson, and Gerald Kenyon. *Sport and Social Systems: A Guide to the Analysis, Problems, and Literature.* Reading, Mass.: Addison-Wesley, 1978.

——. *Sport, Culture and Society: A Reader on the Sociology of Sport.* 2d ed. Philadelphia: Lea & Febiger, 1981.

Lucas, John A. *The Modern Olympic Games.* New York: A. S. Barnes, 1980.

——, and Ronald A. Smith. *Saga of American Sport.* Philadelphia: Lea & Febiger, 1978.

Luschen, Gunther, ed. *The Cross-Cultural Analysis of Sport and Games.* Champaign, Ill.: Stipes Publishing, 1970.

——, and George Sage, eds. *Handbook of Social Science of Sport: With an International Classified Bibliography.* Champaign, Ill.: Stipes Publishing, 1981.

MacAloon, John. *This Great Symbol: Pierre de Coubertin and the Origins of the Modern Olympic Games.* Chicago: University of Chicago Press, 1981.

McIntosh, Peter. *Fair Play: Ethics in Sport and Education.* London: Heinemann, 1979.

——. *Landmarks in the History of Physical Education.* 3d ed. London: Routledge & Kegan Paul, 1981.

Mandell, Richard D. *A Cultural History of Sport.* New York: Columbia University Press, 1984.

Mangan, James A. *Athleticism in the Victorian and Edwardian Public School.* New York: Cambridge University Press, 1981.

Messenger, Christian K. *Sport and the Spirit of Play in American Fiction: Hawthorne to Faulkner.* New York: Columbia University Press, 1981.

Metheny, Eleanor. *Vital Issues.* Reston, Va.: AAHPERD, 1977.

Michener, James A. *Sports in America.* New York: Random House, 1976.

Mihalich, Joseph C. *Sports and Athletics: Philosophy in Action.* Totowa, N.J.: Littlefield, Adams, 1982.

Mrozek, Donald J. *Sport and American Mentality: The Rise of Respectability, 1880–1910.* Knoxville: University of Tennessee Press, 1983.

——, ed. *Sport in the West.* Manhattan, Kans.: Sunflower University Press, 1983.

Murray, J. Alex, ed. *Sport or Athletics: A North American Dilemma.* Seminar on Canadian-American Relations, University of Windsor, Ontario, Canada, 1974.

Nixon, Howard L., II. *Sport and the American Dream.* West Point, N.Y.: Leisure Press, 1984.

Novak, Michael. *The Joy of Sports: End Zones, Bases, Baskets, Balls, and the Consecration of the American Spirit.* New York: Basic Books, 1976.

Noverr, Douglas A., and Lawrence A. Ziewacz. *The Games They Played: Sports in American History, 1865–1980.* Chicago: Nelson-Hall, 1983.

Oriard, Michael V. *Dreaming of Heroes: American Sports Fiction, 1869–1980.* Chicago: Nelson-Hall, 1982.

Orlick, Terry. *In Pursuit of Excellence.* Champaign, Ill.: Human Kinetics, 1980.

Osterhoudt, Robert G. *An Introduction to the Philosophy of Physical Education and Sport.* Champaign, Ill.: Stipes Publishing, 1978.

——, ed. *The Philosophy of Sport: A Collection of Original Essays.* Springfield, Ill.: Charles C Thomas, 1973.

Professional Preparation in Dance, Physical Education, Recreation Education, Safety Education, and School Health Education. Reston, Va.: AAHPERD, 1974.

Rader, Benjamin G. *American Sports: From the Age of Folk Games to the Age of Spectators.* Englewood Cliffs, N.J.: Prentice-Hall, 1983.

——. *In Its Own Image: How Television Has Transformed Sports.* New York: Free Press, 1984.

Remley, Mary L., ed. *Women in Sport: A Guide to Information Sources.* Detroit: Gale Research, 1980.

Riess, Steven A., ed. *The American Sporting Experience: A Historical Anthology of Sport in America.* Champaign, Ill.: Leisure Press, 1984.

Rigauer, Bero. *Sport and Work,* trans. Allen Guttmann. New York: Columbia University Press, 1981.

Riordan, James. *Sport under Communism.* Toronto: McGill-Queens University Press, 1982.

Sage, George H., ed. *Sport and American Society: Selected Readings.* 3d ed. Reading, Mass.: Addison-Wesley, 1980.

Sanborn, Marion Alice, and Betty G. Hartman. *Issues in Physical Education.* 3d ed. Philadelphia: Lea & Febiger, 1982.

Seagrave, Jeffrey, and Donald Chu. *Olympism: A Cross-Disciplinary Analysis of the Olympic Movement.* Champaign, Ill.: Human Kinetics, 1981.

Seiter, Margaret M., and Barbara Kres Beach, ed. *Shaping the Body Politic: Legislative Training for the Physical Educator.* Reston, Va.: AAHPERD, n.d.

Siedentop, Daryl. *Physical Education: Introductory Analysis.* 3d ed. Dubuque, Iowa: Wm. C. Brown, 1980.

Slusher, Howard S. *Man, Sport, and Existence: A Critical Analysis.* Philadelphia: Lea & Febiger, 1967.

Smith, N. J., R. E. Smith, and F. L. Smoll. *Kidsports: A Survival Guide for Parents.* Reading, Mass.: Addison-Wesley, 1984.

Snyder, Eldon E., and Elmer A. Spreitzer. *Social Aspects of Sports.* 2d ed. Englewood Cliffs, N.J.: Prentice-Hall, 1983.

Spears, Betty, and Richard A. Swanson. *History of Sport and Physical Activity in the United States.* 2d ed. Dubuque, Iowa: Wm. C. Brown, 1983.

Templin, Thomas J., and Janice K. Olson. *Teaching in Physical Education.* Volume 14 of the Big 10 Symposium. Champaign, Ill.: Human Kinetics, 1983.

Tolamini, John T., and Charles H. Page. *Sports and Society: An Anthology.* Boston: Little, Brown, 1983.

Ulrich, Celeste. *To Seek and Find.* Reston, Va.: AAHPERD, 1976.

Underwood, John. *Spoiled Sport: A Fan's Notes on the Troubles of Spectator Sports.* Boston: Little, Brown, 1984.

Van Dalen, Deobold B., and Bruce L. Bennett. *A World History of Physical Education.* 2d ed. Englewood Cliffs, N.J.: Prentice-Hall, 1971.

VanderZwaag, Harold J. *Toward a Philosophy of Sport.* Reading, Mass.: Addison-Wesley, 1972.

Vincent, Ted. *Mudville's Revenge: The Rise and Fall of American Sport.* New York: Seaview Books, 1981.

Weiss, Paul. *Sport: A Philosophic Inquiry.* Carbondale: Southern Illinois University Press, 1969.

Welch, Paula, and Harold A. Lerch. *History of American Physical Education and Sport.* Springfield, Ill.: Charles C Thomas, 1981.

Whorton, James. *Crusaders for Fitness: The History of American Health Reformers.* Princeton, N.J.: Princeton University Press, 1982.

Widmeyer, W. Neil. *Physical Activity and the Social Sciences.* 5th ed. Ithaca, N.Y.: Mouvement Publications, 1983.

Zeigler, Earle F. *Issues in North American Sport and Physical Education.* Reston, Va.: AAHPERD, 1979.

——. *History of Physical Education and Sport.* Englewood Cliffs, N.J.: Prentice-Hall, 1979.

——. *Physical Education and Sport Philosophy.* Englewood Cliffs, N.J.: Prentice-Hall, 1977.

——. *Personalizing Physical Education and Sport Philosophy.* Champaign, Ill.: Stipes Publishing, 1975.

RESOURCE PERIODICALS

Academy Papers, The. Published once a year by the American Academy of Physical Education. Human Kinetics, Box 5076, Champaign, IL 61820.

Adapted Physical Activity Quarterly (APAQ). Published quarterly since 1984. Human Kinetics, Box 5076, Champaign, IL 61820.

Arete: The Journal of Sport Literature. Published twice a year. The Sport Literature Association, Physical Education Department, San Diego State University, San Diego, CA 92182.

CAHPER Journal. Published six times a year. The Canadian Association for Health, Physical Education and Recreation (CAHPER), 333 River Road, Vanier City, Ontario K1L 8B9, Canada.

Canadian Journal of Applied Sport Sciences. Published three times a year. The Canadian Association of Sport Sciences, 333 River Road, Vanier City, Ontario K1L 8B9, Canada.

Canadian Journal of History of Sport. Published twice a year. Subscriptions available from Alan Metcalfe, Faculty of Human Kinetics, University of Windsor, Windsor, Ontario N9B 3P4, Canada.

Current Index to Journals in Education. Published monthly in cooperation with ERIC (Educational Resources Information Center) to index the articles from over 700 journals related to areas of education. Available from Macmillan Information, a Division of Macmillan Publishing Company, Inc., 216R Brown Street, Riverside, NJ 08075.

Education Digest. Published nine times a year. 416 Longshore Drive, Ann Arbor, MI 48107.

Health Education. Published eight times a year by AAHPERD. Can be selected as a periodical by AAHPERD members or ordered separately from membership. 1900 Association Drive, Reston, VA 22091.

International Journal of Sport Biomechanics (IJSB). Published quarterly since 1985. Human Kinetics, Box 5076, Champaign, Il 61820.

Journal of Leisure Research. Published quarterly since 1969. The National Recreation and Park Association, 3101 Park Center Drive, Alexandria, VA 22302.

Journal of Physical Education. Published six times a year. The Association of Professional Directors of the YMCA, 40 West Long Street, Columbus, OH 43215.

Journal of Physical Education, Recreation and Dance (JOPERD). Published nine times a year by AAHPERD. Can be selected as a periodical by AAHPERD members or ordered separately from membership. 1900 Association Drive, Reston, VA 22091.

Journal of School Health. Published ten times a year by the American School Health Association, Kent, OH 44240.

Journal of Sport and Social Issues. Published twice a year. ARENA: The Institute for Sport and Social Analysis, Dept. of African-American Studies, Northeastern University, Boston, MA 02115.

Journal of Sport Behavior. Published quarterly. The U.S. Sports Academy, University of South Alabama, Mobile, AL 36608.

Journal of Sport History. Published three times a year by the North American Society for Sport History. Available through Ronald A. Smith, 101 White Building, Penn State University, University Park, PA 16802.

Journal of Sport Psychology (JSP). Published quarterly since 1979. Human Kinetics, Box 5076, Champaign, IL 61820.

Journal of Teacher Education. Published quarterly by the American Association of Colleges for Teacher Education, One Dupont Circle, Washington, DC 20036.

Journal of Teaching in Physical Education (JTPE). Published quarterly since 1982. Human Kinetics, Box 5076, Champaign, IL 61820.

Journal of the Philosophy of Sport (JPS). Published annually since 1974. The Philosophic Society for the Study of Sport. Human Kinetics, Box 5076, Champaign, IL 61820.

Medicine and Science in Sports and Exercise. Published six times a year. The American College of Sports Medicine, Box 1440, Indianapolis, IN 46206.

NAPEHE Proceedings. Published once a year by the National Association for Physical Education in Higher Education. Human Kinetics, Box 5076, Champaign, IL 61820.

Parks and Recreation. Published monthly. The National Recreation and Park Association, 3101 Park Center Drive, Alexandria, VA 22302.

Phi Delta Kappan. Published monthly. The Phi Delta Kappa Fraternity, Eighth and Union, Bloomington, IN 47401.

Physical Educator, The. Published quarterly. The Phi Epsilon Kappa Fraternity, 9030 Log Run Drive North, Indianapolis, IN 46234.

The Physician and Sportsmedicine. Published monthly. McGraw-Hill, Inc., 4530 W. 77th St., Minneapolis, MN 55435.

Quest. Published twice each year since 1963 by the National Association for Physical Education in Higher Education. Human Kinetics, Box 5076, Champaign, IL 61820.

Research Quarterly for Exercise and Sport. Published quarterly by AAHPERD. Can be selected as a periodical by AAHPERD members or ordered separately from membership. 1900 Association Drive, Reston, VA 22091.

Review, The. Published twice a year. ARENA: The Institute for Sport and Social Analysis, Dept. of African-American Studies, Northeastern University, Boston, MA 02115.

Sociology of Sport Journal (SSJ). Published quarterly since 1984. Human Kinetics, Box 5076, Champaign, IL 61820.

Today's Education. Published quarterly. The National Education Association (NEA), 1201 16th Street, Washington, DC 20036.

Update. Newspaper printed nine times a year by AAHPERD. Can be selected as a periodical by AAHPERD members or ordered separately from membership. 1900 Association Drive, Reston, VA 22091.

See also: Darrell Crase, "Current Periodicals in Physical Education and the Sport Sciences," *JOPERD* 56 (October 1985), 76–80.

Subject Index

Organization Index

DATE DUE

5/7/12			

GAYLORD   PRINTED IN U.S.A.